GW00771185

ORIENTAL TRANSLATION FUND
NEW SERIES
VOL. XLV

REAMKER (RĀMAKERTI)

the Cambodian version of the Rāmāyaṇa

translated by
Judith M. Jacob
Lecturer in Cambodian at
the School of Oriental & African Studies

with the assistance of Kuoch Haksrea

Published by
The Royal Asiatic Society
56 Queen Anne Street,
London W1M 0LA

ISBN 0 947593 02 0

Photoset by Trafalgar Studios Ltd, London
Printed by Biddles Ltd, Guildford & King's Lynn

Contents

Preface .... p.vii

Introduction .... p.ix

Abbreviations .... p.xiv

List of proper names .... p.xv

List of Sanskrit and Pali loanwords left untranslated .... p.xx

Résumés of the narratives.

The Main Rāma Story. (The earlier composition. Parts 1–10 of the Institut Bouddhique text.) .... pp.xxi

Later events of the Rāma story. (The later composition. Parts 75–80 of the Institut Bouddhique text.) .... pp.xxix

Translation

The Main Rāma Story. (The earlier composition. Parts 1–10 of the Institut Bouddhique text.) .... pp. 1–194

Later events of the Rāma story. (The later composition. Parts 75–80 of the Institut Bouddhique text.) pp.195–291

Notes pp.293–297

List of Preferred Readings and Emendations pp.298–305

Glossary pp.306–316

References pp.317–320

Preface

The preparation of this translation was begun over a decade ago, before any work on the text of any kind had appeared, apart from a few small passages of translation into French. I was therefore extremely lucky to have, from 1975 to 1981, the help of Mr. Kuoch Haksrea, then just finishing his M.Phil. thesis in Khmer archaeology at the School of Oriental and African Studies. At the end of the task I could see even more clearly than at the beginning how essential it was to have a Khmer assistant. If Modern Khmer prose can be bafflingly inexplicit, Middle Khmer poetry can be more so. The help of someone to whom Rām and Hanumān have been familiar from the cradle was help indeed. But in addition to that, Mr. Haksrea brought to the work many valuable qualities: a real interest in his own literature, a genuine concern about searching for true meanings and a sensitivity about the general import of the poem. His patient, cheerful and constructive co-operation have been very gratefully appreciated.

Towards the end of the preparation of the translation the fine, scholarly volumes of Dr. S. Pou on the *Reamker* were published, providing a revised text, a translation into French and notes. The translation offered here has been corrected and revised by me in the light of the new material contained in Dr. Pou's work and has benefited in numerous ways from her edition. Many of her better readings have been used and I have been grateful for her enlightened solutions to many knotty problems of the text. The responsibility for the choices and decisions made in connection with the revision are mine alone.

I should like to express my thanks to the School of Oriental and African Studies and to the Royal Asiatic Society who have jointly met the cost of publishing this book.

J.M.J. 1986

Introduction

The influence of the Rāmāyaṇa on Cambodian culture, which began to be felt during the Angkor period (9th to 13th centuries A.D.), if not before, and has continued until modern times, has been more profound than that of any other story. The narrative, depicted on the bas-reliefs of Angkor, later became a favourite theme for frescoes on temple walls. The subject of the traditional shadow play, the spaek dhaṃ "large leather (puppets)", was exclusively the Rāma story. The popular masked dance, lkhon khol, which had by this century become associated with the cult of local deities, was based on certain episodes of the Rāmāyaṇa. There was a close link with religion in all these art forms. Offerings were made to gods before performances and the fabrication of objects used in performances, such as the leather puppets and musical instruments, was attended by certain ritual acts. In modern times some episodes of the Rāma story formed part of the repertoire of the Royal Ballet and this was certainly the case in the ancient kingdom. The reverence with which Cambodians regard the character of Rām is not merely for the original Indian reason, that he is a god, living on earth in order to quell evil. In the Reamker Rāma is presented as being more than that: he is the Buddha himself.

Very few versions of the Rāma story have survived to modern times. Apart from the version which is translated here and which is usually referred to as the "classical" or "literary" text, we know only of the texts which were relevant to the popular performances or to the Royal Ballet, which were kept carefully by the masters of the companies but which would now be very difficult or impossible to trace. The literary text is in fact two separate compositions, written in verse, both of which are incomplete. The first one tells the story of the contest of the bow, the banishment, the bridge to Laṅkā, Hanumān's visit to Sītā and the battles up to the death of Rāvaṇa's tenth son. The second composition relates the later story: the drawing of the portrait of Rāvaṇa, Sītā's sojourn in the forest and the events leading to her sons' discovery of their father and Sītā's refusal to be reconciled with him. It is likely that more than one poet was involved in the first composition but that the second was the work of one poet.

The literary text has the form of a dramatic recitative intended to accompany a performance of the mimed ballet. While the moods, situations and actions were mimed, with the prescribed movements of fingers, eyebrows, etc., to an accompaniment of set music, the recited stanzas would describe the thoughts of the characters and narrate events. The text is therefore divided into scenes, often with a change of metre to suit the mood of the new scene and with brief instructions concerning music and dance. Nevertheless, some "scenes" are very long indeed and it seems possible that poets have at some time extended existing passages or included extra material to improve the work. This has resulted in some slight inconsistencies in the narration.

There are many passages where characters re-tell events when reporting to someone else. Such passages would surely not fit into the mimed presentation of the Reamker? The literary text has perhaps gradually acquired the length and, to some extent, the style of an epic poem; it always had the required heroic subject matter. Once the rather tersely written first pages are left behind, the narrative proceeds at a leisurely pace, though events are often put to one side for a descriptive passage or a rather lengthy lament. All the appurtenances of the grand heroic style of warfare and life are present. Heroes going out to single combat are magnificently attired and may have unusual weapons or mounts. Before battle they show off, make threatening gestures, and shout insults at the enemy. The arrows of the two adversaries turn now into snakes, now into *garuḍas* to destroy them; now into fire, now into water to quench it. When they fight at close quarters the ogre champion almost defeats the hero with what seems like a final blow but is then himself slain. But off the field of battle, in this society of divine and royal beings, polite deference is required: people creep on their knees into the royal presence and offer things by placing them on their heads. The characters express grief with writhing, fainting and tears pouring on to the ground. The impressiveness of events is helped by the exaggeration of quantities in phrases such as "a million million soldiers".

The supernatural and the divine elements in the story are constantly brought to the fore. Some of the magic, such as Hanumān's tying together the hair of Rāb(ṇ) (Rāvaṇa) and his wife and casting a spell over them, is fun; but the supernatural power which hermits acquire, through the wisdom gained by contemplation and ascetic practices, must command our great respect. There is no doubt at all of the serious religious importance of Rām himself. Rām's father and father-in-law "knew what Rām had in mind". The Khmer audience needed no more explanation than this vague sentence but Rām spells it out on various occasions, to the demon Rāmaparamasūr, for example and to King Khar. He is Nārāyaṇa and has come down to earth to quell evil. Just hearing this said is enough to convince many of his enemies of his might and to bring them to their knees. On other occasions, to Sītā as they journey through the forest, for example, he explains that he is the Omniscient One, leading the way to Nirvana. In the second composition, relating the later events, Rām, powerfully affected by the ogress, Ātul, seems to be a very different character, hasty in judgment, quick to anger and not so god-like.

The long association of the Rāma story in Cambodia with popular performances helps to account for many sudden changes from grand to comic style or from one mood to another, which take place usually with the changes of scene indicated in the text. The miraculously strong soldiers of the monkey army are on one page literally heaving mountains about as they build the "bridge" and on another are jumping playfully on the beach. The ogres are at one moment really terrifying, evil creatures and at the next resemble villains in a pantomime or, more appropriately, acrobats in the Khmer ballet, as they shout insults at the enemy and leap about, boiling with rage and brandishing their weapons. The source of evil whom Rām will eventually defeat, king of the demons, can feel faint, be bowed down with sorrow or become angry and stamp his feet. Abrupt changes in the style of language occur as one scene gives way to another. Adversaries "thump" and "bash" each other and shout at each other using colloquial terms but bereaved heroines speak in Brahmagīti stanzas, exclaiming "Ah!" and "Alas!" The vividness with which the text makes the characters express their feelings is in marked contrast to the static postures of the ballet and the unchanging expressions in the popular masked dance. In the character of these performances a very close link may be seen with the stylised figures of the Angkor sculptures and with the two-dimensional, stencilled leather "puppets" of the shadow-play. An echo of this stereotyping of the characters is to be found in the regular epithets which abound in the text in proper epic fashion. Kings are always "serene" and therefore we can find a "serene king" in "mental agony". Brothers are loved by brothers and so Bālī (Vālin) is "hostile. . . towards his dear brother".

It has been possible to give only a little indication here and there in the translation of the alliteration which is constantly present as an embellishment in the Khmer. The following is an example in transcription of the sound of the language of one stanza (Part 4, p.36, 11.7–8) in a description of the jungle. It consists chiefly of names of plants, chosen because they alliterate. From both the point of view of subject-matter and of poetic style the passage is typical of Khmer and other South East Asian poetry:

/*kr*o:c *kr*a:y bɔŋ*k*ə̀u phɲìəv
srə*k*ùm *k*ùy *kr*əsaŋ *kr*ah
pè:*k*a: dɔ: *chl*o:k *chl*ah
rum*d*u:əl *d*ao pənì: əlì:/

Other features characteristic of South East Asian poetry are to be observed. There are many instances in the text of passages which almost repeat each other in subject matter. Poets revelled, for example, in descriptions of assembling armies and preparation of the king's carriage and escort. And, where minor points of detail are concerned, the precision expected in the West is sometimes lacking, for example, with regard to how many persons are addressed or exactly what was said. Thus the sage is said to address Rām and Laksm(ṇ) but the import of what he says is directed at Rām (Part 1, p.4). And Dūbhī (Dundubhi) says to Bālī (Vālin), after an exchange of threats, "You say you will shake me and crumble my lungs". In fact, however, Bālī's threats of a few stanzas before were not precisely those, though they might well have been. (Part 4, p.54).

Both compositions contain many passages of fine writing, for the appreciation of which it is not necessary to be a South East Asian: for example, the dramatic account of Hanumān setting fire to Laṅkā, the tender description of the birth and care of Sītā's son, the many vigorous arguments, particularly those between husband and wife (Tārā with Bālī or Maṇḍogirī with Rāb(ṇ)) and the numerous exciting battle scenes.

The whole of the Reamker was written during the Middle period of Khmer literature (16th to mid-19th centuries) but the first composition is much older than the second, as may be seen from even a cursory look at the language of the two. The first is written in a variety of traditional metres (the Baṃnol, the Brahmagīti, the Kākagati and others) while the second is written in one less ancient metre (the Pad bāky prāṃ-muoy) and in a much more verbose style. Both works are anonymous. The first fifth, approximately, of the first composition is written in language of a very much earlier date than the rest of it and there are many changes, such as changes of vocabulary and phraseology, as the work progresses, which suggest, as was said above, that it is the work of several poets. Pou suggests the 16th to 17th centuries as the date for the first composition and the 18th century for the second.

Texts and Translations

When the Institut Bouddhique (I. B.) of Phnom Penh published the literary text, *Rīoeṅ Rāmakert(i) (Reamker),* in 1937 from two very similar manuscripts, each of which consisted of sixteen fascicules of palm-leaf pages, numbered 1–10 and 75–80, the published Parts followed this bizarre numeration precisely. Although many episodes of the story are lacking from the text, their narration would not have filled sixty-four fascicules! Parts 1–10 form the first and Parts 75–80 the second composition.

With its early pages full of archaisms, obsolete vocabulary and unfamiliar words spelt in a variety of ways, the printed text looked formidable even to Cambodians and was not much read or studied until the 1960's. No translation appeared, apart from the short excerpts translated into French (Martini 1938 and 1950), until 1977 with the publication of the first two volumes of Dr. S.Pou's excellent works on the Reamker (1977a and b, 1979 and 1982). These include a translation into French of both compositions (called by her Rāmakerti I and II) and a text for both compositions. For the texts, Pou consulted other MSS, chiefly those of the Bibliothèque Nationale and of the Ecole Française d'Extrême-

Orient and was thus able to make many corrections to the printed text and to add about 100 stanzas to it. Another French version appeared at approximately the same time. F. Martini's translation of both compositions (1978), which he was known to have been working on for many decades, was published posthumously.

The translation offered here is based on the I.B. printed text with many corrections and emendations, set out in the List of Preferred Readings and Emendations, of which a great number are due to Pou's texts and researches and are gratefully acknowledged as such. The translation has been kept as close to the original as possible, being carried out stanza by stanza. The main devices used in order to help the flow of the English have been the frequent omission of repeated epithets or kinship in terms and the addition of conjunctions. The translation is presented with asterisks to indicate the beginning of each stanza. The Part and page numbers of the I.B. printed text are given in the left margin throughout. In order to help students of Khmer, a Glossary of words not, for the most part, in Khmer, Sanskrit or Pali dictionaries is appended. The list of preferred readings and emendations is given to clarify the connection between this translation and the printed text for anyone using both together.

Abbreviations

I.B.	Institut Bouddhique
Khm.	Khmer
l.	line
M–W	Monier-Williams (1976)
Mid.	Middle
Mod.	Modern
N.	name
Ref.	reference
Skt.	Sanskrit
var.	variant form
VK	*Vacanānukram Khmaer* (1967).

List of proper names

All names are transliterated, using the system of S. Lewitz (1969), from the forms appearing in the Khmer (Institut Bouddhique) text. (Consonants in parentheses and the 2nd of 2 written final consonants are not pronounced.)

Ādityasuriyā	King, enemy of Dasarath.
Aggīvās	Arrow of Rām which turns into fire.
Airā, Airābat	Elephant of Indr.
Aiyudhyā	Dasarath's city and kingdom.
Ajapāl	Father of Dasarath.
Akat (Agastya?)	Name, queried in I.B. text, of person who once gave a coat of mail to Rām.
Aṅgad	Son of Bālī and Maṇḍogirī.
Añjanadebī	Mother of Hanumān.
Anujit	A name of Hanumān.
Anuttagrām	Home of Birādh? (Text not clear).
Āriddhacandr	Arrow of Rām.
Asok	Park in which Rāb(ṇ) kept Sītā.
Atikāy	Son of Rāb(ṇ).
Ātul	Demoness who tempts Sītā to draw a portrait of Rāb(ṇ).
Baisrab	God of possessions.
Bājī	Demon who rode in the rear of Indrajit's chariot.
Bālī	Monkey king of Khās' Khin.
Bāyavās	Arrow of Rām which turns into a gale.
Bejayant	Indr's palace and/or carriage.
Bhakkhanes	Ganeṣa, god in the form of an elephant, guardian of Laṅkā.
Bhāradvādy	Hermit with whom Rām, Sītā and Laskm(ṇ) stay.
Bhirut	Son of Dasarath and Kaikesī.
Bibhek	Younger brother of Rāb(ṇ).
Bibitr	Monkey officer.
Birādh	Ogre, King of Daṇḍakāraṇy.
Biruṇ	King of the underworld of *nāgās*.
Biruṇavās	Arrow of Rām which turns into rain.
Bisnu	Viṣṇu.
Bisnukār	Heavenly architect and designer.
Bisvāmitr	Sage, preceptor of Rām and Laskm(ṇ).
Brahm	(1) A god who is an ascetic and who attends the contest of the bow.

	(2) A class of divine beings who live in the abode of the pure.
Brahmās, Brahmāstr	Arrow of Rām.
Brahmavijit	Arrow of Laksm(ṇ).
Citrakūṭ	Mountain on whose slopes Rām, Sītā and Laksm(ṇ) stay. Also called Trīkūṭ.
Daṇḍakā, Daṇḍakāraṇy	A forested region.
Dasamukh	A name of Rāb(ṇ), "Ten-faced".
Dasarath	King of Aiyudhyā.
Dūbhī	King of the buffaloes.
Dūramukh	Demon officer.
Dūs(ṇ)	Younger brother of Khar.
Gandhamād(n)	Mountain situated opposite Laṅkā.
Hanumān	White monkey, officer in Rām's army and his special *aide*.
Harī	A name of Rām.
Hemabānt	The Himalaya.
Indr	Lord of the gods.
Indrajit	Son of Rāb(ṇ).
Isūr	Īśvara, the god Śiva.
Jambūbān	Rām's astrologer.
Janak	King of Mithilā.
Japp-Laksm(ṇ)	Created by Vajjaprit as the twin brother of Rām-Laksm(ṇ). cf. Khm. jap "to create by magic".
Jatāyū	A *garuḍa*.
Jībadvār	A chief in Sugrīb's army.
Kaikes	Kingdom of Kaikesī's father.
Kaikesī	Wife of Dasarath, mother of Bhirut and Sutrut.
Kailās	A mountain in the Hemabānt.
Kākanāsūr	Demon who destroys Bisvāmitr's preparations for a sacrifice and is killed by Rām.
Kāl	Father of Birādh.
Kālatī	A river.
Kāmabālī	Nephew of Rāb(ṇ).
Kāmāvacar	The heaven in which beings are still under the influence of desire.
Kandalī	A mountain on which Hanumān lives.

Kaṅhīṅ	Earth goddess.
Kesar	Monkey prince and officer.
Khar	Demon lord.
Khās' Khin	Kingdom of Bālī.
Kosakalyā	Wife of Dasarath, mother of Rām.
Kosī	A name of Indr.
Krasiṇ	A name which, like Kaikes, represents the kingdom of Kaikesī's father.
Kūkhǎn	A forest overlord.
Kumbhagadādhar	Demon prince and officer.
Kumbhakār(ṇ)	Younger brother of Rāb(ṇ).
Laksm(ṇ)	Son of Dasarath and Sramud.
Laṅkā	Island kingdom of Rāb(ṇ).
Luk Khun	Hall of Justice.
Mahājambū	Monkey king, ally of Rām.
Mahākāy	Demon.
Mahākpāl	Demon officer.
Mahāpās	Son of Rāb(ṇ).
Mahārīk	Son of Kākanāsūr, Rāb(ṇ)'s right-hand man.
Mahodar	Son of Rāb(ṇ).
Maithilī	A name of Sītā, "of Mithilā".
Mālmād	Demon commander in chief.
Maṇḍogirī	Wife of Rāb(ṇ).
Mataṅ(g)	(1) A hermit. (2) The mountain where he lives. (Defective form in I.B. text).
Mekhallā	Goddess of the Sea.
Mithilā	The kingdom of Janak.
Mukharakkhǎs	Demon officer.
Mūlaphalam	Demon ally of Rāb(ṇ).
Nal	Officer of Mahājambū.
Nand	Chief in Sugrīb's army.
Narātǎk	Son of Rāb(ṇ).
Nārāy(ṇ)	A name of Viṣṇu, used as a name for Rām, incarnation of Viṣṇu.
Nerṛati	God who attends the contest of the bow.
Nidrā	Goddess of Sleep.
Nīl	Officer of Mahājambū.
Pañcaliṅg	Ascetic who was challenged by Dūbhī.
Paradust	Enemy of Dasarath.

Pātāl	Underworld of *nāgas*.
Prahast	Indrajit's charioteer.
Prahet	Rāb(ṇ)'s astrologer.
Rāb(ṇ), (Rābaṇā in text, Part 3)	Demon King of Laṅkā.
Rāhū	Demon, enemy of Sun and Moon.
Rakkhås	Demon, adviser of Rāb(ṇ).
Rakkhasen	Demon officer.
Rām	Son of Dasarath and Kosakalyā.
Rām-Laksm(ṇ)	Son of Rām and Sītā,
Rāmaparamasūr	Regarded by the Khmers as a demon but claiming in our text to be of human descent.
Rambhā	Goddess who takes water to the imprisoned Rām-Laksm(ṇ).
Rāmesūr	Alternative N. of Rāmaparamasūr.
Ratanā	Queen of Patāl.
Riktāsī	Younger sister of Rāb(ṇ), guardian of Laṅkā.
Rukkhara:	Monkey prince and officer.
Sahasakumār	Son of Rāb(ṇ).
Santagirī	Mother of Dūbhī.
Såtabalī	Monkey officer.
Sīdantar	Sea between two ranges of mountains round Mount Sumeru.
Sītā	Daughter of Janak, wife of Rām.
Sramud	Wife of Dasarath, mother of Laksm(ṇ).
Sugrīb	Bālī's younger brother.
Sujatā	Wife of Bibhek.
Sujātā	Wife of Indr.
Sumantån	Officer of Rām's army.
Sumeru, Meru	Mountain in the centre of the world.
Sumitr	A name of Laksm(ṇ).
Sūrapanakhā	Younger sister of Rāb(ṇ).
Sutrut	Son of Dasarath and Kaikesī.
Tārā	Wife of Bālī.
Trīkūṭ	Alternative form of name of Mount Citrakūṭ.
Trīmukh (also called Trībhaktr and Trīsir)	Son of Khar.
Trīsir	Son of Rāb(ṇ).

Umā	Wife of Śīva.
Usabh	Monkey officer.
Vajjaprit	Sage at whose hermitage Sītā and her sons live.
Vasiṭṭh	Sage at Dasarath's court.
Viruḷhak	Guardian deity of the southern part of the world.
Virūpakkh	Guardian deity of the northern part of the world.
Yāmatik	King from whom Rāmaparamasūr claims descent.
Yamunā	A river.

List of Sanskrit and Pali loanwords left untranslated

ācārya	Spiritual teacher.
apsarā	Name of a class of female divinities.
avatār	Incarnation of Viṣṇu.
cakravāla	Mythical range of mountains which surround the universe.
dānava	Name of a class of demons.
gandharva	Name of a class of heavenly beings who, in epic poetry, are both musicians and warriors.
garuḍa	Large, mythical bird, enemy of the nāgas.
karma	Former act, leading to inevitable results; fate.
kinnara	Mythical being, half bird, half human.
kumbhaṇḍa	Name of a class of demons.
nāga	Serpent-demon.
rākṣasa	Malignant demon, enemy of the gods.
sālā	Hall, especially used of the reception-room in a hermitage.
śamī	*Prosopis spicigera* or *Mimosa suma*.
tuṣita	Name of a class of heavenly beings.
vīṇā	Indian lute.

Résumés of the narrative

The main Rāma story. (The earlier composition. Parts 1–10.)

1.1–4. Rām kills the ogre Kākanasūr, who, in the form of a crow, has destroyed Bisvāmitr's sacrifice.

1.5–10. King Janak of Mithilā adopts Sītā, found during the royal ploughing ceremony. He holds the contest of the bow in which Rām is successful.

1.10–17. The King of Mithilā gives Sītā in marriage to Rām. An envoy is sent to his father, King Dasarath, to invite him to the wedding. With his sons, Bhirut and Sutrut, King Dasarath comes to Mithilā.

1.17–31. The wedding ceremony of Rām and Sītā is held. King Janak then accompanies King Dasarath and Rām as the whole party leaves for Aiyudhyā. At the gate of Mithilā, the ogre Rāmaparamasūr threatens Rām because he has been given his name. He is reduced to submission.

1.31–38. The journey to Aiyudhyā is completed. A feast is given, after which King Janak leaves to return home to Mithilā. King Dasarath prepares to hand over the kingdom to his eldest son, Rām, but is dissuaded from this by Kaikesī who reminds him of a promise to give the kingdom to Bhirut, her own son.

1.39–42. Rām prevents Laksm(ṇ) from killing Kaikesī in anger. Rām, Laksm(ṇ) and Sītā set off for the jungle and receive hospitality at a hermitage beside a river.

1-42–54. Kūkhǎn, a forest overlord, brings gifts to Rām. He will conduct the three travellers across the river the next day. Kūkhǎn and Laksm(ṇ), on guard outside Rām's sleeping quarters, address the goddesses of the land and of sleep. Laksm(ṇ) is granted the boon of needing no sleep or food for fourteen years.

1.54–63. The travellers cross the river, refusing Kūkhǎn's invitation to stay at his home and his offer to accompany them on the journey.

1.63–2.8. The forest, ravaged by fire, comes back to life as Rām passes through it. He points out flowers and birds to Sītā and shows how they illustrate their own and other human lives.

2.8–15.	The travellers come to a hermitage where they stay the night.
2.15–22.	Continuing their journey, they cross the River Kālati, Rām and Sītā being borne on a raft made by Laksm(ṇ). They pass through a forest where all creatures live in harmony and reach Mount Citrakūṭ where hermits welcome them. Laksm(ṇ) builds a hermitage for Rām.
2.22–34.	In Aiyudhyā, when King Dasarath dies, the sage Vasiṭṭh prepares a message to summon Bhirut to be crowned. Kaikesī alters the message so that it says nothing about King Dasarath's death but summons Bhirut and Sutrut to the coronation of Rām. Bhirut and Sutrut joyfully make the journey to Aiyudhyā to find the city desolate. They guess that Rām has left in anger because he is not to be king.
2.34–43.	Bhirut and Sutrut learn from Kaikesī of their father's death.
2.43–52.	Then Kaikesī tells them about Rām's exile and from Kosakalyā they learn of the message falsified by Kaikesī.
2.53–59.	The sage Vasiṭṭh organises the funeral of King Dasarath and the coronation of Bhirut is planned. Bhirut prepares instead to fetch Rām to be king. He sets off with a large retinue, including Sutrut and the three queens.
2.59–69.	Kūkhǎn sees them, guesses that they come in friendship towards Rām and helps them to cross the river.
2.69–76.	The whole party receives hospitality from the sage Bhāradvādy, with much practical help from Indr. They proceed to Rām's hermitage. Laksm(ṇ), suspecting that Bhirut comes as an enemy, is ready to attack. He is restrained by Rām.
2.77–84.	Bhirut and Sutrut visit Rām and tell him of his father's death. They are joined by the queens and the army. All mourn. They offer the throne to Rām, who refuses. The visiting party returns to Aiyudhyā.
2.85–3.4.	Rām decides that they must move to a less accessible part of the forest. As they proceed they encounter the ogre Birādh, who snatches Sītā away. Laksm(ṇ) goes to rescue her but it needs Rām's help to defeat the ogre. Laksm(ṇ) decides to live alone as an ascetic.

3.4–11. The ogress Sūrapanakhā confides to her brother Khar that she intends to marry Laksm(ṇ). In human form she visits the brothers who, each in turn, send her to the other. Finally Laksm(ṇ), in anger, wounds her. Her cries are heard by Khar, who sends Dūs(ṇ) to bring her home.

3.11–20. Khar marches his army towards Rām and Laksm(ṇ) to take his revenge. Laksm(ṇ) offers to fight in single combat but Rām says he will fight himself. Khar sends first Dūs(ṇ), then Trīmukh to capture the ascetics. Rām defeats and kills them both.

3.20–28. Khar comes himself and is defeated and killed by Rām.

3.28–33. Sūrapanakhā tells Rāb(ṇ) of these deaths and of the beauty of Sītā. Rāb(ṇ) decides to capture Sītā by a trick.

3.33–45. Rāb(ṇ) orders Mahārīk to change himself into a beautiful deer and to entice Rām away from the hermitage. As Rām's arrow strikes him, the deer imitates Rām's voice calling for help. Sītā persuades Laksm(ṇ), against his better judgment, to go to Rām's aid.

3.45–4.9 Disguised as a Brahmin, Rāb(ṇ) approaches Sītā and praises her beauty. Returning to his normal form, he boasts of his intention to take her away. Sītā resorts to praise of Rām's power. Rāb(ṇ), confident that she will later love him, flies off with her.

4.9–20. On the way to Laṅkā Sītā appeals to the gods and to an egret to tell Rām of her plight and ask him to follow. She laments. Jatāyu fights to save her from Rāb(ṇ) but the latter mortally wounds him, using Sītā's ring. On arrival in Laṅkā, Sītā is placed in the park of Asoka trees.

4.20–35. Meanwhile Rām and Laksm(ṇ) return home and find Sītā gone. They set out after her and come across Jatāyu who, before he dies, tells them about his fight with Rāb(ṇ). The princes meet and vanquish an ogre heretic. The egret informs them about Sītā's message and is at first not well received by the princes.

4.35–51. As they journey on the princes pass through the forest where Dūbhī, son of the buffalo king who killed all his sons at birth, has been hidden by his mother and has grown up. He has killed his father. From this triumph he goes on to annoy in turn a sage, the Sea, the Hemabān(t) and the monkey king, Bālī.

4.51–64. After an indecisive battle in the open, Bālī persuades Dūbhī to fight in a cave where his bulk will put him at a disadvantage. Before the fight he tells Sugrīb that if after the fight the blood is light-coloured (i.e. his own) he should block the cave's entrance. When Bālī is victorious, flowers strewn by the gods turn the blood of Dūbhī to a light colour. Sugrīb laments for his brother, presumed dead, and has the entrance to the cave blocked.

4.64–70. Bālī frees himself and, believing Sugrīb intended his death, fights him. The wounded Sugrīb takes refuge in the mountains, attended by Hanumān.

5.1–12. Rām and Sugrīb each know from a portent that the other is near. Sugrīb sends Hanumān to look for a man of merit. Hanumān sees the princes under a mango tree. He scatters leaves on them. Rām prevents Laksm(ṇ) from attacking the monkey, realising that he is special. Hanumān returns to tell Sugrīb.

5.12–21. Investigating the source of some salty water, Laksm(ṇ) finds Sugrīb. He is inside a mountain which collapses at a touch of Laksm(ṇ)'s bow. Sugrīb tells Rām about the quarrel between himself and Bālī. Rām offers to help Sugrīb to defeat Bālī and gain queen and kingdom while Sugrīb says he will help Rām against his enemy.

5.21–29. Hanumān and Sugrīb take Rām to see the body of Dūbhī and to see the *nāga* with the seven palm trees growing on its tail. Rām destroys the body and the palm-trees. Sugrīb, now sure of Rām's powers, asks his help in defeating Bālī.

5.29–41. They go to Khās' Khin where Sugrīb and Bālī fight. Laksm(ṇ) makes a garland so that Rām may distinguish one brother from the other and help Sugrīb. Queen Tārā warns Bālī that Sugrīb, who has already been defeated, is probably returning with some trick. The brothers fight again and Rām shoots an arrow at Bālī.

5.41–50. Rām explains to the dying Bālī that this is his punishment for breaking his promise to Sugrīb to give him Tārā as his wife. He may beg for his life if he wishes. Bālī chooses death. Indr hears Tārā's lamentations and grants that Bālī may live in heaven. Sugrīb is crowned.

5.51–6.9 Rām sends Laksm(ṇ) to remind Sugrīb of his promise to help. Sugrīb takes Hanumān, who has made himself as small as a finger, to Rām. The latter asks Sugrīb to command the forces. Aṅgad is put in charge of a specially selected force and Hanumān is to be in charge of Rām's force. They march off to a position facing Laṅkā.

6.9–18. Rām sends Hanumān, in preference to others whose powers are not so great, to Laṅkā to find out where Sītā is. Hanumān, taking Rām's ring to prove his identity, flies over Laṅkā. He is fed and re-directed by a hermit. He makes himself small to pass safely through the mouth and ear of Riktāsī.

6.18–26. Hanumān crosses over the ramparts of Laṅkā catching sight of various ogre chiefs on his way. He reaches Rāb(ṇ)'s apartments and refrains from killing him in his sleep. He learns where Sītā is by overhearing a conversation and contrives to enter her palace through the roof.

6.26–34. Hanumān gives Sītā news of Rām and then gives her the ring. He is rebuked for not presenting the ring first. Sītā gives him her ring.

6.34–48. Leaving Sītā, Hanumān climbs to the top of the Asoka trees and throws fruit down on the park. He jumps on to the golden rampart and breaks it. He obliterates the ogre army which comes to attack him. Rāb(ṇ), learning this from two survivors, sends Indrajit. Hanumān strikes down the gigantic Atikāy who struggles back to Indrajit to tell him.

6.48–63. Despite warnings given to him of Hanumān's powers, Indrajit marches on Hanumān with his troops. Hanumān raises himself up high on his entwined tail and uses enemy arrows to make a palisade round himself. He is captured and taken to Rāb(ṇ) who orders his execution. He tells the ogres that if they wish to kill him they must wrap him up in cloth and set fire to him. When this is done, he rises in the air, sets fire to Laṅkā and returns to Rām, who rewards him.

7.1–10.	Sugrīb recommends King Mahājambū as an ally to augment Rām's forces. Hanumān and Aṅgad are sent to ask for his help.
7.10–25.	Hanumān and Aṅgad give the message brusquely and are thrown into irons. At night, however, Hanumān breaks their bonds and conveys King Mahājambū back to Rām's camp. The revelation of Rām as Nārāy(ṇ) brings Mahājambū to submission.
7.25–34.	King Mahājambū's two right-hand men, discovering that he has disappeared, look for him all over the *cakravāla* and finally find him. When Rām explains about the attack on Laṅkā, King Mahājambū excuses himself because of his age but offers the two chiefs to Rām.
7.34–46.	When, after a military exercise, and further consultation, construction of the causeway is begun, the fish undo the work. Sugrīb and Hanumān vie with each other in their offers to turn themselves into a bridge, while Aṅgad offers to swallow the sea so that they can march across.
7.46–54.	Rām, explaining that it is essential that his own power should be manifested, shoots an arrow which causes the sea to dry up. The Sea-god appeals on behalf of the sea creatures. It is agreed that the fish shall reconstruct the causeway. Rām's forces cross.
7.54–8.13.	Rāb(ṇ) hears of the approach of Rām, asks Bibhek to foretell the future and then banishes him when he prophesies calamity. Bibhek goes to Rām. When Jambūbān corroborates the truth of Bibhek's prophecy, Rām agrees to accept his services.
8.13–27.	Maṇḍogirī is rebuked by Rāb(ṇ) for telling him he should not have stolen Sītā. A battle takes place in which both generals, Rām's Rukkhara: and Rāb(ṇ)'s Rakkhasen are killed. Rāb(ṇ), overjoyed when he is mistakenly told that it was Hanumān, not Rukkhara: who was killed, has parasols opened to celebrate. They obscure the sun.
8.27–40.	Rām destroys the parasols with an arrow. Rāb(ṇ) takes Sītā with him in his carriage and flies through the air. Rām shoots an arrow which destroys the carriage. Rāb(ṇ) goes up again but, when Rām points a finger at him, he feels

faint. Realising that Bibhek's prophecy of doom for Laṅkā was true, he assembles his army.

8.40–56. Rām sends Aṅgad to tell Rāb(ṇ) to take his demons and leave Laṅkā. On the way Aṅgad quells the elephant, Bhakkhanes. Aṅgad demands to be placed on a level with Rāb(ṇ) when giving his message. Rāb(ṇ) agrees first that he shall be level with Kumbhakār(ṇ), then that he shall be level with Indrajit.

8.56–67. Aṅgad kills the ogre soldiers round him, enters the palace and places himself as high as Rāb(ṇ), by coiling his tail and sitting on it. Rāb(ṇ) sends for Maṇḍogirī, Aṅgad's mother, so that he shall at least pay his respects to her. Aṅgad gives his message, fights his way out, kills four ogres sent to catch him and reaches home.

8.67–9.1. Rāb(ṇ) decides to send Kumbhakār(ṇ) to destroy Rām's army. Kumbhakār(ṇ), wishing to restrain him, reminds him that the whole course of events arose from Sūrapanakhā's wilfulness. However, when accused of being afraid, Kumbhakār(ṇ) agrees to go.

9.1–13. When Kumbhakār(ṇ) surrounds his army, Rām sends Bibhek to invite him to come over to them. Kumbhakār(ṇ) refuses and criticises Rām for killing Bālī. Rām sends Bibhek and Laksm(ṇ) to explain that Bālī's death was due to retribution.

9.14–25. Kumbhakār(ṇ) attacks Bibhek and Laksm(ṇ). His magic weapon strikes Laksm(ṇ)'s foot and from it a huge strychnine plant grows. Hanumān is sent to the Hemabānt to fetch three ingredients for Bibhek's cure for Laksm(ṇ). Then he is sent to Laṅkā to bring from beneath the head of the sleeping Rāb(ṇ) the stone needed to grind the ingredients. When a little more time is required, Hanumān halts the Sun's chariot in its course. Laksm(ṇ) is cured.

9.25–39. When Kumbhakār(ṇ) and Laksm(ṇ) fight again, Laksm(ṇ) kills Kumbhakār(ṇ). Rāb(ṇ) sends Indrajit out to fight. Indrajit's power causes darkness to fall. Bibhek describes the immense power of Indrajit to Rām. Indrajit fails to strike Laksm(ṇ) but succeeds against Hanumān. Hanumān, Laksm(ṇ) and Aṅgad fight against Indrajit.

9.39–52. Indrajit's arrow turns into a mesh of *nāgas* entangling Laksm(ṇ) and the army. Rāb(ṇ) sends for Sītā and, thinking that Rām is also thus captured, accuses her of vain boasting. Bibhek suggests to Rām that he should ask for help from Isūr. Rām declares that if Laksm(ṇ) dies, he will destroy all heaven, except Isūr's dwelling, with his bow. The gods rush to tell Isūr, who says that Brahm is to blame because he cast the magic spell over Indrajit's arrow. Brahm asks the king of the *garuḍas* to disperse the *nāgas* and Laksm(ṇ) and the army are released.

9.51–10.3. Both sides prepare for battle. Rāb(ṇ) brews a snake poison to destroy Rām's army but Hanumān defeats the plan by spilling it all.

10.3–47. Rāb(ṇ) sends 5 sons and 5 generals, one after the other, with an army to fight against Rām. They are defeated in turn by heroes of Rām's side.

- 10.3–12. Indrajit is killed by Laksm(ṇ). Rāb(ṇ) in his anger almost kills Sītā.
- 10.12–17. Mahodar is killed by Aṅgad.
- 10.17–20. Atikāy is killed by Laksm(ṇ).
- 10.20–25. Trīsīr is killed by Hanumān and Usabh.
- 10.25–27. Narātȧk is killed by Bibitr.
- 10.28–31. Mahākpāl is killed by Usabh.
- 10.31–36. Dūramukh is killed by Kesar.
- 10.36–38. Mukharakkhȧs is killed by Chief Nal.
- 10.39–43. Kumbhagadādhar is killed by Chief Nīl.
- 10.43–47. Mālmād is killed by Sȧtabalī.

10.47–48. Rāb(ṇ) assembles the remnants of his army and sends messengers beyond the *cakravāla* to ask Mūlaphalam to bring reinforcements.

Later events of the Rāma story. (The later composition. Parts 75–80.)

75.1–10. While Rām is out riding in the forest, the ogress Ātul in human form mingles with Sītā's court ladies and asks her to draw a portrait of Rāb(ṇ). She does so and the ogress disappears into the picture itself.

75.11–20. When Rām is arriving back, Sītā hides the portrait under his bed. It makes him sleepless and very angry with the court women. Laksm(ṇ) discovers the portrait and Sītā, seeing that her women will be blamed if she keeps silence, admits that she drew it.

75.20–27. The angry Rām orders Laksm(ṇ) to take Sītā away and kill her. Laksm(ṇ) takes her into the jungle but, believing in her loyalty to the king, does not wish to carry out the order, especially as the queen is pregnant.

75.27–39. Sītā tries to make Laksm(ṇ) do his duty by speaking roughly to him. Finally Laksm(ṇ) strikes but the sword turns into a garland. Encouraged by this miracle, they part company, she to wander onward, he to return to the city.

75.39–42. Indr helps Laksm(ṇ) by producing a dead deer, whose liver Laksm(ṇ) cuts out to take to the king, pretending it is Sītā's.

75.42–51. The queen bewails her plight. Indr transforms himself into a buffalo which leads Sītā to a hermitage. There the sage Vajjaprit hears her story and uses magic to produce a hut in which she can live.

75.51–57. Indr sends his four wives and the goddesses down to earth to help Sītā when her son is born. Sītā laments, when they return to heaven, on the loneliness and poverty of herself and her child.

75.57–76.5. Sītā leaves her son in the care of the sage while she goes to bathe but later fetches him unseen by the hermit. When the latter realises that the child has gone, he creates a similar child.

76.6–18. The sage instructs the boys, teaching them to use the bow and arrow. Finding them apt pupils he makes them magic bows. They shoot a huge *Barringtonia acutangula* and shatter it with far-reaching noises.

76.18–25. The boys tell the sage and their mother about the tree. They learn from their mother more about their family history.

76.25–37. Rām consults his astrologers about the remarkable noise which all have heard. It is decided to find the potential enemy by attaching a warning message to a horse and letting it go at will. First Hanumān fetches Bhirut and Sutrut from Kaikes.

76.37–42. The message is placed on the horse's neck, prayers are said for the discovery of the potential enemy and the horse is let loose. Hanumān follows. Behind him come Bhirut and Sutrut with the army.

76.42–52. The boys go off again into the forest where they observe the trees and animals. They find the horse, catch it and, in spite of the warning in the message, ride it.

76.52–77.7 Hanumān makes two vain attempts to capture the boys. They tie him up and scratch a message on his face. He finds Bhirut and Sutrut and tells them what has happened.

77.7–12. Bhirut and Sutrut cannot untie the bonds. Rām sets Hanumān free, hears his tale and sends him, with Bhirut and Sutrut, to fetch the boys.

77.13–26. The boys confront the army, refuse to give their names and claim that their actions were justifiable. They fight Bhirut and Sutrut, using magic, and overcome the whole army at one point. All revive however, and Rām-Laksm(ṇ) is captured and taken back to Rām, while Japp-Laksm(ṇ) runs away.

77.26–33. Hearing what has happened, Rām orders Rām-Laksm(ṇ) to be kept in fetters in a cage for three days and to be publicly reviled. The populace secretly pities him. The gods come down and make him comfortable.

77.33–46. When Japp-Laksm(ṇ) arrives home and tells the story, the sage is able to assure the queen that Rām-Laksm(ṇ) is still alive although in trouble. The queen gives Japp-Laksm(ṇ) her magic ring and he sets out to find his brother. He reaches Aiyudhyā.

77.46–78.3 As Japp-Laksm(ṇ) listens to the crowd speaking of his brother's imminent execution Indr sends Rambhā to help him. She takes to his brother a pitcher of water in which Japp-Laksm(ṇ) has placed the magic ring. Rām-Laksm(ṇ) uses the ring to break his bonds and escape. Reunited with his brother, he returns to the forest, intending to destroy the enemy before returning home.

78.3–12. When Rām hears that the executioners have lost Rām-Laksm(ṇ) he has the army made ready and marches out with it to fetch the boy himself. The boys go out and stand facing the army. The men are afraid of them.

78.12–23. Rām and Rām-Laksm(ṇ) shoot arrows at each other of which the magic properties cancel each other out or turn harmless. Rām finally prays that, if the boys are of his own lineage, his arrow shall become food. It does so and he asks the boys who they are.

78.23–36. When Rām-Laksm(ṇ) reveals that Sītā is their mother, Rām asks Laksm(ṇ) about her execution. He is overjoyed to learn the truth and asks Rām-Laksm(ṇ) to take him to Sītā; he will bring her back to rule the city. Suspicious of his intentions, the boys set off quickly for home, trying to avoid pursuit.

78.36–53. Rām follows the boys home and halts his army near the hermitage. The sage acts as go-between. He fails to persuade Sītā to return to Rām but does prevail upon her to see Rām in person.

78.53–79.12 When Rām asks her to return with him, Sītā angrily refuses, blaming him for believing her unfaithful in spite of the evidence of Hanumān's visit to Laṅkā and her ordeal by fire, and pointing out that she is destitute now and unfit for court life. Rām asks to take the boys with him, thinking that she will soon follow them. When she refuses this, he says he would rather die than return without any of them. Sītā gives in to this and tells the boys. They are unhappy about parting from her.

79.12–24. Rām tells his sons that he will take them to meet their grandmothers and then, if they miss Sītā, they may return. Sītā gives them advice and they part company. The uncles and Hanumān are delighted with them. The party returns to the city.

79.25–32. The grandmothers hear Rām's news and welcome the boys, who tell them about their life in the forest.

79.33–44.	Rām organises companions for his sons and holds a feast in their honour.
79.44–80.1	After some time, Rām overhears the boys express their grief about their mother's loneliness and sends them with Sītā's women to see Sītā and ask her to return. If she will not do so, they are to leave the women there as companions for her. They arrive at the hermitage and speak first with the *ācārya*, then with Sītā.
80.1–13.	When the boys ask Sītā to go back to Aiyudhyā, she says she will not go back unless the king dies, in which case she will go back to his funeral. She refuses to accept the court ladies as her companions. They all return to give the answer to the distressed Rām.
80.13–25.	Rām has a funeral pavilion and urn prepared to trick Sītā into returning. Hanumān fetches her to attend her husband's "funeral".
80.25–35.	When Sītā laments beside the funeral pavilion, Rām comes out to comfort her from where he is observing her. She runs away from him. When she sees that she will be unable to avoid capture she prays that the earth will open for her and descends to the land of the *nāgas*.
80.35–48.	The king of the *nāgas* offers Sītā a home in his palace. Hanumān is sent by Rām to find her and is able to tell Rām that she will be looked after well. Rām, in despair at his separation from her, writes a message and sends it, attached to his arrow, to Laṅkā and from there down into the underworld.

The Main Rāma Story

(The earlier composition. Parts 1–10 of the Institut Bouddhique text.)

1.1–4. Rām kills the ogre Kākanāsūr who, in the form of a crow, has destroyed Bisvāmitr's sacrifice.

1. * Then the supreme prince, Bisvāmitr, most worthy, most high, magnificent as the most elevated of kings, was well pleased. * His anchorite's court, large and lofty, was enclosed, screened by its enveloping walls and by the decorative pillars and door. * In that sanctuary, where an offering was to be made and the Sun's banner was flying, the trees which were burnt in the sacrifices were growing, their foliage luxuriant, shade spreading from their branches. * A stream flowed past, purifying the poisons on the stones, sparkling, mingling, beautiful, its plentiful water splashing up. * Coconuts and arecas grew clustering against the exalted cell, all around — just right, it seemed for plucking — a great variety. * All manner of trees,[1] dense with lush leaves, sprang up there with their ambrosial fruits. * Squirrels crouched and huddled there while gibbons, civet-cats and monkeys jumped playfully on the branches.

2. (2) * At that time there was a base, godless creature known by the name of Kākanāsūr. * She heard, wafted aloft, the sound made by the banner and the notes of the conch, ready for the rite of that lord, the master of Rām, the mighty. * The godless creature changed herself for this occasion into a crow and, using her astonishing powers, flew * there and pecked noisily at the offering prepared according to the Books of the Laws. The trembling flowers and leaves of the *śamī* tree fell off all about. * As the cawing cries of the crow resounded far away, the waving banner was detached — and she hid fearfully, taking shelter, staying close.

* Then the great hermit of effective powers, Bisvāmitr, whose deeds
were mighty, * who built up merit in accordance with the sacred
Books, making offerings and dutifully practising the asceticism which
3. brings power, * saw the great demon crow, that (3) vicious evil godless
creature, scattering his preparations for the power-giving rite. * "I shall
ask for my godsons, those two remarkable princes, that is, for Nārāy(ṇ),
* son of King Dasarath of widespread power. I shall solve my problem
by speaking to the king. * I shall come to the fulfilment of my religious
life." That lord of power and mighty prowess murmured an
incantation from the treatise on the supernatural arts, * that the
supreme Rām and Laksm(ṇ), the strong and mighty, the most high,
might manifest the victorious powers of asceticism. * He spoke to the
princes. "Greetings, Rām and Laksm(ṇ)! I would have you come, for
this very moment is auspicious." * Then the royal anchorite of power
4. led the princely lord and and his young brother * to (4) the hermitage,

(4) to the court for offerings, and produced by supernatural power a most efficacious and mighty arrow. * "O victorious Rām and Laksm(ṇ)," he said, "you are stronger than all. Aim this invincible arrow * to kill Kākanāsūr, to show the lordly power of both of you." * Then Rām held his bow, aimed the arrow at the ogre * and shot. The godless creature Kākanāsūr fell dying. * The mighty arrow went straight on and on. The demoness plunged into Pātāl. The prince's arrow followed. * As she went through every region, every thoroughfare, it pursued the creature until she died.

1.5–10. **King Janak of Mithilā adopts Sītā, found during the royal ploughing ceremony. He holds the contest of the bow, in which Rām is successful.**

5. * (5) Then the King of Mithilā was carrying out a ceremony in the
prescribed way. * On an auspicious day in June, he assembled his chief
ministers for the turning of the soil * in accordance with the ancient
tradition so as to bring peace to the people. * As he took his golden
plough with the royal oxen, his gait was like that of a roaring lion.
* When he had ploughed as far as the bank of the Yamunā river, there
suddenly appeared a divine, golden maiden on a raft, * herself in a
magnificent lotus-flower, completely perfect, of superlative and
remarkable splendour. * The king was highly delighted with this, a
6. royal daughter. (6). *Then the lord of Mithilā assembled his soldiers
for an immediate return to the city. * He took the young lady, so fine,
as his own daughter to his kingdom * where he was an excellent ruler
of his people. Then he held a ceremony to give her a name * and in
accordance with the circumstances she was called Sītā.[2] Pure and
beautiful, she glowed like the full moon. * The royal princess, so noble
in face and character, was, it was plain to see, unequalled by any of the
ten thousand goddesses.

* Then the king, master of men, saw his daughter's remarkable, pure
loveliness. * That learned and august sovereign therefore created by magic
a bow and arrow and he made a vow, * saying, "If any god of un-
7. vanquished power can raise this magic bow with his invincible (7)
might, * I will give the hand of my beloved Sītā, so esteemed, to that
god of mighty deeds." * Miraculously, in all the ten directions, a
tremor went through the earth and through the heaven of the thirty-
three, where heat affected the godly throngs.

* All the gods, overjoyed, hurried eagerly down together all in disorder from the heaven of the thirty-three. * Indr was mounted on Airā, deathless lord of the *nāgas*, bright, splendid, elevated. * The God

(7) of Fire, exalted, of unconquerable might, rode on a rhinoceros of fire of
superlative strength. * The God of the Wind caused havoc in the sky,
for, as he came with his horses, there blew a gale such as to bring death.
* The God of Rain, a huge form, rode on a mighty *nāga*, splashed all
over with water. * And there came Candrakumār, borne on a bird, a
patterned gold peacock. * Brahm, observer of the religious way of life,
8. strong and mighty ascetic, rode on a royal goose. (8) * Neṛrati, lord of
power, was seated upon an ogre as he set forth. * Baisrab, great king and
lord, came in his immense, magnificent aerial palace. * Isūr, whose
power, prestige and splendour surpassed all in the three worlds and in the
dwelling of the divine lords, * was seated upon a great royal ox, having
in his divine being infinitely great might and power. * All the gods, the
kinnaras and the ruling princes gazed at the mighty bow, intent upon
their attempt to lift it. * Isūr of unlimited powers, the representatives of
the gods, and the kings tried out their physical prowess * and were
unable to raise the bow. They remained there with His Majesty.
9. * Then (9) the king, master of men, saw Harī, Prince Nārāy(ṇ) Rām.
* Perhaps he would be able to raise the magic bow with his strength, for
he had force and physical prowess in abundance? * Isūr, leader of men,
saw that all the gods were by now about to return home * but Bisvāmitr
had brought that royal lord and Prince Laksm(ṇ) * to the city of Mithilā.
When they approached him to ask permission to try to raise the bow,
* the king of Mithilā replied, "Prince, do please demonstrate the power
of your right arm."
* Rām had watched all the kings trying to raise the mighty bow. An
10. eager look came into his fine face. * He stepped forward (10) to try what
his strength could perform. All the godly hermits and princes watched
the mighty deed. * Rām, immensely strong and mighty prince of
superlative power and prowess, * raised the bow of victory! All the gods
and men in the world * offered their congratulations to that supreme
lord whose strength was seen to be tremendous. * The prince swung the
bow, raising it up and took aim, sending the mighty arrow up high,
demonstrating his powers unmistakably. * He held out the mighty bow
and arrow. Curving like a wheel, they whirled round in his fine hands.

1.10–17. **The king of Mithilā gives Sītā in marriage to Rām. An envoy is sent to his father, King Dasarath, to invite him to the wedding. With his sons, Bhirut and Sutrut, King Dasarath comes to Mithilā.**

* Then, seeing the surpassing strength and power of Rām, the king of Mithilā * was delighted. He offered his good wishes to him for

11. triumph upon triumph, for the greatest achievements (11) * and
brought the beloved Princess Sītā, endowed with great qualities, and
offered her to Rām, the greatest of all. * He and his chief ministers
ordered an envoy to arrange the engagement with King Dasarath,
* instructing the envoy to go and give details to that king in the city of
Aiyudhyā. * This the envoy did. He approached to inform King
Dasarath of great esteem, supreme lord among princes, * saying,
"Bisvāmitr, the great hermit of mighty powers, whose achievements are
the result of his asceticism, just recently * brought the royal princes,
Rām and his young brother, to * the city of Mithilā, where the king
had assembled his forces for the raising of the bow of supernatural
power. * His Majesty made a vow: if any god or prince, of supreme
physical force, * managed to raise the bow, then in accordance with his
12. vow King Janak (12) would offer the princess called Sītā to him.
* Then all the gods and princes came forward one by one to try their
strength and raise the bow. * They could not do it! They remained
there in the court of the king's ceremonial hall. * But when Your
Majesty's son, Rām, master of men, came forward to try the effect of
his great power, * then, by the might of his arm, he raised the bow and
shot an arrow, there in the arena amidst the assembly of learned beings.
* And there reverberated throughout the earth the sound of a thunderbolt, of a hundred thousand thunderbolts. * The mighty sovereign,
great King Janak, overjoyed, * praising him and wishing him success, is
preparing for marriage the dear, noble Sītā, * to unite her with Rām of
13. great might. I am sent by the king, (13) my master, to inform Your
Majesty, protector of the earth, * and to invite you to come and enjoy
the marriage celebrations."

* King Dasarath heard the envoy tell the story of his elder son,
* how he had demonstrated his surpassing strength, exceeding that of
all other princes of all kingdoms in all directions, * and his joy was
immeasurable. He said, * "O my chief ministers and attendants, hear
the news told by the envoy * about the dear Prince Rām, my elder son.
He has strength greater than anyone's in the three worlds! * He was
able to raise the bow of victory, manifesting his prowess before all
14. men. * We heard a sound (14) at that time and thought that it was a
hundred thousand thunderbolts * striking magnificent Mount Sumeru
and that this was why a tremor went through the earth over a distance
of 80,000 leagues. * But now the envoy tells me about Rām, great
among princes, how he raised the mighty bow * of supernatural power;
how he shot it and it broke[3] with a sound as of a hundred thousand
thunderbolts. * And now at once the King of Mithilā will make
preparations for a wedding — auspicious occasion — between * Rām

(14) and the princess, by name Sītā, who will be his first lady. * O ministers
and generals, please muster a force. Let them mount their horses and
yoke their chariots."
* Immediately the chief ministers respectfully placed their hands
15. together and praised the prince's merit. * They took leave of (15) His
Majesty the King and went out to assemble a vast host of soldiers.
* They made ready the chariots, the big elephants, the horses, all
according to the King's command and went to inform King Dasarath.
* "We have done that which was your bidding. We have diligently
organised the troops so that they are neatly arranged in their military
divisions." * Then the king mounted on a horse-drawn carriage to sit
with his three august wives. * Bhirut rode on a large elephant, its head
held high, accompanying his father. * The elephant, decked with
bejewelled, golden trappings and a beautiful silk embroidered collar,
had brilliant gems placed upon it. * Sutrut, regal as a lion, was seated
upon an elephant equipped with splendid golden trappings. * He held
16. the gold croc (16) proudly, dazzling reflections darting here and there
as he moved his outstretched arm * and drove off, closely
accompanying the king, his father, who was seated in his magnificent
gold carriage. * The whole infantry force gave a shout and moved
forward in procession with the princes * to the city of Mithilā where,
when the king was ready to enter the city, they were ranged rank upon
rank. * King Janak was delighted that Dasarath, foremost of lords,
had arrived. * Leaving his glorious gold palace, so fine and perfect, like
a domain of the thirty-three, * he went to receive that mighty sovereign
17. and great overlord. * The two great kings went into the palace, (17)
with its bejewelled tiers, and spoke in friendship to each other.

1.17–31. **The wedding ceremony of Rām and Sītā is held. King Janak then accompanies King Dasarath and Rām as the whole party leaves for Aiyudhyā. At the gate of Mithilā the ogre Rāmaparamasūr threatens Rām because he has been given his name. He is reduced to submission.**

* Then the two masters of men assembled the divinely wise hermits, whose power came from observing the precepts of asceticism, * the chief ministers and the Brahmin teachers, who had read right through the three Vedas and the Jyotisār, * and had them confer to find an auspicious day, perfect for carrying out the marriage ceremony. * When they had found an auspicious day and a time with excellent portents, stable and firm in the signs, * the king had music played — strings, trumpets, conches, drums — ordering performances by the various

groups, * and he led forth his dear Sītā, most high, and joined her in
matrimony to Rām the god. * The two, prince and princess, paid
18. homage to the two great kings. * The two fathers, (18) seated on
thrones of fine crystal, decoratively bejewelled, * felt they knew in their
hearts what Prince Rām, master of men, had in mind.

* Then the king had the royal drum beaten to assemble the chief
ministers and had them muster the military forces * and order them to
select strong elephants, horses and fine carriages, complete with drivers
to drive. * The ministers hastily bowed low, saluting the king with
respect, * and, taking their leave, departed to gather at the hall of
justice. They took up their stations, all in their places. * Here, there
and everywhere, they were drawing up the troops of soldiers and
saddling the horses, which were provided with fine new saddles. * The
royal carriage, engraved with a design of flowering creepers, was
harnessed with swift horses and waiting in position. * They made ready
the huge elephants, all harnessed, their embroidered cloths firmly fixed,
19. prettily decorating their foreheads, * and gold bands set with jewels (19)
decking their tusks. All was quickly finished and put ready and all the
drivers and elephants assembled. * Every item was prepared. Everywhere the trappings, infinitely numerous, dazzled the eye with their
many colours. * Next the ministers approached the king and informed
him that they had assembled all the troops in readiness, * all according
to the command of that lord, the great King Janak.

* Then the three royal persons, masters of men, * called the
assembly to choose an auspicious time, excellent in respect of its signs
and the accompanying position of the constellations. * When this was
done and a day was found, a watch, a moment, which, together with
the movement of the lunar mansion, was auspicious, * the two kings
20. departed from the ancient royal city of Mithilā. * They (20) ranged
their forces with a company of advance troops to guard against an
attack. * As for Prince Rām's men, he marched them off behind his
father, * following the forces of the great King Janak, who had his
daughter in his care. * The whole host, elephants and horses,
accompanied those masters of men, the three royal persons, as they set
off. * Dust was scattered everywhere. The sky was blotted out with
darkness in all directions. There was not a ray of light! * The sun's
shafts were screened, gone. Earth trembled over a distance of eighty
thousand leagues. * The kings marched as far as the gate to the open
road. The clamour of the infantry, the rumbling of the carriages, * the
noises made by the elephants and horses, the wafting strains of music
and the voices of men * rose loudly to the heavens. The sky and the
21. sun (21) were overcast, the rays of light dimmed and * darkness filled

(21) every corner, a dread and astonishing manifestation of the power of
the divine Rām.

* Then the fierce Rāmaparamasūr, greatly daring, mighty teacher of
the art of the magic arrow, * heard, as the news spread, of the
victorious power of the supreme lord Rām, elder son of King
Dasarath, * of his mighty deed thus manifested and how his given
name was Rām, the victorious. * The ogre gave much thought to that
name, regretting it. * In a temper, he went boldly and imperiously
through the air, armed with all the weapons he could need — * he had
22. arrows, a bow and an axe, piercingly sharp, (22) for destruction — with
the intention of testing this power which was due to asceticism. * A
moment later he was upon the forces of the great King Janak and of
the father of Rām and Laksm(ṇ). * "Hail, Dasarath!" he said, "How is
it that you so uncompromisingly gave your son the name Rām which
was my name? * Your son is a learned man but of no great strength.
Such power as he has is to be classed as human and of this world.
* How dare you set your son up as a god? I would call such behaviour
extremely provocative. It is an act of aggression, a serious offence. * I
am going to cut off the life of your son, do him to death this instant."

* King Dasarath replied, "O divine hermit, you who are governed by
this world's philosophy of truth, * with regard to the name of this son
of mine, I did not decide it for him from my own ideas. * Great sages
23. in their millions (23) with their supernatural powers, all of them being
great hermits of learning, assembled and * gave him this name. And
because this eldest son of mine has mighty power[4] * the assembly of all
the royal hermits and great men of learning endowed him with this
auspicious name, * calling him the august, the divine Rām, who has
achieved abundant merit. That was how it was."

* Then the anger of the ogre Rāmaparamasūr increased most
dreadfully. * Furious and full of animosity, he was up and away,
rushing through the air towards Rām's force. * King Dasarath felt a
shock of fear. He was afraid for the life of his son. * He wept, beat his
breast, his heart feeling tight and full. He moaned, moving restlessly
24. about. (24) * Then he sent a brave messenger to ask news of Prince
Rām, fearing that he might have been overcome by the physical power
of the ogre, that he might be defeated. He might *not* be victorious in
battle! * The messenger took his leave and went straight off, close
upon the heels of the great ogre.

* Then Rāmaparamasūr, ferocious and huge, brandishing his axe
and wielding his bow and arrow, * flew towards the force of Rām,
supporter of the earth, son of the supreme lord Dasarath. * Reaching
his intended destination, Rāmaparamasūr went right up to the gate,

(24) wielding his axe and bow and arrows * and yelled out with loud cries.
He stamped his feet on the ground, making the earth tremble. * He
called out to the master of men, "You ascetic, you! You are ignorant
25. and timid yet (25) thoroughly bad! * How is it that you have dared to
take my name ? — for I have great power in my right arm, tremendous
physical force. * Come out and settle your moral debt with me so that
it shall not be a cause of trouble and unseemly provocation. * If you
behave so arrogantly I shall take this axe and strike you, bashing your
head in. * I shall knock down your glorious pavilion,[5] adorned with
jewels, smashing it to pieces instantly but * if you bow down in the
dust of my feet, placing your hands with palms together, kneeling,
* then I will forgive you and let you keep on with this life." * Rām
replied, "O arrogant great godless creature! Where did you come from,
flying here through the air? * From the skies? From the mountains?
From the forests and caves of the vast Hemabānt? * You come here to
26. my encampment (26) with many demands!"

* Hearing Rām, Rāmaparamasūr grew angry. He blazed with
indignation. * "So!" he said, "how is it that you are not afraid, not
agape at my physical strength for deeds of prowess? * Am I not the son
of a great sage, whose strength is in the precepts, whose manner of life
is elevated above ordinary standards, * and who is known by the name
of King Yāmatik? That is the race of my father. * You are without
understanding, a vulgar ascetic of the forest, a nobody of ill-omened
birth. * You, with your impudence, do not recognise a grand lord when
you see one! Like a blind man, you are confused. You lie * when you
say that I am a godless creature. This might well be called trouble-
making, committing a serious offence."

27. * "O Rāmaparamasūr," Rām instantly replied, "I may have (27) said
that you are * a godless creature lacking in gentleness. Well, what you
just said could be described as thoroughly offensive! * Now it has
never been a normal characteristic of hermits to speak rudely, causing
annoyance. * In all the four continents they speak only with loving
friendship towards everyone. * They are always most kind, they use
words responsibly, they are well-behaved and they follow the Dharma
as it is clearly their role to do. * But now one would say you are
provoking trouble. You are being aggressive, trying to be my rival in
heroic deeds. * I am in fact the son of the great King Dasarath,
supreme among princes — * indeed the kings of all kingdoms have
submitted to him and pay homage at his feet. * As for myself, in the
beginning, in the second age of the world, I lived as Nārāy(ṇ). * All the
28. gods and hermits (28) saw that all kinds of godless creatures were attacking religion * and therefore the gods invited me to come and be born

(28) * as Rām, the strong and mighty, to suppress those evil, godless
creatures who were being wickedly oppressive and destructive."

* Rāmaparamasūr then replied without delay to Prince Rām,
"Divine Rām! You could be described as very conceited, over-
confident and boastful, * claiming to be of the race of Bisnu, of
Nārāy(ṇ), master of men, who upheld the burden of the earth. * If
you are of the race of Harī, the family of mighty Bisnu of great
strength and prowess, * then come and try to raise my bow which I
29. am holding — if you can! (29) * Then I will believe that you are of
the esteemed race of Nārāy(ṇ), lord of the world in the second age."

* Then Prince Rām manifested his prowess and the power of his
physique. * With his left arm only, the supporter of the earth, so
mighty, raised the magic bow up aloft and whirled it round. * He
took great Aggivās, his sharp, powerful arrow and instructed it,
together with the bow. * He swung the bow up and aimed it towards
the body of the ogre. * The latter, agape at the deed, felt a sudden
shock of dread. Trembling, he raised his hands, palms together, * and
30. bowing low in homage, he said, "Please, lord, I beg for my life." (30)
* "I have already instructed my arrow," Rām said in reply, "and I
can shoot it." * Rāmaparamasūr was more and more afraid. His
mind went blank and he trembled as, with palms together, * he
bowed low and said to the lord of compassion, "I beg to be expiated,
lord, of all the wrong I did just now. * I offer you, supporter of the
earth and lord of princes, — for I must reckon with your powerful
bow — * I offer you all my arrows. Please do not continue to be
angry. * I would like to invite you, who wield a sharp arrow, to shoot
it to gather together my own arrows, which I offer you * so that all
shall go into your quiver and you, great prince, will manifest your
great prowess."

* Then the god Rām aimed a sharp and mighty arrow, the great
unconquerable Brahmās, shooting it to gather together all
31. Rāmaparamasūr's arrows on the mountain height of Kailās. (31)
* They came into his quiver of swift arrows as was the command of
Prince Nārāy(ṇ), master of men. * Rāmaparamasūr raised his hands,
palms together, to show his admiration of the perfection of the prince,
lord of power. * He bowed low, taking leave of the lord, and went
through the air to the hermitage which was his own home. * Rām,
exalted by his mighty deeds and great strength, excelling in efficacious
powers, * gained a clear and decisive victory over the ogre
Rāmaparamasūr amid the host of soldiers.

1.31–38. **The journey to Aiyudhyā is completed. A feast is given after which King Janak leaves to return home to Mithilā. King Dasarath prepares to hand over the kingdom to his eldest son Rām, but is dissuaded from this by Kaikesī who reminds him of a promise to give the kingdom to Bhirut, her own son.**

* Then the two princes went to attend upon the two sovereigns.
* Their father experienced the five joys[6] and delightedly congratulated
Prince Rām, * praising his achievement, his prowess and his over-
32. whelming victory on this occasion. (32) * The three royal persons,
protectors of the earth, assembled the vast host of attendants and the
four army corps[7] * and marched their force, at a time calculated to be
the most auspicious, as indicated by the planet Mahāmahendr,
* proceeding all the way to that delightful ancient city, the glorious
royal seat of Aiyudhyā.

* The king provided a feast, as was the custom, with the beautiful ladies of the court at hand in attendance. * The royal family amused themselves pleasantly, together with the numerous grand counsellors and generals. * The king provided a banquet for the army, for the men and for every officer of high or low rank. * The chaplains, Brahmins and poets offered their respects, their admiration and their congratulations to the prince.

* Then the king of Mithilā took leave of his elder, King Dasarath,
33. * and entrusted his daughter (33), of divine purity, to King Dasarath.
* This done, he returned to the ancient city of Mithilā, * to rule his
peaceful kingdom with admirable integrity, constantly pondering on
meritorious deeds.

* Then King Dasarath, foremost of great sovereigns, assembled his
court in connection with the transference of the kingdom, the beautiful
white umbrella * and all the accoutrements, the decorative, bejewelled
crown and the splendid gold sandals * to Rām, his eldest son, for him
to rule the land in his place. * The king had the city tidied up and the
34. roads, every highway and byway, smoothed and flattened. (34) * He
bade the military commanders bring their troops by every route to the
royal citadels within the king's domain. * All the princes of the various
countries were to bring their gifts to offer to the master of men. * Then
the holy hermits, the aged Brahmins, so wise, and the princes and
princesses * of all countries brought their presents and came to offer
them respectfully to the master of men, * reciting praises of the virtue
and the strength of the mighty Prince Rām. * All declared their
allegiance to the great prince, Rām, who would now rule the kingdom
in place of his father. * The king was old now. It was right that he

(34) should thus hand over the realm to Rām * that he might maintain the
35. royal domain, protect the populace and give them (35) peace. * King
Dasarath, their chief, seeing all the princes in agreement and so eager
in their approval, * ordered that an auspicious day should be sought
for the crowning of Prince Rām. * The king would organise a great
feast. He gave instructions for the provision by the various services of
all kinds of amusement.

* When the auspicious day had already been found for holding the
coronation, glorious occasion, * then it was that Kaikesī came to speak
with the master of men, King Dasarath. * "Lord, with regard to your
promise, given to me when you were setting off to wage war and
36. demonstrate your (36) prowess, * and fight victoriously against King
Ādityasuriyā — you gave me your word * that you would give the
kingdom to Bhirut to rule, that *he* would reign in place of Your
Majesty. * But now you are handing it over to Rām. It seems you have
no honour. You are not trustworthy."

* Then Dasarath wept and wailed excessively, unable to control his
thoughts * until he fell, faint and writhing, as though a fire was being
lit in his breast. * The sovereign Dasarath collected his thoughts,
recalled the incident and gave it consideration. He spoke * to Kaikesī.
"The reason why I am at this moment preparing for my elder son,
37. Rām, * to rule the kingdom and protect the people in my place is (37)
that this is in accordance with ancient procedure. * It has never in
history been the royal custom for the younger to rule before the elder.
* And moreover, if I gave the kingdom to Bhirut to rule, it is likely
there would be trouble, criticism from the people."

* Kaikesī, his wife, replied, "Lord, master of men, * Your Majesty
must be regarded as abandoning, in respect of this matter of honour,
the world's code of morality." * Dasarath answered her, "Will you
please let me ask something of you? * I will divide the kingdom of
glorious Aiyudhyā into two separate parts * and give them to my sons,
Rām, the elder, and Bhirut to rule, so as to abide by my agreement."
* Kaikesī, who out of jealousy wickedly persisted in her wrong attitude
to the matter, * did not like the idea and did not heed it. Anger flared
38. up suddenly in her (38) like the blazing heat of fire. * In a furious outburst, she spoke to the master of men. "I am asking you to do as I say,
my liege, * to give the kingdom to Bhirut. As for your elder son, Rām,
and his young brother, Laksm(ṇ), * let them go and live in the forest
ways, leading the religious life as hermits, keeping the precepts for
fourteen years. * Let them build up their knowledge of magic practices
and then let them return to the city." * King Dasarath, supporter of
the earth, grieved and beat his breast and writhed * in distress at parting

(38) from Rām, his eldest son, most beloved, and from that lord, Laksm(ṇ) * because of the request of Kaikesī, who opposed his plans and was unrighteous, mean and jealous.

1.39–42. **Rām prevents Laksm(ṇ) from killing Kaikesī in anger. Rām, Laksm(ṇ) and Sītā set off for the jungle and receive hospitality at a hermitage beside a river.**

39. * In no time this came to the knowledge of the two princes, Rām and Laksm(ṇ). * The latter, immediately angry like a flaring fire, took hold of his diamond-sharp sword * intent upon killing his step-mother, Kaikesī, but * Rām, divine lord, forestalled his young brother with a pleasant smile, * saying, "No, Laksm(ṇ)! Do not think of initiating a wrong against a dear, good parent! Such an act is too serious a crime. Do not do it. Please let your anger subside." * Then the young Laksm(ṇ) made obeisance at the feet of Prince Rām, master of men.

* United in friendship, the elder and younger lords were about to set
40. off. * Then the esteemed Princess Sītā, weeping as she spoke, said, (40) "Lord, I beg you, pity me! How can I stay here like a widow, without a husband? Whether it will mean that I live or die I want to go along with you. * Please be kind and let me go too, to serve you, master of men." * The elder and younger lords were setting off like long-maned lions leaving their fine den.[8] * They bore their splendid bows and victorious arrows, ready to hand, equipped with every kind of armour. * With his young brother and his consort, the prince left the ancient city of Aiyudhyā. * They journeyed through the forests and reached the edge of a great river, difficult to cross. * They could hear the cries of the animals along the range of mountainous forests, those princes in desolate isolation. * The elder, his royal wife and the prince, his
41. younger brother, all three, * came down (41) to bathe in the great river. * When the three purest of princes had finished bathing and come up from the delightful water, they dressed themselves as ascetics, putting their hair in a bun, and walked to the hermitage of a great sage. * All the holy anchorites, learned men, seeing the three fine handsome princes, * felt joy and delight. "Our good fortune is great indeed!" they thought. * "Our merit is abundant, in that we are able to see, appearing here on this day, One who has fulfilled the conditions for the attainment of enlightenment!" * Then they approached and fussed over them, Rām, Princess Sītā and Laksm(ṇ), bearing all three in their arms, * as if they were their own children who had been separated from them and were reunited, seen once again. * They led them to the

(41) peaceful hermitage, soothed them and massaged their bodies.
42 * Delightedly they offered them nourishment in (42) the *sālā*. They
chatted eagerly and enjoyed themselves asking questions. * When he
had partaken of the fruits, the prince warmly took his leave to journey
on. * All the hermits gave their good wishes and their blessing for a
long life and great deeds, * that they might constantly be strong as well
as long-lived, through the power of their blessing.

1.42–54. **Kūkhăn, a forest overlord, brings gifts to Rām. He will conduct the three travellers across the river the next day. Kūkhăn and Laksm(ṇ), on guard outside Rām's sleeping quarters, address the goddesses of the land and of sleep. Laksm(ṇ) is granted the boon of needing no sleep or food for fourteen years.**

* Then there was a man, Kūkhăn by name, who came walking by
and saw the prince. * Kūkhăn was bold and mighty, tall and broad as a
mountain. * His appearance was typically that of a forester, his skin
being unusually dark, his teeth white, though not clean, and his eyes
43. bright. * In the prime of his manhood, strong and vigorous, (43) with
plenty of flesh upon him, he explored the depths of the jungle,
* smelling strongly with a most repulsive, foul smell as of a huge
vulture, horrifying with his colouring and hairy body. * He could look
in a certain direction and that place would become hot and suddenly
catch fire * as if to burn furiously and be destroyed. If he looked at the
sky, heat was diffused in the air. * For clothing, he wore a deer-skin
round him and, as a shirt in place of protective clothing, a tiger-skin.
* He wore around himself as a ready-made belt a strong cord of
python skin. He was equipped with boots of leather. * A band of ten
thousand men, all deliberately dressed like the mighty Kūkhăn himself,
* bearing swords, javelins shaped like buffalo horns and cross-bows,
made the jungle their normal home. * They had every kind of music:
44. strings, trumpets, conches, (44) drums, gongs, large and small, on which
to perform, and * harmonious flutes, mouth-organs and bamboo pipes
to blow and one-stringed guitars to pluck. * The songs which they
sang, on very high notes, seemed like calls, making the forest sound
sad and eery. * They kept a great number of dogs. When they all
barked together the sounds of the forest were drowned by the loud
noise. * They would yap as they fought vigorously or eagerly sped off
in pursuit of other animals and killed them. * The men did not call the
dogs in the usual way by a click of the tongue. When they wanted to
take them out in the forest they gave the signal with a note * on their

(44) bamboo pipes. The dogs, hearing this, would howl loudly in great
45. delight. * All ten thousand (45) intrepid followers accompanied Kūkhăn
when he went out. * They had long forest boats too, a thousand of
them in readiness at the edge of the water. * And the forest king
Kūkhăn was a friend of the great wise hermits. * Kūkhăn was respected
even by the King of Death who did not dare to vie with him in deeds of
prowess.

* On this occasion, as Kūkhăn was going by, he saw Rām in the
hermitage. * Carefully holding a node of honey and a large slab of fish
with some smoked meat, Kūkhăn * approached to offer these things to
the great lord, Prince Nārāy(ṇ) Rām as he sat in the *sālā*. * Laksm(ṇ)
questioned him. "You there! Where do you come from with your fish
and your meat and honey?" * Kūkhăn respectfully said, "I come to
pay homage to Prince Rām. * I am called Kūkhăn. I am a forester and
46. have come to offer my gifts to the prince, (46) most high. * Please allow
me to approach and to pay my respects to your elder brother. * When
I saw just now that the supporter of the earth had come here, my heart
was full of pure joy. * I am the humble servant of the supporter of the
earth, begging your lordship's favour."

* Then the young Laksm(ṇ) went to inform the elder prince, who
was resting. * The latter sent for Kūkhăn and asked his news, chatting
with him with some sadness. * Kūkhăn bowed his head and made
obeisance. The tears flowed freely, dropping on the ground. * Resting
his chin on the earth, not raising his head, not glancing at the prince's
47. face, * (47) he gave expression to his deep grief, bewailing sadly, "O
Rām, manifestly divine, * your father, leader of men, was given the
name of glorious King Dasarath. Your mother, observer of the ascetic
rules, was by name Kosakalyān. * Your father loved your mother as
his true-love. You were their first-born son, the apple of their eye,
* their heart's desire. Day by day they would not let you, their beloved,
suffer any unhappiness. Alas! How can it be that now you have your
hair in a knot and come here, without escort, journeying on foot?
* The three of you, offshoots of a royal line, are used to wearing
bejewelled accoutrements. Alas! How can you dress in bark-cloth and
48. be content in the forests and mountains? (48) * Your merit has
magnified, O joyful princes, greatest of heroes, foremost of great lords.
* You, Rām, are the same person as Nārāy(ṇ), of abundant merit,
sprung from the line of the Buddha, the race of high-born princes.
* Ah! Any land which has Rām Nārāy(ṇ) to rule it will be resplendent
in its prosperity. * Ah! Aiyudhyā's land is like a magnificent, bejewelled
sanctuary, all gold. That it should be your lot, O prince, long-maned
lion, to be parted from it! * O glorious Aiyudhyā is like the heaven of

(48) the thirty-three. How could you leave it, most magnificent lord of lords?
* Alas! I pity you, who have never journeyed through the forests. Your
feet must ache and be swollen, bruised and blistered. * You are used to
sitting in a carriage and to having a military force with officers with
49. you on a journey. How can such a prince simply (49) walk with his feet
directly on the earth? * I would like to be in the service of all three of
you. If you will not graciously take me as your slave * I shall myself
gouge out both my eyes and cast them away because I shall be
separated from you, unable to see you, Nārāy(ṇ). You will have gone."

* Kūkhǎn was greatly distressed, thinking of the three princely
beings travelling through the forest. * When his unhappiness had eased
he raised his hands and made obeisance at the feet of that foremost of
lords, most high. * Carefully holding the node of honey and the large
slab of fish, he offered them to Prince Rām. * The prince
complimented him. "My gratitude to you, Kūkhǎn, is inestimably
great. * But please return now to the spirit-haunted forest, your home,
50. and * at dawn, come and take us three across (50) to the other shore
over there. * Kūkhǎn spoke respectfully. "I should like to look after all
three of you princely beings. * How can you possibly, lordly masters
that you are, live in the jungle? You must miss your comfortable home."

* Then Kūkhǎn busied himself at once assembling all his ten
thousand troops. * Weapons in hand, they all waited for the great
prince who was asleep in the *sālā*. * A party of them went off on foot
to stalk animals; others gathered together with their gongs, large and
small, to make music * for the prince, master of men. The melodious
sounds were wafted along with the calls of animals. * Royal lions,
elephant-lions, lions, tigers, elephants, oxen and buffalo traversed the
forest in every direction, roaring and trumpeting. * Their cries
resounded from one side to the other. There were pagoda-cocks, owls,
51. *Strix flammea* and osprey. (51) And there were gibbons, civet-cats,
monkeys, wild dogs — the barking jungle dogs. There was an endless
variety of noises. * There were snails and there were honey-bearing
bees, which mingled their melodious sounds with the buzzing of the
cicadas. * And the trumpet was played for Prince Nārāy(ṇ), most high,
as he slept * in company with his chief consort, like the brightness of
the sun with the circle of the moon.

* As to Laksm(ṇ), he held his bow and Kūkhǎn, the woodland king, held his javelin, while they remained on guard * at the door of the hermitage, outside it, watching, on duty, looking out for savage beasts. * Kūkhǎn sobbed and said, speaking amid his tears so that the young Prince Laksm(ṇ) could hear, * O Kaṅhīṅ, Goddess of the Earth, you have built up the virtue of a sage times without number. * And thus it

52. was that the divine Rām was to rule the land and that royal city. (52)
* So now, why is it that the prince has not become the lord of that
land, after all? * It seems that you have not completed your acquisition
of merit or your desires. * Because of some retribution, some past sin
of yours, Kaṅhīṅ, * you have made the royal master of men leave the
glorious city of Aiyudhyā."

* Laksm(ṇ) and the king of the forest were guarding the entrance to
the *sālā* and therefore remained sleepless. * But Laksm(ṇ) experienced
an attack of drowsiness which descended upon him from the Goddess
of Sleep, * whose name was Nidrādebī. She covered his eyesight,
bringing darkness to the eyes of the dear prince. * He felt a strong
desire for sleep but compelled his will to overcome the persistent evil.
53. * He called upon her, "O Goddess of Sleep, appear! Come to me!" (53)
Then Nidrādebī flew forth and came to stand in front of him * and
said, "Lord Laksm(ṇ), master of men, I pitied you, weary yet unable
to sleep. * I was worried in case, as you journeyed with your elder
brother, you might be indisposed and troubled. * That was why I came
to you, to let you restore your physical strength a little." * Laksm(ṇ)
made a decision. "O Nidrādebī," he said, "from this day on, remember
* for the space of fourteen years, I would remind you, I have no wish
to sleep. * And as for nourishment, I neither want it nor have a mind
for it. * Let me be quite dissociated from the feeling of hunger, yet let
my body feel comfortable. Let me have the blessing of complete
physical powers. * Let my body be strong, free from sickness and free
54. from blemish, with the desire for sleep satisfied." (54) * Then that
young goddess, Nidrādebī, consented * and bestowed upon the clever
Laksm(ṇ) this wonderful boon, exactly what he wanted. * He went
without nourishment; he went without sleep and his body felt comfortable and content. * He felt that he had had a sufficiency of food without any external help; he was like those bright, handsome divine beings, the Brahm, who have acquired such merit that they live in the abode of the pure, averse to nourishment.

1.54–63. **The travellers cross the river, refusing Kūkhǎn's invitation to stay at his home and his offer to accompany them on the journey.**

* When the morning light had broken and it was day, with the sun proceeding on his journey upwards from the East, * then Nārāy(ṇ) Rām, of superior might, awakened and bathed to refresh his body. * He spoke words of homage, in accordance with the Brahmanic scriptures, making obeisance to the great hermit, made mighty by his

(54) way of life. * Then the prince departed from the hermitage, respectfully
taking his leave of the great anchorite, * and went down to the edge of
55. the river. All the learned sages were downcast for they would miss (55)
the great prince. * They bewailed and wept greatly, their hearts torn
with love for him, not wanting to part from him. * They went down to
the water's edge and wiped away their tears, each individually thinking
fondly of the prince. * But Rām, descendant of the Sun, supreme
among enlightened Ones, was eager for the journey.
* "Greetings, Kūkhǎn," he said, "please bring the boat and take us
across now." * Kūkhǎn spoke to dissuade the supporter of the earth,
saying, "I would ask permission to invite you * to stay and rest at my
home, all three of you most high-born royal persons. * I will serve you
and do you honour, O most high, all three of you. * I will let nothing
trouble you. Do stay in my park, my forest residence. * Should any
56. enemy attack you, it shall be my task to ensure (56) his utter destruction.
* Furthermore, if Your Highness would like to have a deer-skin I will
render one like carded cotton floss. * I will bring a slab of stone to
make a splendid resting-place, an excellent couch for you to sleep on,
* added to which there shall be a fine white parasol, pillows and
cushions of good material, coverlets, curtains, canopy and rugs. * You
shall also have delicious foods of many different kinds, an unusual
variety. * There will be honey, fish, meat, mixed meat dishes, mixed
fish dishes, and tree foods, flowers and plentiful fruits as well. * Even
the gods of heaven cannot surpass or even equal my pleasant garden.
* It has a pool of delightful water, pure and clear for bathing, where
water-lilies are to be seen and lotuses of white and blue. * I beg the
favour of inviting you to come to my heavenly forest home. It is one
day's journey."
57. (57) * Rām heard what Kūkhǎn, the forest king, said, heard his
invitation to him to be a forest-dweller. * "O Kūkhǎn," he said, "I am
touched by the warmth of your welcome. And it would indeed be good
for us to stay with you. * But we journey with the desire in our hearts
to increase our powers of virtue. * In fourteen years' time we shall
come back to the royal city of Aiyudhyā. * If all is fulfilled, we will
come back to see you again, great friend." * Hearing Rām's answer,
Kūkhǎn took the three royal persons across to the far bank.
58. * They went down to bathe and then (58) did not delay, being eager
and happy to be setting off. * Rām enquired of Kūkhǎn, "You know
all about these paths and can show us where to go. * We intend to go
to Mount Citrakūṭ to build up merit and the virtue which comes from
asceticism, finding our food in the deep forest." * Kūkhǎn respectfully
made obeisance, stretching out his hands in salute to the supporter of

(58) the earth, and told him about the way they should go. * "Lord, the
length of that road that you will tread from here! What a long way it
is! * But there are great teachers and a hermitage with large pools full
of water in which to bathe. * I do indeed know all about this path with
its trees, rocks, sharp corners and promontories looming up on all
sides. * I know the territory, having traversed it on foot, every clearing
of it, the bends and forks in the road, the clefts in the mountain, the
caves. * And there are creeks, inlets of water, mountain lakes and
ponds, passes and gullies along the waterways, * steep banks, immense
59. layers of rock. (59) It is all crags, boulders, glistening tarns and
mountain ravines. * I beg your lordship not to be worried. It shall be
my task to take you. * I know the ways, bad and good, the ways with
wild beasts, savage and ferocious. * I shall go along with you to guard
you and to kill all the animals which come to threaten you and do you
harm. * I shall give you my support and ensure your protection against
any animal which comes to attack you. * If aggressive creatures come,
I shall go forth to destroy such enemies. * I shall not allow them to
reach Your Highness, be they hostile, poisonous snakes, venomous
centipedes, stinging scorpions, — evil beasts — * swarming flies or
gnats, horseflies, even midges, large or small, mosquitoes or poisonous
60. flies. * I shall not let them reach you. I shall look after you, (60) all
three of you princes of quality, * whether you are sleeping or
journeying, pausing or setting up a place to stay as the journey
progresses, * I shall bring my armed forces along to protect you until
you arrive at your destination."

* Hearing these most welcome words of Kūkhǎn, so sincere and full
of kindness, * the prince answered, "Well, Kūkhǎn, your kindness is
immeasurable! * It is likely that you are a relative from long ago. I
declare it: we might well be of the same mother! * Since we came here,
having left the city and journeyed through the forest, and met with you
just now, * your kindness to us has been without counterpart. No-one
61. could find a comparison for (61) your great goodness to us. * And I
myself am your elder brother and after you comes Laksm(ṇ), your
younger sibling. * Now Princess Sītā here, so dearly-loved, is your
sister-in-law, my dear old friend. * All four of us are alike physically
and mentally. We live as one person. Do not think of us as being
different from each other. * If I suffer, the pain will affect you and you
will become somewhat ill. * If you suffer I shall not be at ease; I shall
feel perturbed. * I, in my power, declare my promise, my true word,
my vow: * any relatives of yours are the same to me as my own family
— all your kin. * As for my family, all that there are of them, I declare
62. that they are like your own kinsmen to you. * Now my younger (62)

(62) brothers are together ruling the people of our realm, bearing the burden
of the land of Aiyudhyā, * whereas you, Kūkhăn, are King of the Forest,
guarding the periphery of the woods. * It is because they can rely on
you, their protector, that all your kinsmen live in peace day by day. * But
now you would like to go with me. I ask you: who would look after all
your family, your wife and children? * You want to set off and leave
them but I fear some enemy may attack and oppress the kingdom you
govern. * I must say goodbye to you, young brother. If there is any
presumptuous animal or dread ogre with its threats, * I shall shoot to
destroy such enemies with the strength of my bow and the might of my
sharp, powerful arrows." * As Kūkhăn heard the lord of compassion,
63. the tears flowed freely. With downcast face, he (63) stayed behind.

1.63–2.8. **The forest, ravaged by fire, comes back to life as Rām passes through it. He points out flowers and birds to Sītā and shows how they illustrate their own and other human lives.**

* Then the prince set forth, leaving the domain of the forest king. * It
was the hot season, a time when the rays of the sun were just concentrating
on the broken timber on their path. * The ground was dried up and
cracked; the light was dazzling, glaring; flames flashed through the air
* spreading everywhere, blotting out the forest. Fruit and flowers fell off;
2.1. shrivelled, the leaves dropped down. (2.1) * Some leaves were burned,
some reddened. The thatch grass, grasses and reeds wilted and were
destroyed by the raging forest fire but, * by his power obtained through
meditation, Rām, who belonged by his descent to the enlightened, led his
lady onward. * The spreading branches of forest trees on either side of
their path became visibly refreshed, making their way pleasant. * Flowers
of many varieties sprang into sight, growing all around, displayed and
arrayed as though by tasteful intention. * Lofty trees, dried out, stood
silent, their withered leaves clustered round them, stirred by the breeze.
* As the flowers fluttered, their perfume was perceptible, most fragrant.
The delightful scent enveloped, diffused. * Cicadas buzzed and sweet,
honey-bearing bees mumbled as they flew to sip the flowers. * Their
murmuring, like music for enjoyment, was wafted afar in the deep silence
2. to the forest travellers. (2) * The light of the sun, whose beams were
reflected through the sky, was like that of a brilliant full moon, * unable
to make the three royal persons hot. This was because of the virtue of
Nārāy(ṇ) on this journey.

* Proceeding along the path the prince saw a hibiscus which had one flower, just one, of glowing red. * And there was a sprig of creeping

(2) *Luffa*, just one, its flower opening above the hibiscus. † The hibiscus
was growing near a Champaka tree and this too had a flower, just one,
opening above * the *Luffa*. One could see they were entwined in three
close layers, one upon another, their pollen fragrant. * Two coleopters,
close together, descended upon them, catching their scent, to suck and
filter off the pollen of these flowers. * Then the master of men showed
3. this to his lady, saying, "Do look and see how wonderful this is! (3)
These flowers of different colours are symbols. This hibiscus is the
furnace and is alight within, a glowing fire. * The *Luffa* in the middle is
like gold, when they are smelting that metal, so brilliant. * The fine
Champaka on top of the fully-blooming blossom of the *Luffa* * is gold
of high quality, melted down and fused into a mingling, molten mass
of brightness. * The flying coleopters are the unlovely charcoal, black,
blemished, lowly. * The petals of the hibiscus flower, shining red, are
the flames of the fire burning in the furnace. * I myself am like the
hibiscus flower, I am the furnace and I guarantee that I can endure the
heat of the flames. * The *Luffa* is you, Princess Sītā. The fine Champaka
is young Laksm(ṇ). * All three of us, of one mind and heart, are like
the furnace and the gold. * As to the coleopters, who are the charcoal,
4. (4) they are impure like the words of Kaikesī." * The prince wanted to
have the flowers to beguile the princess, dear to him as the breath of life.
* They proceeded on their way, traversing the woods, sorrowing and
sad, travelling through the golden forest, * which called to mind, with
the splendour of its trees, the dazzling reflections of fine emeralds.* The
prince saw the flowers of the *Mesua ferrea* in full bloom, pollinating,
sleekly shining, bearing a sweet scent. * A pair of bees were sipping at
the pollen, sucking constantly as they took it, turning and twisting
amid that fragrance. * The female found her way deep in among the
petals of the *Mesua ferrea*, from which perfume diffused. * The fine
dust of the pollen, which spread everywhere, closed round the bee's
eyes. Frustrated, she blinked, with eyes nearly shut. * Unable to see to
fly away, she remained where she was, turning to this side and that.
5. Grumbling, groping, she went round and round. * Now the male (5)
bee realised how it was that the female could not see the sky and so fly
home. * He darted here and there, crossed over to where she was,
edged along to come to rest near her and buzzed to make her hear.
* The female heard him and flew after him, closely following him, just
as was her desire. * The prince showed this to his chief wife. "Look at
the bee," he said, "He is leading the female bee in flight. * Just so can
you, my treasure, so much to be admired, cross the jungle on foot by
following me, * sharing together, sharing the same road, sharing the
same place to sleep, not thinking of the hardships as we travel in the

(5) forest. * If you were in the city it would be like the pollen enveloping
the bee. * You would seem less perfect owing to the suspicions of the
women folk and the calumny of the world in general. * But you can
persevere with this journey, following me along the way, as the wife of
6. the enlightened Omniscient (6) One. * I shall take you away from here,
beyond this place of ignorance which causes failure and confusion in
the world. * I shall take you, my beloved, to dwell in a country where
there are no involvements: Nirvana, the great cessation."

* The prince encouraged his lovely wife and took her onward until
they arrived at a place with a pool of great beauty, * a lotus pond with
abundant blooms, their buds sprouting out of the water, all their
closely-packed stems ranged level with each other. * There were young
foresters there, enjoying themselves swimming to and fro with much
splashing and calling out to each other. * Some uprooted the lotuses,
flower-buds and all, and let them float to and fro. * As the breeze
blew, making waves, the lotus stems drifted. Their stalks became
entangled and lay one on another. * A peahen flew to the place
7. because, foolish bird, she saw the fresh lotus shoots * in the breeze (7)
looking life-like and thought they were snakes; so she seized them in
her beak and took them off. * She laid them on the nest where she
lived — stupid bird! — having not the slightest idea that they were
lotus stems! * She had two chicks, already covered with down, who
cried to her, demanding something to eat. * The mother peahen
replied, "My darling children, do not cry. Do not begin your plaintive
claims. * Today I have obtained some excellent fare, special food
which you will like." * Then the mother peahen pecked at it and
divided it up. With her beak she spread out the lotus stems. * Unable
to eat them with enjoyment, the chicks were cross with their mother
and started to accuse her. * "We have suffered while waiting for our
food until late afternoon — and to no purpose: we did not get it!"
* The prince listened to the young peacocks lodging their complaints
against their mother, all upset. * He pointed out the birds to his lady,
8. so perfect. "O, (8) beloved, look at the little peacocks. * That one is like
Bhirut. That other one is just like Sutrut, my young brother — * and
they will probably be looking for me, their beloved brother, and
accusing *their* mother Kaikesī." * Rām kept his chief wife amused as he
continued the journey along the forest and mountain ways.

2.8–15. **The travellers come to a hermitage where they stay the night.**

* They came to a hermitage, noble dwelling, where, concentrating

(8) his thoughts in contemplation, walking up and down, there was a great
anchorite, * by name Bhāradvādy. He meditated, cross-legged,
acquiring merit through the four Vedas and * wore his hair in a shining
round bun. Enveloped in a deer-skin made up as clothing, * he wore
slung across his body over one shoulder a bark-cloth sash, for the
power-giving sacrificial rites with which he was concerned. * With all
9. his might (9) and with great constancy, he followed the Laws and
magnified Baisrab in order to become, by perserverance, a great sage.
* With his long beard his face was awesome to behold. He was a great
anchorite of pure learning. * Even thus did the mighty Brahm
accomplish the practices of holy asceticism as a great sage retiring from
the world to ponder. * If he were to study fully the art of the supernatural, he, like Brahm, would possess to a superior degree ascetic
power and merit. * The sage felt a shiver of excitement as he beheld the
Bodhisatva. He was delighted, overjoyed. * He was like a man with a
sickness, close to the point of losing his life, nearing death. * The
ascetic saw Rām as such a man sees the doctor, bringing divine
medicine to sprinkle upon him and save him. * "Even though I have
sinned," he said, "my power enables me to meet with a kinsman of the
Buddha. * All those sins are destroyed; I myself am without fear that
10. any bad fate will (10) return to take vengeance. * Even if there are old
sins of mine which might put their fetters round and round me, I shall
not have to endure such retribution." * Then with these thoughts the
sage took his shady parasol, his walking stick and a bowl for holy
water and left the fine *sālā*, eager to be meditating in his cell, pacing to
and fro.

* Then Nārāy(ṇ), most high, plucked a lotus bud with its stalk * and
approached to offer it, making obeisance to the learned hermit.
* Delighted, the sage embraced the great prince, pleased to be
acquainted with him, and asked with friendly interest, * "O prince of
might and prowess, whence do you come, with your dear wife, so
worthy of admiration? * I would like to know the reason for your
journey, traversing the forest on foot, all alone, you and your family.
11. * And you two princes (11) have turned yourselves into ascetics, leaders
of learning, * wearing bark-cloth and sashes, casting aside the burden
of the kingdom. With what purpose have you come?" * Then the
omniscient prince explained to the ascetic what he was doing, the
whole matter, * and the great anchorite replied, "It is an old sin, a bad
fate, impossible to avoid. * The lot of beings born into this world,
going from one life to another, may be compared with day and night.
* Now there is light, diffusing in all directions through the power of the
sun's rays. * When the sun journeys on and is hidden by the angle of

(11) the great round Sumeru, it is blotted out. * It turns to deep, still
darkness, a gloom in every direction, in which one cannot see. * This is
a suitable comparison for *karma*, the fruit of actions in the past, of
12. merit or demerit, which affects events, (12) giving rise to happy times
and giving rise to sorrow. There is no avoiding it at all. * Only when
we finally achieve Nirvana is there relief. We are freed, leaving behind
old age and death." Eagerly, the great hermit took the supporter of the
earth, his princess and his young brother * into the *sālā* and offered
food and fruit for all three to eat and be refreshed.

* The prince slept at the hermitage in complete content and comfort
for one night. * When the morning light broke through the protector
of the earth awakened readily and bathed to refresh himself * and took
his wife and young brother to pay homage to the hermit, take leave of
him and depart. * The holy sage of great achievement gave his blessing
to Prince Nārāy(ṇ) Rām * and enquired of him, "With regard to your
13. journeying in the heart of the (13) forest, * performing practices laid
down for ascetics acquiring great merit, carrying out the precepts from
the fine Brahmanic scriptures of ritual yoga, * after how many years
and months will you be bringing your lady and young brother,
supporter of the earth, * back across the jungle on your journey to the
city, the capital of your kingdom?" * The prince replied, "I shall be
away for fourteen years. * Then I shall return to glorious Aiyudhyā,
well-established centre of the land. * I take my leave of you, virtuous
lord, learned in the scriptures. Would you indicate the way? * From
here what is the distance to Mount Citrakūṭ?"

* The sage informed him clearly of the facts. "It is exactly ten
leagues, counting this as the starting point. * In the middle is a plain,
14. stretching far, vast and open, its (14) extent just visible in the dim
distance. * It is hard going to reach the far side. The way is cluttered
with sand and stones, parched and hot in the extreme. * I pity this
exquisite lady. I would urge you now not to go, but to stay right here.
* If you would practise the asceticism of the ancient scriptures, I can
myself guarantee that nothing shall disturb your thoughts." * Hearing
the wise man so kindly urging him not to go, the noble prince replied,
* "Reverend One, it would indeed be good to stay. It is wrong to go
against your specific and deliberate advice. * But in my view, this place
is too near Aiyudhyā. In time the news would * reach the ears of my
kinsmen and there would be my relatives coming to look for me!"
* This was his reply. So as not to offend the hermit, * the prince made
15. (15) obeisance and, circling to the right, took leave of the learned sage
and departed.

2.15–22. Continuing their journey, they cross the river Kālatī, Rām and Sītā being borne on a raft made by Laksm(ṇ). They pass through a forest where all creatures live in harmony and reach Mount Citrakūṭ where hermits welcome them. Laksm(ṇ) builds a hermitage for Rām.

* They crossed through the forest until they emerged at the edge of a
deep river, of formidable width. * As to the name of this river, it was
from old times known as the broad, deep Kālatī river. * As he was
going down into it to wash off the dirt and cool himself, the prince said
to his beloved young brother, * "This is a very big river, Laksm(ṇ). I
am worried in case creatures which feed in the water may attack us. * I
am sorry for Sītā, your elder. She will surely be afraid. How ever will
she have the courage to cross?" * Laksm(ṇ) heard and, being attentive
to his elder, * he would not have him worried. He immediately took his
sharp sword to cut down trees and fix them together * as a raft with a
seat for them. And he gathered flowers to lay them, interwoven with
16. small pieces of (16) the stems, * as a fine, seemly cover all in readiness
over the seat on this decorative raft. * He offered it to the prince, his
lord, for the two of them to sit on, while Laksm(ṇ) himself, swimming,
took them across.

* They reached the far shore as they desired, all three royal persons
serene and unharmed, and continued, * traversing the forests and
mountains, until there appeared the path by which they would cross
the vast, far-reaching plain. * Everywhere forest fires were burning,
flashing and flickering, glowing redly, the smoke spreading a heat
comparable with that of the sun's rays. * The prince meditated and
recited a prayer of praise, by the power given him by his teacher,
Bisvāmitr, * a magic incantation, the essence of which was to produce
17. a remarkable boon: the heat of the sun was gone from that place! (17)
* It was as cool as in the moonlight. The trees sprouted and grew.
Flowers and fruit hung there, suspended. * It was like a pleasure-
garden of heaven, a heaven suitable to divert the Lord Indr. * All the
hunters in the jungle, on the trail of wild beasts, changed their feelings
and felt pity for all creatures. * As to the ferocious animals, all enemies
one of another, destructive of each other, * they had a change of heart
and all became friends, affectionate and close, using the language of
animal association. * Young elephants were suckled by royal lionesses;
elephants gave their milk to the sweet lion cubs. * Fawns turned to
tigresses for milk, while the does changed to suckling the tiger cubs
affectionately. * All animals and birds were well-behaved, peaceful and
amicable. They looked after each other with care and affection. * Even
if a poisonous centipede, scorpion, venomous snake — all fierce

18. creatures with (18) virulence of unimaginable violence — * bit anyone,
causing anguish with its venom, then, for that person who had come
into contact with the powerful poison, * it was as though a divine balm
was blown[9] with careful exactitude on the body attacked by the
sickness * and the effects of the attacks were soothed and healed and
the person himself was better! The ugly poison visibly went as by
magic. * Such roots and fruits of the trees as were noxious, their
poison exceeding the venom of snakes in its dreadful effect, * changed
and had instead a honey-sweetness and diffused the fragrance of their
assorted scents. * As the prince set out on the lengthy road, perfumes
permeated, rising up in clouds. * This was due to the power of the
19. perfection of that prince whose (19) role it was to be the highest lord in
the line of the Buddha, * who abandoned his city-kingdom for the sake
of his learning.

* Then Rām proceeded onward and, as the early afternoon sun
moved to the point of setting, * he arrived at Mount Citrakūṭ, a great
mountain indeed, its peak as high as the sky. * On that mountain
height, throngs of deities would come to amuse themselves. * There
were coconut and areca palms with dangling fruit in spacious
surroundings with clusters of tall trees. * All the great sages there,
mindful of the precepts, saw the supporter of the earth, his lady and his
young brother, * on their journey through the jungle, and came out
from their *sālā* to receive Rām and his wife. * A hermit gave his
blessing and good wishes to the master of men, the illustrious lord,
20. greatest of princes. * "I give (20) my blessing for your prosperity and
for a long, pleasant life, my blessing to Rām, the great One."

* Rām and his consort were content. His young brother, so good,
was busy with equipment and designs, * carefully constructing a *sālā*
on the top of the mountain, to be the hermitage for his lord. * He took
gay peacocks' feathers, decorative and dazzling, and placed them
closely one over the other like a thatch to make a roof over all. * Then
he beat a sheet of gold to make a covering entirely over the peacocks'
feathers to complete the work. * It gleamed in all its extent, all golden,
glittering with mottled colours, sparkling, reflecting light far and wide.
* The prince took his consort to stand and gaze at the magnificence of
the beautiful hermitage. * He praised Laksm(ṇ). "You are skilled in
the designer's art! The *sālā* is unique! * But you bear too many of my
21. burdens. My coming to live (21) in the forest does cause you some
trouble!" * The younger bowed his head at the feet of his elder in
acceptance of duty and respectfully replied, * "Lord, I beg Your
Highness not to feel pity concerning this burden and not to be anxious.
* I am a man of action. This kind of activity is no trouble to me. It is

(21) not enough to satisfy my desire to serve you. * To explain: when Kaikesī
wrested the kingdom from you and gave it to Bhirut, * I wanted to
shoot an arrow and kill her and take the kingdom for you — and you
yourself, noble lord, prevented me. * This was because, with your
divine mind, you understood; your brilliant intelligence foresaw that it
would result in retribution upon retribution. * From that day on I
resolved to make myself responsible for your safety, my elder. * If any
enemy attacks, it is I who guarantee to take charge, my lord." * The
22. prince heard his devoted young brother, so cheerful and good, (22)
affectionate and loyal. * The prince and his chief wife, together with
their young brother, all good friends together, * increased their great
state of blessedness and their power on that mountain height through
the practices and prescribed régime of ascetics.

2.22–34. **In Aiyudhyā, when King Dasarath dies, the sage Vasiṭṭh prepares a message to summon Bhirut to be crowned. Kaikesī alters the message so that it says nothing about King Dasarath's death but summons Bhirut and Sutrut to the coronation of Rām. Bhirut and Sutrut joyfully make the journey to Aiyudhyā to find the city desolate. They guess that Rām has left in anger because he is not to be king.**

* When the glorious King Dasarath died, his life, impermanent,
being extinguished, * the wise Vasiṭṭh, great anchorite, knew the
procedures for carrying out the funeral rites. * The queens, the
attendants, the charming young ladies of the court mourned to excess.
* When this was over, attention turned upon the son of the king who
should govern the great kingdom and protect the royal line. * The sage
Vasiṭṭh prepared a royal message to the prince, Bhirut, * that he
should rule the kingdom, undertake the burdens of the land, defend the
23. people and the city-state. * Then Kaikesī redrafted (23) the sage's
message, telling lies with artful deceit. * She secretly sent instructions,
by means of the messengers, saying it was the message of the great
anchorite Vasiṭṭh, man of wisdom. * Kaikesī's message gave her love to
her son, Bhirut, * and invited him and Sutrut to a very auspicious
occasion: * there were to be preparations for the coronation of Rām,
the incomparable, that he might govern the realm of Aiyudhyā * in
place of King Dasarath, his honoured father. The latter had elevated
Prince Rām to this position. * Bhirut was not to delay. As soon as the
message arrived he should, with Sutrut, set off * to the royal city of
Aiyudhyā for the crowning of his elder brother as reigning sovereign.

* Then all the royal envoys took the queen's message in place of the

24. words of the eminent sage. * They journeyed (24) through the forest,
proceeding by day and by night for seven days * and so arrived at the
city of His Majesty, the father of Kaikesī. * They presented the message
dutifully and with friendliness to Bhirut, master of men, and to Sutrut,
serene prince, * saying, "The two ladies, Kosakalyā and the serene
Kaikesī, ask for your indulgence with regard to a ceremony * which
will make the divine Rām and his lady sovereigns of the royal city,
ancient and glorious Aiyudhyā. * Your honoured parents, the three of
them, have ordered us to * bring their instructions with all speed,
inviting both of you dear sons * to be there in good time for the
coronation of your elder brother, the divine great prince Nārāy(ṇ) Rām,
* the great hope of our line of kings, by the authority of the great sage."
25. (25) * Bhirut was overjoyed. He gently raised the golden sandals,[10]
placed them on his head * and turned his face directly towards the city
of Aiyudhyā. Kneeling, he raised his hands in salute. * And Sutrut too
was delighted. Both paid their respects to the glorious country of
Aiyudhyā. * They gave orders to all the military personnel — the many
generals, ministers and lesser officials — to come to them. * They were
to beat the drums to assemble a vast force with all its equipment.
* Aged Brahmins, chaplains and astrologers calculated an auspicious
time to ensure a successful journey.

* At the proper moment for departure on their journey the force was
ranged rank upon rank in procession, their weapons in dense array to
left and right. * Those carrying bows had the arrows for them. Those
holding the cross-bows had arrows in readiness, sticking out of their
26. quivers. * With their shields and swords, their spears and clubs (26)
impeding each other, the huge, cheerful throng, shrilly chattering,
caused the dust to rise in clouds. * The elephant-riders had put the
trappings on their animals and had them ready waiting. The grooms
had carefully equipped their horses * to the sound of much whinnying
and neighing and the pleasing sight of glinting reflections. There were
umbrellas and many-tiered parasols, their fringes blowing all about
them. * Everywhere there were fans of mulberry-leaf shape and
processional fans. The royal carriage, decorated with jewels and gold,
was trim and polished. * There were banners on the princes' vehicle
and fine standards ranged along the columns of soldiers. * Then the
royal order given to all the royal retinue, to make haste to have everything ready, was accomplished. * Bhirut and the handsome Sutrut,
having in mind the time for departure, went to take leave of * their
grandparents, those two serene sovereigns. * This done, they mounted
their handsome carriage, a magnificent vehicle yoked with horses bred
27. in the (27) Sindh. * The two princes were very content, looking forward

(27) happily to seeing their elder brother, Rām.

* Amusing themselves with feats of physical strength, cheerful in each other's company, the princes set out on the road for their long journey. * The music of strings and trumpets resounded afar, mingling melodiously and loudly reverberating in the forest. * The music of mouth-organs gaily accompanied the playing of the violin and the beating of the army (drum). The guitar, the oboe, * the crocodile-shaped guitar and the one-stringed guitar were played as well as the bamboo pipe. The sounds of all kinds of instruments wafted along with the boom of the gongs. * Alcohol was provided in bowls, jars, and pitchers; red wine in jugs. Jugs from the stillroom were arranged in readiness. * First class wine was distributed to all who looked after provisions and the joyous company sang together and held contests for amusement.

28. * By the seventh day the travellers were close (28) to the city of Aiyudhyā. They saw * that it was completely silent, utterly deserted! Everyone was so sorrowful, troubled by a great grief * because they were separated from Nārāy(ṇ). The divine Rām, most high, had gone far away out of their sight. * All men and women in settlements large and small, in the city or in hamlets and market towns, at waterfronts, in distant thoroughfares of trade or * travelling to new places in far-away lands, all spread around them a feeling of woe, as they mourned the loss of the elder prince. * Even the Moon and Sun were upset. Everywhere there was famine. The whole circle of the sky was overcast. * It was now the time of the new year but one did not see the rice-farmers busy working with their ploughs and rakes. * All was bone-dry; pools were waterless. In the paddy fields was self-set rice. The leaves were dried up, shrivelled and limp. * And even the forest trees
29. (29) had wilted, partially burnt, their undergrowth a tangled mass, the reddened leaves falling off. * The flowers and fruit were all scattered near the trees, in fewer numbers than usual. The petals had dropped off, whether they were young or full-grown, * scattered about in the gardens and in the fine pools — for no man or woman would think of picking them up to eat. * Destruction had come to the flowers for adornment too; they had fallen off all around — there was no-one to make a decoration to put round or on the head. * Accustomed to paint themselves with saffron, they wearily gave up and did not insert a flower in their hair or adorn their clothing.

* Since their separation from the supporter of the earth all the citizens felt a deep grief. * Having no comfort or relief they were all silent and glum, with tear-stained cheeks. * Gone too were the singing
30. and dancing with out-stretched arms (30), the happy shouts of laughter.

(30) All was silence. * Because they had lost their refuge and strength, so
treasured, they mourned with unabating grief. * Their sarongs, their
muslin garments, their shirts were not changed, for they had no
inclination to wash away the dirt. * Prayers, the sacred Vedas which
they upheld, they ceased to recite. There was no offering made in the
city. * Men who usually rode off on expeditions on horseback gave up
such outings and trotted confusedly round and round. * Charioteers of
the king's chariots, usually ranged in formation and galloping off to a
great distance, kept all their oxen inactive. * People had disappeared
from the silent paths. Anyone who travelled about went to and fro in
bewilderment. * In every house, every dwelling, people usually burnt
incense. In every household they would light it to let it smoke and
* quickly the smoke would come, fusing, diffusing, merging. But now
nothing happened. It was as if they were dead, as if the houses them-
31. selves were tottering. * As for the rice-farmers, (31) in places where their
land was low, there was water — pools and hollows of water; but * no-
one came to dig channels at intervals to take the water off to the
* village ricefields where it was very dry and hot. The rice was sticking
up as best it could, stark and parched. * No-one thought about
throwing on water or opening up pools to bring water to it. * Buffaloes
and cows came and trampled on the crops or went right away,
abandoning the place, for the fences were broken down all over,
leaving gaps. * One could see that all the rich people who were wont to
look after their persons and make their houses fine, * who had sheets
of gleaming silver beaten and embossed with jewels and gold about
them and casements to their windows, * and sarongs and cloths for
shoulder-carrying of sparkling silk, trousers of flowery, foreign printed
32. cottons, all a riot of mingled colours (32), checked sarongs spread out
in the open, dangling, and * fresh, seemly, dark, rose-apple-coloured
silks and Yamaṇā cloth to put round them, * were, from the time of
separation from the great prince, in utterly desolate silence within the
city.

* Bhirut and Sutrut proceeded towards the north and entered through a gate in the fortifications. * They saw that there were no longer any umbrellas or banners displayed there. There was no array of seed-filled bells swaying suspended from the palaces. * There was hardly a sign of the chief ministers and officials who had waited upon King Dasarath, * or of the aged Brahmins, or of the beggars approaching full of longing, sure to obtain alms, * or of the military officers and men, within and without, the army, who were constantly there to serve the king. * All were behaving quietly, their faces full of gloom. They were suffering from starvation and were weighed down by two matters:

33. * one, that they were bereaved of their (33) victorious king, who had passed away; thc other, that they were separated from Rām, his son, * from Princess Sītā, who was keeping the rules of asceticism, and from Laksm(ṇ), who bowed in loyalty before his elder, Rām, — for * all three royal persons had departed from the ramparts and royal city of Aiyudhyā.

* Bhirut spoke his thoughts. "Why does it look different from the way it has always looked? * No doubt of it — I am afraid our city, royal seat of the land, has suffered some disaster." * Sutrut respectfully replied, "This will be the reason: some serious misfortune must have occurred. * This state of affairs seems very strange to me — and very much to our discredit. * It is because Rām is not protecting our royal
34. line and bearing the responsibility of (34) the city. * He is angry because our mother has asked the king, our honoured father, for the kingdom, * saying that *you* should be king and rule the realm of Aiyudhyā. * I think she had no sympathy for Rām. He is the eldest too. How can the eldest be passed over? * And now probably Rām has departed from the city. * Our father will be lamenting ceaselessly, inconsolably distressed. The whole populace and the army will be saddened at his loss. * In my opinion there will be serious trouble for us." * Thus Sutrut pondered and convinced his elder.

2.34–43. Bhirut and Sutrut learn from Kaikesī of their father's death.

* Then they assembled their entire forces, their elephants, carriages
35. and horses and their gold (35) palanquins, * and stationed them in sections in the fortifications at various points and * entered, intending to pay homage to their father; for * they thought he was still alive and would surely be in the splendid palace, so pleasant, * with Kosakalyā, most high, mistress of the attendant ladies of the court, in loving companionship as usual. * They went quite close to that fine dwelling, the palace of the honoured Queen Kosakalyā, * and saw that it was silent, gloomy, without any attendant or military officer. No sound of music was heard. * Just then Kaikesī caught sight of Bhirut and Sutrut, her sons, * and sent two women running to ask them, panting, to go * and greet their mother, who had been eagerly expecting their arrival
36. day by day. * Bhirut and Sutrut (36) entered the bejewelled palace, home of Kaikesī. * Joyfully she embraced her beloved sons and asked about her father and mother, * saying, "Is the king, your grandfather, still firmly established there? * Are Their Majesties, your grandparents, happy and free from sickness? Is all well with them? * And are all the

(36) relations of the family, the kinsmen, well and happy these days?" * Bhirut and Sutrut bowed respectfully and told her all the facts, all the good news. * Having told her the news, they enquired of her in return,
37. * "Madam, (37) where is our father? We do not see that master of men."

* Then Kaikesī fondly replied to her sons' question. * Narrating with painful gasps, weeping and sobbing, she told them, * "O my own dearest sons, the king your father, His glorious Majesty Dasarath, * has passed away, almost exactly two weeks ago. * I have been mourning in unabated misery for the loss of my refuge and strength, my heart's darling, the light of my life." * Hearing that his father had died, Bhirut felt a tremor in his heart. Shaking violently, he writhed * and fell in a faint there in the palace of his mother, Kaikesī. * And
38. Sutrut too, his younger brother, fainted, almost dying (38) together with his elder as they bore this grief. * Seeing her sons so close to the point of death, Kaikesī, * terror-stricken, quaked all over and swooned on top of them. * Such was the agitation in their hearts that they almost died, the princes and their mother too. * The servants saw them and brought flower-perfumed water and applied it to their persons. * Regaining consciousness, they beat their breasts and wept in great distress. * Their tears penetrated everywhere, flowing freely, spreading onto their breasts, as they fretted.

* "O high-born king," they lamented, "how did it come about that you perished, lost, as the Dharma says, in the middle of life's sea?
39. * Your smile, when you (39) attentively carried out a ritual or made offerings, observing the practices of an anchorite, was of special holiness. You produced four sons * whom you protected and cared for, beloved father, that no harm should come to them, for you loved us as the light of your life. * You did not, in thus leaving us, take pity on us. O poor Rām, your beloved, whom you used never to allow to be troubled! * We are afraid that in fact all four of us are guilty of sins we have committed. Ah! Now we know that you have accused us, grown angry with us and deserted us! * Oh we remember clearly about the life of your father. When you were six years old he came to the limit of his life. * You produced us four sons and abounded in love for us. Alas, now you have forsaken us and gone, totally abandoning us, your dearest ones. * There was a time when there was consternation because
40. a certain godless creature (40) named Paradust had come to seize the realm * of Indr's heaven of the thirty-three. The gods, in fear and horror, came in a body to pay homage to you and ask you to go forth against * Paradust. You went straight to the heaven of the thirty-three — Paradust marched his army away in rapid retreat, defeated by your

(40) heroic deed! * But now you have gone. Perhaps, great king, you have
gone to help Indr? We do not see you. * Oh! Your words, thought out
in a royal message came safely to us. We think most wistfully of those
words, all come to naught. It is indeed sad! * You would have
assembled us all without delay to carry out the grand coronation of the
41. royal ruler of our land (41).* Alas! Your life was completed, then, when
you had had the chance to see the merit of your eldest son, abundant
as your heart desired it to be. * Alas! Can you really have departed?
Were you troubled so much that you died, to be gone for ever from
our sight?"

* The dearly-loved princes, Bhirut and Sutrut, mourned inconsolably
in anguish for their father. * Kaikesī wept and made a great fuss of her
darling sons, holding them against her breast. * "My sons," she said,
"as it is laid down for all men, without exception, * there is no passing
beyond trouble or avoiding it. We have to bear it. There has never
been any other possibility. * There is old age and death. There is birth
42. and growth. (42) * There is no end to it at all. Reaching old age, one
departs, dying. One follows Death's way. * That is how it is with fruit
and flowers. The bud is produced on the stem; the petals, layer upon
layer, * all open and scatter their pollen, puffing up with full fragrance.
And then the scent becomes less and all is released. * The little bud,
brought forth from the stem, is young, then old. Its fruit gradually
becomes ripe. * Then it falls down, leaving the stem. It is like the
succession of births of all creatures, which follow one upon another in
this world. * Young children are there in the midst of the old and
dying. This is how it ends for everyone. * Each person is subject to the
effect of past actions and is surrounded by troubles as deep as the vast
ocean. * Even if King Dasarath had had his lifespan fixed at one
43. thousand million eras, when (43) that time had passed by, he would not
have been able to avoid reaching the moment of death. * O, my darling
sons, birth, old age and death are adjuncts of human life."

2.43–52. **Then Kaikesī tells them about Rām's exile and from Kosakalyā they learn of the message falsified by Kaikesī.**

* Bhirut ended his sorrowing and asked Kaikesī in turn, * "Honoured mother, our father, master of men, has died, then. * But the most divine Rām, his eldest son — where is he now?" * Kaikesī told him, "Beloved son, why should I hide anything from you, the apple of my eye, so dear to my heart? * Your elder, Rām, in a great fury, took away his noble lady and Laksm(ṇ). * They left the city to journey through

(43) the forest. There is no news of their whereabouts." * Bhirut heard that
44. his much-loved elder, princely lord, was traversing the jungle (44) and,
* as if a raging fire were kindled within his very being, he exploded
with anger. * It was as though his heart was being painfully crushed
and would break into pieces. He shook with fury. * Trying to suppress
his rage, he spoke to Kaikesī, saying, "Rām, the divine, ran away? * If
so, the crime of our elder was serious, conflicting strongly with the
ancient ways of kings and * King Dasarath, our honoured father, was
angry and banished him. * Or was it a bad deed of Rām's from long
ago, causing him to want to go and live in the forest, * in accordance
with the final result of *karma*? Or — another possibility — perhaps the
powerful sage * opposed him concerning some matter, making him feel
upset and our elder, master of men, feeling ashamed, did not stay in
the city? * Another possibility: was it the fault of the honoured
45. Kosakalyā? Did she chase (45) Rām away? * And further, was the
highest of princes, King Dasarath, still alive * or had he already died
when the prince, our refuge, fled to the forest?"

* The queen told him the whole story, saying, "O Bhirut, my beloved
treasure, * when your elder, Rām the divine, took away Princess Sītā
and Laksm(ṇ), his younger brother, * your father was still here. He
was, moreover, very upset and suffered great sorrow. * As for all that
matter of a wrong, it was not that your father was angry and drove
your elder to leave the royal city. * Nor was it the words of that sage of
might and power, the great anchorite, going against him. * Kosakalyā,
46. was not to blame either. She was very vexed (46) about it. * The reason
why Rām the divine was angry and fled to live in the jungle was
because of an agreement. * I had asked for a promise from your father,
that he would allow you to be king * and rule our pleasant realm, the
people and the state, protecting the plentiful possessions of the city of
Aiyudhyā. * Furthermore, I asked for an agreement that the prince,
Rām, should leave the kingdom * and perform the manifold practices
of an ascetic in the jungle, as a forest traveller for a period of fourteen
years, * to build up merit, the good produced by holy practices, and,
having done so, to bring his lady and his young brother * back to
glorious Aiyudhyā. And so your father granted me my wish. * Thus it
was that Rām, his eldest son, was upset and angry and did not stay in
the city; * this was why he abandoned His Majesty, supporter of the
47. earth, his honoured father, while he was still (47) alive. * When he heard
that Rām had fled, he mourned the loss of his son and died of his deep
grief."

* Bhirut, as he listened in tears to Kaikesī's narrative, * was at first
respectfully prostrated at her feet. But when he fully realised the

(47) circumstances in which Rām had fled, * his fury exceeded all bounds.
Shaking with rage, * he disrespectfully put both hands over his ears
and did not heed what she was saying. * His eyes gleamed red all the
time like glowing copper. He clapped his hands together — it was like
the reverberating clap of a thunderbolt. * Angrily he rose up and stood
there. One would have thought the city would collapse, for Mount
Sumeru trembled and* the ocean miraculously boiled! Bhirut's fury
48. caused a tremor in the earth. (48) * He said he would strike Kaikesī, for,
evil witch, she had killed King Dasarath. * She had driven him to
death. Vile, stuttering woman! She was entirely to blame. * He
thought, "I myself ought to strike her, cut her in two or three pieces,
kill her this instant. * But she is my mother, who brought me up and
cared for me; it is due to her breast-milk that I am alive. * The wrong
she has done is more serious than that of any other woman. She is
indeed one of the world's doomed spirits. * The proper behaviour for a
woman is to remain with her husband and be content with her family.
* How could she perpetrate such a heinous crime and cause this
chaotic situation? This is not queenly behaviour at all! * Vulgar, evil
witch she is indeed to kill her husband, a noble king! * Because he had
been a party to an agreement, King Dasarath did not hesitate to
49. honour his word and * (49) could not give the kingdom to Rām, his
treasured eldest son. * Because he was thwarted by that promise, the
prince felt embarrassed in front of the people and brought himself to
endure exile in the forest. * My father was extremely reliable. He did
not break his loving promise, even though it led to his death. * If
Kaikesī had never said anything, no wrong would have been done at
all. Is that not so? * To turn to her in time of need would be like
resting one's head on Death! * And further, it must have been due to
an ancient sin of mine that I had to endure the burden of being
conceived * in the womb of Kaikesī, with her woman's wiles and total
lack of truthfulness. * If I reign as king, this fact will be a secret which
50. could lead to my downfall. * And furthermore, enemies would (50)
despise me. They would not respect me because my shameless mother
had caused division in the country. * And, further, I must watch out. I
must try to learn the refined arts of this world. * Then I shall be able to
be my own guide to cross to the far side, passing out of reach of the
bonds of ever-waiting retribution. * I must respectfully take leave of
Kosakalyā, most pure and virtuous queen, * and wipe away this
accursed sin which will bring me retribution, fear, birth and death, so
that all is clean. * And I will build up the pure merit of the ascetic in
practices which wash away the vile blemishes of sin. * I will follow
along the way of Rām. Wherever he is, I will go."

(50) * Bhirut took counsel with Sutrut and they went to the palace of Kosakalyā. * Kneeling and bowing their heads, they made obeisance
51. on (51) the great paved court, * their heads directly on the ground. And where they placed their heads, the earth sank. * Where the head and feet of Bhirut had pressed down, the traces remained permanently. * Kosakalyā called out to Bhirut to go in along with young Sutrut. * She shed tears of grief, stretching out her arms to embrace Bhirut. * She bewailed King Dasarath, sobbing until her feeling of distress had abated and gone. * She spoke even as she wept, in disjointed fashion, gasping and pouring forth glistening tears. * She told the tale, how Rām had fled and the king had sent men after him to stop him going. * But he did not return to the city. Having set off, he went on into the
52. jungle. * King Dasarath (52) had mourned for Rām until he died. * She told Bhirut about the promise and about Kaikesī asking for the favour. * The sage Vasiṭṭh had ordered messengers to convey an invitation to Bhirut to come with his young brother * to carry out the funeral rites for their father who, most unhappily, had passed away. * Kaikesī had arranged with them that they should tell Bhirut that preparations were to be made for the * coronation of Rām as king in place of his father. All this was falsehood. * The queen told the whole story readily. Bhirut was furious * now that he knew the whole story of the message and Kaikesī's order to deceive him.

2.53–59. **The sage Vasiṭṭh organises the funeral of King Dasarath and the coronation of Bhirut is planned. Bhirut prepares instead to fetch Rām to be king. He sets off with a large retinue, including Sutrut and the three queens.**

53. * Then the faultless Vasiṭṭh was approaching (53) the palace of Kosakalyā. * Bhirut and Sutrut saw the great sage coming to ask their news. * They embraced him and wept in the palace until they had spent their feelings of sorrow and felt better. Then they questioned the revered ascetic * who gave them a full account of their father's grief for Rām. * "O illustrious Bhirut," he said, "it is already fourteen days since your father died. * We must not delay. We have mourned and our sorrow has abated. We must hold the funeral ceremony." * Hearing the opinion of the great anchorite, Bhirut and Sutrut
54. * ordered drums to be beaten (54) to summon the chief ministers and the whole military force. * A golden, pinnacled little temple was to be made ready, bejewelled — like a dwelling in the heaven of the thirty-three * on the lofty height of Mount Sumeru — with its ring of jewels

(54) and gold of high quality round it. * Then they offered the body of their
exalted father to be consumed in the sacred flames.

* This done, the great anchorites, eminent sages, aged Brahmins,
teachers and the numerous army officers * were going to prepare for
the grand celebration of the coronation of Bhirut, that he might rule
the kingdom, bearing * the responsibility of the land, governing in
place of the honoured king, his father. * But Prince Bhirut had no
mind for becoming king and raged * as if some poisonous venom had
55. been put on his tongue (55) and he was on the point of death. * "If I
rule over the kingdom, in immediate succession to my father," he
thought, * "and if I do what all these people tell me to do, they will say
I am as brazen as is Kaikesī in what she says. * She went so far as to
kill her husband — so how can it be right to agree with them? * The
proper thing is for Rām, the eldest son, to rule the kingdom in place of
His Majesty, our father. * Only when there is a break in the succession
is the younger brother established on the throne and the realm handed
to him. * It is owing to her arrogant desire to divide us — a grievous
sin — that there has arisen this terrible upset. * As for my ruling this
kingdom, I would disdain to do so. I have no wish for it at all. * I shall
56. either pierce my own breast with this sharp sword (56) and destroy
myself * or I shall go after Nārāy(ṇ) to pay him homage and ask him
to come back. * If our beloved elder brother does not return for the
sake of the royal succession, * then, like Laksm(ṇ), I shall obediently
serve him."

* The great anchorites of power, the Brahmins and the senior
officers thought to direct the great prince but * were unable to
persuade him against this action. Bhirut was very angry. He sent his
young brother, Sutrut, * to beat the drums to announce the assembling
of the royal army with all its high officers. * The masters of the
elephants made ready the elephants. The masters of the cavalry put on
the horses' trappings, decking them out with care. * The masters of the
carriages had the vehicles drawn up in neat array too and busily put
57. the equipment on them. * The masters of all the (57) infantry were here,
there and everywhere, giving orders, all cheerful and enthusiastic. * It
was heard that Bhirut would fetch the prince, supporter of the earth,
back to the metropolis. * It was as though their hearts had been
sprinkled with ambrosial essence, so ready to be off, so fresh in spirit
were they. * And they all felt this eagerness because they missed the
prince, the kingdom's leader.

* Prince Bhirut and Prince Sutrut, their hair knotted, wearing bark-cloth sashes, * changed their appearance to resemble anchorites of
power and blessedness, distinguished for their purity and virtue. * They

(57) mounted the royal carriages. As they proceeded, the reverberations
58. seemed to beat all over the city. * Kosakalyā and Kaikesī, with (58) Sramud * sat in a royal carriage and, as it followed Bhirut, the noise thundered on the earth. * The varied orchestras of strings, trumpets, conches and drums were ready to play en route but * the prince proceeded sorrowfully, his expression grim, his heart constricted with grief. * He would not let the musicians play their percussion or wind instruments or strings as a decorous background of music for him. * When they reached his elder brother, they should play every kind of measure to accompany him in procession. * Seated on the royal carriage, Bhirut was raised high aloft, like the circle of the moon * and the chief ministers of the army and the ladies of the court all round him were like the stars in their celestial courses. * The prince went out
59. from the city gate. His forces, (59) densely packed and teeming, shook the earth, * thousand upon thousand of them. Bhirut and Sutrut set forth and * advanced until early afternoon. Then they pitched camp in the same park where their elder had rested. * They knelt and raised their hands in salute to their elder, beat their breasts and wept for him. * When the morning light broke through and day was come, the princes marched onwards to the bank of the great river. * The noise of the soldiers, of the royal carriages and horses, of the whole force * resounded through the forests and mountains, whence boulders fell into the great river, making waves.

2.59–69. **Kūkhǎn sees them, guesses that they come in friendship towards Rām and helps them to cross the river.**

* Then Kūkhǎn appeared, beating an opening through the trees and straining his neck to look. He saw the soldiers, * the royal vehicles,
60. horses, elephants, officers and the vast (60) force of men. * He shook with anger. "This is Kaikesī!" he thought. * "She has crowned Bhirut lord of the glorious ancient city of Aiyudhyā. * This will most likely be Bhirut bringing an army after Rām and Laksm(ṇ). * He has seized the kingdom and taken over the rule of the people because of what Kaikesī has said. * The prince is not eager for the royal city so he has brought his queen and his young brother, three of them, * to live in the forests and mountains and perform the practices of ascetics, distinguished for their power and blessedness * — for surely it is not possible that Bhirut has brought his retinue and troops of soldiers in pursuit of the prince to kill him? * If Bhirut here, with his relatives and forces, has come to invite Rām * to return and rule the city, then I will be friendly and talk

61. pleasantly with him (61) asking his news agreeably. * But if, not caring,
he acts with arrogance and comes charging to the attack to kill the
prince, * I shall wipe out Bhirut and his whole military force * and I
shall take Rām to rule the kingdom at glorious Aiyudhyā. That is
certain. * Do you think, Bhirut, that, being the son of King Dasarath,
you can escape my arrows?"

* Kūkhǎn blew on his bamboo pipe which echoed through the forest
and his whole force of sixty thousand came. * He bade them haul up
their ten thousand boats, hide them in the trees and bring their
weapons. * He urged them to guard every way, to conceal themselves,
aware of the danger, and stay motionless, to ambush the enemy. * "We
must beware," he told them, "I shall destroy this prince, annihilate
62. him. * Even the gods of the far heavens (62) would I strike and scatter,
destroying the celestial regions too. * How can they allow the divine
Rām to wear bark-cloth? How can they let the three of them be so
forlorn? * This is due to Kaikesī's seizing the kingdom from Rām for
Bhirut. * I shall destroy them with an arrow. No doubt of it. I will send
the whole force flying as far as the sea." * Angry and masterful, Kūkhǎn
ranged his force in line along the river's edge.

* Just then one of the ministers spoke to that illustrious prince,
Bhirut, master of men, * "Lord, if you please, you have marched us
there to this kingdom * where there is a hunter called strong Kūkhǎn, a
63. forest king whose power is immense. (63) * His might is that of a strong
elephant of great vigour, at the peak of its prowess, and he has a force
of sixty thousand men. * Kūkhǎn is of towering height, colossal like a
mountain, impatient and bold. * When your elder brother arrived here
he befriended Kūkhǎn, * who offered his own steadfast devotion,
sincerely from the heart. * And it was Kūkhǎn who took your elder
brother across to the other side of the river. * And now, as you come
with your army, your elephants, your horses, your charioteers and
* your attendants on every side to this river which is on the way to
your elder brother, * I am afraid Kūkhǎn will think you are leading
your columns on as enemies of your elder, Rām. * I fear that Kūkhǎn
64. will strike to defend your brother, protecting him (64) against you,
master of men. * He does not understand the situation, how you have
come in friendship to greet your elder, the noble prince." * Bhirut
heard and understood about the forester of astonishing power and
prowess.

* Then Kūkhǎn approached the river's edge, intent upon engaging in
battle. * He looked at the vast royal retinue in attendance on every side
in dense array. * But Bhirut and Sutrut, with an air of quiet gloom,
were withdrawn into themselves, not eagerly rushing about. * More

(64) than that, they were deeply unhappy. Definitely, they and all their
military force and royal retinue were sad. * Prince Bhirut and Prince
Sutrut wore their hair long and knotted and had sashes of bark-cloth.
* Kūkhằn, astonished, knelt down, prostrating himself completely. His
65. bow and arrows fell from his hands. * Clearly Bhirut (65) had come in
friendship seeking his dear elder, having missed Prince Rām. * Kūkhằn
exclaimed loudly, "I thought Rām and Bhirut * were fuming with
anger against each other because King Dasarath had done what Kaikesī
had asked him to do * and had crowned Bhirut as lord of the royal city
and that the elder Rām was angry about it; * and that then Bhirut had
come with hostile intentions towards Prince Nārāy(ṇ) Rām. * How
could I know that Bhirut was in this mood? In reality he has come full
of sorrow." * Kūkhằn understood the whole matter, the whole course
of events. * He believed that Bhirut was truly well-intentioned and so
he immediately placed his hands together in respectful greeting.
* Bhirut saw Kūkhằn approaching and making obeisance in open and
66. heartfelt friendliness. * The (66) noble prince raised his hands and
greeted the forester in return and chatted with him amicably. * "Lord,"
Kūkhằn said, "the prince is observing the practices of the purest virtue
* together with the young Laksm(ṇ). They have turned themselves into
handsome sages. * And you, sir, have left the city and traversed the
jungle to come here as a traveller and halt in this remote place,
* bringing the royal ladies and the ladies of the court and a great
throng of attendants, uncountable! * You are not exercising your
sovereignty over the kingdom of Aiyudhyā!"

* Then Bhirut replied, "Hail, Kūkhằn, lord of the forest! * The
divine Rām, the dear elder son, is indeed not governing the people
67. — (67) * but how could I possibly be arrogant and acquisitive when it
meant staying away from Nārāy(ṇ), master of men? * As it is, I have
abandoned the city in order to place my head beneath the feet of that
prince, who transcends all men, * to ask our royal master, lord of the
earth, with his lady, * to return to the country of glorious Aiyudhyā
and rule the kingdom, highest lord of our line of kings." * Then Kūkhằn
was delighted. He made obeisance at the feet * of Bhirut, praising him.
"You have forsaken greed, desire, error, fear," he said. * "Your words
are indeed the truth, reliable, unsullied. You walk in the way of the
Dharma, the way of absolute truth, * in coming to pay your respects to
your elder brother, making obeisance before him, inviting him to
68. return. * When your brother (68) came here and greeted all the
great sages and paid them homage, they were delighted to receive him.
* This is the very place where he stayed and slept in the hermitage,
sheltering there one night. * In the morning he led forth his lady and

(68) younger brother, master of men, leaving the hermitage." * Bhirut paid
his respects to the place where the prince had rested. Trembling
violently, * he wept and fell faint on that place. As he rested there, he
thought wistfully of his sovereign. * The prince rested one whole night
at the same hermitage at which his elder brother had stayed. * When
morning came, he knelt and took leave of the venerable, wise
anchorites, who offered him their blessing. * Kūkhăn gave his orders
and all his men crossed the river and went for boats from every creek.
69. * Ten thousand ships came thronging there. They were not enough! (69)
They took all the boats of the hunters * and thus had eighty million of
them, packed together all over a wide expanse of the great river. * The
water brimmed over and flowed here, there and everywhere. The banks
collapsed and caved in amid shouts and cries of alarm. * They took all
the royal retinue across, their horses, the strong elephants and the
numerous vehicles.

2.69–76. **The whole party receives hospitality from the sage Bhāradvā(j), with much practical help from Indr. They proceed to Rām's hermitage. Laksm(ṇ), suspecting that Bhirut comes as an enemy, is ready to attack. He is restrained by Rām.**

* Their clamour reverberated through the forest until they arrived at
the hermitage of the sage Bhāradvā(j). * Approaching to pay their
respects to the wise man, they asked about Rām being angry. * The
sage told the whole story, every detail of the journey of the supporter
of the earth. * Then he welcomed them peaceably, delighted with
Bhirut. * He gave the whole military force a feast, suddenly producing
all kinds of foods, including fresh milk. For he performed a rite and,
* making an offering, he caused the appearance of well-flavoured
70. dishes (70) such that they were never sated or tired of them. * A tremor
in the earth reached Indr, lord of men, greater than all. In delight he
gave orders for instant action: * all sons of the gods, all gods and
goddesses should descend and gather together and produce by magic
* pavilions, couches, everything required for their dwelling place, all
bejewelled and decorated to perfection by Bisnukār. * He sent down
heavenly blossoms in showers over the countryside, their fragrant,
diffusing perfume * rising in a cloud and spreading everywhere. He
sent down innumerable suits of clothing scattering all about. * There
were enough for all their people and they were highly contented with
the soft coverlets of the gods upon them! * It was as if they had
achieved a place in heaven while still alive — for indeed they had not

(70) left their bodies. * And there was the food from the far-away celestial
regions arrayed on golden platters, enough for the whole attendant
71. force. * And hay, too, for the horses and elephants (71) fell from the
middle of heaven on to the ground everywhere around. * Buffaloes,
cows, horses and elephants, as they moved about or lay down, stood or
grazed, had plenty to eat and were abundantly content. * Bhirut
reposed serenely for one whole night in the heaven-sent resting-place,
so perfect. * All the royal officers on the soft, celestial beds which had
appeared slept deeply, profoundly happy. * In the morning the
unblemished Bhirut woke and roused his whole force, to set forth.
* They made obeisance to the great sage, who was pleased to offer
them his warm good wishes. Then they departed. * As the strong
horses, the soldiers, the royal vehicles and the elephants rumbled
along, the earth trembled and * fine dust rose up in clouds obscuring
the whole sky in all directions — an impressive sight. * The excited
clamour swelled up and up; the thundering roar echoed everywhere.
72. * They approached (72) the precincts of the place where Rām was
living, like great waves on the sea crashing down, * boiling, surging,
breaking into white foam — formidable indeed. The reverberations
thundered through the earth.

* Laksm(ṇ), raising his hands above his head, spoke to Rām,
* "Lord, I would ask you to consider, with the divine understanding of
a sovereign: * with regard to Bhirut's taking over the government of
the kingdom, was that the reason for his being discontented? * Why
did he become angry and look for an excuse to quarrel and thus bring
73. his army * after you now for hostile purposes, to kill you, our (73)
elder? * Lord, I beg to take my leave and put myself to the test against
those officers and men of the strong and mighty Bhirut. * Having
acquired the kingdom, how can he change, harden his heart, fail to
think and feel pity? * As for you, the elder, you did not want to join
issue for the sake of our pleasant land. * You left, to build up merit by
observing the practices. Why did Bhirut become so angry as to make
this effort to follow you and kill you? * As long as he is alive in this
world and when he has reached the next, Bhirut will not avoid censure.
* Bhirut will not avoid the four states of loss.[11] His evil ways are
indeed those of delusion and unrighteousness. * Bhirut will not escape
from fear of my powerful and victorious arrow which will this instant
bring about his destruction. * I shall annihilate his horses, his
marching columns, his elephants and his vehicles, raging like the fire
which arose to destroy the eras, * making them be food for the crows
and vultures which hover and turn or dart hither and thither through-
74. out the wide (74) heavens, * until the blood of the elephants is mingling

(74) with that of the horses, the blood of the cows with that of the buffaloes
and with that of the officers and men. * And with it the blood of
Sutrut and Bhirut shall flood and flow like a sea, like a Mount Sumeru
of a sea." * Laksm(ṇ) had spoken to the supporter of the earth, with
his quiver slung over one shoulder and his bow in one hand. * His
sword was tucked into his belt and he held a powerful arrow, just what
was suitable. He was all ready for action.

* Then Nārāy(ṇ) Rām stopped his young brother with gentle words.
* "Laksm(ṇ)," he said, "please listen to me while I remind you of
ancient custom. * In our family there has always been a continuing line
75. of sovereigns * ruling the kingdom in succession (75), their number
great indeed; and they have all acted in accordance with the code of
honour, precisely and properly. * They have ruled in due order: the
father, the lawful eldest son and, next in order, the younger son.
* Never have they come to blows over it, never attacked, killed or
usurped the throne through uncontrolled desire. * And further, to
Bhirut the code of honour is as unreservedly dear as his life's breath.
* He is deferential, full of forbearance, understanding. He is like
Mount Sumeru, which * can withstand the winds of the eight directions
buffeting and blowing without the slightest movement. * And even
when, in her jealousy, Kaikesī, his mother, would have liked to
instigate an evil deed, * she was unable to stir up trouble. Bhirut had a
mind neither for anger nor greed. * Now, when we set out, leaving
76. Aiyudhyā, and came (76) to live in the forest, * Bhirut had already left
the city. We came away to carry out our ascetic practices * and I think
that after we did so Bhirut returned to establish his reign over the
kingdom of Aiyudhyā. * Having achieved that, he levied an army to
come and find me, whom he loves and wants to see. * Now, Laksm(ṇ),
look how his attendant forces are disposed — * and even if they were
our enemies, what need would there be for me to let their strategies
trouble you? * Like the waters of the sea, I would surge and seep right
over them to extinguish the fire they had built." * Laksm(ṇ), the
unsullied, heard the prince of the ten powers speak these gentle words
of truth * and knelt, setting down his bow and arrow straight away and
making obeisance to the older prince.

2.77–84. **Bhirut and Sutrut visit Rām and tell him of his father's death. They are joined by the queens and the army. All mourn. They offer the throne to Rām who refuses. The visiting party returns to Aiyudhyā.**

77. * Then Bhirut marched towards the hill and the hermitage of the

(77) lord and master of men. * Arriving, he stationed his army near the hill and
mustered his men, the whole royal force. * Bhirut and Sutrut, just the
two princes, then set out on the difficult path, * climbing up on to the
mountain height towards the hermitage of the lord Nārāy(ṇ) Rām.
* The latter saw his two young brothers, their tears flooding even as
they walked towards him, * wearing their hair in a knot and clad in
bark-cloth, for they had changed their appearance so as to be dressed
like those powerful beings, the anchorites. * He had no doubt at all of
their friendship and was much moved, his eyes glistening, the tears
flowing. * Bhirut and Sutrut bowed low at his feet and fainted as
78. though at death's door. * The prince (78) embraced and caressed his
young brothers, his tears flowing over their backs * like crystals falling
upon a shining, golden work of art. * He fussed over them, holding
them close and stroking their faces until they regained consciousness
and were able to greet him. * They made obeisance at the feet of the
most high and with great sadness, weeping tears of sorrow, lamented,
* "Ah! We thought we were parted from the beloved Prince Rām, the
strong and mighty Nārāy(ṇ), who was born in changed form to sustain
the earth. * Ah! We are favoured with five blessings. One is our
eyesight, for the pupils of our eyes are indeed rejoicing at being able to
see his immaculate face. * One is our hearing for our ears too are
79. wholly delighted at perceiving the sound of his honey-sweet voice. (79)
* One is for our sense of smell which is constantly overjoyed also, for
our nostrils perceive his fragrant, flower-like scent. * One is for that
part of our bodies, the tongue, which, having the chance to make a
loving reply to the words of that dear one, eagerly moves in our
mouths. * One is for our sense of touch for, coming to dwell in the
forest, we are reunited with the eminent prince, distinguished for his
tranquillity. * All five senses, together with our minds' understanding,
the six means of perception, are fully awakened, keenly alive."

* Then all five princely beings had spent their grief, put an end to
their lamentations. * Rām spoke. "Hail, Bhirut and Sutrut, who lead
the ascetic life and look like anchorites blessed with power! * You have
been able, then, to muster all this attendant throng to come and find
80. me (80) now. * I am afraid that enemies of the king may attack that
most handsome sovereign, supporter of the earth. * How could you
abandon the city and desert that most regal lord, our father? * It must
have been either that the lovely Kosakalyā, Kaikesī and Sramud * have
exerted their influence over you serene princes, so dear to them, or that
His Majesty has some illness of old age." * Bhirut placed the palms of
his hands together above his head and respectfully made reply,
* gasping and sobbing as he spoke, the tears twinkling as they fell, like

(80) the stars of the constellation Rohiṇi. * "Lord and sovereign," he said,
"with regard to our father, master of men, * after you left Aiyudhyā to
81. journey through the forests, * that supporter of the earth (81) grieved
and beat his breast in unabating anguish * and passed to that other
shore, Death's shore, reaching the end of this transient life." * Learning
that his father, manifest king, had passed away, Prince Rām instantly
* felt a tremor in his heart, a quaking which he could not stop. He
lamented until he swooned, writhing. * His lovely wife and Laksm(ṇ)
too writhed and swooned on that mountain height.

* Then Kosakalyā, the beautiful Sramud and Kaikesī * led their
retinue and the soldiers up on to the hill to the hermitage of Prince
Rām. * They approached and clasped that darling son in their arms.
82. Distressed by their bereavement, they fell faint upon that high (82) hill.
* All the lesser officials, the chief ministers and attendants, male and
female, numerous beyond counting, * grieved and beat their breasts
and swooned upon that hill, rolling on the ground and writhing.
* When at last they regained consciousness, had spent their grief and
were soothed, the serene princes, as was proper, were untroubled, they
* and the queens and the anchorites. The soldiers assembled, their
clamour resounding loudly, their officers in a whirl of activity. * All
knelt, all raised their hands to salute the supporter of the earth,
Nārāy(ṇ) Rām, the well-born.

* Bhirut then bowed and with palms together addressed his elder,
master of men, * requesting the lord to return to the ancient city,
glorious Aiyudhyā, * to rule in place of their father, governing the
people and the state. * "At this moment," he said, "the whole people is
dissatisfied. There is unrest because they are separated from you. * I beg
83. you, please (83) have pity! Do not condemn Kaikesī * because of her
vile wickedness which caused you, our sovereign, to become angry and
abandon the city. * When you departed our father lamented for you
until he died of grief." * Then Nārāy(ṇ) Rām kindly explained the
matter of the promise, saying, "O Bhirut, * with regard to our father's
life being ended, it was because he did not break a promise. * He
intended to have you rule the kingdom. How could you nullify his
agreement with you? * If I were to rule before you that would be to
cast aside the pledge made by our father the king. * Please return to
govern the city * so that our father's word will be kept in compliance
84. with his true wishes. * If you want (84) to do my will, you will return to
rule glorious Aiyudhyā. * You will take these golden sandals and keep
them for use in your quarters * and you will observe and obey the
established laws and increase in glory and prosperity. * I shall perform
the ascetic practices for increase in accordance with the precepts of the

(84) sages. When fourteen years have * passed, I shall return to my haven, glorious Aiyudhyā." * When he had finished speaking, without delay the prince took off the golden sandals * and, placing them upon his head, gave them to Bhirut, his younger brother, who accepted them, weeping at the thought of being without the revered supporter of the earth. * This done, he took his leave respectfully and set out to return to the city.

2.85–3.4. **Rām decides that they must move to a less accessible part of the forest. As they proceed they encounter the ogre Birādh, who snatches Sītā away. Laksm(ṇ) goes to rescue her but it needs Rām's help to defeat the ogre. Laksm(ṇ) decides to live alone as an ascetic.**

85. * Then Nārāy(ṇ) Rām took thought (85) together with his younger brother and his wife. * "Living here on Mount Citrakūṭ," he said, "we are close to Aiyudhyā. * Bhirut will, I fear, be coming with his followers to plead and entreat me, pressing me to go and rule the people in succession to our father. * This being the case, we ought to go away. We should leave this mountain and look for a remote locality, where * I shall carry out the ascetic practices and build up righteousness bit by bit, increasing my knowledge in tranquillity." * With this idea, the mighty prince, omniscient, led forth his consort and brother.

* And then the three royal persons journeyed into the heart of the forest ways. * Just at that time there was an ogre which went through the air in search of animals on which to make his swift attacks * in
86. those celestial forests and mountains. He approached (86) the Hemabānt, imitating by his manner a roaring lion. * This ogre, by name Birādh, was of stalwart strength, rugged and rough. He loured and blasphemed outrageously. * In his hands he held a powerful pike to wield for destruction. Stockily built, he was energetic and threw himself about excessively. * He would seize horses and lions and dash them to pieces. He caught tigers as they fled in confusion. He captured mighty elephants for food. * He trampled on the forest trees breaking them in pieces. All the animals — their number was incalculable — were becoming panic-stricken. * With swaggering gait this immensely powerful ogre came crashing through the forest, ill-humoured, fearing nothing and, * as he blundered along he caught sight of a path. He emerged from the trees, proceeded along it and encountered the prince, supporter of the earth, * close by the woodland hermitage where that highest of sages, mindful to build up merit, was acquiring perfect virtue.
87. (87) * And now the loathsome Birādh saw the princess, pure and

(87) comely. * Dizzy with pleasurable excitement, Birādh shaded his eyes.
Then he playfully waved his hand. * Suddenly, there he was, moving
forward, trembling and with a quaking in his heart, but boldly speaking. * "I am called Birādh of Anuttagrām and have come here in
pursuit of elephants, rhinoceros and large tigers. * I am the son of the
great Kāl and have sole authority as king of the forest of Daṇḍakāraṇy.
* My might and power through virtue are great — and now I have
good fortune indeed to have come across you two! * Hail, all you
sages, you with your hair tied in a knot, walking along without fear!
* This forest was given to me by Khar for my enjoyment so your wife
shall be mine — no doubt of that! * As for you there, I shall drive my
javelin through your breast so that the gods will be agape at my
3.1. prowess." (3.1) * With these words, Birādh came and snatched away
Sītā, wife of the prince, master of men, * and bore her off on his hip, his
glee defying all powers of comparison or description. * Then Nārāy(ṇ)
Rām was furious as though set alight with fire. * Setting aside his
ascetic ritual, he took up his bow, with its swift arrow, but * instantly
Laksm(ṇ) asked this favour of his royal elder. * "I beg leave to help
you, to go this very moment on your behalf to fetch back your wife,
lord, most high." * Having spoken he took the strong bow and
powerful arrow of the lord of supporters of the earth to * take aim and
to triumph in the combat. But the ferocious ogre of victorious might
* and mountainous stature, ran straight towards the young brother and
2. (2) the two met, matching might with might. * As when the god of the
wind beats tempestuously over the sea so that it rises up in waves
surging over the land, * so did that young brother go forward to fight
the ogre. The mighty ogre, for his part, hurled himself about, joining
battle, * and leaped forward to seize the prince as he was dispatching
the arrow, demonstrating his astonishing prowess. * Rām of
superlative might could see that his young brother's fight with the ogre
was indecisive * and that the young prince was in a precarious
position, so that esteemed leader of men shot arrow upon arrow,
brought the ogre down and * went to take hold of him. The latter
struggled, twisting and turning, wanting to seize the great prince.
* With his pike of grand victories he moved to grasp the prince, who
brandished his sword, whirling it round. * The ogre, Nārāy(ṇ) and his
brother churned up the ground so that it was gaping open. Such was the
3. amazing force of their encounter! * (3) Rām murmured magic words
over an arrow and shot it, invincible, to bring death and destruction —
Birādh fell to the ground! * Trees in the jungle snapped in two. Mountains
were broken in pieces. All the gods, lords of the mountains, offered their
congratulations on the victory. * The prince had overthrown and killed

(3) Birādh by the might of his arrow. He then burned that wicked, godless
creature. * The prince, his young brother and his wife kept the
traditional laws of asceticism in the forest of Daṇḍakāraṇy.
* Laksm(ṇ) considered how, if he were to depart this life, his whole
body disintegrating, he was but an ordinary person. * He spoke with
respect to his revered elder, raising his hands, "I humbly request to
leave you, most righteous lord. * I would go away to be an ascetic,
following the essential laws of the Books of the three Vedas, as a
hermit, leaving this world." * Rām replied, "No! You are my constant
refuge and strength. How can you go and live on your own? * No! You
4. are like my shadow to me. If I lose you, (4) my young defencelsss
brother, I shall grieve indeed." * The elder prince of glorious victories
was deeply hurt and did not feel at all content * but the august
Laksm(ṇ) went off into the jungle, invincible sword in hand, and stood
still to make his vows * to carry out the rules of ascetics, to meditate
with total concentration, to recite the incantations, to make sacrifices
and to perform the procedures of reflection in unceasing obedience.
* The birds brought fruit in plenty to that hermit, mindful of his
perfect virtue and indifference.

3.4–11. **The ogress Sūrapanakhā confides to Khar that she intends to marry Laksm(ṇ). In human form she visits the brothers, who, each in turn, send her to the other. Finally Laksm(ṇ) in anger wounds her. Her cries are heard by Khar who sends Dūs(ṇ) to bring her home.**

* Then the young demon princess, by name Sūrapanakhā, who lived
and roamed in the forest, * went swiftly across it to the great ocean
and journeyed on to King Khar. Greeting him, she spoke to him in
confidence. * "I have been hearing about Prince Rām and his chief
wife and young brother who are with him. * I am going to change my
form and make myself pretty," she went on, "so that the younger one
5. will take me as his dearly-loved wife."[12] * She then (5) concentrated on
changing her appearance, adorning herself splendidly, very much like a
goddess, * and traversed the forest and mountains to the dwelling of
the princely Rām. She made herself all ready, * combing her hair,
making her body gleam, patting on powder. Then she went up to the
prince and stood there, gracefully swaying, her hands spread.[13]
* Seeing the she-devil approaching with amorous intentions, the prince,
supporter of the earth, * said, "Well, pretty lady! I suppose there is
some reason for this visit?" * Then the demon princess of shallow
brain explained herself to the supporter of the earth respectfully, * "I

(5) am the young sister of the Demon King Rāb(ṇ) who rules over Laṅkā,
that prosperous king of the ogres. * One of my elder brothers is called
King Kumbhakār(ṇ), the other, well-versed in the books of knowledge,
6. (6) is known as Bibhek the astrologer. * I have been thinking about
plans for a marriage alliance and so have almost abandoned my care
for the kingdom's affairs. * But even if one of the race of gods, of
handsome appearance, should woo me, I would not be content to
comply with his feelings. * For I heard about you two lordly princes. I
was delighted. I imagined you, my lord, just as I now see you. * If your
wife were to be angry with me and strike me, I would put up with
blows from Her Highness. * Do, O master of men, Prince Rām, take
me as your concubine!"

* Then Prince Rām began his reply. "O lady, fair of form, * now I
am in a state of perplexity for I have a wife to occupy my attention.
7. * Being already married, I do not feel free. (7) Laksm(ṇ), my young
brother, on the other hand, * is a young fellow without a lady-love. It
would be a good thing for him to have you as his pretty wife. * Indeed
it seems as though Laksm(ṇ) is in luck to obtain you as his blissful
companion in life." * Then Sūrapanakhā said farewell to the prince
and went along the mountain way in the direction of that master of
men. * When she was near the anchorite's hermitage, she displayed her
attractions and her powers, her whole body quivering. * Going up to
him, she knelt and, placing her hands carefully in the lotus position,
she greeted him of the ten strengths, * explaining, "I see that my visit
here is fortunate in the extreme! * I hear that your elder brother,
Prince Rām, has Princess Sītā to serve him to his satisfaction. * And I
hear that you, my lord, are alone. I have an idea that I could wish for
8. you as my divine possession. * If you take pity on me you will rule (8)
that kingdom, the three worlds." * Laksm(ṇ) answered without
friendliness, "I take no delight in royal concubines. * I am content to
increase my merit, leaving the world so as to practise perfect
righteousness like the Brahm in the dwelling of the pure. * You go
back to Prince Rām, that distinguished lord who is content with his
way of life, sustaining the earth. * Sītā is his wife. You could be his
second wife taking the lower place." * Then Sūrapanakhā took leave of
the prince and retraced her way to Prince Rām. * She told him what
had transpired with his young brother. "He did not accept my
invitation! * I thought your brother would accept. Now I am forlorn
for in you yourself, my lord, I have no master." * Rām pondered the
matter. "Madam, it has ever been thus with the man who is increasing
9. (9) his right conduct. * When an invitation is given to him just once,
the wise man would not feel it proper for him to accept it and commit

(9) himself. * You should go and ask him a second time. Use a little
artifice. Tell him of your need for a saviour." * Then Sūrapanakhā
returned to the younger brother, moving with careful grace. * "I have
come once again," she said, "and shall let myself die at your feet. I will
not be separated from you. * That is, even if you do not take me as
your wife, *I* shall take *you* as my husband." * Laksm(ṇ) thoughtlessly
burst into anger. What was this — an ogress amusing herself by lust-
fully enticing him? * He drew his victorious sword, sharp weapon,
seized Sūrapanakhā and trampled upon her on the ground. * He struck
to cut her hands and shave her head. The godless creature screamed.
Earth felt a tremor. * Then she struggled to change her form into that
10. of an (10) ogress, with terrifying demoniac thunder. * She shrieked out
about the master of men so as to be heard in the city in the forest of
Daṇḍakāraṇy. * In her state of shock, she screamed and moaned as she
ran, struggling in frantic haste. * Khar heard the sound of
Sūrapanakhā's cries. In anger he beat the drum to rouse the army
* and sent Dūs(ṇ) galloping off on horseback to Sūrapanakhā to find
out what had happened. * Dūs(ṇ) came through the air, for he had that
power, and reached the place as was his desire. Then he saw
Sūrapanakhā, * saw her body, dishonoured for ever. The good name of
her forbears was lost. The prestige of her family was ruined! * Badly
11. maimed, (11) she was struggling along, crawling. Dūs(ṇ) felt deeply
grieved on her behalf as he saw her. * Weeping, he lifted Sūrapanakhā
up and put her on the horse. The demon princess shed tears of deep
despair. * King Khar was furiously angry. "You were without blemish!
You have lost your good name! You are vilely shamed. * Produce the
name of your enemy — and add the god of Death too, for he helps the
wicked to live on. * I shall pursue that King of Death and seize in my
grasp your evil assailant. * I shall dispose of him in revenge. I shall
cause his life to end as Death creeps in on him."

3.11–20. **Khar marches his army towards Rām and Laksm(ṇ) to take his revenge. Laksm(ṇ) offers to fight in single combat but Rām says he will fight himself. Khar sends first Dūs(ṇ) then Trīmukh to capture the ascetics. Rām defeats and kills both.**

* Khar beat the drum summoning his whole vast force to assemble
within the royal grounds * and, selecting ferocious fighters, marshalled
12. them in readiness, a whole (12) armoury of weapons in their outstretched hands. * They had come forth mounted, some on *nāgas*,
some on sea-monsters, others on deer or * on lions, oxen, buffaloes.

(12) Some rode great antelopes, others royal lions, * horses, or water-
buffaloes, elephants, rhinoceros, great tigers. * They were mounted on
camels, bull elephants and llamas, on lions, donkeys — all many times
victorious in battle. * Their chiefs were experts, each one of them
handling a force of twenty thousand. * They boosted their morale with
hostile cries, "Go into hiding where you will, you ascetics — our right
arms will prevail." * They rode their mounts, while round the infantry
the dust rose in clouds, blotting out the sunshine.

* Seeing the demon host — and more, the huge *kumbhaṇḍa* ogres —
13. * bringing up (13) their unruly forces, those princes of mighty power
were about to go forth to do battle with them. * Laksm(ṇ) spoke with
respect, "Lord, your whole force is of course at Your Royal Highness's
disposal; * but if they hear that we have mobilised the entire army they
will be able to cast aspersions at your powers in that you need to use it.
* Instead I beg to aid you myself, alone, the equal of that mob of
hirelings. * I beg you to be content with this: I will go out to fight in
single combat, offering my life for you." * Then the handsome Nārāy(ṇ)
explained to his young brother, * "O Laksm(ṇ), it was you who
murderously attacked Sūrapanakhā and the godless creatures are filled
with dreadful anger. * That huge army of ogres is so tough and you
would undertake to fight and destroy such tremendous demons!
14. * Perhaps it seems as though I am (14) in your way, this fight being
yours because of Sūrapanakhā, * but in fact you have a brother and
that brother must undertake your fight. Do not worry! * I shall go out
to manifest my might and take that sinful ogre on the battlefield.
* Now you watch my deed of prowess, my glorious victory which will
be famous throughout all the three worlds."

* Then those ferocious godless creatures, so vulgar, drew up their
ranks, scattering the dust so as to obscure the heavens. * They marched
to the boundary of the prince's territory. "Ho there! Rām the prince!
Any moment now it looks like death for you!" * The four branches of
the demon army with their strong elephants and their host of soldiers
shook Mother Earth * throughout her surface and cities were
15. oppressed by their deafening roar. * Khar, in a (15) mighty rage, called
to his own young brother, * "O Dūs(ṇ), the two anchorites have
committed wrongs with their magic bow and its powerful arrows.
* They may live the religious life, seeking the upright behaviour of the
Dharma, but they are errant knaves! * They wronged Sūrapankhā, as
you can see, causing her to lose face and diminish in strength. They
had no fear of our authority. * I would have you conduct our army,
ready as they are for action, * and capture those ascetics of great
victories so that they shall know the strength of our right arms, our

(15) ascetic power. * They are bold, those high and mighty princes, and are
threatening us with their aggressiveness. * They have shot at our
demon army to destroy us, causing a tremor to go through the land.
* They have the blessing of Brahm — the magic arrows of Rām and
16. Laksm(ṇ) number ten thousand. * So use all your might (16) wielding
your magic powers to crush and smash those mighty enemy princes."

* Prince Dūs(ṇ) respectfully took his leave. He made ready the
carriages with their horses, too many to count. * The latter were of
great renown for they flew like the wind. Such was the nature of those
thoroughbreds. * With much kicking, they hovered over the three
worlds or darted with swift turns, accomplishing whatever was desired.
* They were covered with patterned, colourful cloths, gilded and
bejewelled, those mighty horses. * Prince Dūs(ṇ), equipped with magic
devices to attack the two leaders of the world, stood holding his
invincible pike. * Turning vigorously he gesticulated at the two
supporters of the earth while the horde of ogres loudly yelled out their
war-cries. * They beat their victory gongs energetically at Rām and
marshalled their forces ready to attack with daggers, encircle the enemy
or shoot. * They hurled their powerful pikes with all their might — and
17. those powerful pikes turned round and returned, scattering in (17)
the form of flowers! * The ogre prince fired a thunderbolt at the master
of men — and there came flowers for Rām, * in the form of fine
garlands, spreading pollen all about, anklets for his golden feet! * The
horde of innumerable ogres turned from their bows and magic arrows
and laid hold of pointed, sharp-edged weapons and were off in pursuit
of the enemy. * The lord Rām went forth and in reply seized an ogre,
manifesting his might. * The huge creature, fiercely indignant, took
hold of the lord of ten strengths, the lord of power and prowess. * Rām
seized Prince Dūs(ṇ). The ferocious ogre flung out his hands, waving
them about, intent on capturing him in turn. * The lord swung up his
bow, stout and tough, held wide his arms and turned to take aim with
his arrows. He shot * and hit Prince Dūs(ṇ). There he was — fallen!
The horrible ogres were terrified! They sought shelter in the gullies and
caves. * All the gods who dwelt in the great mountains, bearing
18. magnificent garlands, (18) came down from heaven, distinguished
beings, to offer * praises to the leader of men, Nārāy(ṇ), giving their
congratulations on his victory, scattering roasted corn and perfumed
blossoms.

* Prince Khar was furiously angry. He called Trīmukh, his dearly-loved son. * "O Trīmukh, greater than all," he said, "you have been bold, you have waged war successfully, with victory. * Go now and use the power of your right arm in this battle. Gain a great victory over Prince Rām."

(18) * Then the mighty Trīmukh took leave respectfully and went out to
undertake the fight. * The eminent Trīmukh, of gigantic size, held his
bow with care and went onto the field of combat. * In a raging fury,
his eyebrows knit together in a scowl, he jeered with overbearing
contempt. * He was impressive with his three heads and four hands.
He bore weapons, one in each hand. * In his left hands he held
powerful arrows and a sword. In his right hands were a bow and a disc
19. for hurling, crushing its target and (19) returning to the thrower. * His
coat of mail was all bejewelled and of very great thickness, with gems
attached to it in patterns. * With his sash, his jewelled crown, earrings
and ornamented armlets, he was indeed a figure of importance and
power! * He rode on a strong elephant, unconquered in battle, his
weapons in every hand, his spirit eager for daring deeds. * There was
every kind of device to protect his person and prevent his being
wounded by arrows. * The vast horde of ogres roared with a sound like
thunder, to terrify the two princes.

* Rām saw them coming and struck out at them, took hold of them,
cried out loudly with threats, with mighty authority and endurance.
* With his left hand he held his fine elephant; with his right hand, the
prince seized hold of the ogres. * He smote them and they fell limp and
sprawling, with blood flowing all over, like water in a stream. * The
20. blood ran like the river Yamanā in mighty flood (20) pouring forth
towards him, up to * the elephant's belly, welling up. Angrily the
demon prince approached through the air, with arm outstretched,
gesticulating. * He was in a raging fury, compressing his lips and
gnashing his teeth, as he raised the bow to dispatch an arrow. * He
aimed and shot the powerful arrow in an arc. The great disc in his right
hand, he brandished and hurled into the distance, * striking the lord of
men, Rām. The arrows showered down and the ogre, powerful in
contests of prowess, approached to fight, * crashing his way forward
in a great rush. Rām seized the ogre and the ogre struck back. * Rām
shot his powerful arrow striking to kill the ogre — and the ogre fell
dead!

3.20–28. **Khar comes himself and is defeated and killed by Rām.**

* Then that godless creature, King Khar, realised the power of the
supporter of the earth, the august wielder of the destructive arrow.
* He had annihilated Dūs(ṇ) and Trīmukh, the glorious, and a great
army had been brought to destruction, fallen there upon the vast battle-
21. ground. * In a furious rage he (21) spoke contemptuously, "So! I am to

(21) drive up to them myself to take the victory, am I? * So! Dūs(ṇ) and
Trīmukh are dead and a great force too has fallen, their light
extinguished! * I am alone now, bewildered like an elephant whose
throat is being cut for the sake of its tusks. * If I live in pleasure and
happiness, a demon, as it were, without cares, the world would say I
am a man without power, * who has become a weak princeling, foolish
and fearful, with thoughts of protecting his kingdom but no capacity
for seizing opportunities of heroism. * And in this world of beings, that
which one may call the body cannot escape by disguising itself — the
god of Death will take it. * I might live prosperously and peacefully
but this does not mean to say that I would have a long life and escape
Time, * with its power to see far and reach far. Then, in the endless
eras to come, everyone would criticise me for my cowardice."
22. (22) * Khar thought he still had the capacity to think brave thoughts.
He made himself ready and * climbed into his carriage, with its horses
yoked and bridled, wearing a huge diamond and armed with his curved
bow. * He had his crown and earrings, his bow, an umbrella made
bright with peacocks' feathers, to hold for shade, * a shield, a sword,
the bow and a lance. Strings and trumpets murmured melodiously or
resounded shrilly. * His men were mounted on elephants and on lions
which moved menacingly. The ground trembled and quaked
miraculously. * The rays of the sun were obscured in the sky. Even the
god Indr was in darkness, unable to see the sun's light. * So loud were
his army's cries for a glorious victory that mountains were overturned
and layers of earth were piled up. * Khar approached for the combat
against the god Rām. And Rām, possessed of sharp arrows, shot them
repeatedly one after the other. * The carriage was split in two, the
23. wheels and spokes broke up as though crushed (23) into dust. * Horses
were torn loose. Charioteers and horses were separated. The necks of
the horses were ripped. All spattered, they were entangled one on top
of the other. * Shield, sword, bow and cross-bow, all weapons were in
use on that battlefield in the fighting and the fending off. * Enemy
victims slumped down dead, obliterated. Their blood flowed, brimming
over, like the waters of the sea. * The whole fierce force of ogres died,
their corpses piling up. It was like a river of blood. * The demon prince
was in a rage. He twisted and turned with a great effort, foaming at the
mouth, panting and gasping. * Both aimed arrows to kill each other
but Rām's great arrows intercepted Khar's and scattered them! * There
were arrows which tied people up, arrows which scattered poison everywhere. There were whistling sounds here, there and everywhere in the
sky. * But Khar's arrows, when shot, split up and turned into flowers,
while the arrows of the master of men were all genuine weapons, sharp

24. and destructive. (24) The arrows Khar sent were *nāgas* but the arrows
of the prince were *garuḍas* flitting to and fro. * The arrows of Khar
were elephants, loudly trumpeting, but the arrows of Rām, who would
end retribution, were strong elephant-lions. * Khar's arrows, swiftly
flashing by, were flowers but the arrows Rām sent were great sharp
weapons. * Khar's arrows were burning fire but the arrows Rām sent
were water, in marvellous abundance, to quench it.

* The two royal beings, mighty indeed and unvanquished, had great
powers of endurance and strength. * Both shot their arrows to kill each
other but the great arrows of Rām were able to intercept the other's.
* Arrows struck Rām; he shot back. Khar seized Rām but he struggled
free. Khar was unable to come close to Rām. * He dealt a blow and
Rām struck back. The sage seized Khar, who struggled in excessive
rage and fury. * Khar seized Rām but the latter in turn flogged the evil
25. Khar with his bow! * Khar approached aggressively (25), seized hold of
the lord and, brandishing his sword, shouted loud threats at him.
* Then he pulled up mountains and hurled them to hit the body of the
master of men, who pursued him and dealt him a blow. * In anger
Khar broke up a mountain into huge boulders and flung them, shower-
ing them down like arrows, * banging and crashing as they scattered in
pieces. The whole heaven was moved — a most astonishing and
terrifying event! * The sky and the sun were blotted out. A tremor
went through all three worlds. All were aghast at this power.

* The demon prince shouted angrily in a deafening voice as he held
his victorious bow and shot arrow after arrow with all speed. * He
rudely addressed the master of men, "Hey, you anchorite! You repulsive
knave of erring ways! * The whole of my great force, too many to
count, have you shot down to certain death and destruction with your
sharp arrows. * And even now you know no shame! You, who abide
by the good books, you do not consider the manifold retribution which
26. will come. * It is likely that (26) you will, for innumerable eras, reap
sorrow, punishment and fear. I do not know the number of your evil
deeds." * Then Rām replied, "O ogre of erring ways, loathsome villain!
* You do not, then, know the powers that I have, being the god,
Nārāy(ṇ), in changed form? * All the gods of the sixteen celestial
regions invited me to come here as Rām, the god and ascetic. * Did
you not know that I wield the power to descend and wipe out you evil
godless creatures who persecute men? * You are like rubbish or cotton
floss. I am like a fire which bursts into flame and rages wildly across it.
* You do not know the power which I, your master, have. You come
here and resist my supreme authority."

* Then the ferocious ogre, panting and gasping, ran to take shelter in

(26) a cave and prepare to perform a rite in accordance with convention. * He murmured magic, made offerings, meditated reverently, recited
27. incantations from the books, (27) recalling how the prayers went. * He recited the formulae for help as he lay waiting quietly in a sheltering cleft among the caves and crags of the mountains. * Rām knew that Khar was intoning magic. With his bow he struck a blow at the mountain. It cracked! * "Now, Khar, you are being stupid. You lack understanding. Without giving thought, you just run off to escape and hide. * This one would describe as cowardice. Come out and fight in this combat of prowess!" * Listening to this command to take hold of himself, King Khar smouldered with anger like a fire. * Casting aside the ritual practices, he rose up to his immense height and fought with Rām Nārāy(ṇ). * Rocks were overthrown and shattered, falling in pieces. Trees in the forests were scattered about. Great, deep crevasses burst into being. * There was a quaking throughout all heaven. The gods offered their congratulations at the success of the prince, master
28. of men, — * for Prince Harī had struck the malignant ogre (28) to death, to utter annihilation! * The prince was a natural victor on the battle field and thus did the arrogant ogre come to the end of his life. * The prince had carried out a mighty deed: with his devastating arrows he had demolished the army of King Khar, * he had liquidated Dūs(ṇ), that destructive godless creature, and Trīmukh of many victories had died there on the ground. * A quaking had affected the *cakravāla*. The great, regal mountain, Sumeru, was disturbed by tremors. * And the ten thousand righteous gods and the seven thousand fair-winged ones came flying down to offer their good wishes. * They presented fine garlands of divine splendour. They offered lotus flowers in profusion, flowers with stamens and pollen, * to the prince and his young brother and his chief wife, the three great princely beings, eminent above all in this world.

3.28–33. **Sūrapanakhā tells Rāb(ṇ) of these deaths and of the beauty of Sītā. Rāb(ṇ) decides to capture Sītā by a trick.**

* Then the godless creature, Sūrapanakhā, saw that the might of the
29. kingly Rām was might indeed. * She saw Dūs(ṇ) (29), Trīmukh and King Khar, motionless, together with the great demon force, dead. * Alone, she left the kingdom and traversed the ocean, across to the city of Laṅkā, * where she went to give the demon King Rāb(ṇ) an account of the great deeds of Rām, master of men, and of Laksm(ṇ). * "The fact is that those two princes have caused the downfall of Dūs(ṇ),

(29) obliterated Trīmukh and destroyed the lordly Khar. * They have overthrown Birādh the mighty and demolished a host of horses, elephants
and carriages. They fell crushed to bits! * The land of Daṇḍakā was
devastated. The great army was routed. That glorious region fit for
gods was brought to nothing." * King Rāb(ṇ) listened to Sūrapanakhā's
narration. He trembled with emotion. He writhed in agony. * How,
then, had King Khar, that royal chieftain of inestimable strength and
30. might, come to his death? * Then (30) suddenly the godless creature's
eyes lit upon the marks, quite clear, on Sūrapanakhā's head. * "O
good Sūrapanakhā, I see you have suffered injury! It is quite notice-
able. * Alas! You had a fine, perfect form without blemish. I, King
Rāb(ṇ) of the trident, saw that you were magnificent. * Who could
have dared to do this, not fearing me, lord of the three worlds, of the
whole extent of the three worlds? * Who could give you this fright? I
am astonished. Explain to me how it happened. The whole matter
astounds me." * Then Sūrapanakhā made obeisance and told the
whole story. "I heard about the ascetics, pure in righteousness, two
admirable princes * and went to them simply to serve them for the sake
31. of attaining the highest merit (31) and blessedness — and they were
angry with me! I lost my good name. * They said I was not deferential
towards them, that I was following them because I was looking for a
man. Those two ascetics committed many wrongs in their anger,
through not understanding me. * With their swords they cut my hands
and my ears and shaved my head, so that I was afraid I would not live
and would not see your face again. * Khar was incensed! He trembled
with emotion, feeling embittered against Rām until he died. * Those
sages are called Rām and beloved Laksm(ṇ). The former has a heavenly
goddess to serve him constantly * whose name is Sītā. Her face has the
most august features and her behaviour is of perfect correctness. She is
to be admired above all others in the world, * like the moon reaching
its fullness, without blemish. She is able to satisfy the prince's desires
32. and be his loving companion. (32) * Your Majesty, being a man of
abundant powers, ought to have her as your august chief wife, to
increase your well-being."

* King Rāb(ṇ) had the drum beaten to assemble the chief ministers and the numerous demon officers * and pronounced an order to muster the royal troops and have his young sister tell the story to them. * "If we deploy our bold troops, and march up to capture them triumphantly we would have the ascetics with the greatest of ease. * But I am afraid our reputation would be spoilt if we led a huge army to capture insignificant anchorites. * Let us carry out a ruse and have these bragging, upstart hermits succumb to our infuriating trick. * We

(32) will take Sītā by cunning and then capture the ascetic, who will be full of grief and sorrow. * They abandoned Sūrapanakhā in a hopeless plight and Khar, superior to all in the world, died by means of that
33. ascetic's arrow." (33) All the royal ministers placed their palms together and praised their mighty master, * saying, "O wise lord, your idea is excellent. Do have this done straight away."

3.33–45. **Rāb(ṇ) orders Mahārīk to change himself into a beautiful deer and to entice Rām away from the hermitage. As Rām's arrow strikes him, the deer imitates Rām's voice calling for help. Sītā persuades Laksm(ṇ), against his better judgment, to go to Rām's aid.**

* King Rāb(ṇ) gave orders to a capable official, a valued and brilliant man, whose given name was Mahārīk. * He was to change his handsome form into that of a splendid deer, excelling all others. * "You will transform yourself," he said, "into a magnificent deer of large size, admirable beyond all others. * You will attempt to lure the respected Rām, suitably equipped with bow and arrow, to abandon the hermitage and try to shoot you. * It shall be my task to take away the much-blessed Sītā, chief wife of that ascetic. This I shall no doubt
34. achieve successfully." * (34) Then Mahārīk respectfully placed his palms together and replied, "I beg forgiveness for transgressing your command, sire, * but I know the might of the brave Prince Rām. How can I go there and not shrink back in order to stay alive? * The mighty princess, my mother, Kākanāsūr, was in time past a fierce demoness indeed. * She it was who destructively made off with that sacrifice — a test for the ascetic Rām, of exceeding power and might. * He murmured prayers from the three Vedas and manifested his prowess for he shot and destroyed my mother. She flew to take shelter in the great mountains nearby but * the arrow of that prince, like the god of Death, followed her and killed her with speed. The arrows of Rām stuck fast. Her life was over, her body demolished. * Now if you steal
35. his august chief wife, blessed with good fortune, (35) the prince will be angry. Bow in hand, he will demonstrate his powers. * This prince has completed his training in the precepts and in the practices and conduct of an ascetic. The god Rām annihilated Rāmaparamasūr with his powers. * He liquidated Dūs(ṇ) and Trīmukh and eliminated the mighty Birādh. They died as a result of his capacity for success, which is clearly a driving force like fire. * The power of the ascetic Rām, as he intones the magic phrases, is of one who is high above us. We had better start to pray or he will extinguish us, wipe us out."

(35) * King Rāb(ṇ) was beside himself with anger. "So!" he said. "That is
the extent of your bravery and zeal! * You take the line of boasting on
Harī's behalf. You say the ascetic is actually to be praised. He's an
admirable fellow. * You are not afraid of me, your master. You say it
is the ascetic who has the great power. * You are being obtuse and
mischievous. You deserve to come up against my invincible right arm,
36. victorious in (36) all the worlds. * You speak as though you are proud
of his victories! You are pleased that Harī's arrows will be supreme and
remove our chance of success!" * Mahārīk raised his hands, placed
them together. "I was wrong and wilful. How could I extol his
triumphs, as if they were the greatest in the world? * I suffered acutely
and felt great shame when I saw King Khar so sad and then so
piteously killed by those arrows. * But now I most humbly ask to
undertake the order which Your Majesty would have me carry out. * I
would ask to increase my merit by performing this good deed. May I
entrust my family, my beloved sons to you? * My supreme lord, I beg
you to look kindly upon me." * Mahārīk returned home and behaved
with piety, saddened by the prospect of death. * Then, accepting the
king's command, he quickly changed his form in accordance with the
instructions of the ten-necked one. * He set out from the royal city,
37. exclaiming, "Alas! It is obvious that I shall die (37) because of the
immensity of this folly."

* Mahārīk turned himself into a splendid deer, magnificent beyond
all others, * a golden deer which glanced hither and thither, twisting
his neck, turning his body like a shoot of golden creeper. * His dark
eyes gleamed brightly like glittering jewels of deep hue set in the eye-
sockets, * like two morning stars teamed together, like twin Jupiters.
* His two horns together, forking out, round and upright, equal in size,
seemed studded with gems, * as though a stone-cutter had set lustrous
jewels there, arranged in lines. * The shape of his body was fine,
beautiful; his head was alert. * Of superb beauty was his colouring, as
38. if Nature had just borne him (38), just produced him fresh; * as though
Bisnukār had created the pleasing patterns of his adornment * and had
set precious stones of many varieties on him. At a glance you would
say he was multicoloured for * varied rays of light were reflected,
glimmering like rubies and cat's-eye diamonds side by side, like
sunstones. * He was like a precious lotus of gold, dazzling with flashes
of blood red. * Now he seemed like polished emeralds as when lotus-
coloured jewels are worked into a pattern. * As if a jeweller had put
him together, his whole body shone, all high-grade gold. * With supple
movements, he was shepherding his mate in front of him. He stopped to
dally and groom himself * and bent to lick his feet. Then he proceeded

(38) gracefully forward, with a wistful air, arching up, bowing low. * He
went straight towards the august hermitage, near the supporter of the
39. earth, firm in his one purpose. * (39) Constantly he arched up and
bent down, most striking with his dazzling beauty, * as though he had
risen from the heaven of the thirty-three, as though the god Indr might
have brought him into being, * as decorative as an all-golden deer, to
be compared with the newly-risen sun, * of magnificent charm and
brilliance. His hooves seemed to be made of great emeralds. * Trim
and neat, most decorous, he behaved at first as though he might be
scared and run; then he moved towards the great *sālā*.

* Just then Princess Sītā, much-blessed chief wife, caught sight of the
wonderful, golden deer of such beauty. In eager praise of it, * she
spoke to the revered keeper of the ascetic rules, of great merit and
power, "Look at that shining, gold deer, sparkling with jewels, made to
40. perfection! * You should kill it and take (40) the splendid golden skin
for you to rest upon when you are pleased to be crowned king with
undying power. * It shall be laid down, like gold with its bejewelled
appearance, like gold, worthy of the glory of the supreme Indr. You
shall resemble an emperor!" * Then Rām saw the cunning deer of gold.
"Laksm(ṇ), look at the deer — a godless creature in changed form.
* Look after Sītā. I shall kill the demon, demonstrating my power,
using the mighty arrows of a man of victory. That deceitful ogre shall
be destroyed."

* Then, commanding his young brother to guard his wife, the great
prince went out on * foot alone, august supporter of the earth, master
of men, able to take * the powerful magic bow and its quiver of
arrows. Alone he went off to the great mountains and the jungle,
* forcing a way, clambering over the hills, with rocks shaking and
41. breaking into pieces, as he pursued the deer. (41) The demon-deer was
dismayed at the might of Nārāy(ṇ). The lord of men, with his power to
destroy, was causing panic through the forest. * In the late afternoon
the humming of snails and cicadas was heard resounding with the
murmur of horns. * Rām thought of his wife and was most concerned,
for he feared some godless creature, evilly covetous, * might beguile
the princess. By trickery and craft a demon might steal his chief wife.
Thus it came about that the master of men worried about Sītā, the pure
and blessed. * Straight away he poised and shot an arrow at the deer.
It would be killed by that arrow. * The demon-deer gave out loud cries
as if weeping and called out, sounding like the lord Rām, "Sumitr!
This deer is a demon. It is an ogre! * It is powerful enough to attack
42. and kill me!" (42) It called out, "O Laksm(ṇ)! A godless creature is
destroying me! Help your elder brother!"

(42) * Then instantly, hearing this brazen utterance, the princess commanded young Laksm(ṇ), * "O Laksm(ṇ), please go after your elder. He
is suffering and in trouble." * Laksm(ṇ), prostrate at her feet, with hands
placed together, explained how the wily demon was deceiving them.
* "Please, princess, do not have a moment's anxiety about the prince,
your husband. * Rām's arrows are like Death even if a hundred thousand
fierce enemies press upon him. * He alone, he of Bisnu's line, can wield
43. those arrows and kill his foes as they attack, * as your own (43) eyes,
madam, have seen when Rām defeated Rāmaparamasūr. * And he
defeated Khar of ill-famed descent and he eliminated Dūs(ṇ) and Trīmukh
as well. * He annihilated their troops and the gigantic Birādh. He fell
upon these forces, struck at them and demolished them. They perished!
* Please, Your Highness, believe in the arrows and in the right arm of him
who is of Bisnu's line." * Then Sītā was distressed for her husband,
supporter of the earth, mighty with the powerful bow, because a godless
creature was attacking him. * She cried out, * "Laksm(ṇ)! The royal Rām
is our master. * You and I, his servants, minister to him and are his
dependants. * But now my command, issued to you, will conflict with the
command of the prince, * for it compels you authoritatively and prevents
44. you (44) from obeying the prince's order. * Now I am simply giving you a
direct order concerning that godless creature which is attacking our elder.
* If you do not go, I am afraid the world will criticise you and say you
were not true to your own brother."

* Because of some bad fate which was to involve him in lasting retribution, Laksm(ṇ) was not pure in thought. * He raised his hands and
addressed the princess. "I care as much for the prince as for the royal
mother who bore me. * You have thus let me know your wishes, in
accordance with your ideas, madam, and those wishes shall be my command." * Laksm(ṇ) offered a prayer, "O, all you gods of the earth,
* divine spirits of the hills and tree deities who live in the forest ways, * I
beg to leave the princess in your care, I implore you to be merciful and
45. protect her." (45) Then Laksm(ṇ), master of men, took leave of the
princess and went forth * and soon after leaving the hermitage reached his
brother, Rām.

3.45–4.9. **Disguised as a Brahmin, Rāb(ṇ) approaches Sītā and praises her beauty. Returning to his normal form, he boasts of his intention to take her away. Sītā resorts to praise of Rām's power. Rāb(ṇ), confident that she will later love him, flies off with her.**

* Then, when the demon King Rāb(ṇ) saw the younger brother going

(45) after the elder lord, * he transformed himself so as to resemble a hermit of power, with his hair tied in a knot. He walked with the gait
4.1. of a Brahmin teacher, a blessed person. (4.1) * He carried a conch, wore a *śamī* leaf and had a rosary for singing praises while making offerings, hanging from his clothing. His eyebrows were conspicuously trimmed away and he wore a sash. With conscientious attention he was reciting formulae from the scriptures. * Carrying the anchorite's book of the three Vedas, he acted the part of a Brahmin teacher, resembling an ascetic of power, a noble follower of the precepts. * As he came along by a forest path directly towards the hermitage of the princess, this "Brahmin" blew on his conch to indicate his identity.

* Then the eyes of the much-blessed Princess Sītā beheld an aged Brahmin whose clothes and sash proclaimed his calling. * Assuming that he was a Brahmin, devout in the precepts, the princess placed her palms together carefully and greeted the demon, expressing most respectfully her good wishes for his religious fulfilment. * Then Rāb(ṇ),
2. godless creature, seeing (2) the spotless princess greeting him, suddenly became the victim of a burning passion. * "O lady of superb beauty, even among the whole host of goddesses and *apsarās*, heavenly maidens, * it would not be possible to find one comparable with you! I could guess that you are the much-blessed Umā, whose husband had angrily cast her out. * And thus, O lady of virtue, of perfect face and sublime form, whether one was a god or a human one would surely desire, as the wish of one's life, to be united with you. * How is it that you have come to live in the forests and mountains, beset by passing spirits and by animals on the move or lying in wait to snatch you away? * It would be better for you to go and live in the city, with plenty of servants at hand, and to stay in a place fit for you, where your lord
3. was, and attend upon him. (3) * Dearest among ladies, you should be enjoying yourself, holding armfuls of flowers, wearing perfume. * But it was lucky for me, most fortunate, that I saw you. * What can I do? My eyes *will* look at you! With a hundred thousand of them I might look enough! * What can I do to produce mouths and tongues? If I had a hundred thousand I might praise you — you, who are like the moon glowing with burnished light in the heavens."

* Then the much-blessed chief consort thought to herself, "This Brahmin's behaviour is not consistent with the practice of asceticism or with the traditions of morality! * I must praise the might of the divine lord of men so that this evil rascal of a Brahmin shall know the whole story of his heroic deeds." * And the much-blessed princess of noble
4. qualities lowered (4) her eyes, bowing her head, and raised her hands to the lord, leader of men, strong and mighty. * "O Brahmin, I am the

(4) chief wife of Lord Harī, royal prince and established ruler of the well-
founded, august kingdom, glorious Aiyudhyā. * He it was who raised
the magic bow and arrow of victory, famous in all the heavens. He
crushed the great Rāmaparamasūr of mighty power, so huge and
ferocious. * Then he crowned me as his royal consort, when I was
sixteen, and came to the forests to build up merit. * As a hermit of
power he is happy. He is attentive in the performance of the precepts.
He has gone away but any moment now he will be back. * Please,
reverend sir, do take a seat and rest. The two princes have never failed
to return."

5. (5) * With a terrifying ogre's growl, Rāb(ṇ) cast away his disguise as
a Brahmin and presented himself as a real ogre! * There suddenly
appeared, opposite Sītā, a face complete with ornament with glittering
jewels. * There rose up twenty arms, each holding a weapon, gleaming
and starkly visible. * There appeared feet, with accoutrements
attached, stamping the earth. And jewels sprang into sight. * There
appeared the huge, invulnerable body of that lawless being, devoid of
honour — and the princess was alone, defenceless! * The ferocious
ogre, gigantic and powerful, called out to the chief consort, describing
his importance and wealth. * "I am a lord, a great king. All those
precious beings, the deathless ones of the heaven of the thirty-three
* duly pay their respects to me. I was able to snatch away the aerial
6. palace of the god Baisrab. * I (6) was able to chase the god of Death so
that that powerful god took refuge in gullies and caves. * I was able to
take the chief god, Indr, to overcome the deathless *nāga*, complete with
his kingdom and populace. * Mount Kailās was destroyed, glorious seat
of the protector of the world, Isūr. * Being gigantic, I can alone lay low
all the numerous heavens and totally defy the gods. * I have the name
Rāb(ṇ), the demon, and am by descent the ruler of my kingdom, the
splendid realm of Laṅkā. * Hearing about your being alone and
defenceless in these forest ways, forlorn and all by yourself, * I have
come to take you away to rule my kingdom. I plan to be united with
you, jointly to protect my people. * You ought to be seated upon a
three-sided throne, all gold, decoratively patterned with jewels * with
the chief ministers, the generals and members of the royal family
7. coming to ask for our blessing. (7) * To you, seated there as my
partner, all the ministers will pay homage."

* "Rāb(ṇ), you are committing a wrong and outraging the royal Rām
by stealing me! * I am the daughter of the King of Mithilā who made a
marriage alliance with King Dasarath, * mighty in power and deeds of
prowess. The royal Rām and Laksm(ṇ) * are the sons of the prestigious
Dasarath, for Nārāy(ṇ), who governed the world in its second age, * has

(7) now, in its third age, become Rām, great and splendid above all others.
* If you would compare him, compare him with a very great god. If
you would compare him with a king, this precious king is magnificent
beyond all others. * If you would compare his supernatural powers,
they are superlative. Compare his physical strength: it is that of a
8. mighty prince. * I am his royal wife. I am true to my promises (8) and
to the words of the supporter of the earth, * even though the gods of
the heaven Kāmāvacar and the most august among kings might try to
cajole me. * If I do not have Rām the prince, I wish to die! * I have
eyes for no other prince. Even the gods of the Kāmāvacar do not
please me. * And now it seems that you, an ogre, will wrong me and
nullify my vows. * By the great piety of my loved one, shoot an arrow
through my breast this instant and * let my body be there for the two
supporters of the earth to bury! * You boasted just now that you, so
huge, could lay low all the numerous heavens and that even the gods
would pay you homage * but deceitfulness, enticement and parting one
person from another are actions which a great lord would avoid — and
stealing is such an action too!"
9. (9) * Shouting and laughing at one and the same time, Rāb(ṇ)
replied, "You rebuke me! That is just like a woman, quick to anger.
* With your finger-nails you claw at me — at me, your dear heart — to
make me really angry. You scratch me too. * I endure it. I submit. I
am not cross. You think I am stupid like your hermit husband before
me * but when I have taken you away and shown you my goodness
you will be grateful, full of smiles for me." * The princess struggled
angrily. Rāb(ṇ) grasped her — defenceless one — and ventured across
the heavens with her in flight.

4.9–20. **On the way to Laṅkā Sītā appeals to the gods and to an egret to tell Rām of her plight and ask him to follow. She laments. Jatāyu fights to save her from Rāb(ṇ) but the latter mortally wounds him, using Sītā's ring. On arrival in Laṅkā Sītā is placed in the park of Asoka trees.**

* And now the royal Sītā, like the full moon, was stolen away by
Rāb(ṇ). * With hands and body she made obeisance, weeping and beating her breast to raw redness, moaning and sorrowing as * she
10. instructed the forests, the mountains, the gods of the road (10) and
those of the caves, * "O gods, please give news of me to the serene
prince, Rām, my noble lord. * The plundering, villainous King Rāb(ṇ)
has abducted me — has even grasped me in his arms — and is now
taking me away somewhere. * My person is close to an ogre but in my

(10) thoughts I pledge my word that I will endure death rather than be
dishonoured. * Even if the life in this body of mine is ended, the
supporter of the earth, the supreme lord, is my love." * As Sītā
sorrowed for her loved one, her flushed face was covered all over with
tears. * "O Lord Rām, master of men, send an arrow after the godless
creature who came running after me! * The pain I am suffering
concerning you, good Rām, who uphold the Law, is too great to
estimate and is endless. * First, I am in anguish because Rāb(ṇ) has
cruelly wronged me, stolen me away, so that there will be long-lasting
11. ignominy (11). * Secondly I am suffering because you, the supreme
lord of men, will say I am not true and faithful. * Thirdly, I sorrow for
you, my lord prince, who will believe me dead and gone. You will be so
sad about me! * In the fourth place, I am pained for you who have no
blemish, for what can you do but succumb to this bold move by a
deceitful, evil demon? * Fifth, I sorrow because Laksm(ṇ) acted in
accordance with my own orders. It was a deed which was to lead to
disaster. * Lastly I grieve that you, Nārāy(ṇ), will say Laksm(ṇ) had no
respect, no fear regarding your royal command." * The more she
thought, the more wretched she became, miserably unhappy about
leaving home in such disastrous circumstances. * The princess cried
out, groaning and weeping pitiably, constantly thinking of Prince
Nārāy(ṇ) Rām.

12. * King Rāb(ṇ) flew towards Laṅkā with Princess Sītā (12) in a highly
delighted frame of mind. * With arms outspread, he held his weapons,
ready for defence if the supporter of the earth, master of men, should
arrive. * As they flew on in his round-shaped carriage, the princess saw
a bird on the mountain heights, * an egret. She called out, weeping as
she did so, to instruct it to tell Rām, the mighty. * "O egret, if you
should see the master of men arriving and his young brother coming
too, * please give them news of me. At this very moment a godless
creature is stealing me away! * I am at a loss, all alone, suffering
pitiably, utterly defenceless. * O egret, if the prince comes, let him who
has the ten powers and his young brother Laksm(ṇ), * two men of the
line of Bisnu of might and prestige, — let them destroy the harmful,
covetous demon. * Erring and arrogant, determined in the extreme, he
13. is secretly stealing me (13) to destroy me. At this very moment he is
taking me away! * Please respectfully ask the prince to follow me and
catch me up."

* The princess instructed the forests and mountains, the gods of the road, those who dwell in the countryside, * "O all you gods, give news of me to my master, Rām, who is my lord always, * for Rāb(ṇ), vile wretch, is stealing me — even grasping me in his arms! And now, where

(13) will be take me? * My person is close to an ogre! But in my mind I
pledge my word to endure death rather than be dishonoured. * No
longer will it be possible for my dead body to be there for the two
supporters of the earth when they come to bury my remains. * No
longer is it possible for me to see the protector of the world. Why has
all come to naught? Why is all disgrace and infamy?
14. (14) * "Ah lord prince! You will just be returning from the forest.
Have you managed to obtain the deer or were you unsuccessful? A
godless creature has stolen your Maithilī by deceit and is carrying her
off! * Alas! You will be coming from the hot forest now. You will be
calling me, your dearest wife — and I am gone! * I yearn for you as
you now weep and look for me, your treasured love. As it is, your
sweetheart is far away. The godless creature has wrongfully taken me
away. * O my darling master! You spoke and Sumitr responded. He
was to guard me, your wife. * Ah! I am accursed I made Sumitr go. I
did not know the godless creature would try to entice me away from
15. you. (15) Ah! I am used to being near to you, in close companionship,
without discord. I am used to bringing the coverlet for you. It is our
habit to be together day by day."
* The evil Dasamukh, bold as brass, carefully took the princess and
flew up high, mingling with the sun's rays. * They came across the king
of birds, whose power exceeded the eagle's, by name fierce Jatāyu.
* Seeing Dasamukh holding the eminent princess close to his breast
and looking into her face, the bird * understood Sītā's situation and
cried out loudly about it, as he swiftly flew, * swerving and swooping.
Diving hither and thither, he called out, "Ho there! Wicked Rāb(ṇ)!
You are committing a sin in taking this lady away. * She is the
daughter-in-law of King Dasarath and he is a friend of mine. * I shall
therefore destroy you now, once and for all, for taking charge of the
16. princess by evil trickery." * The mighty Dasamukh (16), quite determined on his course of action, boasted arrogantly of his powers, of his
unconquerable sway, of his physical strength. * "You brazen, evil
bird," he said, "wanting to fight for possession of this heavenly
princess! * Since you are a bird, it is not suitable for you to do this.
You should be flying hither and thither over lakes and ponds, carrying
things in your beak together with other birds, * sitting hatching your
eggs until they crack open. You dare to bar my way — I, in my might,
will destroy you! * You are wicked, thieving, lustful and you pretend to
be a friend of a king of noble lineage! * You are a common bird of low
estate, wretchedly lacking in connections, luckless with your
undistinguished birth." * Jatāyu answered, "You ogre! I am of equal
rank with you! How can you brag * and pretend to be of divine race?

(16) You are of base birth, a giant with weapons — and no idea of justice."
17. * Thereupon Jatāyu flew up and opened out his swift wings (17) miraculously, spreading them over the yoke of the carriage. * The sky was overcast. The sun's rays were hidden. It was dark all over; the great heaven was stifling for want of air. * Rāb(ṇ) swooped towards Jatāyu. The latter remained calm and fought to contest the victory. * Both huge and of great strength, they were in different ways victorious in the fight, glancing this way and that, turning upside down, roaring. * Jatāyu pecked at the vehicle, snatching the trembling horses. He turned the carriage right round three times as he fought in the wide sky. * The royal carriage was breaking up as it was attacked. Rāb(ṇ) sent an arrow to ward off the might of fierce Jatāyu. * As for Jatāyu, he destroyed the vehicle and leaped to face his enemy. Rāb(ṇ) sped away, * sending arrows which became a twisting, writhing, poison-spreading, agitating mass of *nāgas*. * Jatāyu carried the horses off in his tough beak and eliminated all of them. He hacked the carriage to pieces with his beak. * He destroyed the carriage and bit the snakes —
18. which were here, there and everywhere — annihilating (18) all of them. He battered the weapons. * Up in the sky Rāb(ṇ) moved through the air and Jatāyu flew. Those great beings met in brisk battle. * The vast skies resounded as though heaven would overturn, as though the earth's surface would be inverted. * There were marvellous occurrences in all directions as the demon lord and master fought, amid a great hubbub, with the *garuḍa*. * There was heard in the wide-open heavens the clamour of the conflict itself and the blast of the thunderbolt. * It was as though a river of water in the firmament were contesting for victory against the ugly sky.

* Rāb(ṇ) fought using his whole body and the might of all his arms but did not win a clear victory. He pondered therefore, seeking a trick to play. * He saw that most precious of rings, unequalled in value, most intricately wrought, * on the hand of Sītā. Its powers were immense. It shone with astonishing brilliance upon her. * And so the
19. godless Rāb(ṇ) (19) hurled it on * to the body of Jatāyu. The wings of the King of the birds were broken, * drooping visibly. Blood flowed, freely spattering all over the ground. * This was due to the power of Rām when he lived as the royal Nārāy(ṇ), leader of men. * A universal sovereign of remarkable magnificence, he completely destroyed his godless enemies. * When he became Rām of kingly dominion he had special magic power in the ring. * As the belligerent Rāb(ṇ) hurled it on to his body, Jatāyu's wings were broken, * drooping visibly. Blood flowed, now separately, now mingling all over the earth. * He lay stricken beside the regal mountain, his life's course, alas, not yet ended

20. in death! * As for Rāb(ṇ), so (20) mighty to look upon, he took
Princess Sītā all the way to Laṅkā. * He put her in royal apartments
but the princess could not rest, through her concern for Rām. * Rāb(ṇ)
was angry with her and ogre officials came to guard her fiercely.
* Then they took her and put her in the park of Asoka trees, a place of
which the beauty was all that could be desired.

4.20–35. **Meanwhile Rām and Laksm(ṇ) return home and find Sītā gone. They set out after her and come across Jatāyu who, before he dies, tells them about his fight with Rāb(ṇ). The princes meet and vanquish an ogre heretic. The egret informs them about Sītā's message and is at first not well received by the princes.**

* Then Laksm(ṇ) went forth in the early afternoon sunlight as the
breeze blew gently. * Birds were darting everywhere, first one, then
another. Pollen was scattered, its perfume diffusing as it fell off.
* Meanwhile Rām had shot his arrow. He got the superb deer — proof
of the arrow's power — and took it. * Turning, he saw Laksm(ṇ) who
put down his quiver, unstrung his bow and * knelt down. Setting aside
21. his sword, he made obeisance (21) and then came to take the deer from
his elder. * Rām questioned him. "You are looking after Sītā. Is it,
then, right for you to come here?" * Laksm(ṇ) explained, "Lord, I was
there attending upon Sītā when * we heard your own voice,
commanding, calling for me, saying a godless creature was attacking
you. * The princess was distressed and ordered me to set off in the
direction of the voice for our master was calling me. * I placed her in
the care of the Earth goddess, asking her to protect her until I
returned." * "Alas!" said Rām, "You were in a dilemma. You did not
think of what was going to happen. * An evil, vicious demon has been
there. So Earth, the protector, was unlikely to stay. The ogre will have
taken Sītā! * How ever could you leave your sister and come on foot
across the jungle looking for one who has the power for mighty
22. deeds?" * Laksm(ṇ) (22) said to the lord of compassion, "Lord, I
placed Princess Sītā in the care of the Earth goddess. * I had explained
to your wife about your powers. She did not believe me at all. * More
and more did she beat her breast and angrily rebuke me, saying I was a
fool and did not care about you. * I believed her and left Princess Sītā,
putting her in the care of the Earth goddess. * I came to seek you, my
lord. Whether it was wrong or right, I did not transgress against you,
the lord of compassion."

* Then Rām commanded his brother to look for the noble Princess Sītā

(22) * and he ran to look for her. Each day according to her habit the lady
Sītā remained at home but when * he opened the door of the royal
apartments and entered the bedroom of the two of them, he did not see
the princess. * He cried out, "Madam! Rām, master of men, is already
23. (23) returning!" * He heard no sound of Sītā. He turned back towards
his elder and told him, weeping as he did so.

* He set down the bow and, with palms together, said to Rām, his
elder, * "Lord, I went and called out to the royal Sītā and did not hear
her sweet, clear voice replying to me. * I called for her nearby, by the
mountains and by the forest thickets but I did not hear the voice of
your chief wife. I called and all was dead quiet. * I looked for her at
the hermitage in the bedroom of the two of you but I did not see the
treasured lady there." * As the prince listened to his young brother, his
heart quaked and he felt a stab of pain. * Then streams of tears, visible
24. far away, poured from his eyes, flowing freely (24) everywhere.

* "Alas! Sītā, you were my sweetheart. How can you have been
separated from me? * Alas! My wife! You are usually here every day.
How can you have gone away now, little wife? * Ah! You are so much
to be admired. Among all the ladies of the three worlds, of the
heavens, of the twelve directions,[14] there is none who can equal you.
* Alas! We three left the glorious city of Aiyudhyā, divine dwelling-
place. Why should it be now, when we come here to stay, that you are
lost? * Alas! It must be due to some wrong that we have committed,
both you, who are like a sapphire, and I. We must have caused some
lovers to be parted, ruined or lost. * And so it has come to us to be
separated in our turn, the two of us, to suffer calamity and loss. Now
25. you are lost from my sight. * I recall your hair, (25) black and thick,
and you, with your arms extended round it, tying it and braiding it
with flowers, adding further garlands, with all kinds of flowers, round
it. * I recall your forehead, shining like the gold of a candleholder,[15]
like the full moon, whose great light is visible to the whole world. * I
remember your eyebrows, arched like the curve of a victorious bow,
attractively crescent-shaped, as though Bisnukār had designed their
form. * I remember your beautiful white ears, like gold flowers, on
which you wore the most splendid shining jewels. * I remember your
eyes, pure and clear, like most precious corals; your round white nose
without a blemish even as big as a particle of pollen. * I recall your
black teeth, close together, as though precious sapphires were so
placed. I am concentrating on bringing to mind your whole
26. appearance, my loved one. * I remember your colouring, so like (26)
the ripe yellow and green *Telesma minor* which changes hue prettily
three times a day. * I remember your waist, to be grasped with one

(26) hand round it, your breasts like ripe golden kaki fruit with the skin
removed, placed upon you. * How I regret that you wanted the
magnificent demon-deer and that you asked me to go after it! You did
so wish to have that decorative deer. * I took my bow and arrow, in
accordance with your desire, my loved one. And now, because of your
wishes, I have the deer!" * The prince mourned exceedingly, almost on
the point of death. The master of men rolled on the ground, writhing,
in the forest. * He was in anguish within himself. He shivered and
could not straighten up; he felt a quaking in his heart as though he
27. would die and be at an end. He suffered (27) torturing pain, * grieving
deeply, reaching no end of it, because he was parted from his lotus. His
lovely princess was lost!

* The two princes set out immediately to follow the treasured
princess whom that godless creature had stolen away. * They made
their way, clambering over and into the dense jungle, unceasingly
striving to make headway. * Traversing the forests, they climbed up the
mountains. Boulders crashed down. The whole disc of the earth felt a
tremor. * In the heart of that master of men there burned an anger like
the fire which consumed Sumeru, lord among mountains. * The prince
journeyed on with all speed, weeping, distressed about his wife,
choking with grief. * By far-away paths in the forest they proceeded,
the two princes, lonely and forlorn indeed. * Most sadly and sorrowfully did they lament among the rocks and pools of the mountain
28. forests. * And cries were heard as (28) the animals called, in those far-
away, isolated places. As Prince Nārāy(ṇ), great master, * was
hastening to follow after the princess, using his great powers and
physical strength, the two unvanquished princes * suddenly came upon
the *garuḍa* for, to their astonishment, they saw blood welling up,
seeming greater in quantity than the waters of the ocean. * The prince
questioned him, "O king of the *garuḍas*, whatever enemy was it that
fought so mightily with you?" * Hearing the prince's question, the king
of the *garuḍas* * replied, "Lord, most holy, fine princes both, * the
Princess Sītā was being taken by the demon Rāb(ṇ) * venturing
through the air. They came across me and I fought with that godless
creature. * I spread my mighty wings. When Rāb(ṇ) shot a sharp arrow
29. it did not touch (29) me. * I was up in the air darting, intercepting,
destructively breaking up his carriage, demolishing it. I detached the
horses from it and flung them off to their death. * Rāb(ṇ) constantly
shot arrows everywhere throughout the sky and they did not touch me
but * then he drew off the ring from the hand of the esteemed Sītā, so
much to be admired, * to strike and defeat me, through your power,
Your Highness, and now I am on the point of death." * Listening to the

(29) story of the king of the *garuḍas* the prince was himself deeply grieved.
* He opened his mouth to speak, weeping at the same time for that
most pitiable King Jatāyu. * "O Jatāyu, you have indeed earned my
gratitude. There is no equivalent for your good deed with which I
30. might repay you. * I will give you the boon of going to heaven (30) to
be attended by handmaidens and to possess a bejewelled palace in
tiers." * After listening to the prince's words, the king of the *garuḍas*
died and went away to be born in the domain of heaven. * This was
made possible through the power of the words of the victorious prince
of the lineage of the Tathāgat.

* The prince performed the funeral rites for King Jatāyu, now in a dwelling-place in heaven, kingdom of treasures. * They mourned him in great sadness, both the prince and his young brother. Then they pressed on with their journey. * Along the far-distant tracks of the jungle they forced their way urgently, pursuing the princess.

* They chanced to see an ogre who was known as a heretic. He
roared loudly at the masters of men with bold cries. * "This forest is
my domain. Any being so overweening as to * come within my
31. boundaries I shall eat for the satisfaction of (31) my belly. * And now
here come you two! It just happens that I fancy a taste of human
being. * If you turn angry then you will even more surely be defeated
and I shall tear you in pieces." * Then Nārāy(ṇ) of the line of Bisnu
replied quickly, informing him of the facts. * "So! Brash ogre! Heretic
of renown! Your habit it may be to catch animals to eat daily for your
food but * you do not know the mighty prowess of us princes. It is to
be dreaded as were the great fires of past ages. * You brag about
contending against us in a fight, not realising that you will die
immediately and fall for all to see." * The *kumbhaṇḍa* chief, in a
furious rage, roared out confidently, loudly threatening the prince.
* Then, with arms extended, he approached and seized the prince's feet
32. — but the prince with his hands snapped the fangs of the ogre (32) in
two! * The princes beat him, trod on him and kicked him. They pushed
him and stabbed him. They demolished him, tearing him in pieces
which fell here, there and everywhere. * Blood flowed in deep rivulets,
gleaming brightly, flooding, covering and overwhelming everything. It
was like the ocean. * Having overcome the ogre by means of their
prowess, the masters of men gave their minds to proceeding with their
journey.

* And then, as the two princes traversed the jungle, they suffered the direst hardships. * The egret caught sight of them and flew down to make correct obeisance to the two lords. * "Sirs, the princess — your chief wife, O master of men — has been taken off by King Rāb(ṇ)

(32) himself! * The princess beat her breast until it was red raw, bewailing and calling out to me amid her tears. She told me * to inform you both
33. that she wants you to send poisoned arrows after him. (33)" * Laksm(ṇ) was very annoyed. "You wretched egret, how dare you give yourself such airs and tell lies? * You are normally along the mountain streams and by the ponds, pecking at things to eat. That is the behaviour which befits your nature." * The egret listened to the younger prince, deriding him in unseemly anger, and replied with a further rebuke, * "O princes, you both lack understanding! How can you insult me as if I were vulgar and common? * I possess a pleasant city and have servants too, although I am a bird. * I was afraid for you, O prince, you, who have only Princess Sītā as your royal wife, * because you are rather foolish and did not grasp the situation and were overcome by the demon's trick so that the ogre was able to take your wife away. * This one might indeed call 'vulgar and common'.[16] How can you malign *me*, saying I am common?"

34. * Then Rām (34) listened as the egret ridiculed him so pointedly and * realised with his keen intelligence that these words would be spoken of far and wide. * He should destroy the egret utterly before the rumour could spread. * He raised his great bow in the direction of the egret. The disc of the earth quaked. All the forest trees were miraculously overthrown. * When he saw that the power of the unvanquished prince was so superlative the egret feared his life was at an end. * He fell down at the feet of the august prince. "Lord, supporter of the earth, I beg to expiate my guilt. * I myself who am a bird am the one who is vulgar and foolish to have given offence to you who have perfect virtue. * If you will exact retribution I will bow my
35. head for you to take my life. * If you (35) take pity on me it shall be my task to help you, repaying you for sparing my life. * As to myself, I am daily most dreadfully accursed — a Rāhu,[17] bringer of bad luck — but * you will take Laṅkā, O prince, and on that day, whenever it may be, think of me. * I shall fly three times round the great citadel of Laṅkā and after that the city will be brought to ruin." * When he heard the egret's account of himself the prince relented and forgave the bird.

* Two aeons ago Nārāy(ṇ) transformed himself and, as the god Rām, came down to live, * to manifest his prowess, defeat and destroy the godless creatures and achieve success as a divine hermit. * The two princes, masters of men, were parted from the comely princess, distinguished for her purity.

4.35–51. **As they journey on the princes pass through the forest where Dūbhī, son of the buffalo king who killed all his sons at birth, has been hidden by his mother and has grown up. He has killed his father. From this triumph he goes on to annoy in turn a sage, the Sea, the Hemabānt and the monkey king, Bālī.**

* As they journeyed on, the lord told his young brother that in that
36. forest (36) there had been a buffalo, an invincible fighter. * In that lofty, silent forest of the Hemabānt, all tangled and dangling, pleasantly spreading, * were all manner of trees[18] springing up prettily round the masters of men, bowing before those diving lords. * There was the scent of the ironwood flowers, of the eaglewood, sandalwood and mangosteen; there were sprigs of creeper sprouting up, entwining. * There were various plants dotted about, thickly-growing, forest-dwelling, their flowers mingling, mottled. * There were myriads of trees and little white lotuses, their flowers strewn in great numbers; and birds of the woodland and bees, gracefully playing; there were * deep lakes and creeks, gulleys, ravines, paths and clear streams, where the animals spent long hours at play or leading one another along.
37. (37) * The forests of Hemabānt long ago, they say, were Oh! so serene everywhere, so pleasant. How peaceful and delightful for all the animals! In those far-off times, there had lived there with his stolen wives, content beyond measure, a ferocious king of the buffaloes. * He was a powerful lord, used to success, with a vast force of soldiers; * he had under his protection innumerable wives and a throng of attendants. * Having unvanquished power in his immense horns, his aggressive attacks made mighty elephants and strong lions recoil and * when he marched on lions and tigers and did battle with all the animals of the land, they were agape with astonishment at his power. * He defeated all the *dānavas* revealing a triumphant might which was
38. astounding (38). * The buffalo king — thus was he known — was horribly frightening, stubborn and overweening. * Whenever he had a son born to him, this buffalo father attacked and eliminated his own child! * This was the result of actions long ago, of erring greed and passion.

* Then one of his wives brought forth a son, called Dūbhī. * In the forest where they lived the mother — by name Santagirī — made haste to conceal him in a hiding place. * When he had grown big, he used to steal off to graze in the deep thick jungle when the sun was at its strongest. * He would eat huge amounts for he appreciated his own remarkable physical strength. * He ate three fields of grass every day
39. and swallowed three pools of water, drinking until the (39) earth was

(39) visible. * The so-called Buffalo Prince Dūbhī had a proposal to make
to his mother. "The king is a man of power. * I would like to ask to
serve my father day by day, making obeisance at his lotus feet. * I ask
Your Majesty to allow me to go. If I might take upon myself some of
my father's burdens I would achieve my heart's desire. * If some enemy
attacked him it would be my task to give aid to prevent any loss of
prestige for him." * But his mother replied, "Because of his unbending
arrogance the lord king * does not treat us as his protégés or give us
the least consideration. On each occasion he has fruitlessly annihilated
his own sons!" * Dūbhī reflected on his own weakness and readily
concerned himself with keeping hidden. * He became huge, cruel and
ferocious. He would toss his head and spring into menacing postures.
He was vigorous and virile indeed. * As he crushed and churned up the
40. mountain-side, boulders fell in pieces (40) and tree upon tree was
uprooted. * His invincible power made itself known all around.
Resounding reverberations echoed far and wide. Earth was shaken by
tremors.

* The news reached Dūbhī's father whose anger leaped like fire. That
great buffalo marched off to the search, * flinging back his head in the
wind and calling the buffalo-call. All the animals took shelter, afraid of
the buffalo's might. * "I am he who is known as the 'Brave Buffalo',
whose great prowess is a marvel!" * Then the buffalo king came
prowling along straight to the place where his son lived * and saw the
mighty Dūbhī, whose body was astonishingly huge, as big as a high
mountain, * as he walked along the way through a gulley, tossing his
head, calling the buffalo-call, crumbling the earth and sniffing the
41. ground. * The mighty buffalo king approached (41) Dūbhī to address
him with menaces, "So! Inconsiderate, arrogant son! How dared you
challenge my strength just now? * How can you have such confidence
in your physique? That is as good as offering your life to the King of
Death! * If you are not already dismayed by my power, I shall strike
you down and make you fear it in no time at all!"

* Then Dūbhī of great might fell down on his knees and paid his
respects properly to his father * and spoke to the mighty king of the
buffaloes. "I am at this present time requesting your indulgence. * I am
your servant, sire, to be here day by day to wait at your feet. * I
humbly ask for a place to live in the forest, deep within it." * Instantly
the buffalo king became more furious with him and replied in a
42. disgraceful manner, * (42) "So! You live hidden away in secret, making
yourself an enemy to me, your father! * You have been hiding in the
jungle, taking the mountain gulleys as your shelter to live in from day
to day. * Now that you are grown to this enormous stature, you would

(42) contest for a great victory over myself, the mighty one. * So! You ignorant, wayward creature! You would offer your life to Death, would you? * I shall destroy your body utterly in combat. My mighty strength is ready for use." * Thus did Prince Dūbhī hear his father threatening him beyond the limits of proper behaviour, acting without honour or friendship, * attacking his own son without feeling shame, committing an error through the evil poison of his desires. * "So!, Dūbhī!" he continued, "You brag that your strength is the greatest in
43. the world — but I shall put you to death in (43) the forest here and now." * At this Dūbhī raged with implacable fury. Adopting a superior manner, he said, "Let whoever can manage to kill the other here and now be the victor and govern the whole herd." * The mighty, powerful buffalo king, absolutely resolved in his obsession, boldly contesting to kill his own child, was, all would say, of overweaning arrogance, * sinful and vicious, quite depraved. He had erred, he had forgotten himself and had spoken words which were cruel and imperious. This had turned him into a dread and terrible enemy. * Dūbhī thought to himself, "I am weak. My father is not a good man at all. He is drunk with an evil desire for power." He said, * "You use your power for evil ends, having no respect or fear of others. You are unable to feel pity for your son. * I shall go and attempt to fight for what is right even if my action, compared with the actions of people in general, seems to be
44. terribly evil (44)."

* Both the father buffalo, putting his strength to the test, and the son, Dūbhī, were cruel and arrogant. * The two adversaries approached for the conflict, their horns sharply pointed, one destructive weapon upon another. * Their massive, fleshy forms resembled Sumeru, grandest of mountains, two of them on the field. * Gone were the rays of light, overcast. A tremor shook all the sixteen heavens; the Brahm were disturbed. * Moon and Sun stood still to watch, departing from their course. Time was not as usual. * They fought from first light until just mid-day. Then the father fell dead.

* Dūbhī acquired the whole buffalo herd and, full of pride, mingled
45. happily among his attendants. * His body was virile and powerful. (45) Arrogant, immense, he would walk along with the moving herds of mighty elephants and strong lions. * The noise was like that of the thunderbolt. The earth almost cracked and the whole jungle resounded. * His four legs, as he stood stock still or moved along, resembled pillars of rock in the great mountains. * His claws were like emeralds. When his feet trampled and stamped, the great earth trembled. * His two horns were like pikes, pointed like the powerful weapon of mighty Isūr. * Sniffing, he would open his mouth. His

(45) tongue was arrayed with colours, all flashing like a bright tongue of
flame. * His eyes burned redly like the rising sun, the shafts of light
darting marvellously in the ten directions. * When he pawed the
ground, head down, there arose a stormy wind from the skies high
above, causing dreadful havoc. * He bent his body, terrifying to see,
his form huge like a rampart, high as a mountain peak. * He came
46. crashing along, running to chase the animals. They were (46) separated
from each other and unable to feed. * They lost their mates, their
families, their territories. They lost their peace and quiet. Their various
homes were lost to them. * From their silent cave the lions fled in all
directions, scattering as he pursued them with his formidable strength.

* He proceeded on his way, eliminating the animals, knowing he was
going in the direction of Pañcaliṅ, a sage of efficacious power. * With
his horns he butted into the mountains with their five circles of hills.
They split! Boulders rolled down, shattered. Trees were uprooted and
overturned. * Spirits and ogres of the road all turned to the righteous
hermit, all trying to stop Dūbhī. * The hermit spoke to him, addressing
him with words of truth, "O bold buffalo, * we are persons who seek
out the right way, coming to this mountain as to our home, to its caves
as to its cells. * Long ago it was created, at the same time as the earth
47. and Mount Kailās, where the god Isūr lives. (47) * I have never bragged
and tried out my strength for I have never had a mind for aggression
towards other beings. * O Dūbhī," he continued, "if you want, if you
would like to try your might against a person of prowess, * I will take
you to the divine goddess who protects the great ocean. * She is
powerful and has a host of attendants thronging round and sea-
dragons and *nāgas* in great numbers." * Dūbhī listened to the hermit's
words and set off on his way to the goddess of the sea.

* The water splashed up as spray, spurting all around, reverberating
like thunder through all the ten directions. * Waves were flung
crashing up to the sky. The sun, moon and stars were gone from view.
* This remarkable occurrence affected all creatures. All the sea-
dragons and *nāgas* quietly hid themselves away. * The waters of the sea
48. grew thick and the goddess (48) almost died of shock. * She brought
the creatures of the sea to cajole and soothe Dūbhī with friendly words.
* "Greetings, most powerful Dūbhī," they said, "You are unique
among gods and bold creatures. * Having destroyed all the strong lions
you now wish to contend in battle with the ocean! * The sea-goddess
has been supremely kind to the unnumbered sea-dragons; she protects
them and the *nāgas* and fish. * She is mistress of all waters, of all rivers
and lakes, countless myriads of them. * Creatures of all regions and
throughfares have lived together quite happily, maintained by the

(48) goddess, their patron. * You have already been feeding upon us. Now
you trespass on us who should have your gratitude. * O Dūbhī," they
said, "listen to us. Do go back to the Hemabānt. * If you are able to
49. defeat (49) that one, you will attain the position of head of those
throngs of creatures and of the gods! * All will be happy in the
Hemabānt and it will be a serene dwelling-place for you with a host of
divine handmaidens. * Take the Hemabānt for yourself; it is a pleasant
city in which to amuse yourself with your buffalo concubines."

* Then the buffalo king set forth, leaving the sea, and went straight
to the Hemabānt. * He trampled his way over the mountains in haste
and, as he approached those crags, a tremor was felt through the great
earth. * There were rumbling reverberations as when the fires burned
in the fourth age of the world, astonishing and awful to behold. * He
called, "Hail, Hemabānt! Your praises were sung by the sea-goddess.
Bold you are and of vast powers, but not kindly. * Come out and I
shall be there, ready to destroy you, demon of ill fame. I am a buffalo
50. with excessive venom in my horns." * The noble divinity (50) was full
of fear in case the huge, wicked buffalo attacked him. * He pleaded, "O
dānava, great lord of all creatures, * do you come here now with the
desire of taking my kingdom to rule or to try out your strength? * With
regard to my kingdom, it shall be as you wish. What we are afraid of is
this mighty power of yours. * Your might should be matched with
someone else's. You should fight with King Bālī, offspring of the Lord
Indr. * The divine king named Bālī captured the savage King Rāb(ṇ),
godless creature, and bound him. * He contentedly rules the kingdom
of Khās' Khin, protecting the monkeys, whose number is uncountable."

* The buffalo listened to what the Hemabānt said. He made his way
to the distant place where the monkeys were, * pleased with himself, in
his mood of ignorant confidence, just as the sea-goddess had tricked
51. him into being, * (51) and easy in his mind, just as the Hemabānt had
tricked him into being. He did not know that the monkeys were terrifying, like the fires of ages past in their destructiveness. * The city known
as Khās' Khin, always a delightful place, unrivalled for its tranquillity,
was where * Bālī ruled, with benevolent power, his realm of tens of
thousands of monkeys.

4.51–64. **After an indecisive battle in the open, Bālī persuades Dūbhī to fight in a cave where his bulk will put him at a disadvantage. Before the fight he tells Sugrīb that if after the fight the blood is light-coloured (i.e. his own) he should block the cave's entrance. When Bālī is victorious, flowers strewn by the gods turn the blood of Dūbhī to a light colour.**

Sugrīb laments for his brother, presumed dead, and has the entrance to the cave blocked.

* "There is an ill-natured *dānava* of vast powers and physical force, a
demon-buffalo," the Hemabānt Mount Sumeru told the assembled
forest monkeys, "of great prestige and ability. * He is successfully
finding his way to Bālī. Three times already has he gone out to fight
with someone." Bālī then called out masterfully, * "Hail, ferocious
dānava, persistent in your lawlessness! You are making enemies with
your bragging. * I, by name King Bālī, come from a family of immense,
52. widespread prestige. * I shall not bring my troops. (52) I shall come out
alone since I am a match for you." * "And I am known as Dūbhī. I
went after the mountain Sumeru. I butted the sea and made it splash
up as spray. * O greatly daring Bālī, come out! Let us contest our
might now without delay." * Well, *dānava*, you wait impatiently. Bālī is
ready. You are bold like a forest overlord * but just you so much as
take a step forward and it will be tantamount to offering yourself to
the god of Death!"

* "Ho, you helpless creature! I, Dūbhī the mighty, have churned up
the sea. The mountains have changed their form — yes, it was I who
did it, I whose name is Dūbhī. * When I churned up the sea, the fish all
sank down, dead, and the waters became dry. Well, if you say that in
53. the kingdom of Khās' Khin there is (53) one, Bālī, let him come forth to
be spokesman and to fight in single combat!" * "Ho, Dūbhī! I am the
great Bālī who will break your neck, fell you at one go and jump over
you. I shall snap off your horns and brandish them. * Oho, buffalo!
You have not yet heard of the strength of Bālī's right arm. I shall
cleave your body in two. I shall lift you up, carry you on one shoulder.
54. (54) Let Bālī alone. He is bold and fearless." * "O Bālī, I am Dūbhī.
You say you will shake me and crumble my lungs — but you have not
yet been up against my horns. You, a monkey, will die instantly, no
doubt of that." * "Ho, buffalo! You have not yet heard about my right
arm, in your ignorance. I shall break your neck in one go. Then I shall
be putting your powers, if you have any, to the test."

* Bold King Bālī, boasting of his superiority, was undismayed by the
mighty Dūbhī. * "Well, Dūbhī, you are no more than a buffalo who
struck his own father to death. * You do not know the mighty power
of those who are of simian descent. When they enter a contest they
most certainly persist until they match the enemy's standards. * I shall
cause your death. In your ignorance, you will be destroyed and this
55. will be through my unvanquished power." * Bālī, (55) furiously angry,
went through the air back to his residence. * He went up into the palace

(55) with its seven tiers, bedecked with jewels, with gold, much gold, and with crystal. * He adorned his face, setting glittering jewels, gleaming, magnificent, all over it. * With his diamond-studded sword in his hand, he went through the air straight towards Dūbhī, who was on his guard, ready for the fight for victory. * They were involved together, those two different beings. Dūbhī the fearless moved to this or that position, speedily fending the other off. * He pitted the earth, churned it up, making swift attacks with his horns and darting glances to each side. Trees were uprooted and overturned. * Battered and crushed, the hills came falling down in pieces. Heads arched upwards. Arms were raised threateningly. Sharp horns were shaken free. Glances were cast to each side. * One turned to avoid the other, one swiftly tossed the other, forcefully removing himself out of the way. They leaped to bar the way or swooped sideways, glancing and turning, suddenly airborne. * King Bālī, advancing for victory, was thrown back as though flung, failing to
56. close with the (56) buffalo. * The two sharp, destructive weapons, those close-set horns, met with the magic art of King Bālī and were unable to penetrate the flesh. * It was as though a javelin — sharp weapon indeed — were skilfully thrown to pierce another weapon! * Bālī's sword struck the horns, one weapon upon another, as they goaded each other to deeds of prowess. * Bālī darted away up in the air. Dūbhī fended and stayed on the defensive, turning to throw the other from his horns. * Dūbhī and Bālī were both proficient, both most eager for victory, intent upon the fight, now taking aim, now fending off. * Earth subsided, slumped, cracked, quaked. A tremor was felt through the jungle with distant reverberations. It was a marvel. Even the gods of heaven * came down through the air, leaving their aerial palaces, filling the sky as they flew by magic to watch and admire the great deeds. * The light of the sun and moon went away completely. There was no certainty in the shadows. All was dim and not as usual.
57. * There was consternation (57) because Dūbhī met Bālī, might met victorious might.

* Bālī now knew what were their individual powers, that the physical might of the buffalo king was equal to his own, * so he left Dūbhī and went away to give the matter intelligent consideration * as follows: "If I fight against him out here, I fear that I shall not beat the great buffalo. * His frame is gigantic and of immense power. Out on the open ground he spreads his whole body out widely, uncontained. * At will, he whirls round, tossing his horns, and uses them most effectively to butt. It would be a good thing for me to find a ruse to overcome him and end his life. * I will take him into a cave," he thought. "I will make the cave a fine coffin to hold his body. * And thus that persistent

(57) idiot, Dūbhī, will go into a cave which is small for his body. * I shall
have my wish: the pleasure of stabbing him, feeling no awe of him. I
58. shall strike him down dead. (58) We shall fight from the very first light
until the first moment of dusk. Then we shall rest."

* After this Bālī went back through the air to the palace in Khās' Khin and, summoning Sugrīb, gave him instructions. * "My brother, this Dūbhī is too much for me He whirls round, gets away to left or right, steps forward, takes his stand, has no fear. * I engaged with him for a while to try him out. I jumped forward and felt the ends of his horns. They cut like sharp swords! * He is gigantic, that buffalo, enormously fat and his strength is superior to mine. * I am going to carry out a plan. I shall take him to a sacred cave and inside it we will fight out our contest. * But one more thing. In case he beats me you
must come with a force and bring rocks and stand by in readiness. * If
59. you (59) see dark blood that is the blood of the mighty buffalo king.
* But if the blood is light it is mine, your elder's, and you will take rocks from the great mountains and block up the cave * and you will reign over the kingdom of Khās' Khin, doing everything properly just as I did when I was there."

* When Bālī had instructed his young brother, he went off to Dūbhī, who was waiting for him out there with the open ground on all sides. * "Ho there, mighty Dūbhī," he said. "You, who have dared to come here and take up your position on the battlefield, are King of the buffaloes. * And I too am a king, of the simian race. Why then do we place ourselves out here on the open ground to die? * It would be better for us, we being kings, to choose a place in the mountains as a site for our coffins to rest. * If we die there it will be a worthy place, a
temple for our royal corpses." * The aggressive Dūbhī was a foolish
60. fellow. He agreed that this was a good idea and complied with (60)
Bālī's suggestion. * They entered the splendid cave to fight. The buffalo had difficulty in turning and changing position. * Bālī was able to achieve his aim and kill him owing to the cunning of his clever mind. * Blood flowed like water, flooding, brimming over, spreading wave upon wave, a great ocean of it. * When they saw this mighty deed, manifested by a monkey, throughout the heavens of the Paranimitta, the Nimmānaratī, * the Tuṣita, the glorious celestial domain of the Yāmā, the Tāvatiṃsa, right to the Cātumahārājikā,[19] * all the gods of all the six Kāmavacara were amazed. They rained down showers of heavenly blossoms, * filling the skies as they strewed them, scattering all about, diffusing clouds of perfume. * And they offered their congratulations
and praised the heroic deed of Bālī, the monkey king. * Petals and
61. pollen (61) fell off from the heavenly flowers, fluttering on to the vast

(61) earth, * and were soaked in the blood of Dūbhī, changing it to a light
colour, exactly like that of a monkey!

* Then Sugrīb and his host of attendants met together to confer.
* "This is not the blood of a buffalo. This blood is clearly that of the
mighty King Bālī. * It is to be feared that when the elder master of men
met with the mighty power of Dūbhī, the latter killed our dear king."
* They believed it was the blood of Bālī, the great Sugrīb himself and
all the attendant monkeys. * Sugrīb wept, on his knees, bewailing the
harsh deed. Choking with emotion, he thought about his dear brother
and lamented in abject misery. * "O King Bālī, your dominion was
manifestly greater than that of other kings. You ruled in prosperity
62. with goodness (62) in abundance. All was as desired. * Greater than all
the others in your deeds of prowess, you were indeed renowned far and
wide, with distant echoes of that fame reaching even to heaven itself.
All felt respect for * your scintillating mind. How could you succumb
to the power of the buffalo king, Dūbhī, who was afraid of the fray?
* Even the evil Dasamukh was defeated by your mighty deeds — and
the *nāga* of the seven palm trees, when you seized him in fun, just in
your usual way. * O king, how could you come to die, to be
annihilated by the strength of Dūbhī? Alas! It has come about that the
glory of Bālī has succumbed to the greater might of the buffalo."
* Sugrīb gave vent to his grief and mourned deeply, his eyes glistening.
63. * Angrily he said, among all his officers, soldiers and ministers, (63)
* "I have no mind for governing the kingdom in place of my elder,
King Bālī. * I shall go after that erring buffalo who came here as a
plundering enemy and I shall slay him." * The officials spoke against
this. "We implore Your Majesty not to decide upon revenge. * If you
go after the buffalo you will be throwing away your army, the people's
force; * the whole city would be deserted, and all of us monkeys would
be without refuge. * You have lost your brother — just that. So why
not rule the kingdom?"

* When Sugrīb had listened to the remonstrations of the royal
officials for the sake of the succession, * he commanded his attendants
to lead off the dense, sprawling throng of people and the army in all
64. haste. (64) * They led the simian host from the city of Khās' Khin. They
fetched the mountain rocks. * They blocked up the entrance to that
splendid cave, closing it tightly by hurling rocks at it — as much, one
would estimate, as a mountain of rocks! * And when he had blocked
up the cave, Sugrīb returned to the city of Khās' Khin * to grieve with
his chief ministers, with Tārā the queen and with the dear court ladies.
* All mourned deeply, bewailing the loss of King Bālī with loud
lamentations.

4.64–70. Bālī frees himself and, believing Sugrīb intended his death, fights him. The wounded Sugrīb takes refuge in the mountains, attended by Hanumān.

* And now, having felled Dūbhī by his mighty power, the intrepid
Bālī * went to the entrance of the cave and saw nothing but rocks,
blocking it up tightly. * Bālī shouted and called but the rocks were
65. thick on the outside and his cries were not heard (65). * Hearing no
reply, he stood back and roared out a lion's roar with all his strength.
* He cut off the buffalo's head and pulled it along. Holding it up high,
he rushed forward with great force * and hurled it at the rocks, which
fell down, broken and crushed! The entrance to the cave was opened
up, the rocks and boulders scattered all round * in little bits, all
shattered and rolling down to the distant sea, through the might of the
simian king. * Bālī came out of the cave, went to the city and entered
the palace. * His fury was unimaginable. He did not utter a single word
to his queen or his ministers. * Flushed all over his face in his grievous
vexation, he seemed about to burst into flame.

* Then Sugrīb was full of fear for himself, afraid he would die. He
66. went to offer his respects, * saying, "Lord, I myself (66) called an
assembly to discuss the matter and look into the facts. * That blood
was not buffalo's blood. We saw clearly what it was like and it was
your blood flowing out towards us. * And so I gave the order to bring
all those rocks and throw them so that they blocked up the cave, * not
to transgress your command, O king, that special idea of yours which
you had just thought of so cleverly. * I beg you to go yourself and
look. If you see that blood you will realise it does not demonstrate that
we were stupid. * And further, we saw you involved in the fighting. We
saw it quite clearly. We heard terrible noises and then — nothing. * I
was going after you, great king, but all the ministers stopped me for
fear that panic might arise in the city for * if Dūbhī had killed you,
honoured lord, they feared there would indeed be turmoil."

67. * And now Bālī, greatest of all, was haughty and hostile too (67)
towards the young Sugrīb, his dear brother. * "You do not know the
power of my right arm. You said I had been beaten by Dūbhī, a
buffalo animal! * Your reason for this utter lie was that you wanted
the kingdom and were looking for a way to kill me. * You had them
bring rocks along and hurl them to close up the cave, blocking it so
that I would not be able to come out. * And you put on an affable
manner towards me, all friendly and pleasant — and I did not recognise
your guile. * You would betray your own brother. You are a
despicable, pleasure-seeking, lying, stupid villain!"

(67) * In his excessive anger King Bālī slapped Sugrīb's head.[20] Sugrīb, unable to prevent this, * bounded up into the air and departed from the palace. Bālī flew after him, not letting him go * but following in pursuit right to the ramparts of the *cakravāla* booming loud threats of
68. anger with all his might. * He caught him up, shouted at him and (68) hit him. Sugrīb received blows so terrible that he was near to death. * Turning to escape, he flew down through the sky; but he did not get away from Bālī, who followed closely after him. * Catching him up, Bālī attacked him, beating him from behind, most miserably. He did not let Sugrīb escape from the blows. * Sugrīb, suffering wretchedly and struggling, went down into the mountains to take refuge among the gulleys, the cracks and crevasses of the rocks. * Bālī flew down to the mountains, following closely. He reached out, grasped both Sugrīb's feet and whirled him round, * about to bang him on the mountain-tops. Sugrīb, still conscious, took hold of something and tore himself away. He flew off, * freed from Bālī's grasp. Then he went through the
69. air and into the mountains of Mataṅg. * Bālī (69) could not enter there because it had been officially given to the hermit, Mataṅg * who had been angry when Bālī killed Dūbhī and the blood flowed over his hermitage. * The hermit Mataṅg, who built up merit on that mountain, would not let Bālī come near. * If he approached he would die. Bālī, realising that he could not therefore go there, * returned to his palace, which resembled a celestial residence of the gods.

70. (70) * Sugrīb hid in the mountains enduring pain and sorrow, forlornly awaiting death. * He had been shamed in the eyes of his elder brother, the monkey king, shamed in the eyes of the mass of the people in the city of Khās' Khin. * Tears like the waters of a river flowed freely from the mountain gulleys and caves. * There was only Hanumān, his young nephew, to care for him and be his companion day by day. * Sugrīb was very glad to let his own welfare be in the hands of that dear nephew.

5.1–12. **Rām and Sugrīb each know from a portent that the other is near. Sugrīb sends Hanumān to look for a man of merit. Hanumān sees the princes under a mango tree. He scatters leaves on them. Rām prevents Laksm(ṇ) from attacking the monkey, realising that he is special. Hanumān returns to tell Sugrīb.**

1. * And now the two princes were journeying in pursuit of the august princess, the esteemed Sītā, * continuing on their way without halting to rest at all. * They had come to a mountain forest, had crossed a

(1) plain and had arrived at a jungle-covered area where * there was heard the sound of buffaloes, lions, whole herds of them, male and female, standing stock still, sending their calls to each other, * their growls and howls resounding through the still, dry forest. Roebuck and rhinoceros hastened to shelter, to curl up and hide.

* The princes heard a mighty buffalo calling as it approached. It was a great and authoritative portent. * Rām stopped and turned his head to look at his dear young brother. * "Laksm(ṇ), in this place where we have arrived I hear the call of a demon-buffalo. * He is crying, almost
2. groaning. This is a clear sign, a splendid portent indeed. (2) * Soon we shall meet with a fine person who is enduring pain and suffering and who will come to turn for help to our mighty resources. * He will increase our prosperity and glory. More than this: in time to come we shall be able to capture Laṅkā with ease." * The prince pronounced this divine prophecy for the benefit of his intelligent young brother and, * when he had foretold the future from the portent of the buffalo, the two princes proceeded silently along their way through the forest.

* There was a mango tree of enormous size which had put forth shading leaves on spreading branches. * Its scent, the perfume of its pollen, was perceived in all directions through the wafting of the wind. * The calls of birds were audible, their cries echoing pleasantly as they flapped their wings and preened themselves at leisure. * Some perched, some flew as though for pleasure. Their chirruping was like the music
3. and song of heaven. * The princes slept beneath the great tree (3) whose pleasant shade * enveloped them closely so that they were constantly cool in the gently-wafting breeze. * Rām slept with his head resting on the lap of Laksm(ṇ), as a pillow. * Then, owing to his perfection, the sun was unable to set. * The Sun-god drew his chariot to a halt. All the trees round about them gave shade, spreading pleasantly, * like an umbrella fashioned by magic here below to be useful at the prince's sleeping place.

* Then the lordly Prince Sugrīb saw this admirable, clear portent and was highly delighted. * "Hanumān!" he said, "What is this? Look at the sun. It has lowered its rays to set. * Why then are there shadows as
4. of the mid-day sun? What is it, Hanumān? (4) It is probably because a man of merit * is coming here to stay in this forest. Thus it is that the sun's afternoon shadows are all around us * and all the trees out there stand silent, straight and motionless with their burden of fruit and flowers * so extraordinarily sweet to the taste. Hanumān, would you help your uncle, please? * Go and look everywhere. That man of merit who is coming to us has reached our territory over there."

* Then Hanumān of extensive powers prostrated himself and

(4) respectfully took leave of the monkey prince. * Through the air he
went to the borders of their land and saw the master of men, Nārāy(ṇ)
Rām, * asleep on the lap of his young brother beneath the shade of the
tree, both princes isolated and without protection. * Hanumān flew up
to the top of the mango and looked at the lines on the palms of Rām.
5. * When he saw (5) the lines clearly curving in wheels, traced across both
his august hands, * Hanumān thrilled with happy excitement for he
was firmly convinced that it was the supporter of the earth, Nārāy(ṇ)
of surpassing power. * Hanumān was delighted; this was just what he
wanted. "This man," he thought, "is to be my master. * All Prince
Sugrīb's pain and grief will simply slip away from him by the power of
this prince and master of men."

* Hanumān pondered the whole matter and eagerly plucked young
mango leaves to honour Prince Rām. * As he picked them, he threw
them down and they fell thickly, spreading all about over the two royal
princes. * The younger prince constantly brushed the mango leaves
away from Prince Nārāy(ṇ) Rām but * Hanumān scattered them down
all the more and the young brother, with weary hands, swept them up!
6. (6) * Glancing up through the quiet mango, the prince saw a beautiful
white monkey. * Furiously angry, he grasped a powerful, sharp arrow
to aim at the royal monkey but * the tough and powerful Hanumān
jumped to snatch the bow from the lordly young Laksm(ṇ) * and then,
huge and daring, sprang up into the silent, shady tree to hide in the
branches. * Laksm(ṇ) seized Nārāy(ṇ)'s bow and arrow and was
aiming the arrow to strike down the royal monkey * when suddenly
Rām, the princely master of men, awoke and asked his brother,
* "Laksm(ṇ)! What is this? You are aiming an arrow — at what?"
* Laksm(ṇ) put down the powerful arrow and bow and respectfully
7. spoke to the supporter of the earth, his royal lord and (7) master. * "A
most unpleasant monkey, lord. It is pure white like cotton floss which
floats away as the cotton is carded. * He is dropping mango leaves
onto you. When I brushed them aside he was all the more eager to
drop them down in profusion. * I was angry and raised my victorious
bow to its full height to shoot him down to his death. But that wicked
monkey * has the strength for deeds of prowess. He is mighty indeed!
He managed to snatch the bow away out of my hands! * He jumped up
into the branches and hid, climbing onto them and concealing himself
close to them at the top of the tree and there he still is. * I was
shooting an arrow in the direction of the monkey, taking your bow,
lord prince, supporter of the earth, when I tripped over your feet as
you slept. * This monkey is most aggressive. He has stolen my bow and
hidden it too, put it in a secret place. It is not to be seen."

(7) * Then Nārāy(ṇ) Rām of the ten powers, whose virtue had
progressed to its final stage and who had attained full power for deeds
8. of heroism, * protector of men, looked up and saw the simian (8)
prince, * pure white and shining, wearing bejewelled earrings on both
his ears. * And the prince of the line of Harī understood and spoke
immediately, restraining his young brother. * "O Laksm(ṇ)," he said,
"do not be angry. Just look at the monkey. * It is outstanding among
simians. It wears beautiful, coloured earrings on its two ears!"
* Hanumān, of mighty prowess, came down from the tree, paid his
respects to the master of men * and then presented the bow to that
lord, bowing his head and body as he prostrated himself at his feet.
* Speaking respectfully to both princes, he said, "You, O prince, are to
be my honoured master. * Your goodness exceeds that of all princes
and you are endowed with gentleness. * Lord, my mother told me, 'If
9. any (9) man is able to see these precious, divine earrings, * then that
man, having that ability, will quite definitely be your master.' * And
now you, royal prince and lord of men, strong and mighty in deeds of
prowess, are my master. * I will undertake to do good deeds to help
you and repay your very special kindness to me, lord of compassion."
* The young Laksm(ṇ) did not say a word, just then. He smiled to
himself. * Hanumān quickly realised, "Laksm(ṇ) does not believe what
I said." * So the powerful Hanumān then opened his mouth and
yawned. Flashing sparks were visible! * The twelve directions[14] glowed
with a divine brightness and the light of the sun reached out towards
10. the three underworlds in the ten directions. * Then (10), seeing this
marvel, the Lord Harī of the line of Bisnu, prodded the young Laksm(ṇ)
to draw his attention. * "This monkey," he said, "is quite remarkable.
By birṭh he is a prince among monkeys, a lord of the lower creatures."
* Then the handsome master of men questioned the monkey prince,
* "O simian, tell me: what was the name bestowed upon you? * I
should like to know about this: were you born of a hermit or a god?"

* Hanumān made obeisance and replied, "I was born the child of the
god of the Wind. * My exact name, given me by my father, is Hanumān
the Bold. * With regard to my coming here, the reason is as follows.
There are two monkey princes * between whom there is a bitter
quarrel. One is the king, Bālī by name, superlative in power. * The
11. other is the royal simian named Sugrīb, young brother of Bālī, (11) born
of the same mother. * Both of them are my uncles; that is what they
are to me. * King Bālī, the elder, is very angry — mistakenly so, for he
is not within the limits of the ancient laws. * He furiously reviled his
young brother, the prince, and banished him from the kingdom. * And
now Prince Sugrīb is writhing in anguish. He seems to have reached the

(11) point of wanting * to stay alone in the haunted forest, weeping sorrowfully in lonely seclusion." * Then Rām replied, "My own grief is deep indeed." * The quick-witted Hanumān, understanding what was in Rām's mind, * how he wanted to see Prince Sugrīb, took leave of the masters of men * and went, darting swiftly through the air by virtue of
12. his powers, to Prince (12) Sugrīb. * He addressed his uncle. "My lord prince, you told me to look for a man * of merit, endowed with the signs of heroism. I have clearly seen a man of this kind, a man of merit. * I beg you, uncle, do come straight away to pay your respects to him." * Sugrīb was delighted, having just what he desired, and thought about venturing through the air to the place where the prince was staying.

5.12–21. **Investigating the source of some salty water, Laksm(ṇ) finds Sugrīb. He is inside a mountain which collapses at a touch of Laksm(ṇ)'s bow. Sugrīb tells Rām about the quarrel between himself and Bālī. Rām offers to help Sugrīb to defeat Bālī and gain queen and kingdom while Sugrīb says he will help Rām against his enemy.**

* Then the princely Rām sent his young brother to look for water. * "Ah Laksm(ṇ)! Would you please go and look for some water for me to drink and to use for bathing?" * His brother knelt and raised his cupped hands in salute to his elder and set off. * Making his way through the jungle, he saw a stream which had formed from the tears
13. of the brave Sugrīb. * He (13) drew water and ran quickly back to offer it to his elder, master of men. * Then the prince drank some water and noticed that it was salty. It was not like water! * "Laksm(ṇ)! Where did you take this water from just now? It is saltier than other water. * This water is miraculous, not at all like normal water. * Go and try to find out the source of this water, see from what place it flows." * Laksm(ṇ) took his leave, went to the water and looked for its origin. * He saw there was a vast mountain from which a torrent of water flowed out in copious streams. * He heard most plaintive moaning sounds and sobs of grief, quite unmistakable. * Laksm(ṇ) returned
14. and, prostrating himself before his elder brother, gave him a clear (14) account. * "Lord, as to your command to me to investigate the course of the water, * there is a vast mountain and a torrent of water flows from it * and I heard loud cries of lamentation and deep distress." * Then the most high, the Omniscient One, graciously spoke, giving his beloved brother this command, * "Now Laksm(ṇ), please go and strike that mountain and then you will see who the person is."

(14) * Accepting the royal command, the young brother went into the
jungle straight to the mountain. * He raised up his bow and used it to
strike the mountain. * There was no breach or dent in it at all!
Laksm(ṇ), strong and mighty in powerful deeds, rested and then struck
15. a distinct blow. * The mountain resisted (15) the force of the blow
firmly and did not break up. The prince struck an unmistakable blow.
Earth trembled and stirred. * All the animals, seeing this, were afraid
of this might; they fled, some tumbling together, some scattering far
and wide. * Sugrīb reacted by giving this advice, "Lord, do not strike
blows. Do not go to this trouble. * Just flick the mountain with the
curved end of your fine bow and a hole will appear. Do not trouble
yourself to strike blows." * The esteemed prince heard the brave
simian's words of advice * and flicked the curved end of his bow at the
mountain. It collapsed, completely demolished! * Then the royal Sugrīb
bowed low in obeisance to Laksm(ṇ), master of men, * and the latter
took the monkey to present him to the supporter of the earth.

16. * Laksm(ṇ) and the monkey prince left the jungle and went to (16)
Prince Rām, master of men. * When Laksm(ṇ) presented him and the
great lord of monkeys paid his respects to Rām, * the latter instantly
felt a tender compassion for Prince Sugrīb who was suffering such pain,
for, * owing to his own perceptiveness, Rām understood. "If you have
sorrows to bear," he said, "they shall be my burden. * Now what is the
reason why King Bālī is so angry as to banish you?"

* Sugrīb sadly knelt close to the feet of the prince, leader of men, his
hands in the lotus position. * "Lord, I will inform you of the whole
matter, that Your Highness, who supports the earth, may know. * In
the first place, there was a buffalo king, boastful of his power, vigorous
and strong indeed. * His name was Mighty Dūbhī, of powerful
physique, lord over strong animals, even lions. * He roamed through
17. the kingdom of Khās' Khin and called out Bālī, challenging him (17) to
a combat. * Bālī came through the air and went out to fight against King
Dūbhī, the mighty. * He fought with the buffalo king from first light to
the end of the day. * Both in their different ways had their victories on
the field of battle. Neither reached the point of death. * Bālī and the
buffalo king displayed great prowess in the fight as they provoked and
engaged each other on the field. * When the two princes were weary,
their vigour for heroic deeds waning, * Bālī came through the air to
Khās' Khin, to the great city, to rest. * He gave me instructions to
organise a force of monkeys and wait outside the ramparts in the air
* and to tell them to pull up mountains, rocks, boulders and slabs of
stone in sections according to their duty. * He devised a plan in full
18. detail. He proposed to the wicked Dūbhī to fight (18) in a cave * and

(18) his instructions to me were as follows: 'If the blood is the buffalo's it will
be a dark red colour. * If there is clear-coloured blood it will be mine
and I shall by ill-luck be dying. * In such a case, bring mountains and
boulders to fling down and close up the entrance to the distinguished
cave.' * Having instructed me, he went through the air to where the bold
Dūbhī was and approached to engage in combat. * And in that cave he
gained his desire; the king, my mighty elder, * managed to slay the royal
buffalo in accordance with his plan, being of extraordinary greatness.
* As he did so all the gods of heaven called out their congratulations and
rained down showers of fragrant blossoms * which caused the blood of
the buffalo king to flow out clear-coloured — and I thought it was the
blood of King Bālī! * So then with the chief ministers I made the monkey
19. force (19) bring rocks and close up the cave.

* "After slaying the buffalo, King Bālī kicked away the rocks, scattering them about. * The boulders blocking the cave fell in bits. When he had kicked them to pieces, the king brandished his sword of glorious victories * and came through the air to the city of Khās' Khin. He was in a furious temper as though fire raged in his kingly breast. * Angrily he laid false charges against me in the middle of the hall among the generals and ministers and the assembled forces. * He said I was intending to usurp the kingdom and to seduce his wife! I was put to shame by the slanderous accusations. * His fury overstepped the limits of royal behaviour. Without any reflection he went to the length of driving me forth as an outcast. * Disgraced, I endured my sorrow all alone. Thus it was that I came over here to live in this region." * The
prince heard Sugrīb explain his situation and tell how heavy was his
20. burden of grief. * Then he spoke words of great value, "Hail (20),
Sugrīb. I too have sorrows. * Here am I, just come to this forest and with
the chance now to meet you, who have * to bear your unhappiness
alone, bewailing piteously and suffering physical hardship. You are very
like myself. * O Lord Sugrīb, do not worry now. * It shall be my task to
fulfil your wishes exactly as you yourself require. * Come, just observe
my powers. I will attempt to demonstrate my might. * I will take the city
of Khās' Khin and Queen Tārā as well to give to you." * Sugrīb heard
these kindly words, spoken with sympathy and a special friendliness,
and * delightedly replied, putting his head below the august prince's
21. feet, * "I offer (21) myself as your servant, lord prince. * If fierce
enemies wickedly approach to surround you, protector of the earth, with
intent to oppress you, * I shall bring the forces of the simian race,
invincible on the field of battle and infinite in number, * and we shall
fight to prevent their reaching you two princes to trouble you.
* Furthermore, I should like to speak to Your Highness about another

(21) matter." * Just then Hanumān prodded Prince Sugrīb, his uncle, to
prevent him from saying anything more. * He was afraid that he might
say the wrong thing and spoil everything and then not be able to have
what he wanted. * Sugrīb and Hanumān took leave of the supreme
lord, Prince Rām.

5.22–29. **Hanumān and Sugrīb take Rām to see the body of Dūbhī and to see the *nāga* with the seven palm-trees growing on its tail. Rām destroys the body and the palm-trees. Sugrīb, now sure of Rām's powers, asks his help in defeating Bālī.**

22. * As they left, (22) Hanumān thought hard and realised what his
uncle had had in mind; * there was indeed a certain matter which
Prince Sugrīb had not yet broached. * "My lord uncle," Hanumān
said, "I know you do not believe in the power * of Prince Rām but he
is in fact Nārāy(ṇ) himself. * If you simply do not believe me, please
try looking at his two hands. * They have clear lines on them, curving
in wheels traced all over them. His mighty prowess is quite obvious.
* This man is undoubtedly Nārāy(ṇ) who, by a divine decree, has
23. descended to be born as Rām. * If we would know his might (23) and
judge his strength against Bālī's, whether his mighty power is greater,
* let us take the prince, master of men, to see King Dūbhī, felled by the
might of Bālī. * And another thing to do, if we desire to know precisely
the power of the magic arrow of Nārāy(ṇ) Rām, supporter of the earth,
* is to take him to see the seven palm-trees growing on the tail of the
nāga, old as great earth. * Let the prince take aim and try out his
might. Then we shall know the powers of that master of men." * After
this consultation Hanumān and Sugrīb went to seek audience of the
prince.
* Now Nārāy(ṇ), most royal master of men, highest of sovereigns,
understood with his divine understanding * and said, "Hail, Sugrīb!
24. Where was it that Bālī slew (24) the buffalo? * I should like to see with
what power King Bālī felled him in that cave." * Sugrīb made
obeisance and replied, "Please, prince, do follow the direction of your
wishes." * Then lion-like, the two princes, younger and older, set out
* and went to where the corpse of the buffalo Dūbhī, huge like a
mountain, lay overthrown. * The prince aimed from his victorious bow
a most powerful, destructive arrow, Aggīvās. * He aimed at the form of
the royal buffalo which instantly burst into great flames and was burnt
to fine ash. * Then Rām took Biruṇavās and aimed it to quench the
fire of that destructive, magic arrow. * And then he took from his

25. quiver Bāyavās, which he raised up * and shot to (25) gather up all the ashes and throw them to the bottom of the great ocean.

* Hanumān and Sugrīb, royal princes, clearly saw that the mighty prowess of Rām was indeed superlative. * They knelt down at the feet of that most worthy prince, so eminent and distinguished, * and said, "O lord whose meditations bring increase, there are some trees, seven palm-trees which came into existence at the same time as earth. * We should like both of you to come and try out the might of your most powerful sharp arrows." * The most worthy prince listened as Sugrīb explained his desire to know his mighty power * and replied, "O Sugrīb,
26. tell me: in what region (26) is this place? * Please lead the way. We two will go and test our powers."

* Then the royal monkey, Sugrīb, raised his hands in respectful salute to the prince, glorious Omniscient One, * and invited the two princes to leave that forest and go and see. * Younger and elder, they journeyed along the path through the forest * until they reached the place of these seven great palm-trees which grew on the tail of the *nāga*. It was like a succession of jewelled coils. * Then Nārāy(ṇ) Rām of abounding strength and sparkling intelligence, ennobled by divine understanding, saw * the palm-trees growing without ground support
27. and he of the ten powers thought (27) in his divine wisdom * as follows, "It is probable that these seven palms are growing on the back of the great king of the *nāgas*." * The prince then manifested his power, causing the demon-*nāga* to feel fear of his physical strength: * he trod firmly with his most noble right foot upon the *nāga's* tail, pressing down on it. * The *nāga*, struck by fear at this heroic feat, was incapable of slithering away. It stayed there perfectly still. * The palm-trees were spread out in a line. The prince then directed the sharp arrow, Brahmās, accurately to disappear into those great palms — and they broke up into little bits, the pieces scattering everywhere. * The sound made by Nārāy(ṇ)'s mighty arrow, resembling that of 100,000 thunderbolts, was heard far away in the world of the Brahm. * All the gods, the god of
28. Death, Brahm and Indr presented (28) garlands of heavenly flowers in congratulation. * The foolish, venomous king of the *nāgas* made his way into Pātāl and hid himself in the very middle of the ocean.

* Then Sugrīb, the monkey prince, kneeling, raised his hands above his head in salutation * and crept close to speak at the feet of the compassionate Nārāy(ṇ), lord of men, whose power was so great, * saying, "Dear lord prince, you who are master of the three worlds, you are greater than all with your mighty deeds. * It is quite clear to me that your powers are immense, astounding in their magnificence, * exceeding those of all gods and godless creatures. Please do come to

(28) Khās' Khin. I beg you to shoot at Bālī with your arrow, master of men,
eminent for your invincible might, and destroy him. * If Bālī is
defeated by the strength of your arm and loses his life through your
29. arrow, (29) O prince, * I will humbly offer you this whole vast monkey
force, whose number is infinite, a complete army of great magnitude,
* to pay my debt of gratitude to you, most royal master of men. Your
kindness and gentleness * are remarkable, exceeding those of princes in
general, because you are of the lineage of Nārāy(ṇ), of the Buddha."

5.29–41. **They go to Khās' Khin where Sugrīb and Bālī fight. Laksm(ṇ) makes a garland so that Rām may distinguish one brother from the other and help Sugrīb. Queen Tārā warns Bālī that Sugrīb, who has already been defeated, is probably returning with some trick. The brothers fight again and Rām shoots an arrow at Bālī.**

* Then the two princes went to Khās' Khin. * Rām commanded
Sugrīb to call forth his elder brother, Bālī, and to pester him so that he
would be irritated. * This would make Bālī, the strong and mighty,
come up into the air to do battle with Sugrīb * and would give a
chance to Rām to shoot his sharp arrow, Brahmās, and fell King Bālī
with it. * Sugrīb made proper obeisance to the prince, graciously took
30. leave and (30) went * through the air to the great city of Khās' Khin to
call forth his elder brother.

* And now the two princely lords were standing silent, their arrows ready aimed to achieve deeds of heroism. * The prince prodded Prince Sugrīb to make him call King Bālī out to the middle of the battlefield. * The immense Sugrīb made threatening movements, fierce sword in hand, and imperiously stamped his feet. * "Hail, brother Bālī! You are quietly ruling your peaceful kingdom — but *I* am here now! * You drove me out — and I was blameless — to live in the jungle in daily hardship and pain. * Come out and fight hand to hand! Let us know which of us two has the final victory!"

* Bālī became very angry as he listened to these harsh, imperious
31. words. (31) A tremor went through his breast. * He took his invincible
sword in his hands, whirled it round swiftly and attacked with his
mighty strength. * There came sounds of blows, of knuckles beating, of
palms slapping, of roars like thunder, of bold encounters with swords.
* They were heard trampling over the mountains, contending for
victory. * Then they flew through the air, gathering speed, and ran
across the skies. * The two simian princes brandished trees in their
hands, waved them about and struck blows with them. * The forests

(31) and mountains fell in pieces as they battered each other with might and main, using tree-trunks — which split in two! * There was the sound made as they trampled over the mountains with high-pitched howls, angrily biting and tearing at each other, their claws clasping as they bit. * Mountains and forests were crushed to bits and trodden down with reverberating thuds, owing to the violence of these angry princes. * In their rage the monkey princes were clamorous. Their strength was a marvel. Their fits of fury were horrifying. * King Bālī was in his prime,
32. his vigour exceeding that of his (32) weak young brother. * Gasping for breath he went through the air, this way and that, overtaking the other. Nārāy(ṇ) saw that the elder monkey's strength was greater. * Sugrīb and Bālī, bold monkeys, made mighty efforts and engaged in furious altercation with each other. * They were like mighty lions in a contest for prowess. It was like a war fought between them. * They prodded each other and were entangled together, huge and in full vigour. With fierce boldness they hurt each other, clashing together in the battle, speaking to each other at the same time. * Rām could see, confusedly, that the two lion-like monkeys, speeding hither and thither, were very alike and so he pondered and did not aim his arrow.

33. * Sugrīb lost to the might of his elder and returned (33) to kneel at the feet of the lord prince. * "Lord, you sent me to the great city of Khās' Khin — and you were going to shoot Brahmās. * But in the event, I have been up in the air, quite obvious to the view up there in the sky. * So why did you not aim your arrow? As it is, I am at death's door and have come to pay my respects, master of men."

* The prince heard the royal monkey, heard how he had been beaten by King Bālī and had returned to the place where he, Rām, was * and he said, "You two monkeys are like twin lotus flowers, * or just like one strong elephant with another — or like twin mountains, both level with each other. * More, you are like suns with brilliant light in the heavens, both side by side, indistinguishable, * quite dazzlingly beautiful and in full strength. It is impossible to recognise each of you.
34. * The great Laksm(ṇ), foremost among men, (34) must make a garland to distinguish the elder from the younger. * Then I can dispatch the sharp arrow, the great Brahmās of invincible force."

* Then Laksm(ṇ), master of men, quickly went off and made a garland for Sugrīb. * The latter made obeisance, asking for a blessing on his life, and then went back through the air to Bālī * and cried out in the night, "Hey! Bālī! Come out and fight our battle!" * Bālī was furious and full of menace. With eyes glowing redly and his face blotchy, he was horribly frightening. * Seizing his bejewelled sword, he brandished it and took up a position with both arms rigidly extended,

(34) imperious. * His huge form resembled a fortified rampart, a daunting
35. obstacle (35) indeed.

* Then Queen Tārā approached the monkey king, greeting him
respectfully. * "Lord, do not let things slip your mind. The cheerful
Sugrīb here is provoking you to anger. * Was he not beaten? Why, if he
is not playing some trick, has he come here to beg you to fight? * Do
you not see this as a ruse? It looks as though some man of great deeds
is crossing swords with you. * I entreat you to consider carefully and
not to be angry because of what your young brother says. * You might
be compared with a forest which catches fire — and the grasshoppers
are killed. Death may come about because of anger. * Do not be angry
with him. This anger itself will cause you to neglect important matters.
* You will abandon truth, righteousness and good. You will do wrong
36. and be changed by your anger into an evil person (36). * I beg you not
to be so excited. You may slip up this second time." * King Bālī
shouted out instantly, "Your words are most aggressive" — and he hit
her on the head with his fist — * "I am not afraid. From a long time
past no one ever surpassed me in deeds of prowess. * Even King Rāb(ṇ),
the mighty, who laid low the heavens, causing turmoil to arise, * even
that king of limitless strength took to his heels, unable to stand up
against my might. * There are powerful princes who would not hazard
a guess as to their power to attack me and match their prowess against
mine."

* Bālī was in a mighty rage. Sharp sword in hand, he went with a
37. vigorous bound off through the air. * He met his young brother (37) for
the contest and sprang forward with great forcefulness. The two
contesting monkeys, both in their prime, struck one another, heads
together. * Both in full vigour — and with the sharpest of weapons —
they sped through the air twisting out of the way, each striking the
other, pursuing each other swiftly round and round. * They
approached for the fight, noisily contending for victory against each
other. They passed each other through the air; they whirled about.
They grasped each other, bit each other. * They dashed through the
air, their arms outstretched. They hurled themselves violently about
with loud, piercing cries. * The land sank down and cracked open.
Mountains were dented, broken up, overturned, leaving gaping ravines.
* Boulders, crushed to pieces, were hurled down, to fall and be
scattered afar, dropping all around, in horrifying confusion. * Strong
lions were separated from each other. Elephants fled in all directions.
The deer were terrified. * The tuskless elephants, oxen, and buffalo,
strong tigers, rhinoceros and roebuck became caught up on each other
38. as they ran away to hide. * In panic the birds flew off in different (38)

(38) directions. All creatures called out in awe at these deeds of prowess.
* The heavens were overcast, the rays of the sun obscured. In the sky,
criss-crossed by radiant rainbows, there was thunder. * The calls of the
gecko were muffled. Devout, aged hermits blew on their conches to
acknowledge the event. * The marvels resounded afar because those
monkeys of royal birth, distinguished from each other, were contesting
against each other. * Bālī jumped right over his young brother and
leaped forward to take rocks, supporting them in his hands. * Boulders
were hurled all about, scattering in their thousands, dropping everywhere. Bright sparks of fire flitted to and fro among them as * they fell
to the ground. Trees were littered about, crushed to pieces. A cloud of
dust rose up. * Sugrīb parried against Bālī, boldly brandishing a sharp
pinnacle. He uprooted trees * and hurled mountains down. As they
struck each other, rocks were cast far and wide. * There was a sound as
39. of the thunderbolt. * Flames glowed redly (39) over all the earth, like
fire catching alight in cotton floss, flashing to and fro across the
heavens. * They fought, seeming like two long-maned lions positioned
on an open piece of ground. * The two brothers were like two great,
tough diamonds. With reverberating cries, they approached and
grasped each other. * They screamed out as though earth had split
open or was overturned in a mighty, dreadful upset! * They fought,
jabbing at each other with might and main, turning swiftly up in the
air, revolving like magic machines. * They sprang forward, leaping
with strong bounds, through the power of magic incantations, sworn
enemies, their gesticulations full of menace. * In raging fury they
struggled fearlessly to bite sharply at each other's mouths and noses,
their gleaming eyes glancing, glaring.

* The marvel echoed as far as Pātāl. The whole of great heaven felt a
tremor. They brandished their swords, arms raised in threat. * The
earth trembled as if shaken. Mount Sumeru was like a little shoot at
the top of a cane bush where the bark flakes off in the heat. * The sea's
40. (40) waves boiled up. The Hemabānt seemed to be uprooted and
annihilated! All heaven was aghast. * In the clouded sky thunder
rumbled and reverberated and the sunlight was obscured. The whole
disc of the *cakravāla* was overcast. * All the world was misted over, the
whole sky obscured. Loud cries and calls rang out. * The gods of the
ten directions shuddered and crept away through the air to the outer
areas of the *cakravāla*. * The gods of the six levels of heaven rushed to
offer their congratulations and resounding praises. * Consternation
spread as far as the sixteen levels of the Brahm who, in their astonishment at the power of the monkey princes, forgot their meditations.

* The lord Nārāy(ṇ) Rām saw that Bālī's power would certainly

(40) overcome the young brother — and soon. * Just then King Bālī leaped forward and boldly grasped Sugrīb. Holding him by the head, he flung
41. him about, * hurled him (41) and hit him with force. The simian King Bālī whirled his brother round until he was at the point of death. * Then the younger monkey was terrified. He cried out to the invincible Prince Nārāy(ṇ) Rām, * "Lord, I am winded now! I beg you, prince of princes, shoot your arrow, fight!" * The prince was close by a Bodhi tree, under its spreading branches with their new shoots and myriads of leaves, when * he aimed the great Brahmās from the bow, piercingly sharp, and shot it at the monkey king. * The sound of the bow driving the powerful arrow was like reverberating thunder. A tremor moved through the earth.

5.41–50. **Rām explains to the dying Bālī that this is his punishment for breaking his promise to Sugrīb to give him Tārā as his wife. He may beg for his life if he wishes. Bālī chooses death. Indr hears Tārā's lamentations and grants that Bālī may live in heaven. Sugrīb is crowned.**

* Bālī fell back from his younger brother and snatched at the sharp arrow of the prince, the undoubted Lord Harī. * Seizing the mighty arrow, King Bālī cried out, "Who is it who has this ascetic's power? * Was it Indr's arrow? Or Brahm's? Or was it the arrow of a godless
42. creature possessing an evil magic? (42) * I think this arrow may be that of Baisrab or of Prince Nārāy(ṇ) Rām." * Not having the owner of the arrow to tell him, King Bālī stared bewildered at the point of the arrow. * He saw the traced letters steeped in gold indicating the great Brahmās of Rām. * Bālī seized the sharp Brahmās, placed it above his head and made obeisance. He gave an account of himself. * "Lord, I am without fault, without any guilt at all. As for you, our master, Prince Nārāy(ṇ), * manifestly a man of this world, why do you come like a craven coward and use evil trickery? * Such a one might be called a man of no real might. If you are a man, how can you be afraid to fight on the field of battle? * Come out, I ask you! Let me see you! Then I shall learn about your family and their deeds of prowess of long ago."

43. (43) * In his right hand Bālī held the effective arrow of the great prince which had struck him. * In his left hand he held his sword. He sought somewhere to set himself down and then said what he had to say. * "Greetings to you, who are strong and mighty in deeds of heroism, you who come to make your savage attack with your destructive arrow! * While we two brothers, victorious in fighting, are

(43) stubbornly engaged together on the field of combat, locked together in raging fury, * why do you come secretly creeping up close to us and, with your great strength, shoot your arrow Brahmās?"

* Then the lord and protector of the three worlds spoke to the king, * saying, "Greetings, great Bālī! You have wronged your brother Sugrīb, the monkey prince. * You broke your word, given in friendship, that he might have your queen, Tārā, if he wanted her. * This was the reason why I took aim to destroy you: because you did not remain true
44. to (44) that word, given in friendship. * When she was first born, the queen, Tārā, you were going to give her to young Sugrīb. * You broke your promise and took the Princess Tārā as your own wife. * Retribution from long ago comes now to destroy you, making you succumb to the arrow, Brahmās."

* Bālī made a respectful salute, prostrating himself at the feet of the princely Nārāy(ṇ) Rām. * "I have done no wrong to you, royal lord and master of men, * to you, whose aims concern the three worlds, who live the life of a hermit, carrying out deeds of righteousness. * You wear a rosary and study the art of the supernatural, dress yourself in a tiger skin, a band of temple grass over one shoulder. Attentively, for the daily sacrifice you blow your conch, carry out the ritual and perform the practices as in the treatises. * Meditative and mild-
45. mannered, you have been living the religious (45) life in accordance with the Brahmanic scriptures, reciting, reflecting, murmuring prayers daily. * But now you have abandoned the Discipline, cast this burden from your heart. You have no mercy, no pity. * I have seen you in anger, transgressing the traditional code of behaviour, aiming your powerful arrow to end my life. * You are the lord and protector of the world and yet you come to kill me when I am guiltless!" * The prince had listened to Bālī's words and as he and Laksm(ṇ), lion-like, were proceeding on their way, * he said, "Well, King Bālī, hurry up and ask for your life. * I will call back the strong Brahmās and your life will be spared."

* Hearing this fine proposal, Bālī pushed away the victorious arrow, prostrated himself and replied, * "Lord, it is right that I should endure
46. to the death (46) for I was struck by your arrow and there, on my body, is the mark of it. * And it was only so long as he was not defeated that the renown of King Bālī would still be distinctly heard of far and wide. * I am afraid that it would be rumoured throughout the three worlds that Bālī feared death and asked for his life to be spared. * I would prefer to die rather than live with this stain for ever on my character. * Lord, I will leave in your care my young brother, Sugrīb, and Aṅgad. * They may perhaps go a bit far with their thoughtless

(46) behaviour but I beg you to give your support to these charges whom I, your humble servant, place in your care." * When Bālī had finished speaking about putting Sugrīb and Aṅgad in the care * of the two great and noble princes, he was exhausted and weakened, his strength ebbing away. * As the lord of the monkeys tried to push away the arrow Brahmās, he could not hold it. It pierced him and brought him to his
47. (47) death. * Brahmās of mighty power was seen to go far beyond all the lords and beyond Indr and Brahm * and to fly through the sunlit skies, then plunge down as far as the rampart of the kingdom of the sea. * Washing itself until it was thoroughly cleansed and pure, it set off back eagerly to return to Nārāy(ṇ) Rām.

* When Bālī was felled by the sharp arrow, his queen, Tārā, fretted and bewailed him with loud lamentations. * With all her handmaidens she mourned the loss. She ran hurriedly through the mountain forest, * afflicted by grief, her body trembling, and fell at his feet with terrible cries. * "O great king, mighty in deeds of prowess, my dearest, how is it that you are dead, * that you have abandoned this life, dear prince, and fallen in the forest, to lie there on the ground, reduced to nothing?
48. (48) * And it was from this that I would have kept you! I said that the intrepid Sugrīb here was determined on some plan; * that it was likely he had some person of another race, of superlative power, as his supporter. * Absolutely furious, you raged and said that I was practically the enemy of the king! * Some wrong you committed long ago, bringing retribution, has now ended your life on this remote pathway. * You have abandoned all the charming young ladies of the court and your delightful kingdom to come to this forest and be annihilated! * You lie fallen, alone here on the ground, gone from your palace. * So now you have the moon as your torch and the forested mountain as your pillow on which to rest! * And now you take the ground as a royal couch on which to sit, a royal bed for sleeping!
49. * Now you have the sky as a spreading canopy (49), resplendent with stars strewn all over it! * Now you take the wailing of the wind as your music, lightly wafted to do service to your corpse! * Alas! You were tall and handsome, fair of face, of magnificent strength. * In war you were capable of victory on the battlefield. All the gods did you honour with heavenly blossoms, dazzling white. * You were able with your power to capture and tie up Rāb(ṇ), that most terrifying godless creature, and quell him so that he was afraid. * You were possessed of invincible might. Your powerful deeds of prowess defeated the buffalo. You were an ascetic of power. * And now you die here in the forest, abandoning your beloved sweetheart, your most humble and devoted true-love."

(49) * Then the lamentation of Tārā made the kingdom of Lord Indr
quake and tremble. * Up above the lord of men, Indr, opened his
divine eyes and raised his hands, lotus-fashion, praising Bālī. * Holding
50. a conch with perfumed water, (50) he went through the air to where
Bālī was, sprinkled him with the water and kindly * granted him the
boon of being conveyed to heaven to be born then and there in that
dwelling of the gods; * the aged hermits, who practised right behaviour
with great diligence, stopped to come and hold the funeral rites,
* granting him a passage to that state of freedom from pain, the state
of extinction, and giving him their good wishes for enlightenment in
the domain of knowledge.

* They all sprinkled the perfumed water on him and recited from the books to bestow this glorious boon upon him by means of their divine understanding. * Bālī, who had succumbed to the power of his enemy, was really to dwell in the celestial kingdom * and enjoy complete happiness, just like the gods who attained this through their perfection.

* Having slain Bālī, the prince crowned the simian Sugrīb. He was to
51. rule the kingdom in succession * and protect (51) the populace and the
whole monkey army, uniting them as had the kings of old. * The two
princes set out, traversing the jungle full of loudly-calling animals.
* Along a stream where there was a clear pool for bathing they saw
peacocks and geese which called out in answer to each other. * As the
princes walked with pleasure among the animals, the lords among
animals brought flowers and fruit to offer to them, * presenting the gay
mixture of flowers and fruit to Nārāy(ṇ) as he rested on the forest way.

5.51–6.9. **Rām sends Laksm(ṇ) to remind Sugrīb of his promise to help. Sugrīb takes Hanumān, who has made himself as small as a finger, to Rām. The latter asks Sugrīb to command the forces. Aṅgad is put in charge of a specially selected force and Hanumān is to be in charge of Rām's force. They march off to a position facing Laṅkā.**

* Sugrīb, king of the monkeys, now ruled all the land as Bālī had
done and * in his contentment he forgot about his debt of gratitude to
the two masters of men, who had long been expecting him. * Rām
therefore ordered his young brother to go to him and the latter made
52. the journey to the city of Khās' Khin. (52) * "Greetings, simian Sugrīb!
Have you forgotten your debt of gratitude to your sovereign lord, that
you give no thought to it at all? * It seems you want to fall like Bālī!
After having your royal master carrying out your wishes, * you are
forgetting to be grateful. The prince himself might slay you there on the

(52) forest path." Reminded of Rām's command, Sugrīb respectfully gave his reply. "Lord, I beg you to be indulgent * for I have only just begun to rule recently. The monkey ministers have been coming to ask for my blessing. I will indeed at once draw up my troops, the whole force, to offer them to our lord but * some monkeys live in the mountains; some by the sea. These have not yet come. * I will muster the whole force, after which I will set forth * and bring them with me to offer them to
53. the prince, (53) great master of men, who is my own lord. * Please, Your Highness, be so kind as to inform your elder brother, my master, who is distinguished by his kindness: * after one day's interval I shall set out, bringing the monkey host to offer to my lord, the prince." * The good Laksm(ṇ) considered this and then returned to give the information to the elder prince. * "Lord, King Sugrīb will be assembling his simian force to offer to you. * He is going to Mount Kandalī because Hanumān is there, not yet having come to join him. * May it please you to be kind to him and not rush into an angry quarrel with him."

6.1. * When young Laksm(ṇ) had completed his mission and gone away, the monkey king * left the city of Khās' Khin and proceeded through the air in haste to where Hanumān lived * in the forest of Kandalī, a woodland home to be compared with a royal garden in the heaven of the thirty-three. * Sugrīb approached quite near to Hanumān's bed and * saw that that son of a royal chief was fast asleep. Not daring to wake him up, * he blew loudly on his conch, a resounding note. All the wild beasts were afraid and did not dare come near! * Hanumān rose. "What strange event brings you here, Uncle?" he enquired. * Sugrīb
2. explained, "The messenger of Nārāy(ṇ), of the lion's roar, (2) who slew Bālī * has asked me to march our great monkey host to him. That is why I have hastened here now to your home. * I wish to invite you to go with me immediately to present yourself to the master of men."

* Hanumān, of brilliant powers, became as small as a finger! Sugrīb then tucked him away in a fold of his clothing. * He presented his army to Rām, thousand upon thousand of men, all of surpassing strength and each in his own way invincible. * He opened out a fold of his clothing and stretched up his hand, holding Hanumān on it, putting him near his own eyes. * Then he made obeisance to the master of men. "Lord, this monkey is my nephew. * I would like to leave him with you even though, begging Your Highness' indulgence, he may not be very well behaved."

3. (3) * The two princes were sitting in their splendid pavilion with its bejewelled tiers. * The handsome Rām spoke eagerly and with authority, * "Hail, King Sugrīb! Whatever is this? A monkey, so

(3) exceedingly small? * There must be some powerful magic, some
incantation of tremendous efficacy, some clever craft?" * Thus he had
finished speaking, that Omniscient One, serenely enlightened, who had
completed his acquisition of merit. * Having listened to the royal
words, Sugrīb bent low to make obeisance, dutiful and loyal. * "Lord
Nārāy(ṇ) Rām of great might, hermit of ascetic practices, distinguished
in the world for your purity, * as to the power of this small creature of
4. the simian race, I cannot (4) tell you about it * for fear that I shall tell
a lie. I beg you not to be annoyed but to keep him a little bit and see."
* "Our intention in being here at the present time," Rām replied, "is to
destroy Laṅkā, * for me to defeat and eliminate that godless creature,
Dasamukh, of most evil deeds and false philosophy; * for me to
annihilate him now, so that all godless creatures shall know about the
enlightenment of Nārāy(ṇ). * But just now in your reply to me you
raised a difficulty, suggesting that I should stay and look after Hanumān
until he should be grown up. * I would be afraid of the censure of the
gods. They might be very disapproving of me. * For are they not
expecting me to think out my plans and find a way without fail to cross
over for this battle? * How can I think just now of changing plans and
5. waiting, of keeping Hanumān until he grows up?" (5) * Hanumān, with
both hands placed together, made obeisance before the lord, Prince
Rām, * and, having heard what he said, opened his mouth wide,
straight away, and pretended to yawn. * Twelve glorious shafts of
sunlight, resembling sunstones, were seen * to appear out of his mouth,
with a brilliance which was visible in every dwelling of the heavens of
the blessed! * The light reached upwards to the highest peak of
existence, that of the Brahm; to the sides it went to the ends of the
cakravāla; downwards it reached the boundary waters. * The prince
was highly delighted to see Hanumān using magic to demonstrate to
him his powers in deeds of prowess and * said to his young brother,
* "Laksm(ṇ), just look at Hanumān's might! * We shall be able to take
Laṅkā with ease and subject it with no trouble at all! * And now, will
6. you please go and begin to (6) supervise the arrangement of all our
troops in their sections of the left and right, * letting Sugrīb be the
commander-in-chief who will bring up the vast forces to wait for
battle, ready to do great deeds."

* Laksm(ṇ) took leave straight away of his most honoured elder, to assemble the soldiers and have them organised in their ranks. * "Greetings, Sugrīb, foremost of kings," he called, "The prince orders me to see to the mustering of the vast simian host under you, their king." * Then King Sugrīb was delighted at having achieved the boon of this royal command * and he busied himself rounding up the

(6) enormous army of monkeys into its four fighting corps. * He selected soldiers of geat daring and handed them over to Aṅgad, as chief of the
7. (7) main force. * As to Hanumān, the mightiest of all the monkey lords and ministers, * he let him stay close to the two lords, master of men, to command their own forces * while the kingly lord Sugrīb and his vast army followed Rām as rear-guard.

* When the preparations were made, Laksm(ṇ) approached respectfully to inform his elder brother, Rām, the lord, * that, whenever he announced his distinguished intentions, he could set forth. * Rām commanded the astrologer, Jambūbān, to calculate an auspicious time, reliably to the second. * When he had found the auspicious day, the best time with regard to the attendant position of the constellations, precisely according to the times, * Rām had the gongs of victory beaten,
8. twice, thrice, grandly; the sound rose high up above. (8) * Then he marched his invincible army forth in its sections to fight the royal war. * All the monkeys ran along after him in procession as had been decided, arranged according to their military sections. * At a glance, they resembled the waves on the four thousand seas surging forward in line with each other.

* Then the prince came to Mount Gandhamād(n), truly the most august and glorious of mountains, distinguished for its nobility. * He pitched camp at that place, excellent for its fruit, * which was sweet to the taste, most delightful and abundant enough for all needs. The monkeys enjoyed them. * The prince built a grand pavilion close to the
9. sea-shore, facing Laṅkā. (9) * When the two princes of royal descent, mighty in deeds of prowess, were seated in their pavilion, * with the chief monkey ministers and attendants here, there and everywhere, waiting upon them, * the waves on the surface of the deep ocean, breaking like hosts of white tufted reeds, came to salute the masters of men.

6.9–18. **Rām sends Hanumān, in preference to others whose powers are not so great, to Laṅkā to find out where Sītā is. Hanumān, taking Rām's ring to prove his identity, flies over Laṅkā. He is fed and redirected by a hermit. He makes himself small to pass safely through the mouth and ear of Riktāsī.**

* Then the lord Rām, prince of manifest power, gave his royal command, * "O mighty Sugrīb, you, who are the chief of all the simian lords, * please just pick out one monkey to go and enquire for me where Sītā is living. * I must, however, send someone who can go to

(9) Laṅkā and be back in a twinkling." * Sugrīb made obeisance and said,
"Begging your indulgence, lord, I have only Chief Jībadvār here. * I
pray you, give him your command; he will go with your enquiry."
10. * But Chief Jībadvār said with respect, (10) "Lord, I can go through
the air across the sea * but, as for returning in one day, as you
command, lord prince, I cannot do so. * To say this seems ungracious
but it is because I am old and my strength is diminishing. * The mighty
Chief Nand here, though, could accomplish your command, lord,
supporter of the earth." * Chief Nand prostrated himself, his hands
placed together in respectful salute, and said, * "Lord, I can go
through the air across the sea to Laṅkā and come back straight away
* but I cannot do as I would wish to do, that is, change my form, as
Prince Hanumān can. * Now on the way to Laṅkā there is a young
11. sister of Rāb(ṇ), named (11) Riktāsī, * guardian of royal Laṅkā, city of
the evil Dasamukh. * This she-devil opens her mouth at the city gate.
The upper part of it reaches across to fill the sky, * while her jaw below
stretches across the great earth. Birds are unable to fly over it!
* Because the vile Riktāsī guards the way by which one would make
this journey, * even an ogre, *gandharva* or godless creature, crossing
over to Laṅkā, would enter the mouth of this female, * would turn this
way and that, losing his way completely and would die in her stomach,
12. lost, never to come out! * Lord, in time long past (12) the way to Laṅkā
was never difficult like this * but from the time when he acquired the
princess, Rāb(ṇ) has been watching over every approach with constant
vigilance. * There is nothing for it but the powers of Prince Hanumān.
Hanumān can do it. He will go with your command."

* Having listened to Chief Nand's description of the difficult way to
Laṅkā, the prince * said, "O Hanumān of mighty power, * will you go
and visit Princess Sītā, my honoured wife, my heavenly consort?" * Rām
spoke brokenly with much emotion, distressed in his anxiety for his
princess. * His eyes filled with tears. Embarrassed in front of the
simian prince, he wiped them away — but not before they were seen —
and * with an effort controlled the expression on his unblemished face
so that it was like the pure and unclouded full moon. * The clever
13. Hanumān could (13) understand what was in the prince's mind: concern
over his princess and * fear that she was not observing the virtuous
behaviour proper for a woman, that the demon, full of lust, was
coming to harass her or cajole her. * Having achieved the favour of the
royal command, he fell at the feet of the supporter of the earth to
accept it. * "Lord, I will go to Laṅkā. But perhaps your royal lady will
not trust me? * I will take something of yours as proof, supporter of
the earth. As it is, I have nothing as evidence. * This will allow the

(13) princess to know me. There would then be no anger on her part or any suggestion that I was inventing the royal command. * Her Highness might think King Rāb(ṇ) had transformed himself into a monkey and was coming to coax her." * Prince Rām listened to Hanumān. His well-spoken words, setting out the facts, were respectful and in accordance with what was right. * The prince drew from his finger his invaluable ring, set with cat's-eye diamonds, * and gave it to Hanumān

14. (14) to take for the noble princess, to explain his purpose when she should ask him about it. * "You are to go to where the evil Dasamukh is and investigate everything, including his activities and plans. * Do have a thorough look at all the surroundings of Maṇḍogirī and Rāb(ṇ). * Look at the whole military force, observe all the godless creatures who are guarding the princess. * Go to the apartments of my chief consort so that you will have a chance to speak with her directly and explain * and give my wife the bejewelled ring. She will quite certainly recognise it." * Hanumān bowed very low in reverence and took the jewel-covered ring and put it on his head. * Then, placing the palms of his hands down on the mighty Gandhamād(n) mountain and pressing down on it with his great might, * he bounded upwards through the air. The mountain was crushed to bits, flattened just like the earth!

15. (15) * The simian prince ventured into the sky, flying far and taking with him some monkeys, who stayed close to him. * When, out there on the vast expanse belonging to the master of the ocean, great waves crashed down and dispersed as spray and * they saw *nāgas* and sea-monsters, first one then another, the little monkeys were terrified! * Hanumān put them to stay in a forest and then off he went, high through the air. He came across a demon-lion * which Rāb(ṇ) had sent to guard the beaches along the coast of Laṅkā. * The demon-lion saw Hanumān arrive through the air and engaged him in combat in the sky. * Hanumān, fighting his very best, felled the lordly demon-lion to death. * Proceeding, he saw the *nāga* of the seven palm-trees, which blocked the way, not letting him pass across, and rose up, venomous, to the attack. * Hanumān darted forward and snatched away its head

16. (16), twisting it off and dropping it in the sea!

* Then he went on through the air and passed beyond Laṅkā. He lost his way and came to a hermitage. * Seeing an august anchorite, who had built up merit through the ordained practices, he approached with devotion to pay his respects. * "Wise lord, most godly hermit, distinguished for purity and goodness, * I beg you just to be so kind as to show me which is the way to Laṅkā." * The hermit of power replied, "You have already passed Laṅkā as you came through the air! * Now, my friend, I think you are hungry. Come and have some food.

(16) Have plenty." * Then the sage rolled three balls of rice in his hands
and offered them to Hanumān. * Hanumān took the rice and ate it
hungrily. He thought it would never be enough! * He suddenly
17. laughed, as he ate, as though in derision of (17) the great anchorite.
* But, through the mighty power of the hermit, he could not manage to
eat all three balls of rice! * Hanumān felt quite put to shame by the
great hermit and took his leave respectfully. With the rice in his mouth
he went off through the air.

* Next he came to Riktāsī, guarding the gate just outside the
ramparts of the city of Laṅkā. * Halting for a while, Hanumān
considered the situation. "If I let her realise that I am here," he
thought, "she will fight me * from now until the morning. Then she
will be defeated by my right arm for it will be able to destroy her.
* However, I am sent by order of Rām and, if I cannot go there and
return instantly, he will not succeed in his plans. * But another point: if
I enter her mouth I am afraid for the bejewelled ring. That wretched
creature is unclean. * The vulgar, base-born, vicious ogre would have
18. (18) the royal ring in her mouth!" * Hanumān thought he would not
stay there, delaying. He threw the ring far away up into the sky. * He
transformed his body so as to be very small and entered her mouth.
Then he emerged through her ear, * darted through the air far into the
heavens and, as he flashed past, caught the bejewelled ring! * He put it
on his head straight away and went on swiftly, arriving next at the
ramparts of Laṅkā.

6.18–26. **Hanumān crosses over the concentric ramparts of Laṅkā, catching sight of various ogre chiefs on his way. He reaches Rāb(ṇ)'s apartments and refrains from killing him in his sleep. He learns where Sītā is by overhearing a conversation and contrives to enter her palace through the roof.**

* As he was about to enter by the eastern gate, Hanumān saw an
ogre, godless creature. It was difficult, then — impossible! — to enter
there. * He turned away to the north-east gate and looked all about
him at the whole place, considering whether there was a gap. * Just
then, he saw a branch of a fig-tree which had pushed its way through a
crevice in the stone rampart. * He made use of that branch, climbing
on to it and walking along it. He edged his way along, came out at the
19. iron rampart and went inside that. * He saw (19) the nephew of the
godless Rāb(ṇ), son of a demoness, known by the name of Kāmabālī,
* giving audience with high-ranking chief ministers, so resplendent, and

(19) with splendid ladies of heavenly beauty arrayed beside him. * He did
not see the noble Sītā. Then he left that position and went within the
bronze rampart to look for her. * He saw Atikāy come forth to a hall
to which demons were taking the most horrifying objects of warfare for
his preparations. * Hanumān climbed on to the rampart of the copper
fortification, went within it and saw Mahākāy, * one league in height,
as one could see from a distance. He was holding audience, arrayed
with weapons of those godless creatures. * Hanumān did not see the
esteemed Princess Sītā. He proceeded until he came to the five-metal
rampart,[21] * where he saw the ministers of the despicable ogre forces
whom the conceited Dasamukh had guarding the heavenly ladies, * all
20. of them goddesses, celestial maidens, whom Rāb(ṇ) had stolen (20)
away. * He did not see Sītā there. Hanumān crossed over it and came
to the diamond rampart. * Proceeding to the gate at the north, he saw
Rāb(ṇ)'s son, the mighty Indrajit, * who was holding audience, glowing
with burnished light, with a flickering brightness as of flames, a
marvellous radiance, * making preparations in a hall, deliberating and
explaining matters to his attendant troops, demon captains and
soldiers. * Hanumān did not see the esteemed Sītā. He proceeded to the
gate on the east * and saw the master astrologer who calculated the
dangers to the glorious country of Laṅkā and to the lord of Laṅkā.
* Finding it difficult to enter, he went right round from east to south,
all the way * and saw the great Kuṃbhakārṇ, a prince of the godless
creatures, and his attendant ogre soldiers. * Going to the west gate, he
21. saw Sahaskumār (21) who protected the park of Asoka on the west.
Looking about as he went on a little way, he saw that at the side of the
gardens a gap had appeared. * He became small by magic, slipped
through and came to a treasure-house where there were twelve caskets,
* a splendid store of jewels. He did not see Sītā. He crossed the golden
rampart * and saw a palace, dazzlingly bejewelled with fine, sparkling
crystal and bright gold in twinkling tracery.

* Round the regal couch of the mighty Dasamukh were the young
women and attendants of that lord of godless creatures. * Old women,
unmarried women of the household, pretty concubines and ministers'
wives, of divine beauty, were simply everywhere. * There were many
burning torches placed at intervals and in the light of their flames one
could see clearly. Hanumān looked upon * the ten-faced Rāb(ṇ),
22. sleeping in deep content on (22) a couch beside Maṇḍogirī. * Thinking
she was Sītā, Hanumān stealthily took the sharp sword from beneath
the royal head on its pillow. * Drawing it, he raised it up to strike,
holding it over the neck of the great King Dasamukh but * he heard a
snore and put the sword back down in its place.[22] Then he looked at the

(22) features of the other person * and saw that without a doubt it was Maṇḍogirī, the wife of the ogre, who would be separated from her husband, would lose him * — and would be an unwanted widow. They were not the features of Sītā, distinguished for her nobility! * Hanumān murmured a magic spell of special intent. Instantly the hair of Maṇḍogirī and Rāb(ṇ) became entangled. * He wrote down on the doorway a warning that it would be difficult to free their hair since it
23. was a magic device; * he told them to have the lady slap the head (23) of Dasamukh[23] three times with her left hand; * then the knots would be undone; if she did not do so, they would be tied up together until they died.

* This done, Hanumān went out and had a look over the golden rampart. * He saw a score of young ladies, close companions, chatting pleasantly to each other. * "Ah! The mighty Dasamukh, prestigious lord!" said one. "He has an abundance of possessions, attendants, * divine women of beauty, shapely concubines and innumerable servants, young demonesses. * He should be so happy and contented! Why ever does he do wrong deeds? Has he not reached the point at which he can feel satisfied? * He goes so far as to steal the much-cherished Sītā, an extremely wicked deed. He gives no thought to the scandal and censure! * He has no pity for Rām who had only Sītā to attend daily to his needs. * He should be worried in case, deprived of
24. her, the lord of the world below (24) should destroy Laṅkā." * Then another joined in. "Princess Sītā, they say, is to be admired more than all other women. * I do not yet understand it at all. When the ogre king stole her from over there, where did he put her?" * "He put her in the park of Asoka trees to the north," one replied. * The prince of simian descent heard what the girl said and was overjoyed.

* During that night the sleeping princess dreamed a wonderful dream. * She seemed to see her sovereign lord riding upon an elephant equal in size to the great Sumeru. * The elder prince was wearing white clothing and had a host of attendants waiting upon him. * In her dream it seemed that as the prince proceeded on his grand elephant,
25. the fine white beast of immense size, * with a lion-like roar (25), the intrepid elephant, so high, with grim expression and raised trunk, crushed the walls of Laṅkā! * They were broken to pieces, falling down in bits! He chased the ogre soldiers and routed them. What consternation! * The esteemed princess woke instantly and told her woman, Sujatā, * wife of Prince Bibhek, and she gave the following precise interpretation: "Your dream, madam, is most satisfactory. * You will have news, some word, some sweet message from Prince Rām by messenger." * The delightful Sujatā thus completed her careful

(25) interpretation in the quiet of that night. * Just at that very moment
Hanumān had come through the air and had reached the bejewelled
tiers of the royal palace in the park. * To enter by the door was too
26. difficult because there were young demonesses (26) in attendance in
great numbers. * Hanumān transformed himself and became small. He
edged his way up to the top of the high pinnacle of the palace * and
then picked leaves. He pulled them off and scattered them down on to
the sleeping quarters of the princess.

6.26–34. **Hanumān gives Sītā news of Rām and then gives her the ring. He is rebuked for not presenting the ring first. Sītā gives him her ring.**

* Then the royal princess awoke and saw a parting in the fringe of
her canopy. * She came to the conclusion that it was King Rāb(ṇ) who
had changed himself into a monkey and come there. * "There is no
way in," she thought. "No gap ever appeared in this beautiful building.
* Where could this monkey have entered and come down? I fear it is
the demon king who has come in disguise to carry on with his
coaxing." * Then suddenly the great monkey, Hanumān, dropped
down to where the spotless princess was and, falling at her feet,
* greeted her with hands close together and knees bent, bowing low
27. and saying most respectfully, * "Madam, honoured (27) consort of the
prince, I am his trusted, faithful messenger. * My name is Hanumān
and I come from His Highness. Prince Nārāy(ṇ) Rām * bade me visit
you, his dearest wife. Your husband is most anxious about his royal
consort."

* The esteemed princess then replied, suspecting that * this monkey
was telling lies, "I do not believe you. Do not speak words of guile.
* When the most regal prince of the ten powers left the city and set out
and * I, with his young brother, Laksm(ṇ), was his attendant on that
journey through the forest, * I saw no monkey following the supporter
of the earth as his devoted servant." * "Madam," said Hanumān,
"most righteous consort, princess of royal lineage, most beloved,
28. * when Dasamukh stole you away, the prince came back (28) and went
looking for you in vain. * Your husband and his young brother grieved
to excess in their distress at this adversity. * The two princes went on
foot through the forest, calling for you, sadly lamenting." * Hanumān
related the whole story, not leaving the princess uncertain about
anything. * He told here all about Sugrīb and Bālī, who, though they
were beings of the same kind, had fought each other. * Sugrīb had
turned for help to the mighty Prince Rām and the prince had defeated

(28) and killed Bālī. * Sugrīb, who ruled over the monkeys, thousand upon
thousand of them, in the city of Khās' Khin, * had come to offer them
to the lord. Hanumān told the story well and clearly, making it
pleasant to hear. * "This Sugrīb is my uncle, a lord above our heads,
29. the elder brother of * my mother whose name is (29) Añjanadebi. My
father is the god of the Wind, a leader and protector of men. * I do not
tell you any untruth. May I humbly inform Your Highness, I have not
departed from the truth at all."

* Listening to what he said, the princess realised that he spoke
honestly and put things in proper sequence * but she was troubled and
explained this, as she spoke to him. * "Greetings, Hanumān. I would
believe you — yet I have a feeling of doubt and suspicion. * Have you
any proof, something that I might recognise as being from the prince
of royal descent?" * Then straight away Hanumān took the jewelled
ring from the parting in his hair * and, treating it with great care,
presented it to the royal lady. Princess Sītā took it * and was quite sure
she recognised it as being from the prince, the ring which he wore.
30. There was no (30) doubt at all. * She put it on her own head. The tears,
unremitting, flowed on to her breast. * The princess wept in grief and
lamented for her prince with loud sobbing. * Then Sujatā remonstrated.
In the quiet of the night she was afraid the godless creatures would
waken. * It would reach the ears of Dasamukh and he would know
that someone had entered the fine palace. * The princess tried to
control her distress. In the midst of her tears and sobs she scolded
Hanumān. * "Bold Hanumān, when I received the news and message
from the prince, * his precious words, so auspicious, I was in doubt.
You might have failed in the whole task! * Why ever did you not give
me the ring when you first arrived? * You came nonchalantly along as
31. if you had plenty of (31) time to play with, used all your charm upon
me and then gave me the ring afterwards!" * Hanumān answered
respectfully, "Lady, I was at fault if I caused you any worry * but it
was the command of the honoured prince, spoken by the lord, my
master, himself. * The ring is from the noble prince's finger. The
command came forth from his lips. * The ring has value but the
command of that most honoured and godlike prince is invaluable.
* And that is why I gave you the news first and presented you with the
ring later. * If I had given you the ring straight away, failing to follow
my orders and not fearing to upset you, * you would have felt quite
sure it was the prince's but then you would have wept with grief and
32. fretted. * Only when your anguish had abated would you (32) have
asked for the actual message. * I came here in secret and am returning
immediately in accordance with the prince's orders. * I caused you to

(32) suspect me like that but that was how I could tell you everything. * As
it is, I see you, dear madam, trying to control your voice, while gasping
for breath, choking with sobs, * even though you are having your weep
afterwards! What guarantee have I that it would have been possible for
you to have the news quickly?"
* Listening to this proper and well-spoken reply, the princess felt
admiration for the clever Hanumān. * He fell at her feet and most
respectfully made obeisance. * "Madam, royal consort, what is there of
your own as reliable proof * that I may present to your husband to
make him quite clear in his mind and without suspicion, in case he says
33. I did not come to you?" * Then the (33) high-born princess took off the
sparkling gold ring * from her little finger and handed it to Hanumān.
Amid copious weeping she gave him her instructions. * "O Hanumān,
go tell my great lord, my most dearly beloved, * that if he thinks kindly
towards me, as he did in time past, I beg that compassionate prince
* to feel love for me now as he did in those days; * not to think that I
am tainted, that I have been close to the masterful ogre, that I have
been blemished. * I have been looking out for my sovereign's arrival
for ten months but have not seen his face. * Now you know the whole
story. You know how, reduced to nothing, I have reached the shore of
the god of Death in Laṅkā." * The prince of simian descent received
34. the princess's instruction willingly and attentively (34) and thought
about his journey.

6.34–48. **Leaving Sitā, Hanumān climbs to the top of the Asoka trees and throws fruit down on the park. He jumps on to the golden rampart and breaks it. He obliterates the ogre army which comes to attack him. Rāb(ṇ), learning this from the two survivors, sends Indrajit. Hanumān strikes down the gigantic Atikāy who struggles back to Indrajit to tell him.**

* Then Hanumān took his leave of the royal consort. Manifesting his astonishing powers, * he went out and took the tops off the Asoka trees, with their profusion of leafy branches and top-shoots, fruit and flowers. * As he left the princess and the Asoka trees, he uprooted coconut and areca palms, stretching out his arm to grasp the ambrosial fruit. * He dropped the fruit of many colours and kinds all over the surroundings, tumbling them down in showers. * He plucked fruit from the trees on each side, stretching up or bending his head, glancing, turning upside down.

* All on his own that mighty one swung round with great force, twisting his body and, with a great spring forward, reached * the

(34) golden rampart and smashed it! Turmoil broke out and there was brisk
action among all the *kumbhaṇḍa* ogres. * They gave assistance, looking
most belligerent, holding all kinds of weapons: shields, swords, bows,
35. cross-bows, knives and buffalo-horn spears. * Some, the archers, (35)
aimed their arrows. The four ogre captains stood in the midst of the
demons, stirring them to action. * Four thousand ogres gave their
support, each pulling Hanumān's tail this way and that. Hanumān dug
his toes in, crouching, and then leapt forward to trample these godless
creatures to death on the ground. * He was like a *garuḍa* swooping to
snatch a *nāga*. He was like a fierce, regal lion seizing a strong elephant.
* The ferocious, evil godless creatures came thronging all around,
toppling over one another.

* When Princess Sītā heard the noise, she was greatly perturbed and
cried out to stop Hanumān, saying, * "O thoughtless Hanumān! Why
do you not reflect? You bear the instructions of a great prince. * You
came here intending to maintain secrecy, return straight away and
arrive back in accordance with the prince's orders. * Oh! Why are you
being so careless, causing such a hubbub? How can that be the right
36. thing (36) to do?"

* Hanumān did not heed her. He went away from the princess, tried
his luck and caught the thunderbolts of those godless creatures.
* Snatching them away, he dangled them, burning, over the earth,
scattering the lions and other animals in different directions. * He
uprooted coconut and areca palms and battered the godless creatures
with them. They scattered here, there and everywhere not daring to
remain guarding the princess. * The ogre generals drew up their ranks
which resembled the waves of the sea. * Ogres were closely surrounding the monkey but he resolutely stood his ground and obliterated the
gardens completely. * Grandly wielding his sharp weapon, Hanumān
swung it at the soldiers with good aim. Those godless creatures slumped
down dead, * their heads cut off, their bellies opened and distorted,
heaped on each other all about. * He chased after that force, chased
the ogre chiefs, pursuing the combatants with blows. He caught up
with Sahasakumār * who rode in a great chariot yoked with aggressive
37. lions which (37) he prodded, as he shouted loudly at them.

* Sahasakumār was raised up high and accompanied by the music of strings, trumpet and conch. His shady umbrella was fixed in position with dangling fringe and there were high, pointed umbrellas and gold parasols. * There were bold elephants of gigantic size which moved and turned aggressively as they were driven onwards. * The captains of the lions, all mounted on lions, were calling out with frightful cries. * The ranks of soldiers, skilfully drawn up in their sections, came forth in ten

(37) divisions, behind each other. * There were soldiers, bold as brass, able to strike with great force in the fray, mounted like conquerors on various mounts: * on fighting lions, strong elephants, oxen and great *nāgas*; * on aggressive goat-antelopes, tigers, evil eagles and lofty buffaloes; * on bulls, lions and fiery rhinoceroses. They went very far through the air, flashing to and fro across the skies. * They drew up
38. their ranks, as vast as a flood (38) of water welling up all at once.

* Boldly the evil creatures took lengths of iron and bore them up high to use as bludgeons, shouting at the monkey with animosity. * Hanumān snatched these weapons, brandished them and threw them at the troops, who were flattened, rolling on the ground. * The blood flowed like the River Yamunā, overflowing in rivulets, with turbulent waves. * The whole force of godless creatures was struggling fiercely. Victorious in the contest, Hanumān caught hold of the chariot, overturned it and made it fall down. * With one hand he snapped the chariot in two so that it hung down, trailing along. With the other hand, he grabbed Sahasakumār himself. * He struck at the lions, the elephants, the horses, beating the demon army flat, to roll on the earth. * He beat the lions, the oxen, the buffaloes, the rhinoceroses, the tigers and the goat-antelopes. The horses and drivers died too. * He came and snatched the eagles, grasping them firmly as he swished swiftly by,
39. (39) and he killed those mighty birds. * The great elephant-lions and king-lions, he grabbed — they tossed about on the ground, bespattered with the flowing, pouring blood. * He snapped the carriage in two and cast it away and, falling upon Sahasakumār, he held him and squeezed him to death. * The whole force of 500,000 officers and men was entirely destroyed, along with their vehicles and mounts.

* Only two of the godless creatures remained alive, escaping the terror, and they ran to inform Rāb(ṇ). * Rāb(ṇ) listened to their tale. "It began with a monkey lord coming to attack us. * He destroyed our chariots, our royal horses, our ogre army — he destroyed all the ten corps! * He also destroyed your beloved son, the demon prince, great Sahasakumār." The mighty Dasamukh was indeed angry.

40. * Hearing of the loss of his son, Rāb(ṇ) boiled with rage and (40) felt
deep anguish too. * He called for his eldest son, Indrajit, a huge, strong youth whose right arm was of surpassing power. * "O, Indrajit, hear this news, the story of the monkey prince. * Please lead forth the army and destroy this evil ape which has ruined the park." * Indrajit respectfully replied, "I can take him. He's just an ordinary ape with big ideas, whereas * I am the eldest son of the king. The power of my right arm is superlative. There is no doubt about it: I shall win renown. * But in case we might resemble an old race horse and an old jackal

(40) encountering each other, * I beg your authority to pick out some soldiers. In lineage, they will be the monkey's equals! * This may sound as though I am not happy to help you, O supporter of the earth. I would not wish to go against Your gracious Majesty." * "If you
41. eliminate this one ape," King Rāb(ṇ) said, (41) "letting it know the might of your right arm, * and realise fully your invincibility, your victory will be great indeed, a victory over Prince Rām."

* Then Indrajit took his leave respectfully and led off the ogre troops, * five complete armies of them, bold and determined, well-versed in all kinds of craft. * Appointed as commander of their splendid force was Atikāy, a great military chief. * A chariot was made ready with its horses bridled and yoked — horses which gleamed like huge emeralds. * Indrajit climbed into the chariot of which the gleaming magnificence might properly be compared with the rising sun while * the light reflected in the bodies of the horses seemed at a glance like the glow of the rainbow. * The driver of the glorious chariot was a fierce ogre, on his own, by name Prahast. * At the rear of the vehicle
42. was placed an enormous old ogre known as Bājī. (42) * There was the music of strings, conch and gong. As they advanced along the way in a great mass, a tremor went through the earth, * as when a gale is blowing down trees and, one after the other, they totter and are dashed to pieces on the earth's great open spaces. * In all ten directions it was dim. The sky was dark, all sunlight obscured. * Some soldiers bore shields and brandished swords. The ranks of the horses were drawn up, bringing the weapons into close proximity to left and to right. * Some soldiers held *nāgas*, swaying with dancing movements, biting their lips in anger — terrible, menacing forms. * When the army came close to the trees they deployed their lines and surrounded the monkey prince.

* Then the simian lord, whose master was Nārāy(ṇ), saw the army of ogres of gigantic size suddenly in an angry mood. * The intrepid monkey prince, strong and imperious, whose power for victory was so great, thereupon * curled his tail and wound it round and round, up
43. and up, making it look like a wall of defence. (43) * With the long coils in many layers he raised himself up, his body high on the Asoka branches. * Standing with arms outstretched, he plucked fruit, put it in his mouth and ate it, quite dauntless and unconcerned as he did so! * He was like a great lordly lion which had caught an elephant and was eating it without any fear, * not scared of other animals, having no presentiment of doom or any feeling of dread affecting him.

* Then Hanumān saw Indrajit, the impeccable, standing in his horse-drawn chariot, * magnificent with his glittering brightness like the sun, newly risen, shining in the east. * The prince of simian descent

(43) considered. "Is this Rāb(ṇ) or some other godless creature?" * The
ogre troops, close-packed, were surrounding the monkey on his huge,
spreading Asoka tree. * They went up close to it and the gleaming
44. monkey saw (44) Atikāy. Undaunted, he shouted out a question.
* "Hey! Who is that wicked ogre, so bold, standing in his horse-drawn
chariot? * Is that the evil demon, the misguided Rāb(ṇ), himself or is it
some other godless creature?"

* Then the mighty Atikāy, the dauntless, was furiously angry and
gave his reply. * "Hail, monkey! Hear me. You do not know all about
the ascetic power and superlative might of * that person. He has the
skill to wage war with victory, to be invincible time and time again,
* to go and capture the gods of heaven, even the god Indr, and indeed
to bring them under his authority. * That is why the god Indr granted
him his name, * to be known as great Indrajit.[24] He is the eldest son of
45. the king, His Majesty the lord of Laṅkā (45) * and is the apple of the
king's eye, his pride and joy. * As for myself, my name is Atikāy
because I can change my form[25] and disguise myself by numerous
tricks. * It is my nature to meditate alone. So there, you see! I have
that exalted tranquillity and the especial purity of the scriptures."

* Then the mighty Hanumān replied with a laugh, poking fun at
him, mocking him quite disrespectfully. * "Ho there! What a stupid,
demoniac quadruped you are! Why are you not overawed, as you enter
this contest of mighty deeds? * You cast aspersions! Your army and
their chiefs, who have come thronging here with their great might, think
I am all of a dither, curled up small. * As I look at your silly faces, you
are like mosquitoes and mites settling on an elephant's feet, * flying all
together in a dense swarm, persistently biting the elephant so as to
cause instant death; * they are united in their eager effort but, meeting
46. with a puff of wind, (46) they come to a bad end; * some find their way
to where the mucus is and are submerged in the liquid; thus, dispersed
in the water, they collapse in death! * You do not know Hanumān. His
body is all furry but he is hard as iron. * If you come to the attack, it
will be tantamount to bringing yourselves to Death here in the park.
* You come like vulgar, stinking corpses advancing upon me for this
contest of heroic deeds." * Then the mighty Atikāy was in a tearing
rage at the reply of the monkey. * There he stood, furiously making his
body spread out, large, long, huge, transformed. * His height was, one
would estimate, three leagues. The changed Atikāy was an immense,
gigantic form. * He moved his body and arms as though to attack. He
47. knit his brows, frowning with belligerent hatred. (47) * He made
threatening gestures, louring. His eyes glowed redly, enlarged and
glaring. * Hanumān looked at the awful, enormous changed shape of

(47) the ogre Atikāy * and then, with superlative power, the monkey prince
sprang out from the Asoka tree. * Bounding forward, he kicked Atikāy
down and stood on him! The ogre fell to the ground and lay on his
back, almost dead. * A sound was heard as of the thunderbolt. Earth
sank down and was shaken by a horrifying tremor. * Atikāy shivered
and shook and, with a struggle, slumped vacantly into unconsciousness,
eyes closed. * Then he made a mighty effort, dragging himself along as
fast as he could. He was on his feet, reaching forward, stretching out
his arms, weaving a tortuous course. He moved off at a run, * breaking
up trees and hills. Mouth agape, almost there, he reeled, put his feet
astride for balance, moved on. * Amid panic and confusion, a deafening
48. turmoil, Atikāy rushed to the invincible (48) Indrajit.

6.48–63. **Despite warnings given to him of Hanumān's powers, Indrajit marches on Hanumān with his troops. Hanumān raises himself up high on his entwined tail and uses enemy arrows to make a palisade round himself. He is captured and taken to Rāb(ṇ) who orders his execution. He tells the ogres that if they wish to kill him they must wrap him up in cloth and set fire to him. When this is done he rises in the air, sets fire to Laṅkā and returns to Rām, who rewards him.**

* When Atikāy told him what had happened, Indrajit was very angry. He roused the charioteer, Prahast, * and mounted his horse-drawn vehicle, blazing with rage as though with fire in his heart. * Then Prahast spoke. "I beg you, my lord, to be indulgent to me, humble creature that I am. * It may seem from what I say that I would restrain you from this action. Indeed, I do beg you to guard against an encounter with this monkey. * He is quite intrepid and, what is more, he understands the art of warfare. He is unshakeable, a valiant hero. * If one would compare his great strength, I think one would take for comparison yourself, my lord and master. * If, in your anger, you try to kill this powerful ape, what kind of opposition to him will you contrive?"

* Then Indrajit replied, "I am pleased, Prahast, with your very
proper suggestion, which it would be right to take. * But when we took
49. leave of the king it was to come here to (49) seek an engagement on the
battlefield * and even if it were not just with one monkey — mighty
hero, powerful and confident adversary though he be — * but with ten
thousand times ten million monkeys, still we ought not to be overawed
by the power of mere apes! * When we came here we said to the king,
'Even if it is a person with great ascetic power, * we will fight with all

(49) the might of our right arms to the death, each one of us without fail.' * If we retreat we shall dishonour the king's command and detract from the glory of his great deeds. We shall be censured forthwith. * It will seem that in our ignorance, we are scared of the enemy: of one monkey! As it approaches we scurry away! * It will reach the ears of our proud and mighty king and he will be very angry. As time goes on, shall we be able to bear to live?" Indrajit was furious with the enemy and in dread of him. He roused the troops and they swept forward.

50. * Hanumān (50) observed the ogres running up in hordes. Unconcerned, he tossed his head up and down nonchalantly. * Then the august monkey prince, lord of monkeys, struck out with terrible blows and threw them into a state of alarm. * He slapped and bashed the evil force — they died as though laid down on the great earth. * He sprang forward to capture lions, horses, strong elephants and turn them upside down in his wake. * He smashed the royal chariot and flung it down to one side. Tossing his head up and down, he made threatening gestures as he turned back or dashed forward. * He jumped up and grasped the top branches of an Asoka tree and entwined his tail right round them, * just like many thousands of snakes wound round, interwoven. He was safely supported up there! * The ogres shot showers of arrows which, like rain, filled the vast heaven in all directions. * The monkey did not flinch or curl up small. He pulled out the arrows and stuck them closely round himself as a
51. palisade! (51) He watched the army, thinking, "I am glad that Indrajit is coming to match his heroic exploits against mine. * Now, if I go fiercely to the attack to annihilate all the ogres, killing them off completely, * there is no doubt about it: Indrajit will not die. He will not succumb to the power of my right arm. I cannot destroy him. * If I fight, I fear it will be for a long time and I shall not return quickly to Prince Nārāy(ṇ) of royal descent. * The prince will be looking for me eagerly at this very moment. I should go straight away as he commanded."

* Then an old ogre prince took a revered and trusted adviser to Indrajit. * Being very old and wise, he was anxious about protecting their far-reaching reputation. * Taking the whole matter very seriously, he had pondered deeply and was ready with * his opinion. * "I beg
52. you, my lord, to hear me," he said. "I will (52) inform you of the whole circumstances of Hanumān's origins. * In the beginning the Wind-god, a lord of extraordinary power who has the might of a virtuous ascetic, * took as wife a lady whose name was Añjanadebi, of singular purity and loveliness, * and produced the bold and mighty Hanumān, a child with clear signs: * there were bejewelled earrings in his ears; there were

(52) twelve round suns * in the mouth of the lucky Hanumān. When he opens his mouth wide, the suns may be seen, radiant as the moon, beaming * brightly in all directions. Such is the glorious power of the ferocious, proud Hanumān. * If you can kill these twelve suns, thus
53. located, my lord, * then, through your own great (53) powers, you will be able to bring to Hanumān the terror of death * but he is the son of the lord of the wind and no one can put the mighty Wind-god or his entourage to death. * You were able to have a chariot driven up and halted there but it has meant death and destruction to the ogre force! * He smashed the royal chariot to pieces. It fell to one side, shattered, and all the weapons were scattered far and wide. * He sprang out and kicked down Atikāy himself, who, almost overwhelmed, faint and shaking, managed to make his way to shelter. * And there was Sahasakumār too, cherished son of the king. He caught him and crushed him to death! * I implore you, my lord, not to think lightly of him. Ignorant though I am, I offer you my thoughts, though I would not go contrary to your intentions." * Then Indrajit replied, "I am pleased, reverend sir. Your ideas are very proper indeed. * Under our present circumstances, however, we shall not debate the strength of this simian of wide powers. Our mind is made up, whether it means life or death."

54. * Indrajit was a lord but was in body a (54) base ogre and so he became furiously angry, * a mighty fire, like that of an age long ago, seeming to burn in his breast. * Everywhere on the field, his numerous chiefs, attendants and soldiers came thronging. * Indrajit raised his sharp, magic arrow and shot it in the form of serpents, tightly twisting, too numerous to count. * Hanumān endured them, staying quiet and still, crouched in a small space, letting the ogre wind countless serpents round him in numerous layers. * The demon force of four thousand gave their assistance, closed in and caught hold of Hanumān, pulling him this way and that. * He lay low just where he was. Then he sprang out and kicked at their legs. The godless creatures fell flat! * The ogres picked themselves up and quickly moved off again. They captured him again, pulling him to and fro, * making such a din with their strident
55. noises. They struggled fiercely, closing in on him. * There was a (55) rock to tie him to — that was how they got him!

* The ogres went to the palace and presented Hanumān to their lord, Rāb(ṇ), showing him their power for heroic deeds. * The evil Dasamukh was overjoyed. He congratulated the victorious Indrajit on his might. * In delight, King Rāb(ṇ) said, "Now, all of you of the ogre army, * let us take this wretched ape and kill him with all haste." * Some had axes handy. Some took tight hold of him. Some hacked at

(55) his chest. * Some struck his head with clubs. Some stamped on his
head. Some took iron pestles and mortars * and hit at his head to split
it open, to crush his brain-marrow to bits and tear it up to eat. * Just
56. at that moment all the four (56) thousand demon executioners, hurling
themselves about with great energy at high speed, * pulled Hanumān
first one way and then another — four thousand of them acting
together! — closing in on him, squashing him and grabbing him.
* They dragged him from side to side until they were out of the palace.
Some ogres attacked him with whips, some with sticks or iron bars.
* They laid him flat. Some stabbed him, some trod on him. Some
aimed great axes, which, thrown from afar, would split his head open.
* But the mighty Hanumān did not flinch! He controlled his body,
turning over, turning face upwards, whirling about. * He snatched the
iron bars from their hands and went off in pursuit. Bravely he hurled
himself about, brandishing weapons and striking at the ogres. * Some
had their heads pierced through or crushed. Some had broken legs or
dislocated joints. All staggered and tottered together. * Some died.
Some, alive, endured their distress. Hanumān kept quite still and silent.
57. * The ogres surrounded him in a body (57). They surged round and
held still. They hit him with pestles.

* Hanumān felt neither fear nor pain. Much amused, he laughed
gaily and said, with mischievous intent, * "You stupid ogres! Coming
to surround me with all this hubbub and confusion is getting you
nowhere! * Baseborn and ignorant, you blindly believe in the magic
spells of devils. You use iron to strike against diamond * and you have
a fierce spirit but no strategy. Your mental powers are slight, your
ignorance bottomless. * I am loath to distress myself. I will not conceal
from you — why should I? — that it will be torment for me not to die
quickly. * If you want me to die, go and tell that godless creature the
lord of Laṅkā * to take Yamunā silk, foreign flowered prints and silks,
good ones, and soak them in oil and wrap them round me, * thousands
of times round my body, that is. Then kindle a fire and set me alight
58. with crackling flames. * Then I shall die, do you see? You devils (58)
are so ignorant — such untutored dunderheads! * How can you, even
joining your forces, match the victorius power which I, with my
supremacy in strength, have all alone?" * Then Hanumān tore away an
iron mortar with a resounding clatter and dented and broke it. * He
grabbed an iron pestle and chased after the ogres, dealing blows at
them. The ogre force was miraculously broken up and routed in
consternation.

* Those vulgar godless creatures instantly beat their breasts and
trembled, their hearts quaking violently. * They huddled together,

(58) crouching low, dejected, full of fear, aghast. Then they ran off to tell
the ten-necked one. * "We surrounded the monkey closely, all four
thousand of us, holding iron pestles, and we struck him. * But he stood
his ground and managed to stretch out his arms, turn round and arch
his neck like a majestic lion, * roaring, huge and strong! With an easy
manner, he laughed and spoke in a pleasant tone of voice. * The
59. monkey (59) turned back to tell us what to do: if you want him to die,
kill him by means of fire. * He told us to soak in oil some fine new
cloth and wrap it round his body. * Having wound it round the whole
of his body in many layers, with no space left bare of cloth, * we
should then kindle a fire and set light to it. As it rapidly catches fire, he
himself will without a doubt be extinguished!"

* Rāb(ṇ) was highly delighted on hearing what the soldiers said. He
felt very content. * Because he was so ignorant and bad he did not
know that the imminent destruction of the kingdom of Laṅkā * was
connected with his words, as he commanded the demon pages to
disperse at a run * and quickly bring great quantities of materials from
60. the storehouses to wrap round Hanumān's body. * Hanumān (60)
changed his form, making himself mountainous, using a secret, divine
craft. * The materials of all twelve storehouses were not sufficient!
Even when 16,000 concubines, * with arms full, brought their sarongs
to help, it was not enough, owing to the supernatural power of the
cunning magic. * They constantly added numerous layers, wrapping
them round his immense form. One could see it would still not be
enough!

* "It's no good, you stupid ogres!" Hanumān said, "Think. What
else is there? The sarongs of Maṇḍogirī, * including the lady's muslin
shawls. What were you thinking of, not bringing them to wrap round
me to finish the job?" * The pages ran off to speak to Maṇḍogirī. She
could not make any objection. * Because she was so upset about her
son, she gave the things to tie round the monkey for his destruction.
* Receiving the sarongs and muslin shawls, the pages ran straight back
with lightning speed, for they had the physical strength of demons.
61. * Then they wrapped the cloth round, kindled (61) the fire and set it
alight. It caught fire, flickering with a red glow. With a crackle, it shot
upwards.

* The mighty Hanumān went higher and higher, swaying about, fire and all, as he went up into the sky. * He called out a warning. "Hey there! King Rāb(ṇ)! Watch out for Laṅkā! This fire will spread in all directions." * Then he went through the air directly over the splendid, bejewelled palace, decorated with gold, lofty and pointed. * It burst into flames which leaped angrily to the top, high aloft, with a loud

(61) crackling, blotting out everything with * thick, black smoke fusing,
rising up. The fire blazed up, obliterating all. With loud crashes the
palace fell down, bit by bit. * There were explosive bursts as sparks
shot off and were scattered to shower in all directions and to flit, redly
glowing, across the sky. * The fire rose and spread, hotly raging. Every
ogre house was in turmoil, as it flared up with great heat. * The fire
62. glared, throwing light to a great distance (62), to the heavens beyond.
Far up above, it blazed brightly. * It spread to the apartments of the
demon Rāb(ṇ), who sprang up and ran out, hot and terrified. * The
bejewelled royal couch caught fire. The sleeping quarters of Maṇḍogirī
caught fire * and the women, faint from shock — being women — and
fearful, their minds a blank, went here, there and everywhere in a state
of consternation. * Amid the bangs and cracks and the tremors, they
ran, falling over one another, heaped up over each other. * Some ran
for their belongings, to take them along. Others carried their children
on their hips, their muslin shawls falling off, torn and not covering
them. * The point came when the various thoroughfares of the city
were wiped out and all the valuables in it were destroyed utterly. * The
ordinary ladies of the court beat their breasts and wailed loudly,
shaking. * Even the evil Dasamukh supported himself from falling,
63. shamefaced and (63) downcast, deep in thought, saying not a word to
anyone.

* The mighty Hanumān, the one and only, returned to the prince and told him about his clever deeds and feats of strength, * how he had craftily played a trick and how the ignorant Rāb(ṇ) had not understood that what was being done would lead to disaster. * Hanumān related the whole story in precise detail. The eminent Nārāy(ṇ) listened to him * and that mightiest One of all was pleased. "O Hanumān," he said, "these ideas of yours were excellent. I am delighted. * I am giving you a bejewelled diadem and bracelets for your arms and a set of clothing, as a reward for a monkey prince." * Hanumān bowed his head respectfully before the master of men, as he received the royal reward, and * the ministers and soldiers who were waiting upon the prince made obeisance to him reverently.

7.1–10. **Sugrīb recommends King Mahājambū as an ally to augment Rām's forces. Hanumān and Aṅgad are sent to ask for his help.**

1. * Then Nārāy(ṇ), protector of men, was living high up on Gandhamād(n) in his fine pavilion. * The noble princes, elder and younger, both of superlative might, had assembled the monkey forces

(1) for a conference * concerning their intention of going to Laṅkā to attack the demons there. * "Our present idea is to take our glorious army and station it on the beaches by the deep sea * but we have in all only a modest force of some tens of thousands for what we plan. * We intend to build a causeway to cross over and thus be able to go right to Laṅkā, overcome the ogres and kill them. * Your force will probably be too small. How do you think we shall manage to make a stone construction and cross the ocean? * O Sugrīb, simian king, being by birth of a powerful monkey family, * you must know by name some
2. influential simian ruler (2) of some other country? * We would send to him a friendly message of good will, cordial and warm, * inviting this king to come and join us with his army and chief ministers * and give immediate consideration to the building of this causeway, to the planning of our procedures and to the protection of our interests in this battle."

* Sugrīb listened to the words of that eminent supporter of the earth, the master, Nārāy(ṇ) Rām. * He bowed low, his head on the ground, his hands respectfully saluting, and said, * "Lord and master, there is one royal family, a line of kings of simian race. * The unique and mighty king, greatly blessed with power, is by name Mahājambū. * He is most handsome of form, his body of astonishing toughness and
3. strength. * His fur is fine and long, close and thick, with a shine (3), a lustre on it. * He is magnificent, with a splendid brightness like the red-glowing sun. His fine beauty seems * like sunshine reflected as burnished light on clouds which lie closely banked in an overcast sky. * His eyes give the impression that, if he were angry and looked keenly at something, it would catch fire and be destroyed. * If you would compare the might of this monkey king, he is like the mighty King Bālī.

* "One might take, for example, the time when the *nāga* of the seven palm trees, whose power lay in its inimical, virulent poison, * was out there in the middle of the sea. There really were seven palm trees growing on its back! * Every time the *nāga* curled up the palm trees went round and round into a clump on the spot. * When the *nāga*
4. swam away the palms did not stay still. They opened out (4) into a line, one after the other, * a row of seven palms along the long, trailing *nāga* as it struck the water and splashed it about! * Bālī would come through the air and seize the head of the *nāga* even as it rose to strike with its poisonous venom! * Seizing its head and tail, he would manage to wind it round, twisting it up into serpentine coils. * If the *nāga* stayed in that position, Bālī would stay in the air by magic, catch hold of it and tug at it to spread it out. * And the palm trees would be arranged

(4) once again in a line! The *nāga*, disgruntled at Bālī's playfulness, would
give up the struggle. * Bālī would treat it as a game and laugh with
great glee, without the slightest fear or respect. * Now the daring King
Mahājambū came through the air to have a game with the *nāga* of the
seven palms * and he had the same power as King Bālī for playing this
5. frivolous game to the full. * The two kings of (5) similar physical
prowess sought with each other's company and became excellent
friends.

* "Now King Mahājambū has numerous senior ministers to the left
and right of him. * There are special officers of the highest rank
looking after their innumerable forces and guarding the realm. * One is
called Chief Nīl, the imperturbable, and one Chief Nal, the faultless,
determined like a roaring lion. * They are in very close harmony with
His Majesty and never leave his side. * As to the royal city of this
powerful king, this grand and elevated lord and ruler, * it is in the
tranquil region of the Hemabānt that he rules in peace, with an
abundance of possessions and attendants. * All round his diamond
fortress, at every gate, are pavilions with turrets, one after the other.
The ramparts are seven concentric circles, close together, * with moat
and dry banks. There are varied thoroughfares, all decorated with
diamonds, most delightful avenues, * grand highways, majestic roads
6. crossing to and fro, (6) magnificent, winding esplanades. The lofty
ramparts of the city * in splendid succession encircle it seven times like
the Sea of Sītandar which presses closely upon great Sumeru.

* "There is a five-towered palace, resplendent, shining with dazzling
brightness with its seven tiers. * Gems, crystal and gold are arranged
upon it. It is studded with jewels and glittering with gold reflections.
* There are sunstones and dark pearls, shining flower-stones,[26] red
gems and valuable lapis lazuli, seeming to whirl round, * precious
rubies and great sapphires, vividly glowing, huge emeralds set in gold.
* Everywhere there shines a brilliant red light with the sparkling
precious stones, the coral and the patterns composed of the nine
jewels.[27] * The curved ends of the buildings are elegant indeed with
garlands of gold lotuses far up at the top. * The regal couch of the king
is finely wrought in gold. *Garuḍas* support the bed, which is decorated
7. with pictures (7) of famous ogres * in conflict, cheek by jowl, bold and
daring, their minds set on the struggle. * Flowers and creepers, enlaced
together, intertwined, are embossed in conspicuous gold with lotus
petals dotted about here and there. * A chain of them of varied hue
among the diamonds flashes reflections with dazzling brilliance,
* gleaming with brightness, resplendent, sparkling, glistening like drops
of water. * Higher and higher up, sculptures have been worked on the

(7) royal couch, depicting the towers of a pleasant palace, a beautifully-sculpted residence. * On this side and on that are fans and horse-hair fly-whisks, polished and inlaid. Cushions and pillows with embroidered corners are spread under canopies. * Silken mattresses and rugs with golden fringes, suitably grand for a royal palace, make it like a bed for the gods. * There is the music of strings, of the trumpet and conch, a
8. decorous accompaniment played for the king. (8) There is singing, with high-pitched notes, sounds which harmonise and float upon the lightly-blowing breeze. * Guitarists play, while the sound of songs of response, soft, sweet messages, are wafted along. * Each palace has a gate of seven thicknesses, seven sheets of iron with a lock for each one. * Charming young ladies, row upon row of them, and chief ministers, keeping their appointments, throng there in attendance. * An army of monkeys, a great company of servants, quite uncountable, is there to surround the king protectively * while the powerful King Mahājambū himself rests on a bejewelled royal couch alone."

* The prince listened as the high-born Sugrīb praised the mighty King Mahājambū * and then, after reflection, he said, "Who will take the
9. royal message? * We should send (9) great Hanumān, so confident and powerful, a strong, intrepid youth. * He is steadfast and understanding — but he is very strong-willed and will not be tolerant if he is involved in a scrap. * I am afraid if anyone thwarts his plans Hanumān is obstinate. He gives no thought to the relative importance of a matter. * It is usual for a royal messenger, whether the message is important or trivial, to be tolerant and well-behaved. * I will choose a companion for him. Then if anyone is obstructive the friend will make Hanumān patient. * It would be a good idea to let Aṅgad go with him. If there is any wrong done, any bad behaviour, he has the right ideas and is very reliable. * He understands, as well as if they were his own, both the quarrelsomeness and the superior qualities of his dearly-loved friend, Hanumān. * If Aṅgad
10. makes a suggestion, Hanumān will accept it and find it suitable." (10) The prince had finished speaking. The whole gathering, having listened, gave its approval. * They would send the two monkey lords with the royal message to the forests of the Hemabānt.

7.10–25. **Hanumān and Aṅgad give the message brusquely and are thrown into irons. At night, however, Hanumān breaks their bonds and conveys Mahājambū back to Rām's camp. The revelation of Rām as Nārāy(ṇ) brings Mahājambū to submission.**

* Hanumān and Aṅgad made the journey and arrived near King

(10) Mahājambū's residence, a most splendid and lofty palace. * The two
intrepid monkeys came upon an army Chief of Staff, * who questioned
them. "Greetings, monkey princes! You come to our fine city from
what region?" * Aṅgad and Hanumān explained in their reply.
"Greetings, great minister. * We bring a royal message in friendship
11. from the Prince Rām. * Please take (11) us at once to King Mahājambū,
as is appropriate, considering the royal command we bear." * Thereupon the minister went to inform the monkey king, * who, learning the
facts, gave orders to his officials * to make ready the royal rugs of
wool and lay them down in the place where the envoys would
approach to pay their respects. * They were to prepare the chief
ministers' meeting hall and arrange for a suitable orchestra to be
provided to left and right. * Then they were to receive the messengers
and bring them up to attend upon him as was the custom for royal
messengers on any occasion.

* The valiant Aṅgad and Hanumān, without a trace of fear, went
12. along with bold gait. * Concentrating (12) on their mission, they
entered, lion-like, the palace precincts of the royal ally. * King
Mahājambū of royal lineage opened the fine window of red copper for
the orchestra to be heard * and spoke. "Greetings, simians. From what
kingdom do you bring your message?" * "We have the honourable
duty," they replied, "of bearing a royal message * from the august,
divine Prince Rām. He sent us to fetch you instantly * because he is
setting off with his armed forces to destroy his enemies, the ogres of
Laṅkā. * He plans to construct a causeway as soon as possible with the
help of his thousand upon thousand of men. * But he is afraid they will
not be enough for that sea. So the master of men sent us here now
13. * with his instructions to Mahājambū to bring his (13) armed forces to
our aid in this glorious war. * If this message arrives at night, he is to
go at night; if by day, then he is to go that day without delay. Such is
the royal command." * Aṅgad and Hanumān had shown no deference
to King Mahājambū at all and he was very angry. * His whole face
reddened. He boiled with rage, extremely agitated. * The fuming fury
in his breast was like flames fanned and suddenly flaring. * His eyes
glowed red, the colour seeping as he heard the displeasing message, not
in accordance with propriety. * Like a man beating a serpent's tail with
an iron hammer, he roared out their severe punishment, thundering
out his threats. * "So! Let us take these enemy monkeys captive and
give them the most severe punishment, sevenfold." * Instantly the
executioners bustled in, took hold of Aṅgad and Hanumān and
whisked them away, * pulling them this way and that out of the royal
14. apartment. The valiant Aṅgad and (14) Hanumān could not resist and

(14) escape. * They endured it all, letting the triumphant executioners thrust
them into chains and into weighted-down shackles, secured round
them seven times. * An iron cage kept them crouching, closely
confining them. Head pillories of wood and iron were fixed on them
with tight chains, seven times round them. * They enclosed them,
thrust all the bolts firmly home, hammered sheets of iron up against
them and brought armed monkeys to surround and guard them.

* When this bad fate had made Aṅgad and Hanumān prisoners for a
whole day, * Aṅgad thought about himself and became afraid. Tears
fell. * "O Hanumān," he said, "just think! * We two have brought the
message by royal command, have helpfully come here to take
Mahājambū — * and we haven't got him to go! What we have got is
15. severe punishment from (15) His Majesty! * We have brought disgrace
upon our noble prince's command. It is clear we have spoilt his good
reputation. * We knew his wishes, his brilliant idea, his carefully-laid,
suitable plan. * We came here to help the supporter of the earth. How
can we just die, bringing slander and disrepute — all for nothing? * We
should be ashamed on two counts: first, we seem to have been
irresponsible, stupid, lacking in resourcefulness — to have caused this
calamity to ourselves. * Second, we have clearly spoilt the glorious
name of the two princes and diminished their authority. * And there is
not even anyone who has escaped to return and tell them! * Why ever
did we come dashing along, so careless of ourselves? It made it
impossible for news to reach them!"

16. (16) * And now Hanumān saw Aṅgad deep in thought, brooding
unhappily about the things they had done wrong. * "Aṅgad," he said,
"don't worry about yourself. Don't be afraid that we shall never
escape. * It is my responsibility and no one else's to take King
Mahājambū and present him to our lord." * Hanumān set his mind
with determination to wait for night time. Then he cast sleep in the
dead quiet. * The monkey force drawn up around them lay asleep —
grouped like bunches of bananas! * He murmured an incantation, a
divine verse to keep the whole monkey force quiet, sprawling everywhere without a sign of life. * He snapped the links of the chains,
broke the wooden and iron shackles and tore away the bolts, scattering
them about. * The cramping iron cage was smashed completely. The
17. sheets of iron were destroyed and fell about, battered to bits. (17)
* Owing to the efficacy of the superior magic spell from the sacred
treatises, none could stop him. * Freed from their painful restraints,
Aṅgad and Hanumān went swiftly off through the air. * Aṅgad was to
fly quickly back, going ahead to give the news and report, * while
Hanumān controlled his body, turned round and darted suddenly at

(17) great speed through the air * to open the doors of the golden palace. As there were many of them, all close together, it was difficult to find the way in. * The royal sleeping quarters too were cluttered, with no easy approach to the front. * Hanumān went up in the air and cut off the topmost pinnacle of diamonds so that it was opened as far as the spreading canopy. * When he had dismantled the gold pinnacle he
18. murmured a superior magic spell to cast sleep (18) to keep everyone unconscious. * The charming young ladies in attendance here, there and everywhere slept as though dead, unable to stir and waken. * Very gently Hanumān approached the couch. Then, holding the whole bed of the stormy Mahājambū on his hands, he went magically through the air * and caught up Aṅgad on the way. "I have no more strength for flying quickly," said Aṅgad. * "Come and hold tightly on to my shoulder," Hanumān said. "Don't fly if you are out of breath and finding it hard work." * Aṅgad clasped Hanumān's shoulder and the latter went through the air by magic to where the prince's fine pavilion was. * He found a place for the royal bed to the east of the elder prince's quarters.

* Then he spoke to the great prince, the lord Laksm(ṇ), young
19. brother of the wise Nārāy(ṇ). * "Lord, I (19) have just been and fetched Mahājambū here as the prince commanded me." * Hanumān told how King Mahājambū had, in his excessive rage, punished them with such dreadful severity. * Laksm(ṇ), apprised of his elder's wishes, addressed Sugrīb and the royal generals. * "Hanumān has just brought the mighty Mahājambū, as the prince commanded him. * Mahājambū is so strong! How can we manage to make him docile? * He did not arrive here with bars of gold to hold friendly discussions! * Hanumān has managed to bring him — an angry Hanumān who had been spitefully punished and who then thought of the ruse * of sleep. Supporting the whole sleeping quarters, the royal couch with its abundant jewels, he has just arrived without waking him."

20. * (20) Sugrīb knew well the powers of Mahājambū, whose heroic deeds had been clearly demonstrated. * "Lord, I am myself aghast at the arrogance and ill-temper of this fellow and the bold look in his eye. * He becomes so full of wrath that his glance is like flaring fire which is swiftly reduced to ashes and crumbled to nothingness. * There is only Nārāy(ṇ) to whom he will pay respect and to whom he will submit. * There may be superior kings of great power — Mahājambū is not a bit afraid of their might. * I beg you, lord prince, to give a command directly to the son of the Wind, sending him * to ask Isūr of far-reaching dominion and mighty prowess to transform Nārāy(ṇ). * Then King Mahājambū of the simian race, on seeing the transformation, will

21. do him honour; * (21) and will change and shake off his anger. He will
find it possible to end this wrong-headed mood of enmity."

* Then the young brother of the lord, Nārāy(ṇ), gave full instructions to the son of the Wind * who took his leave and was gone in a flash through the air to Mount Kailās. * Approaching the great Isūr, he said, "Lord, I, your servant, am sent here by Laksm(ṇ) * to beg this favour of you, who are of superior might and eminence: the transformation of the honoured and powerful Nārāy(ṇ) * because King Mahājambū, the strong and mighty, is with the lord, Prince Nārāy(ṇ) Rām, * and will not submit to his authority! I ask your indulgence, to
22. grant, with your powers, this boon." (22) "It shall be my task to under-
take help for Rām," Isūr replied. * "When Mahājambū comes out of his sleep, I will let him see that he is the unique Nārāy(ṇ) of complete power." * Then, having made obeisance at the feet of Isūr, protector of men, while the latter gave him his powerfully effective blessing, the son of the Wind * returned to inform the lord Laksm(ṇ). Hearing that Isūr had indeed been kind, * the young prince gave orders to the officers to make everything ready, * to prepare the hall for the numerous chief ministers and have attendants drawn up in due order to left and to right. * The simian forces stood guard all round, bearing their full
23. equipment of weapons. * Laksm(ṇ), from his position at the (23) much-
bejewelled window, * ordered Hanumān to place the sleeping quarters of the forceful Mahājambū gently in the fine pavilion. * Then he informed the beloved, godly Rām, serene prince, whose delight showed in his face * and told Hanumān to undo the spell, his magic device.

* The peacefully-sleeping King Mahājambū suddenly started awake and saw where he was, saw the fine pavilion, * looked to left and to right and became very angry with a sudden rush of feeling. His teeth grated together. Shaking, he compressed his lips. * The lord, the royal-born prince, the most high, then opened the bejewelled window of the apartment. * Trumpets, conches and strings very quietly and
24. decorously made music as (24) an accompaniment which floated, wafted
far away heavenwards and * King Mahājambū beheld the vision of Nārāy(ṇ) of the ten strengths in his pavilion, * with four mighty arms, holding a wheel, a club, a globe and a trident, powerful for victory. * He saw the very person of the noble Nārāy(ṇ) — and shook with fear, trembling in every limb; * and finally he went down on his knees, his hands placed carefully with the fingers in the lotus position above his disordered hair, * high up above his head, as he respectfully saluted the great lord and master. * "I think Aṅgad and Hanumān played a trick on me and easily deceived me by their wiles. * If they had said it was Nārāy(ṇ)'s orders, would I — I ask you! — have been so unconcerned,

25. so lacking in respect for the royal command?" * (25) Then the eminent Rām saw that Mahājambū was feeling more submissive * as he knelt, bowing and scraping, with hands outstretched, crouching low down and paying his respects * and, casting away his transformation as Nārāy(ṇ), was quite clearly again the divine person of Rām, * who, because of his abundant merit and virtue, had become enlightened, the highest One in the three worlds. * Mahājambū saw that his powers were supreme and said, "This person is the mighty Nārāy(ṇ) * together with the divine Rām, both in one. I thought they were different beings." * He turned it over in his mind, deep in thought, but did not change his opinion. He became all the more submissive towards the power of the prince.

7.25–34. **King Mahājambū's two right-hand men, discovering that he has disappeared, look for him all over the *cakravāla* and finally find him. When Rām explains about the attack on Laṅkā, King Mahājambū excuses himself because of his age but offers the two chiefs to Rām.**

* When the sun's circle was stationed in the east and its brightness was shining forth gloriously, * it was then usual to begin preparing the
26. many halls in accordance with daily routine; (26) * but on the occasion when the monkey Hanumān had taken away the powerful King Mahājambū and presented him to Prince Rām, * his well-founded city was in frenzied commotion! * There were two great military officers, by name Chief Nīl and Chief Nal, * the right-hand men of the mighty lord, the great King Mahājambū. * Both of them were chief ministers of glorious eminence. Both had great skill. In any situation it was an advantage to have them. * To King Mahājambū, one might say, they were exactly like two sharp ivory tusks. * If ever there was any trouble or wrong-doing, the two loyal chiefs were there, intelligent and dependable. * On this occasion these chiefs of many victories were, each one separately, busily making their way to attend upon the king. * They saw the pleasant room quite empty and silent! His serene
27. Highness the king — and his (27) bed — had disappeared! * The queen and the court women were weeping and wailing, the sound of their sobs echoing through the palace. * The two chiefs heard the facts in amazement. * "Astonishing! His Majesty has vanished by magic! * We shall have to fight to get him back without giving up — to the death. Then others may tolerate us. * That we can still be alive! How, this being so, could anyone so easily capture our master and take him off? * It is better for us to throw our lives away. To have our enemies

(27) despise us could hardly be satisfactory, could it? * And there would be disapproval in this world and the next, the slander spreading for ever! * Let us go after His Majesty, protector of the world. Let us fall and lose our lives fighting." * The chiefs deliberated thus about the whole question. Then they set off to look for their king.

28. (28) * Chief Nīl went up in the air and moved round in the sky as far as the six Kāmavacar levels of heaven and the sixteen heavens of the Brahm beyond * and then to Indr and all the general Brahm. He saw everything far and wide — but he did not see the king! * Chief Nal of mighty power pushed a way into the great earth which bears us, breaking it and going through it * as far as the eight great hells with their sixteen subsidiary ones of unlovely aspect. * He asked all the *nāgas* of that world — he did not see the sovereign, his wonderful lord and master. * The two of them came back through the air to the peaceful place where they were before and met each other. * Chief Nal flew to the east and the mighty Nīl to the west. * They did not see the king! Chief Nal ventured into the skies,
29. going straight to the south. (29) * Chief Nīl swiftly returned, darting through the air, and went off to the north to seek the king. * Chief Nal used all his strength going first here, then there. The two reliable chiefs went to look in all ten directions * both inside and outside the borders of the *cakravāla*, in every place far and wide, the empty spaces, the mountain ravines, * disturbing the base of lovely Sumeru, decorous dwelling-place of Isūr, furnished with fine palaces. * They did not see the king. They returned quickly to their own homes. * The two of them conferred together. "Where can His Majesty be, that we cannot find him? * We shall try our best to follow him, whether we know the place or not, and so find our king."

30. (30) * Just at that time King Mahājambū was full of sorrow — sad to see — and quite helpless and forlorn, * waiting for the two ministers to come. They had been missing for so very long and there was no sign of them at all! * He was silent and glum in his great anxiety. He brooded continually, thinking to himself, * "Alas! Chief Nīl and Chief Nal! Why are you not rushing here straight away to find me? * You have let me be all alone with the soldiers of the supporter of the earth, the lord, Nāräy(ṇ) Rām. * Should I stay or go away somewhere? I am helpless, though I am comfortable here. * I think of you, equally beloved to my heart, every day. You must have met with some wicked villain!" * As King Mahājambū thought these thoughts, it was as though the news went straight to the two chief ministers.

31. * At just that moment, Chief Nal (31) and the sturdy Chief Nīl, with the strength for glorious victories, weapons in hand, whirling their clubs, * came through the air or broke through the earth, pushing a

(31) way through with great might, and arrived at the royal pavilion,
dwelling of Rām. * Suddenly they were there next to King Mahājambū,
paying their respects to him, one to his left and one to his right. * They
compressed their lips, most formidable in their anger and eager for
action, and * with a sudden start, they made as if to grasp hold of the
king, with the intention of protecting him and fighting a battle for him
* for they saw the princely Rām seated there, with his chief ministers
and the brilliant white monkeys attending upon him in great numbers.
* The two chiefs were incensed. Not afraid, not dumbfounded by his
power, they thought to launch an attack upon these forces!

* Then King Mahājambū saw that Chiefs Nīl and Nal were at the
ready for an encounter with Nārāy(ṇ) the mighty. * Alarmed, dismayed
32. (32) and afraid of disaster at the hands of Rām's powerful soldiers, * he
made obeisance to the prince. "Nīl and Nal," he said, "pay your
respects to His Highness! * You think this is a prince of ordinary
descent but this is the beloved Rām Nārāy(ṇ) of mighty power."
* Then Chief Nīl and Chief Nal placed their hands together and put
them on their heads and, * with great respect, arms outstretched, they
saluted the great Rām of the line of Nārāy(ṇ). * The lord, Rām, sweetly
spoke soft words of friendship. * "Well, King Mahājambū, great
master of your royal monkey family, a line of pure descent, * I sent
Hanumān and Aṅgad to invite you here so that we might take counsel
together about building a causeway. * I would like you to consider
joining in this great task, leading your own monkey forces as
33. auxiliaries to our simian (33) troops. * You will overthrow mountains,
breaking them up, and fix the rocks, large and small, to form a
causeway to Laṅkā. * I shall lead the monkey princes, great simian
lords of widespread authority, with their armies * to destroy the vile
rākṣasas, to annihilate them together with the demons of Laṅkā."

* King Mahājambū heard the sweet words of special import, as the
prince of compassion spoke. * With hands curved together, he spoke
against this. "O lord, I am an old man. My powers have already
declined. * I do not think I am as I was before. I would ask you, on
whom we depend, to be content * if I respectfully take my leave. I beg
you, most distinguished and gracious lord, to allow me to go back
home. * Chiefs Nīl and Nal, of far-reaching power, the equal of my
own, I present to you, great prince, to go with you * to the city of
34. Laṅkā to destroy that demon Dasamukh, (34) horrible to behold. * I
would leave them with you. If they do anything wrong or improper,
please, prince, forgive them." * King Mahājambū of the monkey race
made respectful obeisance to the great and powerful One, * offering
Chief Nīl and Chief Nal at the feet of the powerful lord of men, the

(34) divine Nārāy(ṇ), * and bowing low on his knees. Then he left and went through the air to his home city and his own palace.

* News of all this reached Laṅkā. It was said that the great princes, Rām and Laksm(ṇ), masters of men, * would build a causeway in the sea and would destroy the ancient city.

7.34–46. **When, after a military exercise and further consultation, the construction of the causeway is begun, the fish undo the work. Sugrīb and Hanumān vie with each other in their offers to turn themselves into a bridge, while Aṅgad offers to swallow the sea so that they may march across.**

* Then Nārāy(ṇ) Rām, feeling very happy, set about rousing his men ready for the conflict. * This done, the two invincible princely lords took their seats in their decorative pavilion. * There he was, the lord,
35. Rām, in his palace which was made beautiful with many-coloured (35) jewels and with gold, * near the shore where the sea came flowing. A fresh breeze wafted gently, diffusing a perfume * which spread everywhere instantly through the royal quarters and the enclosure for meditation. * There was the music of strings, trumpets and conches, of drums, gongs and cymbals for the delight of the princes. * The simian ministers were all seated in attendance upon the princes like ripples on the great ocean — * and the ripples on the vast sea were as numerous as the host of monkeys, noisily attending upon them on the upper shore. * It was like two seas, just alike, ordered by some ferocious being for the use of the princes, * elder and younger, the two royal lords of powerful prowess.

* Now Jambūbān, who had a good grasp of the situation, looked far out over the multitude of monkeys, as they paid homage to the lord of the ten directions, * all making the five-fold obeisance[28] as their
36. offering (36) to Bisnu. He spoke as follows: * "Lord, I have considered carefully and my conclusion is that the demon troops are indeed formidable! * They know how to fight and vanquish the enemies of their king. They know the main features of the road and how to deceive us with their cunning tricks. * At that time when they went to take possession of heaven, they came upon a host of gods and fought with heroism. * With their abounding strength the demons in fact overcame the gods and took Indr himself! * But now, monkeys from old times have plucked fruit to play with as they jumped and climbed on the branches. * They can pick fruit and hold it in their mouths — but do they know how to use force and military strategy? Will they gain

(36) victory in this encounter? * Let them have a chance to learn about the corps which fight with round discs, about the four corps which protect the army, that is the army of the great lord Rāb(ṇ). * Let them learn how to
37. avoid Death and vanquish your enemies by the use of clever (37) craft."

* The prince took heed of Jambūbān's suggestion and gave orders to a force of specially bold soldiers. * They were to choose troops for the right-hand side, powerful soldiers. For the left, too, they were to choose some. * They were to wrap up their heads in white or red cloth respectively, as a means of recognition. They were to measure the area to and fro for suitable distances, taking the sharp rampart as their guide. * Rām gave his orders with great firmness, calling loudly for them to press forward with determination, strike blows at each other and take the initiative, in search of glory.

* Then all the monkeys took leave of him and went up into the air to display their powers for the battlefield. * They flew to snap off mountains, each one of them holding four mountainous rocks, their arms outstretched! * They came along in dense array, bold as brass, fighting each other, stamping on the mountain peaks, making them fall to pieces. * They uprooted trees as they overturned the mountains, scattering them about. Monkeys banged and hammered at each other with the trees. * The trees were broken down, destroyed. They took
38. mountains (38) and chipped and dented them. They banged and broke them against each other with the result that fire sparked off. * All ten directions were dimmed as they attacked and lifted slabs of rock to hurl them down with all speed and with perfect aim to a great distance where they leaned up on each other. * The mountains were spread out in pieces, by direct hits from rocks. The monkeys waved their arms to keep their balance, swaying in the air, as they trod them down. * Dust rose, obscuring the sky, spreading in a cloud all about, as the great mountains were crushed finely by the rocks. * There was wild confusion as the monkeys darted energetically in all directions, dealing blows. Earth stirred and the movement * miraculously echoed through the borders of the *cakravāla*, so that men stared agape in wonder. * Then those monkeys, of manifest power, exceeding that of the demons, paid their respects and gave their account to Rām.

* "As they have demonstrated on the field of action, the monkeys are mightier in deeds of heroism than the ogres!"[29] * said the elder and
39. younger princes, standing in their decorative (39) pavilion.

* The simian Aṅgad, lord of men, was there in attendance amid the chattering throng, to confer about the question of building * the causeway with the two princes and all the monkeys: they would rouse the men for the attempt on the waters and would make haste to gain

(39) their victory; * let those monkeys who strove for success be off to fight the whirling *rākṣasas*; they must be urged to be off to quell the enemy; * then, when the godly lord of men led forth his five monkey hosts to the sea he would conquer its waters.

* Rām gave orders to the monkey generals and ministers to assemble their forces * and spoke about crossing the water and letting the demons realise their trick. All the monkey lords would like that! * The prince of exceptional intellect and widespread fame spoke of what had been determined. * "Greetings, all of you humble monkeys. You will have renown and praise for crossing this coastal water. * It behoves us
40. to demonstrate our power and build this road (40) for our crossing. We must use the mighty strength of our simians." * The prince, with his authority, had spoken his wishes. He and young Laksm(ṇ) busily sought out their men. * They sent for Chief Sugrīb becaue of his knowledge: being the commander of a force, he knew the army of Laṅkā. * They sent for the Chief of Inspectors and the Chief of Command, the Chief of the Records and the secretaries and officials. * They sent for the Chief directly concerned with routes to estimate the length of their approach and know the depth by calculation. * Once they had the depth clarified they would be capable of making the sea crossing to the farther shore. * They sent for these people so as to estimate the 100,000 leagues of the ocean's expanse. * They distributed the tasks equally with the same amount of responsibility — and off went the monkeys, eager to be the first to be ready.

41. * Then, they were drawn up in (41) ranks, spreading like 100,000 suns close upon each other, far into the skies. * The monkeys set about breaking off mountains, transporting them with extraordinary strength. * Flashing past like sunlight flitting across the sky, they rapidly brought the mountains. * Some lifted them and, carrying them on their hands, vaulted over the columns of soldiers before breaking the rocks to pieces! * As the boulders were smashed, sparks of fire flew off. The din was heard far away, causing consternation to the numerous gods. * Deer, lions, great tigers were afraid for their safety, alarmed by the force of the simians. * As the monkeys daringly brought the mountains, flying through the air, they seemed to treat it as a sport. * They held the mountains in their hands — great mountains complete with their forests! — and came through the air to
42. the sea. * Mountains, (42) rocks, water were flung in all directions. The sea was lashing, its waters dark. * Great numbers of *nāgas*, whales and sea-monsters were upset by the monkey forces churning up the sea. * Then the Sea-god became angry! Fish, *nāgas*, sea-monsters and the Chief Supervisor of fish * came and bit at the lumps of rock and secretly

(42) stole them away, carrying them in their mouths, destroying the arrangement of the mountains! * He of the race of masters of men had given
his orders to the panting and puffing monkey force but was seeing no
positive results. * The god of the Sea, deep and clear, made waves like
strong elephants and, with crashing breakers, was about to fight them
and chase them away. * White horses broke out on the sea's surface.
Rām's host was aghast. Then the sea was emptied of its waters! * The
water seemed to be the sky and the sea-bed to be clouds, as the waves
were inverted and turned to white foam[30] — * a marvel! The numerous
forces of monkeys stood still, their hearts beating fast, all together.
43. * Then the monkeys assembled (43) and reported to the younger
prince, who was violently angry. * When he had heard what the
auxiliaries said, the young prince went to his elder's dwelling to repeat
the message. * He bowed low respectfully at his feet and said to the
lord of compassion and protector of men, commander of their forces,
* "Lord, I see that all the monkeys are exhausted by their extremely
hard work. They have used up all their strength for this road of
mountains. * I beg you be merciful and, using your divine understanding, speak to the Sea." * Then that god who was highest on earth bade
him beat the drums and rouse the monkey soldiers. * They came at
once in throngs, monkeys, young princes and the young master,
Laksm(ṇ). * When the august god of the three worlds permitted it, the
monkey princes and their ministers and soldiers * approached, filling
the court with all their numbers, to wait upon him, rank upon rank,
44. armed and proud. * The prince spoke (44) to them, resembling the
bright moon speaking among the stars, * "Greetings, simian princes
and officers. You have lost all your energy! * A little while ago we
tested your powers to build the causeway over the sea for us to make
the crossing so that we would see the strength of you soldiers —
* because you monkeys said you would capture the sea of Laṅkā and
even subdue the four continents!"

* Then the simian king, Sugrīb, placed his hands together and asked,
amid the troops of soldiers, for his life to be of use. * "Lord, may I
help you? I will change my form — it is, I would explain, a power I
have — * into that of an immense Brahm. I will turn my palms face
upwards and place on them all the monkey divisions, * to be a bridge
to convey you two princes across there, O supporter of the earth,
together with all your host of troops * and including your most noble
quarters, your exquisite pavilion, decorated with jewelled patterns. * I
will raise this road above my head and go through the air straight to
45. (45) Laṅkā. In the twinkling of an eye we shall be there."

* Hanumān, seeing Sugrīb letting his powers be known among the

(45) groups of monkeys, bowed low. * "Lord, I ask the favour of serving
your cause. O supporter of the earth, I will convey your throng of
soldiers across. * Do not let this be a bother to my uncle! It shall be
my task to aid you, O glorious prince, lord of lords. * My tail shall
twine round the shore over there and my arms, clinging tightly round a
mountain peak, shall seize hold of the shore here. * As for the depth —
84,000 leagues — my feet will tread upon the sea-bed and be
supported. * This will allow the countless monkey forces, the whole
army, to go across, as is your desire, prince. * It will be just as though
you are on the ground, as you go to Laṅkā to destroy the vulgar
demons."

* Then Aṅgad paid his respects and spoke at the feet of Nārāy(ṇ)
46. amid all the asembled soldiers. * "Lord, I ask to (46) demonstrate my
powers as the foremost and greatest of your soldiers. * Do not let
Hanumān be troubled. I ask to help you, O master, Prince Nārāy(ṇ). I
will swallow the water. There shall be dry dust. Not a drop of water,
even as little as to come to the tops of the temple grass, shall remain.
* Thus shall the whole great sea be drained dry, all its depths of
countless leagues becoming parched and arid. * This will let all the
forces, men and commanders, the whole esteemed host, cross over.
* As the vast force marches over to the incomparable city of Laṅkā, a
cloud will cover all ten directions." * So ended the rivalry between the
simian king and the young princes of invincible powers. * They had
made their offers of help, all three, and had explained their suggestions
most properly.

7.46–54. **Rām, explaining that it is essential that his own power should be manifested, shoots an arrow which causes the sea to dry up. The Sea-god appeals on behalf of the sea creatures. It is agreed that the fish shall reconstruct the causeway. Rām's forces cross.**

* Then the fine-looking lord, Rām Nārāy(ṇ), resolved the matter
47. admirably with his profound understanding. * "O (47) simian king and
you leaders who wield great might and have offered for my use your
ideas and your powers, * I am afraid that the ordinary people would
say that Rām and Nārāy(ṇ) and Laksm(ṇ) are dependent upon the
strength of monkey princes * and that it is by using your powers that
they are able to gain the great victory over the lord of Laṅkā. * 'This
invincible might of Rām and of his young brother too,' they would say,
'— we do not see them demonstrating it!' * O simians, all of you, I
would wish to make manifest the magnificent powers I wield, my

(47) superiority in courage, * so that the enlightenment of Prince Nārāy(ṇ)
may be clearly comprehended in the midst of the troops of soldiers."
* Then Prince Nārāy(ṇ) left his pavilion, glorious with its fine jewels
and gold. * He stood there among all the many thousands of soldiers,
resembling a royal lion, a magnificent, roaring lion. * Next, he raised
48. his bow (48) and poised that arrow of immense power, * of which the
name was Aggīvās, the invincible, undefeated in the three worlds,
renowned throughout the world as a source of wonder and awe. * And
by its power when he shot it, the sea dried up, a cloud of smoke was
diffused and a noise was heard as of 10,000 thunderbolts! * It set fire
to the sea which burst into flames while everywhere the sun's light was
misted over by a great cloud. * During the whole time of daylight there
was complete obscurity, as though the sun might have been destroyed
and darkness filled the heavens. * A movement stirred the mountain
home of Indr, the bejewelled Kailās and the forests of the Hemabānt
too. * A tremor went through the centre of the three worlds and
through the great sea, mighty domain of pure streams. * By the power
of the arrow which was despatched, the vast extent of the ocean could
clearly be seen — empty!

* The whole company of creatures who lived in the sea and the
49. tutelary gods (49) of the sea too were aghast. * The waves of the Sea
explained the situation to him. The Sea-god saw clearly how it was and
was shocked and dismayed. * He ran to look for his beloved Mekhallā,
the goddess who protected the sea in a general way. * All together they
went to tell the divine Nārāy(ṇ), prostrating themselves at his feet.
"May it please you, prince, to have pity on us! * We beg you to be
kind and help the unnumbered beings of the sea who are dying." * The
Sea-god then produced a bejewelled diadem and cloth of many kinds
* to serve as gifts to offer to the great master, Rām, the highest lord.
* He placed his hands together and spoke dutifully. "May it please
you, this great ocean is a splendid kingdom * but if you wish, prince,
you can overwhelm the water and its depths will disappear * so that it
50. will be the end of the shoals of fish (50) and the sea, which, since old
times, has been the entrance to this shore, will be gone."

* Rām answered by referring to the past, when he was seated on the back of the powerful *garuḍa* * and overcame many demon lords who in that second age of the world were seen to possess most formidable fighting power. * "And now," he said, "a demon, by name Rāb(ṇ) — an arrogant and savage demon lord, moreover — * in the third age of the world has been attempting to vanquish the might of all the gods. This demon, moreover, is still living. * That is why the king of all the gods invited me to come and be born here and vanquish the race of

(50) demons. * While I was building a causeway to cross the water, you, Sea, were sending the *nāgas* to destroy that highway so that * we saw it become sea-water again! As for Rāb(ṇ), he is concerned to seize the
51. initiative and destroy our approaches. * That is why I (51) am conquering the sea. The drying up is in fact due to those very powers of mine with which I shall lead my vast force across."

* The Sea-god bowed low before the highest of men and spoke, trembling, to the lord of the earth, raising his hands respectfully. * "Lord, with regard to the beings which live here, I beg you to think kindly of the lives of all these humble creatures. * Let me, I pray you, build your road for you. Please calm your anger and be appeased. * I ask you, then, out of kindness to spare these creatures. Their plight is appalling." The prince then opened up for the host of fish the clear waters of the sea's highway, of great depth and purity. * Sea-monsters, and whales, cat-fish and sharks swam along, ready for their food, relieved and happy.

* And now the Sea-god bustled about, mustering the force of sea-creatures, the shoals of sea-monsters and whales. * They brought the mountain-boulders in their mouths and built the causeway for the
52. prince, vying with each other as they set the rocks in order. (52) * They arranged the slabs of rock, laying them out in the sea, flat and close together in the ocean's midst. * It was magnificent, all the leagues of its length, a triumph of power, a highway for the Lord Harī to tread. * They built a palace, bejewelled like the heavenly dwellings of the gods, strewn with precious gems, * which they asked the favour of presenting to Rām for when he reached the farther shore, a magnificent structure, all jewels and gold, finely wrought. * They created a parasol of peacock's feathers to shade him; they constructed a canopy for him, put up banners and formed a procession, prettily swaying. * To all the monkeys — 100,000 in number — and to the two exalted princes, who had manifested powerful deeds of heroism, * they raised their hands, expressing their good wishes for success. They would follow the prince when he left.

53. * The simian officers in great numbers drew up the 100,000 men (53) who were there to serve in their fighting sections * and organised the troops and the equipment. In their outstretched arms they held parasols, seats, shields, swords — every requirement for the prince on the march. * They had guards for defence and the music of strings wafting along with the sound of conches. * With a noise which caused all Earth to feel a tremor, they beat their victory gongs, for the princes were about to cross the ocean. * Each of the princes was seated upon a shoulder of the great Sugrīb and the two mighty beings were just * like

(53) Indr on his mount Airābat, with a vast, fierce force of tens of thousands thronging round and offering their good wishes, * or like Bisnu journeying on his mount, the *garuḍa*, with wheel, conch, club and globe, roaring through the spacious skies. * Now the prince on that sea-road looked magnificent with the closely-crowding throng of monkeys. * It seemed as if the splashing waves of the sea made obeisance to the two commanders. * There were waves of banners,
54. waves of shady parasols (54) and wave upon wave of weapons for they were equipped with tens of thousands of arrows! * The prince proceeded across to the sea-shore of Laṅkā and there he stationed his army, in that place of glorious victory. * He was exalted by his own person, by his descent, by his virtue and had an ascetic's powers and strength for heroic deeds. * As he organised his officers and men, the vast monkey army, * the uproarious clamour reverberated in the ten directions. Earth was stirred by a tremor.

7.54–8.13. **Rāb(ṇ) hears of the approach of Rām, asks Bibhek to foretell the future and then banishes him when he prophesies calamity. Bibhek goes to Rām. When Jambūbān corroborates the truth of Bibhek's prophecy, Rām agrees to accept his services.**

* King Rāb(ṇ) heard that the lord Rām, highest of princes, had crossed the ocean * right to the shores of the land of Laṅkā and that the two lords Rām and Laksm(ṇ) were busily urging their men to the battlefield; * they were lining up their troops in proper order, wrapping up the heads of their elephants and putting on their trappings; they were seated most grandly, each one on his elephant; * their wish was to engage the enemy and fight; and when they fought on the field of battle
8.1. they were bold indeed and utterly unflinching! (8.1) * He had the drums beaten and he made a loud proclamation, putting the whole royal city into a state of commotion, * to the effect that, at that very moment, young Laksm(ṇ), the Lord Rām Nārāy(ṇ) and the simian king — Rām, lord of men, and Laksm(ṇ) * both wielding the supernatural power of Bisnu — intended to destroy the demons in Laṅkā.

* Rāb(ṇ) spoke to his young brother. "Greetings, Bibhek. I want you to make a prophecy about the country's situation. * I am afraid a time of turmoil may be imminent, when total defeat will obliterate the kingdom of Laṅkā. * Is it possible that we may have a heroic victory or will Laksm(ṇ) and Lord Rām over there be triumphant? * I have a feeling that we shall be defeated by them, cowering as they annihilate
2. us on the battlefield. * You must prophesy according to the Books (2)

(2) quite openly. Don't try to please me, your brother, through fear of me. Don't you hide anything! * It is undeniable, Bibhek, that you are brilliantly clever and, with your divine capacity for clear perception, you are knowledgeable about the world. * But I am afraid you may fear some danger threatening me and may restrain me from action — and that might cause the obliteration of the kingdom of Laṅkā. * Perhaps, though, our mighty deeds will bring a great victory over our royal enemies? * If we have success in the deployment of our troops and establish supremacy over them, * I will do you honour and elevate you. You shall be there in our delightful, bejewelled hall, shaded by a white parasol."

* Bibhek bowed respectfully. "Lord, I would ask Your most gracious Majesty's permission * to look in the learned books of astronomy, which will provide us with a clear answer."

* Bibhek consulted the books of horoscopes with great attention and
3. looked at (3) the auspices of all the stars and at any danger looming over the people of Laṅkā. * Jupiter, Venus and Saturn were in conflict. The Moon and Sun, with Rāhū and Ketu, had become brilliant even in the daylight. * Their light glowed and flashed like banners all over the sky. Their glaring brightness represented the destruction of the kingdom of Laṅkā! * The whole horoscope was full of portent; in every direction there was nothing but villains, omens and thunder, terrifying to the demons. * Having made his consultations, Bibhek respectfully explained the portents for the information of the lord of Laṅkā.

* "O lord, I who am by name Bibhek, your young brother, would ask you to be indulgent with regard to this answer from the Books. * I have looked at the horoscope of yourself, sire, and of the people. Rāhū
4. is seizing (4) the Moon and the Sun! The configuration of the planets is suppressing our good auspices. * Ketu may be seen filling the sky with smoke and a variety of colours, overshadowing any chance of a glorious victory for us. * So I beg you, my lord, to consider our whole kingdom and have a sense of regret for Your Majesty's glorious renown throughout the royal realm of Laṅkā. * O lord prince and brother, when you took the Princess Sītā you were like a crow which has no power to reflect and carries off in its beak a sunstone * of purest white, quite perfect, and goes off to put it away in its nest. And when it is touched by the heat of the sun the sunstone catches fire and demolishes the nest completely. * Or, alternatively, it is as though a person strives to fix his bait carefully on his fishing line. The fish swallows it. It is not long in its mouth before it is dead. * When you,
5. lord, took the Princess (5) Sītā because of what Sūrapaṇakhā said, it

(5) became the cause of this attack upon our kingdom — all because of a woman's words! * When kings were ruling the realm in the past they never acted upon a woman's words! It has never happened before! * So I beg you, sire, to think about handing over Princess Sītā to Prince Rām, that serene lord. He will then be appeased and not angry. * That would be right and in accordance with the Law; there would be no retribution in the other world. You would entirely avoid any evil action or disgrace.

* When King Rāb(ṇ) had heard Bibhek explain from his calculations the bad omens of horrifying danger, * which he had seen in the Books of astronomy, the King of Laṅkā was furious and paid no heed to the
6. Books. * Boiling with rage, he yelled at the top of his voice (6) with terrifying effect, * "You are evil, Bibhek! How could you make a prophecy which is slander and calumny? * You likened me to a common crow! You went on to compare me with a horizontal fish! * But you praise the bold Rām, comparing him with a sun-crystal and then with the hook on a fishing rod. * I ought to kill you outright for I fear you do not appreciate my triumphant powers. * You, who have praised the enemy of your king, be on your way! Be off and stay with them. The enemy is on his way here. * I shall destroy the royal Rām, Lord Harī. I shall destroy Laksm(ṇ), his young brother. And I shall instantaneously destroy you, * if you do not get out of the way. This blunder of yours, this offence, in defiance of a royal command, is so serious that * I shall attack your head with an iron club and break it
7. into seven pieces. (7)"

* Seeing the king so outrageously angry, beyond the limits of established kingly tradition, Bibhek could not oppose him. * He knelt to take his leave and went away to divide his belongings and give them away, thinking sorrowfully of his wife and children. * He set out alone and left Laṅkā. He went to where Rām's victorious army was stationed * and came across the fearless monkeys who were on guard that late afternoon and who could see him quite clearly.

* They saw before their eyes a figure of great grandeur and knew it was a demon prince. They urged each other to surround him and capture him. * Some, of feeble wit, wanted to kill him; others could see a good reason for not letting him come to any harm. * The monkey captains thought it proper to present Bibhek to Rām and so they led
8. him (8) there. * The assembly, including Sugrīb, Chief of the force of all the monkẹys, saw and recognised the astrologer Bibhek. * They led him in and said to the prince, "Lord, this is the younger brother of Rāb(ṇ), of one and the same mother. * He has come to say that he will stay as your royal servant, supporter of the earth, and that he will not

(8) transgress against you. * We ourselves, simple beings, have our doubts.
We suspect this is some trickery of the demons to deceive us. * Since
this is the younger brother of the king, our enemy, we ask to kill him
and have done with him."

* And then the astrologer, Jambūbān, spoke against what the
soldiers had said and fearlessly made reference to the following
prophecy. * "When you entered your fine pavilion, O prince, the
accompanying position of the constellations was excellent and the time
was propitious. * According to the words of the prophecy, a man of
wisdom would come to stay with you as a loyal and trusted officer.
* Even if things do not go just according to the accompanying
9. auspices, you *will* have a miraculous victory and take (9) the kingdom
of Laṅkā."

* Then Rām Nārāy(ṇ), powerful in mighty exploits, aloft in his fine
pavilion, * spoke eagerly and pleasantly, questioning the astrologer
Bibhek. * "Hail, demon! Is *this* your fortress, then, that you, our
enemy, are with us here? * I think you have come to carry out some
trick in connection with the battle, to destroy us and end the glory of
Rām? * Or have you come for the sake of your own good name, to
prevent our victory by your magic craft? * Come, tell me the truth
—no lies! — have you come to attack us, to beguile us or to play some
trick? * You are like a burning tree trunk which falls into the middle of
an expanse of water. * If you have come to make us fail dismally, to
jeopardise our chance of victory, your life shall end. * If you have truly
10. come to assist me, I am delighted. I shall want to know all about (10)
you."

* Bibhek bowed his head respectfully and made obeisance at the feet
of Rām, saying, * "I will tell you, as I told Rāb(ṇ), King of the
demons, about all the bad omens for Laṅkā. * Lord, I looked at the
whole astonishing horoscope and explained the situation quite frankly
to * King Rāb(ṇ). There was an unfortunate conjunction of signs,
utterly horrifying: the Moon and Sun, with Rāhū seizing hold of them!
* There were clearly divine portents of evil. I tried hard to explain. I
thought Rāb(ṇ) would be grateful but * he was beside himself with
rage! He said he would drive me out. In fear of death, I came to pay
homage to you, master of men. * Alone, as I am, I ask to place my life
in your hands. You are my master. * If I am to live, I ask to help you,
to repay your kindness to me, my lord. * If you do not trust me, I
would ask that the monkey king should summon those entrusted with
11. (11) the sacred books of horoscopes. * Now Jambūbān, he of the simian
race, who calculates the hours, is a trusted and learned member of your
council. * Please let him examine the astrological conditions, the

(11) birth-date of your royal enemy and the prospects for the kingdom of Laṅkā. * If what I have said is true, I ask you, Rām, to believe that I really am a man of honourable intentions. * If it is not so, if I am false and desire to attack you, * I ask you to kill me, prince. Have not the slightest pity on me."

* And now Jambūbān spoke. "Lord, I have already made my consultation and what Bibhek has said is true. * According to the disposition of the heavens, Bibhek does wish to be your trusted servant, to take up your burdens and help you." Then Rām thought he would be as loyal and close to his own heart as a young brother * and
12. he would give him a suit of clothing and food (12) which he might have pleasure in using and enjoying at his ease. * Rām, the magnificent, spoke, readily giving his reply, * "Bibhek, I shall undertake to give you the whole of Laṅkā to rule * as its king in succession to the preceding king. This gift I shall make to you out of gratitude." * All those of the simian race placed their hands together in approval of the prince's mercy * and they gave sets of clothing to Bibhek to wear, as an adequate recompense.

* It was just when the evening sun was inclining and when, in full assembly, Rām was working out the procedures for the war * that Bibhek fled to the prince. Rāb(ṇ), who had led his forces after Bibhek but had not caught him, was in a furious temper. * Bibhek had made his approach to the army of victory and to the noble princes,
13. distinguished for their (13) calm compassion.

8.13–27. **Maṇḍogirī is rebuked by Rāb(ṇ) for telling him he should not have stolen Sītā. A battle takes place in which both generals, Rām's Rukkhara: and Rāb(ṇ)'s Rakkhasen, are killed. Rāb(ṇ), overjoyed when he is mistakenly told that it was Hanumān, not Rukkhara:, who was killed, has parasols opened to celebrate. They obscure the sun.**

* Rāb(ṇ) returned to his throne and assembled his chief ministers, * his eyes glowing red like the constellation, Taurus, or like fire — for hot flames raged in his breast. * No one spoke against him. Only his dear queen, his chief consort, * by name Maṇḍogirī, spoke against his course of action, intent upon protecting his widespread reputation. * "O lord, Bibhek is not unreliable. He is thoroughly conversant with the diverse magic arts and with the Books. * He has given a clear prophecy and it will very soon be fulfilled. He was upset for you because you are both his brother and his master. * When he made his calculations and saw the situation quite clearly, he was full of anxiety

(13) and fear about the destruction of Laṅkā. * He was distressed on the one hand for yourself, his brother, and on the other hand for himself and your people in every thoroughfare. * He was afraid there would be
14. a holocaust (14) which would bring about the destruction of the ancient city of Laṅkā. * Even if you did not accept what Bibhek said, you should have given it consideration and borne it in mind. * Why did you rage so furiously, exceeding the limits set by our noble kings of old times? * And why did you go so far as to take off your gold sandals and beat Bibhek's head with them, there in the bejewelled hall, * where so many of the chief ministers were gathered together? You had no pity for him, who was born of the same mother's womb. * He was disgraced before all the army officers and before his king. To remain here was impossible for him. * And so, he has changed sides and abandoned you, fled to be with Lord Harī Rām, your enemy. * So, what of Rām now? We have heard of his power and ferocity — now he has Bibhek as well, to be his master astrologer! * And they will be back here to pester us. I fear that when he comes to destroy Laṅkā there will hardly be any city left!"

15. (15) * King Rāb(ṇ) listened to these words and then angrily rebuked her. "Indeed, Maṇḍogirī!" he exclaimed. "The world disapproves of women extolling the powers of the enemy! * Just recently you were praising Rām because he knows the art of the bow and shot Bālī by stealth. * Those brothers had their quarrel. Why ever did Rām listen only to Sugrīb's pleas for a mighty deed? * That was how it came about that he went secretly, shot Bālī, took the city of Khās' Khin * and gave Queen Tārā, the people and the chief ministers to Sugrīb to govern. * You go too far with your praises of Rām's powers just because he has recently, with a shot from his bow, killed off that monkey's elder brother. * You extol Rām's triumphs — but tell me, when does such power as that prove destructive in warfare? * Now just watch me and Prince Rām exchanging arrows with each other. Then
16. you will see a mighty deed (16) and no mistake! * There are only Rām, Laksm(ṇ) and that horde of monkeys who stay with them — and what a fine lot they are!"

* The queen again remonstrated with him. "Please, my king, do not be so quick to anger. * Rām may seem stupid to you but that is because you yourself tricked him by a ruse, * by telling Mahārīk to change into a deer and have Rām shoot his arrow at him. * Laksm(ṇ) went after the supporter of the earth. Off he went, deserting the precious princess; * and you, taking the guise of an ancient Brahmin, sidled up, stole away * Sītā and put her in the park of Asoka trees. You may well be compared with a thief! * If, O scion of a glorious line of

17. kings, you had gone forth fearlessly, roaring like a lion, (17) on to the battlefield * and, hurling yourself about energetically with your great might, had met him face to face and fought him, challenging him to deeds of prowess, * striking each other, hand against hand, body against body, one man's strength against the other's, and had completely destroyed Rām and Laksm(ṇ) * and won Sītā by the power of your arm, then obviously it would have seemed a splendid deed. Your name would have been made glorious. * But, as it is, I do admire your lordly power! You don't fight him; instead you secretly steal his wife! * This is the cause of the destruction of Laṅkā, as Bibhek said when he gave his prophecy. There is no doubt of it."

* King Rāb(ṇ) had listened as his queen expressed her adverse opinions and revealed the truth more and more tactlessly. * In rising fury, Rāb(ṇ) replied, "To judge by your words, woman, you are hand
18. and glove with Bibhek! * Go on, take Bibhek as your lover (18), the object of your passion. * I tell you, be off and live with him. Let Bibhek look after you when you are the servants of Rām and Laksm(ṇ). * I shall be going forth to destroy Rām, young Laksm(ṇ) and the monkey forces and * I shall destroy the brazen Bibhek and yourself too. You shall die together. * You do not appreciate how the mighty Dasamukh, the Lord of Laṅkā, enjoys the wealth and grandeur of gods, * consumes magnificent repasts and has heavenly women of divine purity to love. * You applaud the exploits of Rām and young Laksm(ṇ), those masters of monkeys, * who keep themselves alive by means of the trees. They pick fruit for their meals! * All of them — the princes and their men — eat the food of the forest trees! * You
19. commend the power of Rām, regarding it as equal to mine but I (19) am going to find a way to repel that entire force and make it fail in its attempt.

* "They have all eagerly shared the burden of building the road; they have striven constantly night and day without respite * and, after a long time, they have finished building it and have crossed over to the Laṅkā shore on our side. * The monkeys, officers and men, with their restricted rations, have been in disorder. They will be taking counsel together, ravenously hungry. * As is the habit of monkeys, they will make straight for the forest, scatter in wild confusion and climb the trees. * They will pick fruit and eat their fill and will be absolutely delighted with their safe woodland domain. * I will order the ogres to drive them together and attack them; to guard the wood at every point, intercept them and seize them. * If they come into the forest our ogres will kill them. If they flee in retreat to their army base, they will die of hunger. * Even if they survive, they will be thin, weak and

20. wobbly, deliberating wretchedly (20) about the return home. * When they march their army in retreat, to make that move home, we shall intercept them on the sea-shore and chase them on their way. * As for the bold Rām and Laksm(ṇ), however great their strength may be, I would liken it to fire without wind * and without a single bit of kindling. * The fire catches alight but has no means of burning and is completely extinguished. * Rām is like the fire itself. His monkey forces are like the kindling and the wind."

* Rāb(ṇ) was conferring with his chief ministers just when the prince had made the crossing. He banished his young brother in anger and * was also angry with his wife, scolding her crossly, making out that her offence was very grave. * Owing to his bold, bad ways, his erring ignorance and his base nature, a poisoning jealousy was relentlessly inflaming him. * He sent his general, Rakkhasen, at the head of a military corps and a force of over a hundred thousand ogres, * bold,
21. (21) brave and capable, to keep guard along the forested areas and intercept the monkeys, * keeping a close watch, taking every precaution, so as to cut them off as they passed to and fro through the forest. * The demons were to block their way imperiously and ward them off by dispersing in crowds throughout the forest and guarding the shore. * They were not to let any of the monkey force succeed, try though they might, in taking fruit to eat.

* When Rām had built the road and crossed over to the side of famous Laṅkā, * the monkey force had come teeming across. They had jumped about as they played on the beach, showing off, full of fun. * Happily calling out as they enjoyed themselves, they had taken up postures of combat with their arms and heads, vigorously stretching out their arms and striking each other playfully. * Rām now gave orders to a simian lord, a warrior of great valour, whose name was Rukkhara:
22. (22) * to lead a force of 50,000 resolute men, who would fight fearlessly if they encountered the enemy. * They marched forth from the glorious army base and spread out as they entered the forest in order to look for fruit. * Some climbed up and plucked fruit. Some grasped the branches and swung to and fro with cries and calls. * Others climbed on to forks in the trees where they stood on the branches, swaying this way and that, trying to be the first to reach the fruit. * They met with General Rakkhasen with his vast ogre force who were smouldering with anger as they moved in to intercept them. * Rukkhara:, determined and steadfast, with his 50,000 well-trained troops, fell to and fought the ogres.

* The ogres were tough and resolute, with weapons in every hand. Hurling themselves forward, they surrounded the monkeys closely from

(22) all directions. * The monkey troops chased them away — astonishing
23. feat! — hitting and attacking them, banging and bashing them. (23)
* With shrieks and yells they joyfully slipped through the forest. They took hold of tree-trunks, snapped them off, uprooted trees and shouted loudly at the enemy. * They approached with unconquerable ferocity to seize the demons. They swerved with speed, dealing blows, overturning them, jumping on them, slapping them. * Broken trees fell down. They hurled mountainous rocks, turning and jarring against each other violently in the struggle. * Utterly intrepid, Rakkhasen, of massive build and gigantic height, did not flinch. * He took hold of those monkeys and squashed them. Rukkhara: went close and bit Rakkhasen's head. * Rakkhasen swung round and flung him off, compressing his lips in anger, and gave him a hammering with an iron bar. * With resolute determination, Rukkhara: sprang forward holding pieces of mountain and rock in his hands, and flung them down on him, scattering them in heaps. * Rukkhara: and Rakkhasen contended against each other with ferocity, first limbering up and then going all out for victory. * Ogre and monkey soldiers were killed. They lay in great
24. numbers all through the forest, writhing, slumping down, dying. (24)
* Rukkhara: and Rakkhasen fought each other for a long time, expertly, unyielding, covered with dust, thrusting out their arms to strike. * Both were in the flower of youth when they met on that battlefield, each one intent upon the effort to kill, each one full of menace. * They received blows all over their bodies and were both reduced to a very low state, until finally both died at the same time.

* Many of the monkey force escaped alive but the ogre force of 100,000 was annihilated * except for just one ogre, who fled into the distance and went to inform Atikāy of the course of events. * When that ogre had seen bold Rukkhara: he had thought it was Hanumān himself fighting against Rakkhasen. * "Hanumān had no fears," he explained, "he brought his troops to amuse themselves in the forested area. * This monkey force invaded the wood and purposefully climbed up to grab the fruit to eat. * 100,000 ogres, with the ogre Rakkhasen,
25. approached to seize that force of (25) monkeys and Hanumān himself
as well. * But Hanumān fell upon them, flung them to the ground and trampled right through their ranks, hurling them upside down here, there and everywhere. * He uprooted tree trunks and struck out with them, causing them to fall in pieces with a mighty crash, overthrown. * Rakkhasen thumped and slapped the monkey troops. They drew back and he fought with Hanumān himself. * He defended himself bravely, contending with great ferocity for a triumphant victory. * They both died together, Rakkhasen and the mighty Hanumān, there in the

(25) forest. * All the ogres and all the monkeys died without exception. They are all over the forest. * When Rām heard that Hanumān had been slain he moved his fine army away and departed in retreat. * I had a clear view close by the shore where the army was stationed. They have gone away. It is dead quiet."

26. * Then Atikāy, highly delighted, took (26) the news straight to King Rāb(ṇ), * telling him what the ogre had said, that General Rakkhasen had fought to the death with Hanumān. * Rāb(ṇ), extremely pleased, stood up and clapped his hands and waved his arms about. Then he put on a fine outfit of clothing. * In his glee he was quite above himself. "Ha ha!" he laughed happily. "Now, madam Maṇḍogirī! * You were full of praise for Bibhek, who is an ignorant scoundrel, full of boldness and not very attentive to duty. * Can you look at me, Rāb(ṇ), and have such thoughts as those? How do you regard me now, Rāb(ṇ), your husband? * You extolled Rām, saying that he knew what he was doing in military matters. You thought you were right about the tactics of mighty Rām, * who has been making a great name for himself through his determination in crossing the vast, gleaming ocean * and sincerely believed that he would attain his desire, which — poor
27. Rām! — has come to (27) nought. * So now he has scrapped the whole idea, gone away and is lost at sea! * I have removed his chief support and they have decamped. They have fled, flustered and frightened!"

* The evil Dasamukh was full of overweening confidence. He had the parasols of victory put up, enormous, tall umbrellas * filling the great heavens! They were so high up there that it was dark throughout the skies and thus * the light of the sun's orb was hidden away, entirely obscured and invisible. It was light night. * Rāb(ṇ)'s retinue of officials, thronging from all sides, opened their parasols and put them up, each for his own separate use.

8.27–40. **Rām destroys the parasols with an arrow. Rāb(ṇ) takes Sītā with him in his carriage and flies through the air. Rām shoots an arrow which destroys the carriage. Rāb(ṇ) goes up again but, when Rām points a finger at him, he feels faint. Realising that Bibhek's prophecy of doom for Laṅkā was true, he assembles his army.**

* Then, as the unvanquished elder brother, lord of the three worlds, whose name was Nārāy(ṇ) Rām, * lay on the gold-covered couch on the lap of King Sugrīb, who cherished him while he slept, * his serenity
28. was disturbed (28). The lord, most high, was tenderly watched over by the two monkeys; * Hanumān lovingly held his right hand; Aṅgad kept

(28) watch and held his other hand. * Bibhek was stationed behind him.
The prince now woke up, looked up at the sky and saw the darkness.
* Then the lord, protector of the world, roused himself and eagerly
questioned the astrologer, Bibhek. * "O Bibhek, the sun is excessively
clouded over. Its course is not just as usual. * What is the reason for
this present darkness? All the directions are sombre and unlit. We can
see no sun." * Bibhek paid his respects, bowing his head, and, with
hands placed together, gave careful answer, * "O lord, this is the
demon Rāb(ṇ) of our race. He has proceeded, roaring like a lion, * out
to the northern palace. And the ministers and pages, 16,000 of them,
29. * are commanded by him to open parasols (29) of victory, which fill the
surface of the sky. The heavens are entirely obscured! * They have
come to have a look at the monkey troops. He has heard that you,
lord, supporter of the earth, have marched your army off in retreat.
* And the reason why the sun is invisible, clouded over, on every side
just as though it was night time * is because they have opened their
parasols and umbrellas and these form a cloud right across the
radiance of the sun's orb." * Rām listened to Bibhek's explanation.
Then he proceeded to demonstrate his victorious arrow, Ariddhacandr.
* He flexed the precious arrow of victory in his hands, regarding far
into the sky. * Directing his bow and powerful arrow, he shot towards
those parasols of victory and demolished them!

* Before this, King Rāb(ṇ) had been thinking cheerful thoughts and
30. feeling very pleased with himself. He had questioned (30) his master
astrologer. * "Prahet, my minister, those ascetics, Rām and Laksm(ṇ),
have by now set in motion the retreat of their army, have they not?"
* "No, not yet," answered the astrologer Prahet. "At this moment Rām
is sleeping * tranquilly on the lap of Sugrīb. At his illustrious feet, the
two supreme monkey princes are guarding him with care. * Hanumān
is tenderly holding his right hand, while Aṅgad is watching lovingly
over his left." * When Rāb(ṇ) heard Prahet tell him this different story,
he grew angry and anxious. His eyes glared. * "I heard Atikāy himself
say that General Rakkhasen had fought with the monkeys; * both
Hanumān and Rakkhasen died and many others, both ogres and
monkeys, came to their end in that forest. * Why, then, does the
prophecy from the books of astrology declare quite clearly that
Hanumān is still alive? * Atikāy, you said Rām had marched his army
31. away — but Rām (31) is still there! Why did you come and tell me lies?"

* Atikāy crouched down low. "Royal lord," he said, "I beg you to
consider. * I did not distort the facts — I would not dare. It was indeed
one of Rakkhasen's men who came running to me saying that he had
fought beside him. * Our ogres and the horde of enemy monkeys,

(31) striving mightily for victory, had fought each other to the death. * It
seems that they saw a different monkey, a particularly tough and
powerful one, and they just imagined that it was Hanumān." * The
astrologer Prahet cleared the matter up. "The monkey which fought
against General Rakkhasen," he said, * "was called Rukkhara: the
mighty. He was large, fleshy and bold — just as Atikāy suggested.
* Lord, all the monkeys who are in the service of that Prince Rām * are
huge, resolute and daring; they are conversant with the books of the
32. magic arts; their race is that of the monkey kings. (32) * And there are
some superior monkeys of great power, eighteen of them, valiant
indeed. * All of them are audacious and tough. They have performed
heroic deeds, showing a power equivalent to that of the determined
Hanumān. * They lead a force of soldiers, thousand upon thousand, of
great physical strength, supporters of the lord Rām."

* Rāb(ṇ) considered. "Prahet, my minister! With regard to the
ascetics, Rām and Laksm(ṇ), what do you think about them now?"
* The astrologer Prahet made his calculations and then said, "He has
closed one eye and is flexing an arrow * of which the name is
Ariddhacandr, the august. Rām is holding it in his hands and stroking
its shaft. * Look straight up in the sky! It seems he has aimed the
arrow at the heavens! * Now he has turned to look behind him and is
chatting with Bibhek, whose skills are manifold. * And now he is
turning to look. He is looking over here! It is probable — or certain! —
33. that there will now be destruction and (33) confusion." * Prahet cried
out, "Look! It strikes! Rām has shot his arrow straight here!" * Prahet
had not finished speaking his warning to take care when the great
heavens were rent. * Rām had sent off the sharp Ariddhacandr. The
deafening noise of the arrow crashed through the skies, resounding like
100,000 thunderbolts at one time, with their rumbling reverberations.
All the palaces of heaven felt a tremor. * The regal Sumeru made a
mumbling noise as if the heaven of the thirty-three would be uprooted
and the earth would turn over, upside down.

* Then the eminent master of men stationed his glorious army and
went into his pavilion. * His young brother was with him and all those
uncountable monkey soldiers * were in attendance here, there and
everywhere, thousand upon thousand of them, thronging round.
* They approached to speak jovially with their sovereign, feeling
34. pleased with (34) their own great powers and forthcoming triumph in
battle. * "Laṅkā is within our very grasp," they said, "whatever the
number of King Rāb(ṇ)'s demons." * Rām replied to his simian
officers and men, saying that he really depended upon their immense
strength. * All had the power and vigour of youth, the strength to kill

(34) the enemy ogres and put an end to that race for ever.
* Then that godless creature, King Rāb(ṇ), descended from the
ogres, showed off his powers for victory. * He yoked horses to his
carriage, dressed himself splendidly and travelled up into the air across
the sky, * taking with him the noble Princess Sītā, royal consort, chief
wife of Rām. * Flying magically by means of his demoniac powers, he
came to flaunt her in front of Rām. * He raised his victory parasol high
above him in the sky and floated along close to Rām's fine
35. encampment. * The afternoon sun was just going down as (35) the
high-born prince caught sight of the ogre's carriage, * its royal horses
haltered in their yokes, grand and elegant, as it went through the air.
* It shone with dazzling brightness, glittering with colours, resplendent
in the sky. * Rām questioned the astrologer Bibhek, "What is that
brilliant object which is approaching?" * "It is a royal carriage,"
Bibhek answered with respect, "and in it is the demon Rāb(ṇ). In the
back of the carriage is your treasured consort, Sītā!" * Rām felt
furiously angry with this demon of overweening might. * He who
possessed great power in his sharp arrows, took the mighty Bāyavās of
astounding properties * and sent it speeding forth to the ramparts
which hold the *cakravāla*. * The fine diamond-covered carriage was
36. dented (36). The banners and parasols of victory were flung in all
directions, quite ruined! * The sky was clouded, obscured by a
darkness. All the corners of the heavens stirred, trembling dreadfully.
* The whole troupe of divinities, dumb-founded and in terror, flew
away, struggling against each other in their haste, quaking with fear,
* while the arrogant demon, Rāb(ṇ), summoned Bisnukār to come and
mend the carriage * and make it beautiful as before with decoration
and glorious banners and parasols of exactly the original form. * Then
Rāb(ṇ) drove his horse-drawn carriage straight up into the air again!
* Because of that demon's overweening arrogance, he attempted acts of
aggression without a thought about the consequences to himself.
* Rām's anger knew no abatement; it raged increasingly, deep within
his divine, intelligent mind. * "Bibhek, my astrologer!" he said,
37. "Laksm(ṇ), my brother, (37) and all of you men of the army, * this
arrogant demon has now gone too far! This is an added affront and
harassment. * I would send my sharp arrow Brahmās to strike the
demon but it would cause poison to spread and reach the princess."
* Laksm(ṇ), Bibhek and the attendants all with one voice spoke to
dissuade him. * And so he used magic craft and divine power, mighty
strengths of that lord. * He pointed his finger of supreme supernatural
power at Rāb(ṇ) — and the latter felt as if he had overeaten, very faint
and trembling. * He tossed and turned, shivered and shook and lay in

(37) the carriage as if he would die that instant! * The driver turned the carriage and horses round and drove back through the air, high in the sky. * Rāb(ṇ) reached home and considered the matter. "I might have
38. died! (38) * The power of my perfect virtue protected my life. That was how I escaped and arrived home. * I am amazed at the power of Rām's virtue; his strength and performance of magic are magnificent. * I was very lucky indeed that I did not die! This Rām *is* Nārāy(ṇ) in changed form. * He is making an attempt upon the land of Laṅkā. He has already crossed over. However can I stop him? * He is making an attempt upon my person. He can do this — the stars, all-powerful, are counteracting my birth-horoscope! * The signs of the zodiac are against me. The Moon is against me. All are distinctly in conflict with the whole of my established kingdom. * And the outlook for Laṅkā is very bad indeed; the outlook for the whole people and for all our populated areas is bad. * This is what Bibhek prophesied according to
39. (39) the Books, while I myself did not accept what he said! * I went so far as to drive him away in anger. Alas for me! What an ignorant fool I was! * Brothers should stay together, whether they act rightly or wrongly. I have let the enemy take him under their wing — and they will have him as their eyes and ears! * As a learned teacher, familiar with the treatises on the magic arts, he will be making his calculations, conferring with them and giving victory to them! * I shall most likely fall into their hands — my life is at stake; Laṅkā too will go to them. * It would seem that the time has come when I shall die because of Sītā. I shall die and destruction will come to my country too. * Destruction will come to the generals of the royal family and to all the army, the whole force of servants and soldiers. * And all the princes too, powerful and bold, are now likely to meet their death."

* Then the lord of Laṅkā sent word to the generals to assemble 3,000
40. (40) men. * They came in densely-packed hordes, a vast and mighty host, rank upon rank, endlessly * and waited deferentially in attendance upon the king. The assembly hall of the evil Dasamukh had been made ready. * Rāb(ṇ) was seated upon a magnificent rug in the bejewelled regal hall, in his extensive palace, * where gems were set in the glittering lattices. It resembled the residence of Indr * in the blessed heaven of the thirty-three when all the gods in that far-off heavenly place come to attend upon him.

8.40–56. **Rām sends Aṅgad to tell Rāb(ṇ) to take his demons and leave Laṅkā. On the way Aṅgad quells the elephant Bhakkhanes. Aṅgad demands to be placed on a level with Rāb(ṇ) when giving his message. Rāb(ṇ)**

agrees first that he shall be level with Kumbhakār(ṇ), then that he shall be level with Indrajit.

(40) * Now the victorious elder prince required Aṅgad to go with a
message to King Rāb(ṇ). * The princes had assembled the huge force of
simians, too numerous to count, thronging round them, and * were
seated, handsome lords, on thrones in their fine pavilion, their bright,
bejewelled dwelling, with a breeze wafting over them. * Aṅgad was to
be a royal envoy, taking the message to Laṅkā and acting as spokes-
41. man. (41) * Magnificent as the sunlight, possessed of invincible power,
the simian Aṅgad * could rapidly memorise the matter and keep it in
his mind and was clearly well acquainted with the ways of the world.
* He could remember, provide answers, give explanations, speak
pleasantly and be proud and dignified. * He was a descendant of the
monkey race and also of the line of the great, glorious ogre kings;
* and further, he was so immense that, when it was an occasion for
being forceful, he was superb. * In the grandeur of his physique, of his
family, of his successes and of his personal prestige, that monkey
prince was exceptional.

* The prince spoke words of sweet sincerity, serenely giving * his
instructions. "O Aṅgad, you will take my command to the evil
Dasamukh. * You will bear the royal message of Prince Nārāy(ṇ) Rām.
42. * I am sending you (42) to King Rāb(ṇ) to give him my explanation of
the whole situation: * 'Rām is Nārāy(ṇ) himself in changed form, come
to live here in this transformation. * The evil Dasamukh is an erring
enemy, a villainous vandal and coward, who has committed the sin of
adultery. * His passion has led to a wickedness which is clearly
increasing, knowing no abatement or satiety. * And so all the gods
have invited Nārāy(ṇ) to be born as the great lord, Rām. * Now the
wicked Dasamukh has stolen the princess, beloved of the lord Rām,
* and the prince has followed his wife, Sītā, and has just now, after a
long time, arrived here. * Why is Rāb(ṇ) still so full of pride? He gives
not a thought to the prince's arrow, hungry for its food! * The prince
sends this command to the evil Dasamukh: that he should assemble his
43. attendant forces and then depart from (43) Laṅkā. * Otherwise, the
prince will take Dasamukh himself as food for his sharp arrow — no
doubt of that — out on the battlefield. * Let the evil Dasamukh not
delay a moment because the prince is waiting for him.'"

* When the instructions had been given Aṅgad set off, bearing the message of the protector of men, * and proceeded fearlessly as if to attack everyone in the demon city! * Through his great power he turned himself into seven mighty mountains which sparkled with

(43) burnished light, * their brightness reaching out, copper-coloured, like the red glow of the sun's rays flashing through the forest. * The glaring light shone as far as the ogre Dasamukh who was astounded when he saw its dazzling radiance. * Then Aṅgad waved his tail round seven times, beating the ground with it, almost smashing the earth, * — and the vast ocean was turned to spattering spray, crashing waves and
44. white horses (44)! * A mighty tremor went through king and kingdom. It seemed as though the quaking, shuddering Laṅkā would be overturned. * "This is extraordinary," thought Rāb(ṇ). "What monstrous noise is that, resounding with mighty reverberations?" He sent an official galloping off on his horse to look at the gate of the fortress. * The ogre saw the radiant Aṅgad, his tail lying trailing along the ground, * and informed the demon lord, Rāb(ṇ), that there was an enormous monkey there. * Then Rāb(ṇ) commanded him to tell the demons on guard at all the gates of the fortifications, * officers and men, to barricade the entrances of the fortresses, their weapons ranged together in close formation at the ready.

* Aṅgad, moving forward swiftly and smoothly, intrepid, undismayed by the ogres, * broke down the gate with a kick and, lion-like, pro-
45. ceeded to destroy (45) the fortress of many ramparts. * Five thousand ogres were beaten and crushed to death in the outermost stone ring of the fortifications. * Aṅgad crossed straight over that fortification and proceeded as far as the rampart of iron. * He considered it quite unnecessary to kill the very ordinary demons who guarded the gates * and therefore stepped forward across the iron fortification and across the bronze fortification * to reach the decorative brass rampart and cross, without a care, to the copper rampart. * But there, his expression wild for he was in rut, was the powerful Bhakkhanes, keeper of the central area.

46. * The teachers and aged Brahmins (46) were making sacrifices outside the city. They had begun their ritual there and were murmuring prayers, meditating and praying for victory: * that the country might have peace and be without fear; that any sinister threat to them should vanish; that they should vanquish such foes as attacked them; * that the king and people of that pleasant land should be content and the royal family well and happy; * that the army, officers and men, should be free from illness, every one, through the power of their virtue; * that such peace should come to the royal city as the Brahmanic scriptures foretell — with accuracy as a general rule — for the king; * that there should be peace and prosperity at all times with the forests fruitful and food of all kinds in plenty.

* And just then Aṅgad proceeded towards the centre of the mighty

(46) city. * He brandished his sharp, bejewelled sword and called out
threats. "So, you demons! I am here! * I shall capture the whole city of
47. Laṅkā. I shall thump your heads until they are bruised and swollen (47)
and all the hair drops out! * I am Aṅgad, the mighty, and I bring the
royal command of Prince Rām Nārāy(ṇ)." * Then Bhakkhanes' oil burst
forth and flowed from its sac, spreading, seeping as far as his mouth.
* As it flowed he approached, with mouth agape, to fight fearlessly with
Aṅgad, both of them with mighty strength. * Those adversaries met and
fought against each other while the demons fled, raising the dust in
clouds. * The *kumbhaṇḍa* ogres scattered, terrified, in all directions into
the far distance, all quaking inwardly. * A rumbling sound like that of a
storm reverberated in the skies while the waves of the sea brimmed over,
pouring in different directions. * Everywhere, earthquakes were felt. All
the animals scattered. Elephants and horses went off from their stables
in all directions. * And the people were fleeing away all around. The
magnificent Aṅgad was fighting with Bhakkhanes. * Aṅgad fended him
48. off and attacked him with casual (48) ease. He grasped hold of
Bhakkhanes by the neck, applying pressure and said, * "Bhakkhanes,
you evil good-for-nothing, I would put you to death this very moment
* but I fear that in every foreign land the word would go round that, as I
brought the royal command, * a strong elephant came out to fight me.
This would seem to degrade that royal command of my master for my
person would be sullied * and the heroism of the master of men would
be clouded over by this fight with the wretched elephant who guards the
city centre. * And what honour will result from this which might be
sufficient to elevate me in time to a position of glory? * Well,
Bhakkhanes, pull yourself together. In the course of time, you will suffer
the most fearful terror. * The lord Isūr gave you your name, letting you
be called Bhakkhanes. * How can you treat so nonchalantly the special
49. order of (49) Prince Nārāy(ṇ) of mighty power? * It was Nārāy(ṇ) and
the lord Isūr himself who placed you in this world to be born with this
form. * Tomorrow word will reach Rām. He will destroy Laṅkā and
Rāb(ṇ) too, will be eliminated. * He will liquidate all of the demon race,
all the arrogant ogres. It will be the end of the kingdom of Laṅkā.
* Where will you put yourself to escape from that sharp arrow, the
great, unvanquished Brahmās?"

* Then Bhakkhanes was afraid as he heard those words from the
prince's royal messenger. * Quivering and quaking, he ran pell-mell
into the hermitage where he stayed in the shade. * "Aṅgad," he said,
"you go. I will stay in this outer place. I cannot oppose you. * You
bring a message of authority from the great Nārāy(ṇ). Off you go, then,
50. in your own way. (50) * It seems likely that you will capture Laṅkā and

(50) destroy Rāb(ṇ) as well. O why did he steal the prince's wife? * It was because of his vile baseness and failure to realise that the prince would destroy him completely and that * death and destruction would come to his beloved young brother and sons and to all the military force, officers and men, all of them. * And now it is hardly likely that we shall remain alive, we and Lord Rāb(ṇ) himself and all his kinsmen! * Destruction will come to the whole city of Laṅkā as it falls straight into the hands of Rām and Laksm(ṇ)!"

* Then the mighty King Dasamukh had heard the excessive noise made by Bhakkhanes and Aṅgad * of victorious power, as they fought each other. He sent a page to run and have a good look. * Aghast, he
51. came to report to Dasamukh. "A bold monkey (51) is fighting against Bhakkhanes! * But it will not be very long now before he is dead for he will be defeated by the might of his arm. Bhakkhanes will get him!" * A further page returned and approached to tell his news. "Lord, Bhakkhanes was just now * butting but with diminishing strength — to the point of defeat! Aṅgad pursued him, sending him running off to the shelter of the hermitage! * For Aṅgad is extremely angry. He is an important messenger from Rām. * At the gate he met with Bhakkhanes and wildly went after him. He is a huge, determined, loudly menacing creature. * Aṅgad crushed him almost to death but Bhakkhanes struggled free and managed to reach the hermitage in a dejected state. * Aṅgad has now gone off to stop and rest in the court of Law on the right."

* Rāb(ṇ) heard about the messenger of Rām and gave orders to lay rugs in the bejewelled hall, * to have plenty of chief ministers duly
52. present and (52) paying attention in case the message caused hostilities to break out. * Royal lions and elephant-lions went stamping along and strong elephants with their marvellous trappings, rank upon rank. * The driver of the royal carriage and horses waved an iron rod. He was armed with sharp arrows and all kinds of equipment. * Military officers were distributed along the way, guarding every point of entry. * When all was ready, a messenger was sent to tell Aṅgad to approach and pay his respects to His Majesty. * Aṅgad made it clear in accordance with protocol: "I, the important royal messenger of the overlord, Prince Rām, * and, moreover, the son of Bālī, am sent by my sovereign, the lord Rām. * When Dasamukh gives me a seat, with whom shall I be on a level, in view of the honour due to my royal
53. orders?" * Then the messenger went to inform Rāb(ṇ) of (53) Aṅgad's instruction.

* Rāb(ṇ), shaking with rage, made an effort to suppress his feelings and replied, * "My chief ministers and officers, you must take care,

(53) each one of you, and not be forgetful of yourselves. * In the past a common white monkey came and engaged in a fight about taking fruit. * The result was the destruction of our army, including my beloved son, Sahasakumār, for he died too; * and when the proud Indrajit shot arrows to surround him and they dragged him this way and that, trailing him as they brought him along, * he kicked them down, chased them until they sulked and hid. They only just got him here — and then he tricked us with his lies! * He destroyed our whole city — our fault for not using our brains! * And now the son of Bālī himself! We should regard him with circumspection and protect ourselves rigorously. * We will carry out a ruse so as to capture him successfully. As he approaches
54. (54) we will give him a good beating, all of us helping, and we will kill him. * We will not let him escape to reach the palace. We will have him put to death in the courtyard. * First, however,[31] we will tell him we are treating him as a person of substance with a most elevated seat, while we receive the royal command * and that we shall let him have a place equal to that of the great Kumbhakār(ṇ), the young prince, our brother, who has no equal among the ministers."

* Then King Rāb(ṇ), having thought it out, sent an official to go and arrange a room for receiving Aṅgad, * saying that now he had prescribed that Aṅgad should have as elevated a seat as that of his own young brother, * the mighty Kumbhakār(ṇ) himself, born of the same womb, his second king, who was great indeed. * Aṅgad instantly replied with a rebuke, * "You rascal of a demon page! * I ought to be placed on
55. a level with Rāb(ṇ) because (55) the command of Rām, my magnificent lord, * has pervaded my whole body. His divine command is quite clearly in every part of me. * My body or mind, as I wait to expound the message, or my words as I do so are all an essential part of his command. * How can you let me be placed on a level with Kumbhakār(ṇ) as though my visit to Rāb(ṇ) were a social one?" * The ogre official went to inform Rāb(ṇ) of Aṅgad's message. * "Well then," said Rāb(ṇ), "run and rouse Aṅgad and have him come straight here. * He will be placed as high as Indrajit, my eldest son, of surpassing nobility, scion of a royal line of kings."

* The official went back and respectfully approached Aṅgad, inviting him to go along. * "His Majesty King Rāb(ṇ)," he said, "has sent me to
56. speak with you, Aṅgad (56) of great might. * He will allow you to be seated as high as Indrajit, his own eldest son, * close to the grand, royal throne, raised on a royal rug and beneath a canopy of white parasols * in the forecourt of his palace of bejewelled tiers, very close to the great king and beside the prince. * His Majesty would have you go straight there because he wishes to hear the message you bring."

8.56–67. Aṅgad kills the ogre soldiers round him, enters the palace and places himself as high as Rāb(ṇ), by coiling his tail and sitting on it. Rāb(ṇ) sends for Maṇḍogirī, Aṅgad's mother, so that he shall at least pay his respects to her. Aṅgad gives his message, fights his way out, kills four ogres sent to catch him and reaches home.

* Then Aṅgad, in the middle of the troops of soldiers, had no fear of the demon throng and was ready to be off. * Lions, elephant-lions, tigers, elephants and horses and uncountable ogres crowded round him. * They wielded every kind of vicious weapon, drawn or raised, here, there and everywhere, athwart each other and impeding each other, in densely-packed array. * Aṅgad knew them; they would kill him. So, bawling out loudly, he went to the attack, bringing them, terrified, to an abrupt halt. * The ogres received a shock and went
57. quite pale with fear. (57) In their bewilderment, they stabbed and struck at each other! * The elephants went off after each other, noisily contending against each other with their tusks and going swiftly round and round in tumbling confusion. * The royal lions, elephant-lions, lions, horses and charioteers were overturned in a tumultuous whirling mêlée. * Loud yells resounded from their gaping mouths as ogres fled, moaning. Piercing shrieks were heard as, in a daze, they turned frantically round and round. * They hacked with their knives and, with heavy, thudding sounds, they ran, forcing a way, flinging, beating, stamping, pounding. The din was excessive. * It seemed as though there was a tornado with the wind whirling, whistling and whisking up objects.

* Hearing this noise, the evil King Dasamukh thought the ogres had surrounded and captured Aṅgad and had just put him to death * but, when he opened the window and stood up at it, he saw his forces dead. He signalled by a wink to all his officers. * "Let us take no notice," he said, "and behave as if we did not know. Let us pretend we have
58. assembled to wait for him." * He sent a (58) messenger to go and summon Aṅgad, telling him the king wanted to hear the actual message. * Aṅgad should come immediately; the king was expecting him. He should proceed there that very minute.

* The huge Aṅgad, so capable, resolved to go into Laṅkā alone. * Eagerly he looked at the magnificent city through the gate by the high eastern rampart. * Glittering jewels of all nine kinds[27] adhered as a decorative design to the pinnacles of the glorious palace. * In a myriad traceries of gleaming gold were set forth tongues of flame, stars of splendid brilliance. * The royal couch of gold, bejewelled, was beautifully sculpted in the form of flowers; and in the court were

(58) sparkling mirrors. * Everywhere there were dignified attendants in
great numbers, beautifully adorned. * Aṅgad looked at the superlative
women of the court, like divine *apsarās*, godly ladies of the heaven of
the thirty-three. * Some held lotuses for garlands; they were plucking
59. and shaping the flowers (59) and petals and spreading them out to plait
them. * Some were smoothing their pretty faces; some were combing
and braiding their hair and putting in it the golden flowers of the
Crinum asiaticum. * With garlands entwined round their necks and
with eyebrows like bows, they were the most elegant of women. * They
were amusing themselves. Some were laughing delightfully, some
chattering in a happy crowd together. * Their eyes were bright in their
eager faces. Their lips were covered with betel. They smiled prettily
with blackened teeth. * The beauty of some was in their lithe bodies;
their breasts were like golden fruits placed upon them. * Their cheeks
were full; their ears, decked with earrings, gleamed with comely
whiteness. * The evil Dasamukh, the high and mighty, had heavenly
maidens ready to hand in attendance upon him. * Aṅgad saw all these
splendid indications of high rank, the numerous important ministers
60. and the possessions in endless plenty. (60) * No bird of any kind could
fly high enough to pass over the ramparts of Laṅkā!

* Then the prodigious Aṅgad, undismayed by the demon throng,
went straight into the palace, * past Indrajit, and approached to take
up a position level with the evil Dasamukh! * He saw Dasamukh
raised up on the coverlet of his throne decorated with crystal,
sapphires, coral and other gems. * To make the royal message seem
more important, Aṅgad wound his great long tail round and round,
writhing, encircling. * He folded it round to sit on it, winding it up in
many, many layers. When he sat down, he was raised up very high,
* higher than Dasamukh! The latter, furiously angry as he perceived
this, glared directly at him. * Aṅgad put his feet astride and leaned
backwards. Rāb(ṇ) felt crosser and crosser but suppressed his anger
61. and affected a mild manner (61) * because it was his intention to ask
questions about the message and then, when he had everything clear,
he would of course capture and kill Aṅgad.

* "Well, Aṅgad," Rāb(ṇ) said, "since, my boy, you are the son of Maṇḍogirī, * fathered by King Bālī, and I am your mother's husband, why do you not show me some respect? * After all, I am your step-father. Was there ever anything so stupid in the world as your behaviour? Don't put on such airs. * Even if you do not raise your hands politely, do at least consider sitting properly. * If you want to know the answers to questions about your origins, my lad, they are low! I fear you are not on a level with princes. * But your mother,

(61) Maṇḍogirī, attends upon me as my beloved queen. * Even if you do not show respect to me, what about her, then? How could you not show respect to your mother?"

62. (62) * Rāb(ṇ) sent a page to summon his treasured queen and Maṇḍogirī arrived. * Aṅgad thought deeply. When he looked at her and definitely recognised her as his mother, * he raised his left hand as far up as his stomach in greeting to her. "I am happy," he said, "to offer my respectful greeting to you, mother. * You are equal to five lotuses. I bear a most profound sense of gratitude to you, as deep as the ocean. * As for offering one hand in giving my respects, it is in recollection of what you have done for me, O queen. * When I was conceived with all my five parts and lay in your womb, * the simian king, Bālī, scooped me out of your womb and took me away to care for me. * I am taking the opportunity offered by Rām's command; this left hand of mine salutes your revered womb. * Even the enlightened Buddhas, numerous as the grains of sand,[32] would not have avoided
63. (63) being conceived. * They praised the great good done for them by their mothers. This is called the 'maternal benefaction' and it is unique, matchless.

* "As for you, Dasamukh, lost soul that you are, what good have you done me that you should dare to tell me to show respect to you? * All you have done is great harm to all beings. You have gone so far as to steal a wife, heaping crime upon crime. * When my father was still alive he captured you, tied you up and put you at the foot of my hammock * to swing it and rock me. Your ten mouths sang suitable songs — rather loudly and clearly! * If I raised my hands in salute to you, it would really be totally ridiculous — an act of forgetful muddle-headedness! * To greet with deference the servant who had to rock the foot of my cradle would be to besmirch my honour.

* "Now, evil Dasamukh, the lord Rām sends me to speak with you.
64. (64) * Kindly listen to the royal Word, the command and message of the prince, our noble lord. * Rām is no other than Nārāy(ṇ) himself. The gods of all the ten directions invited him to come * because you, the evil Dasamukh, plundering villain, came guilefully to steal and ravish the wives of the gods from all regions * including the six far-away heavens of desire. All were the lovers of the crafty demon Dasamukh. * And it was not only goddesses that you stole; you stole Rām's wife, his noble consort and loved one. * At this very minute, the prince is coming after you, intending to find his noble consort. * The prince has been on his way here for a long time. All his unvanquished arrows are at the ready, starved of their food. * The prince instructs you to prepare your throng of attendants to be off to the war at the

(64) double! * The prince will have you as food for his sharp arrow out there
65. on the battlefield — no doubt of that! * Do not (65) think of dilly-
dallying because the prince's arrows are all hungry for food, their
stomachs hurting." * Having made his speech, Aṅgad stretched out a
hand for some betel from Rāb(ṇ)'s tray and nonchalantly chewed it
there and then!

* As to King Rāb(ṇ), he was in a furious temper once again, his
uncontrollable anger renewed. * He rose and went to slap Aṅgad but
Aṅgad slipped out of the way and knocked Rāb(ṇ)'s hand away. * He
struck back at the evil Dasamukh who received the blow and fell over in
a deep swoon. * The vast horde of godless creatures warily prepared
themselves and then surged forward pell-mell, all jabbering, to surround
* Aṅgad, who let them encircle him closely. Some grasped him; some
came round him and pressed tightly upon him; * but, as Aṅgad steeled
himself, his long tail, which he flung round and round, tightened firmly
on the demons, enveloping them. * Then he leaped up in the air,
66. whisking away the sunstone from (66) Rāb(ṇ)'s head! * As the powerful
Aṅgad sprang up into the air, all the demons enclosed by his great tail
* were torn loose and scattered in pieces as though someone had cut
them up with a sword. * And the pinnacle of the palace was dented as
well, as Aṅgad gave it piercing blows before flying far into the sky.

* Meanwhile Rāb(ṇ) became conscious and opened his eyes. He stood
up and seized his sharp sword and his great bejewelled weapon, the
wheel. * Just then four *kumbhaṇḍa* ogres, who were *aides de camp*, of
enormous size, bold and brave, * approached to dissuade Rāb(ṇ). "Let
us do this for you. We can capture Aṅgad. * Lord, we beg you, please be
calm. Let your mind be free from worry." * Then the four gigantic ogres
67. went in a flash far up into the air and (67) strove mightily to catch up
with Aṅgad. * The latter, as he flew, looked back and, seeing the ogres
pursuing him, turned unhesitatingly and waited for them. * The
kumbhaṇḍa ogres swiftly came through the air and caught him up. They
fended and countered, all fighting together, hovering up there in the sky.
* The ogres joined forces to enter the contest, vying with each other. The
mighty monkey, transfixed, motionless, did not flinch. * He gave forth a
deafening cry at the demons, turned and assailed the heads of the *aides
de camp*, the great *kumbhaṇḍa* ogres. * They were destroyed, all four!
Their severed heads fell down to earth. * Aṅgad turned back home to
tell the news to the great master, Prince Nārāy(ṇ).

8.67–9.1. **Rāb(ṇ) decides to send Kumbhakār(ṇ) to destroy Rām's army. Kumbhakār(ṇ), wishing to restrain him, reminds him that the whole course**

of events arose from Sūrapanakhā's wilfulness. However, when accused of being afraid, Kumbhakār(ṇ) agrees to go.

68. * Then the demon king, Rāb(ṇ), learned how (68) his officers, ogres of royal descent, * had died, how all of them had slumped down annihilated. Rāb(ṇ) shook with a fury like the fire which burned in that bygone age. * He spoke. "My great prestige as a man of substance has turned sour. My distinguished reputation as one of the line of the most mighty Brahm has turned sour. * It is not right that they should be killed, that they should admit defeat at the hands of mere mortals and four-footed monkeys. * So now I will obliterate both those men and their feeble-minded jungle apes. * We will have our revenge — and just let them see what a shock it will be for them! We will not have this ridiculous behaviour, this unawareness of the might of Rāb(ṇ). * This time, to quell them, I must use the powers of Kumbhakār(ṇ). He shall go forth to fight and achieve a heroic victory. * For he has mighty strength. He possesses a sharp club[33] of great efficiency which can lay
69. low all the (69) three worlds. * Brahm granted him this, placing it in his hand, to make him the foremost man in the army of the demons."

* Then Rāb(ṇ) commanded an officer to tell his princely young brother, * Kumbhakār(ṇ), to come with all haste to attend upon his king and elder, Dasamukh. * The ten-necked one explained what had happened so that his beloved brother had a good grasp of the situation. * Kumbhakār(ṇ) was a prince who adhered to what was right and, when he thoroughly understood the matter, he begged to disagree. * "Lord and elder," he said, "do not start this enmity. * The whole reason for this situation is Sūrapanakhā's saucy desire for a human husband — in conflict with our conventions. * And you, my lord, did
70. not keep to the ten-fold law of kings when you were a party (70) to the furtive stealing of Sītā, * chief consort of that prince who is journeying on foot through the forest as an ascetic, the great and powerful Nārāy(ṇ) Rām. * To act like this was out of keeping with the practice of kings, out of keeping with the way of the Law. I beg you, cast aside your lustful passion. * Please hand Sītā back to Rām. From then onwards there will be peace and tranquillity. * The whole people, both within the city and outside it, will be content; the chiefs of the demon kingdom will be content. * Rām is the *avatār* of Nārāy(ṇ). There is therefore no one who can defeat him in battle."

* Listening to these reminders from Kumbhakār(ṇ), Rāb(ṇ) was terribly angry and stamped his feet with resounding thuds. * "What temerity the rascal has! To dare so lightheartedly to oppose me! To say that I go so far as to be lustful in passion! * He would be subservient to

71. monkeys! He is afraid of two humans. He does not dare (71) to hold up his head and go out to fight! * He comes to tell me of his disapproval and oppose me, not daring to confront them in battle. He extols the might of the tough Rām. * I am sorry for the race of demons. They admit defeat at the superior hands of Rām and Laksm(ṇ)!"

* Kumbhakār(ṇ) heard these words of clear purport from the ten-faced king and spoke eagerly. * "I am not afraid of anyone! If it is your royal desire, send me to fight. Then I will offer * my life, with no thought of myself. I will endure death and destruction. I will do battle, offering my skills to you, my lord." * Hearing this, Rāb(ṇ) was delighted. He changed his attitude and said, "Well now, *this* is my own young brother! * I want you to go out to the contest and win an outright victory. The achievement of your powerful right arm shall be remembered until another age." * He gave orders to Mahodar to marshal the army; to have it done at the double, so that they would be able to march off on their mission in good time.

72. (72) * Then Kumbhakār(ṇ) took his leave and decked his person handsomely in the ogre style with the trappings of war. * He led his men directly towards the dwelling of Rām and Laksm(ṇ), feeling eager to join battle. * And so, with much clamour, their army went forth, a vast force indeed, dispersing through the forest. * At that time the princely Rām, resplendent as the moon's circle, was in his pavilion, * in the midst of this army, of which the fighting sections, reaching out in all directions, in close formation, waited in attendance upon their lord.

9.1. (9.1) * The monkey host, vast beyond all norms, was eager and excited, ready to strive in the contest, blow for blow, giving of their best.

9.1–13. **When Kumbhakār(ṇ) surrounds his army, Rām sends Bibhek to invite him to come over to them. Kumbhakār(ṇ) refuses and criticises Rām for killing Bālī. Rām sends Bibhek and Laksm(ṇ) to explain that Bālī's death was due to retribution.**

* The whole demon army, with its sections of the left and right all combined, accompanied Kumbhakār(ṇ). * A deafening clamour resounded. Overweening in confidence about their attack, they were eager to contend and deal their blows. * As they invaded the forest with crashes and thuds, their noise rose up aloft and the earth was stirred by a tremor. * They marched up close to the army of the master of men, drawing up their ranks, paying attention to the formation of their troops, * distributing them and stationing them so as to face the

(1) royal enemies and join battle along every route, in every gap and at every
point of infiltration. * When night came to the heavens and, with its cover
of darkness, made the sky disappear from view, * Kumbhakār(ṇ), the
mighty, had completed his encircling action. He approached to take a
secret look at the army of the great Rām.
2. * (2) The two princes were seated in their pavilion of victory with its
bejewelled decoration, their large, lofty palace of gold. * Like the
shining moon, glowing with burnished light amid its throng of stars,
* so was the Lord Nārāy(ṇ), attended by all the royal simian soldiers
and their officers and ministers. * The prince looked up at the distant
sky and saw it was as if the glowing star of Venus, twinkling * at the
other brightly-shining constellations had no disfigurement in its radiant
beauty * but had two orbs set closely together! No cloud was there to
mar or cover them. * The prince, the great, enlightened One, spoke to
the astrologer Bibhek, questioning him. * "O Bibhek, we have come
here, bringing our army of great simians, * and have built a road to
3. cross (3) the mighty sea, uniting to capture this kingdom and to fight
for victory. * Now Venus has two stars rising in the heavens side by
side! * What is this: bad or good? Do investigate how things are, using
your capacity to explain events."
* Bibhek saluted the master of men and addressed the great princes,
* "Lords, this is the young brother of the demon Rāb(ṇ), mighty in
deeds of surpassing heroism. * He is known as Kumbhakār(ṇ), the
great, the victorious, and is second in rank only to King Rāb(ṇ).
* With regard to the appearance of these two stars of Venus close
together, they are the gleaming gems * set on the top of the crown of
the royal Prince Kumbhakār(ṇ). * At this moment, august lord, he is
4. himself approaching to look at your army." (4) * The prince heard
Bibhek's able description of the appearance and heroic might * of the
great and renowned ogre, Prince Kumbhakār(ṇ), of his prodigious
physical strength, * of his determination and of his fine, large build. He
was clever, quick and bold. He was astonishingly — splendidly —
immense.
* Then Rām spoke with words of sweetness to Prince Bibhek.
* "Please go, Bibhek, to your elder brother. You will speak out against
his plan. * You will not let him now wrongfully contend against my
mighty power. It would not be easy for him. * I am Nārāy(ṇ) and this
arrow of mine, my usual one, is Death. * Even if there were as many as
a hundred thousand arrogant enemies, none would succeed in passing
beyond my arrow! * And that is why I am rather unhappy concerning
5. (5) the great Prince Kumbhakār(ṇ) whose descent is from the race of
royal ogres. * I would have you go straight to him now and tell him to

(5) come and stay with us. * *I* will give him a position of greater honour
than that of any demon lord of Laṅkā." * Bibhek had bowed and
clearly heard with pleasure the honey-sweet message of the lord of
compassion. * Showing great deference, he committed the message to
memory. * Bibhek took his leave respectfully and, bearing the
command of the lord, Rām, * went to the place where Kumbhakār(ṇ)
was, renowned ogre of the ancient line of the ten-necked King.

* Then Kumbhakār(ṇ) urged his ogre captains, in charge of all their
6. soldiers to the left and right, * to (6) select groups of ogres, choosing
those who were courageous and likely to be useful at striking blows on
his behalf. * He had them place every officer and every ordinary soldier
in a section with a commander. * When this was done, Kumbhakār(ṇ)
saw his young brother, Bibhek, arriving. He smouldered with anger.
* "Well, Bibhek," he said, "I would say that, in turning insolently into
an enemy of your own elder brother, you commit a heinous crime!
* You have dared to betray me, your elder, by bringing Rām across the
ocean[34] to crush Laṅkā. * I shall put you to death, because you are in
league with him."

* Then Bibhek replied to him, "Lord and elder, do not be so quick
to anger. * I am not here with the desire of doing harm to you, my
7. august brother. * I bring (7) a kindly message from Rām of mighty
strength, who has brought to perfection his power for heroic deeds.
* The prince's heart is wonderfully merciful and mild. He is
exceptional! * He is outstanding for his adherence to the Law. He is
leading all beings across to the delights of heaven. * Just now his royal
command has been graciously given to me, his servant, to come
directly * to you, whose power surpasses that of other demons, to you,
the mighty, the much-admired. The lord Rām has now acquired, by his
power for deeds of prowess, the greatest authority. * The prince
observes the precepts in the practice of asceticism. His performance of
the magic arts is always as efficacious as he wishes, * because in the
time of the second age of the world, he was Nārāy(ṇ), lord of the three
8. worlds. * Now in this third age of the world the prince has become (8)
Rām. * And now Rām feels particularly kindly and welcoming * towards
you, my august and princely brother. He is afraid you may be killed by his
sharp, destructive arrow. * That is why, my lord and elder, the prince has
sent me as his envoy to bring his command to you. * If you set your heart
on being the loyal and devoted servant of him whose merit deserves
praise, and go to be the attendant of the lord and protector of the world,
the Prince Nārāy(ṇ) Rām, * he, in his serene compassion, will elevate you
with the greatest honours, * letting you be shaded by a fine, tiered, white
canopy and sit on a throne on a level with his young brother."

(8) * Then Prince Kumbhakār(ṇ), having heard the will of the lord, Rām,
9. * spoke. "O Bibhek, you bring (9) a message which is sweet to hear and bears the mark of the prince's compassion. * But I bear the order of the king, our elder, my great sovereign and lord. * How can I cast aside the command of my dear king? I fear that would be to go beyond the limits of the established laws for service to the king. * I would be ashamed on three counts. First, there was that time when the royal Prince Rām * shot his arrow and himself felled King Bālī, — very wrongfully, to all appearances. * Bālī had been without a single fault upon him. It was just a quarrel between two brothers. * Why did Rām let himself, who was so great, be the subject of slander? * As for the retribution, Rām could not escape it; it bound him. * Second, if I were
10. to stay with you as his servant, Bibhek, * what if you and I (10) who are brothers should quarrel? It is probable that I should be like Bālī! * And it would be a source of calumny for me as for you, to have abandoned an elder to go over to Rām. * I say it is transgressing the ancient established laws for you to go and be the enemy of your elder brother. * The elder is equal to a father. You should not have done him a bad turn in return for his bad turn to you. * He is our lord. How can you have the temerity to treat your elder brother with scorn? * And then, it is not right that you should be the bearer of this royal message or lead this crowd of apes * who have struggled to build a road in the sea to come and destroy the ancient city of Laṅkā. * Your attitude, as I see it, is extremely hostile. You do not realise what a disgrace this will be in future times and far-distant places. * Matters involving dishonour are not usually regarded lightly by the wise.
11. * Thirdly, take the demon King Rāb(ṇ) (11) the mighty, of surpassing prestige and prosperity, * whose charming court ladies, in their tens of thousands, are so fine, divine beings, every one. * Now, Rām had just the Princess Sītā as his royal consort * and Rāb(ṇ) went to the length of stealing that chief wife from the master of men — a quite lawless act as one can see. * Because greed is his first consideration, he gave no thought to the great suffering which would have to be borne. * O, Bibhek, this is why I feel afraid that now I also may be affected by his disgrace. * I would prefer to die instantly now rather than become the servant of that great prince, Rām! * Now you go and give this information in accordance with my instructions to those two princely lords of the earth, will you? * I ask the prince to make his force ready
12. with care and come out on to the battlefield to fight. We shall be (12) rivals in the performance of heroic deeds. * As for my becoming the servant of Rām, I have no thought of joining him!"

* Bibhek took leave of his brother respectfully, returning directly to

(12) Prince Rām. * Bowing and saluting with palms together, Bibhek told everything to the prince as Kumbhakār(ṇ) had told him to do. * The two princes reacted with annoyance. "We must send a message concerning this slanderous criticism! * Bibhek, will you please go and inform him of the following matter. With regard to my shooting Bālī, * the reason for this had occurred much earlier. For King Bālī had made a promise * that he would give his queen, Tārā, to his young brother, Sugrīb; and having done so, he broke * that promise, made on oath. Since he was not true to his word, retribution came to cut off his life. * And so it was that he was destroyed by the sharp arrow, Brahmās,
13. (13) the great magic weapon of superlative victories, * which gave the august King Bālī the chance to reach the kingdom of heaven, abundant in riches." * Then Bibhek bowed in obeisance and respectfully spoke to his sovereign, "O supreme lord, * with regard to conveying your most righteous words, the expression of the distinguished thoughts of your marvellous intelligence, * I cannot go alone, because he has no mercy, no forbearance, no power of reflection. * I beg that the young prince may go with me. Then he will be respectful." * The prince realised that this was true and sensible. After reflection, therefore, he of the line of Bodhisatvas * ordered his young brother to take with him a large force of monkeys, with their officers and ministers. * Bibhek and the master of men raised their hands, bowed and took leave of the elder prince.

9.14–25. **Kumbhakār(ṇ) attacks Bibhek and Laksm(ṇ). His magic weapon strikes Laksm(ṇ)'s foot and from it a huge strychnine plant grows. Hanumān is sent to the Hemabānt to fetch three ingredients for Bibhek's cure for Laksm(ṇ). Then he is sent to Laṅkā to bring, from beneath the head of the sleeping Rāb(ṇ), the stone needed to grind the ingredients. When a little more time is required Hanumān halts the sun's chariot in its course. Laksm(ṇ) is cured.**

14. * Bibhek and Laksm(ṇ) took the message commanded by the lord Rām, who observed the Law, * to the dominating, cruel Kumbhakār(ṇ), who glared at them as he caught sight of * them arriving. Angry and taken unawares, he summoned his men. * Instantly his forces were everywhere about the place. There was nothing but ogres, a gleaming sea of them! * Some swaggered in groups, raising their arms in threatening gestures. Some displayed their confidence in their javelins or their spears or stropped their sharp knives. * Some made obeisance, giving their good wishes to Prince Kumbhakār(ṇ), most capable of fighters. * Kumbhakār(ṇ) watched his retinue of soldiers of gigantic

(14) size, eager and excited to a degree. * He bore a club[33] of superlative
15. power. Immense to look upon, (15) he stamped on the ground.
* Unafraid, he whirled round his combined missile and pike with all his
might. The earth was shaken by a tremor. * He hurled this pike at the
feet of Laksm(ṇ). The prince lost consciousness with the terrible shock.
* Then, attached to the pike, there grew a shoot of the strychnine
plant! It sprang up and up, clearly seen in the sky, while * the other
end of it went deep down into the earth as far as Pātāl! Rām, the elder,
was filled with fear. * He came down from his pavilion of victory and
comforted his young brother, placing him on his lap. * Embracing and
caressing him, he wept in sorrow. He shook with emotion, losing all
sense of what he was doing. He spoke his thoughts.

16. * "Alas! My young brother, I grieve for you, struck (16) by that
terrible magic pike! Some wrong-doing of yours is manifested in this
awful retribution, this most cruel suffering. * Yet while you have been
with me you have been blameless! In all the words that you have
spoken to me, my darling brother, you have been loving and honest.
* You were as close to me as the shadow which accompanies my body.
And even then it can come about that I should lose my dearest
brother!" * The prince lamented most plaintively, thinking of the good
deeds which his brother had done for him — good deeds without equal.

* As Rām mourned increasingly, writhing on the ground, Bibhek
spoke to his sovereign. * "Lord, do not be troubled so about the young
prince. It shall now * be my task, as your servant, to stay and look
after your young brother, lord of the earth, until he is recovered."
17. * Bibhek expressed (17) to Rām a request that Hanumān should be sent
to the Hemabānt to fetch some precious medicaments of the gods.
* Hanumān, the mightiest of all, understood and was ready to help.
* Bibhek had consulted the treatises. He gave orders to Hanumān, the
trusted confidant of their lord, * to fetch the ingredients for a divine
prescription: first, to fetch a beautiful lotus bloom with stamens; and
* next, to fetch clean, pure water from the nine pools, and some urine
from the king of the oxen.

* Mighty and dependable, Hanumān took leave of the prince and
18. went through the air towards the forests of the Hemabānt. (18) * He
made his way over all the mountains and reached the place of the nine
celestial pools. * The royal *nāga*, who was keeping a watchful eye for
the demons, caught sight of the princely lord of the simians, soldier of
Rām, * about to go and draw water from the nine pools, source of the
special ambrosia. * Realising that this was an instruction of Bibhek,
the *nāga*, carefully attentive, reared with opened hood to cover and
guard the water * so as not to let Hanumān approach and draw it as he

(18) intended. * Hanumān, powerful in deeds of prowess, darted through the
air, demonstrating his might. * With an effort he changed direction and,
with enormous power, jumped on to the reared head of the *nāga*, so that
it sank down * and he reached the group of pools. Hanumān, the
successful, was able to draw the heavenly water * and go through the air
19. to the region of the king of the oxen, whose power was (19) like that of a
royal lion.

* Seeing the monkey prince, the king of the oxen shook his head,
waving his horns round, while he blew a gale through his nostrils, * a
gale as strong as the whirlwind which ends an age within an era! * It
blew the strong son of the Wind-god swiftly and speedily to a distance of
many leagues, * all the way to the far-flung *cakravāla*, like a bit of
cotton floss blown up high into the air. * Hanumān, the strong and
mighty, inflamed with anger, so that his breast burned with his fury,
instantly used his great powers to fly all the way back. * He managed to
creep along behind the king of the oxen, with great bravery, and, seizing
his tail, to twist it tightly, * winding it round with a sudden spurt of
force. The king of the oxen almost died! He could not help but make
20. water all over the place! * The unique Hanumān (20) grandly gesticulated with outspread arms and brandished his sword triumphantly.
* Having acquired the urine of the king of the oxen, he quickly went
through the air to obtain the beautiful lotus bloom with stamens.
* Now, for this ingredient for the prescription, the mighty Hanumān,
not knowing the plant, * broke off and lifted up the whole mountain!
Taking it in his hands, he went back through the air to Prince Bibhek,
using his great strength. * When Bibhek had received the divine herb
and, having all the medicaments for the prescription, had expressed his
21. gratitude, * Hanumān picked up the mountain and returned (21) with it
to where it had been. * Bibhek respectfully gave an account of this to
Nārāy(ṇ), praising Hanumān for his good deed.

* All the medicaments were there in accordance with the treatises, but the grinding stone was lacking. Bibhek respectfully informed the prince that * there was in existence a stone, a fine jewel, an emerald, the exact requirement for the cure. * Other stones would give rise to poison and were no good, but this gem was in Laṅkā and the lord king himself guarded it. * His palace had seven ramparts and the gates had numerous locks all over them and were extremely thick. It was very difficult indeed. * Rām commanded the courageous Hanumān, who overcame all obstacles, to go off through the air in the quiet of the night.

* Hanumān went off through the air immediately to that bejewelled building and saw that all was quiet. The hordes of demons were asleep. * He opened the door and pushed aside the feet of the ogres — 100,000 ogre

22. (22) soldiers — yet not one stirred! * He prised open the chains, snapped off the locks and pushed against the doors of the palace. They gave way, breaking in pieces. * Owing to his most effective magic, Hanumān, boldly confident in his powers, caused the whole force of ogres to slumber. * He entered the sun-stone palace, with its jewels like flames, and glanced at the pretty women * sleeping crowded together on either side of Dasamukh's couch, where Maṇḍogirī slept beside him. * The bejewelled couch, with its elegant cushions and pillows, had a white canopy spread above it, grandly opulent. * Hanumān rummaged among the clothing and found the gem under the king's head as he lay. * Stealthily, he took it. Then, enjoying himself, he tied Dasamukh's hair to Maṇḍogirī's. * Next, he left and wrote instructions on the door for the wicked ogre, a message about his magic: * that he should tell
23. Maṇḍogirī to pat him on the head with her left hand (23). Then their hair would be freed. * If he did not follow the instructions something untoward would befall him; his power would be crushed. * If he acted in accordance with the instructions he would have happiness in plenty; his customary success and his power would remain supreme. * When he had written this, Hanumān flew home and presented the lucky gem with a merry laugh, pleased with himself.

* Bibhek considered Laksm(ṇ)'s critical condition, the poison of that powerful club-missile and his life-chances, and said, * "We do not need long. In one third of an hour, the young prince could be freed from this affliction and in good health." * When he had spoken to Rām the latter gave orders to Hanumān the bold, who was ready and willing to help. * Hanumān took leave of the prince and went through the air up
24. into the sky to the palace of the round Sun, * proceeding (24) by means of his astounding powers. Arriving all in an instant, he blurted out, * "Master! Do not proceed! Halt for the time being. It is on the authority of Rām that I come to stop you. * The young Laksm(ṇ), highest of princes, is undergoing the most cruel suffering for he was hit by the pike of Kumbhakār(ṇ). * There is the most frightful commotion. The earth is trembling. The gods are in sympathy. * The astrologer, Bibhek, has unmistakably prophesied that, if you proceed, Master, on your journey of breath-taking brilliance, * if the Sun in the east sees the day, then Laksm(ṇ) will die. That is why I am begging you to take pity. * We do not need long. If we had only a third of an hour, the young prince could be freed from his affliction and in good health."

* "O Hanumān," the Sun-god replied, "if you make me stop you
25. will confound Time itself! (25) * It is arranged with precision; all the twelve months have their proper time. Any deviation from this would make it difficult to proceed. * Night will, I fear, soon part its shadows.

(25) I shall not do what you say. Do not say any more to stop me." * Hanumān was furious! He struck the great, strong horses and coachman and flung them aside. As for the carriage, he managed to hold it firm. * The sky was clouded; a rumble of thunder was heard; the sun's circle was overcast; the heavens were in turmoil.

9.25–39. **When Kumbhakār(ṇ) and Laksm(ṇ) fight again, Laksm(ṇ) kills Kumbhakār(ṇ). Rāb(ṇ) sends Indrajit out to fight. Indrajit's power causes darkness to fall. Bibhek describes the immense power of Indrajit to Rām. Indrajit fails to strike Laksm(ṇ) but succeeds against Hanumān. Hanumān, Laksm(ṇ) and Aṅgad fight against Indrajit.**

* Then the news came round to the demons that the young prince was in good health; * for Rām had sent Hanumān to fetch the grinding stone together with the divine herbs * and Bibhek had in person carefully administered that rapidly effective medicine. So it was that the young prince was well. * There was a mighty outburst of anger
26. from Rāb(ṇ): "So! By his (26) untrustworthiness Bibhek has wrongfully harmed his loved ones! * Kumbhakār(ṇ)," Rāb(ṇ) said, "you see this miracle? Bibhek has done us a great wrong. * Laksm(ṇ) was hit by your invincible, prestigious club and nearly died. But he is not dead yet — he has escaped! * And it was Bibhek who gave the instructions. Hanumān came to steal the grinding stone so that he had all the things. * Without delay they concocted the medicine and applied it and now Laksm(ṇ) of princely parentage is well again! * Now, this time, no carelessness! Destroy Laksm(ṇ). Let him reach the shores of Death and no mistake!"

* Then the great ogre Kumbhakār(ṇ), making obeisance, took leave of his elder brother. He roused his soldiers for departure * and assembled his demon army, with his chiefs of the left and right. There was force upon force of loyal * men, unflinching, bearing their power-
27. ful weapons all athwart each other, tough fighters (27) and bold. * Their shouts of rivalry rose high and, as they beat their gong of victory, in their eagerness, they made a deafening, resounding din, which caused the earth to tremble.

* Then the high-born Laksm(ṇ) bowed at the feet of the elder prince and asked to try again. * "I am most ashamed that the tale should be told: 'Thus did Laksm(ṇ) cower when he was wounded by the brave ogre'. * May I please leave you immediately and take that enormous ogre for you without delay? * I will shoot my most powerful arrow and finish him off with his head split open, as though hacked down. * I ask

(27) you the favour, prince, of looking kindly upon my request. And now I beg to take leave of you." * Then the prince spoke fondly in reply, "O,
28. Laksm(ṇ), I give you my permission. Off you go and fight. (28) * I will watch the triumph which your heroic deed will give you. You take that ogre now, the great Kumbhakār(ṇ)." * Laksm(ṇ) took leave of the supporter of the earth. With his powerful bow and matchless arrow, he set forth, * towards his army. As he marshalled his simian force of soldiers, bearers of the banners of the Sun, their noise reverberated loudly through the earth. * Laksm(ṇ) marched the glorious army, while the lord, master of men, looked on at his young brother, setting * off. All those courageous monkeys were asking to help him and the lord Laksm(ṇ) was agreeing. * When he had marched them up close in full view, monkeys and ogres struggled with might and main in confused turmoil. * They threw each other about, hurling insults; attacked, fended, rushed to trample the foe, surged stalwartly forward with
29. force. * They shot down showers of arrows; swords (29) and other arms were everywhere. Daring, foot near foot, they closed to strike each other in combat.

* Kumbhakār(ṇ) bawled out thunderously as, step by slow step, he approached to begin a fight against the young prince. * Holding his powerful, sharp club, Kumbhakār(ṇ) stretched out his arm, and leaped about, stamping the ground and compressing his lips. * Laksm(ṇ) shot his arrow — it dashed that powerful club out of Kumbhakār(ṇ)'s hand. It fell in pieces to the ground. * The ogre seized another powerful club-cum-pike and brandished it, swaying as he took aim and hurled it. * But just then, Laksm(ṇ) sent an arrow which split open his head and the ogre Kumbhakār(ṇ) was destroyed! * The ogre horde were knocked over, crushed and battered. They fell with twisted limbs, scattered about, heaped on each other, flat out. * Heads were off, as though hacked through. Some ogres, injured in the chest, collapsed, flopping down on each other.

30. (30) * King Rāb(ṇ) listened as the demons told him that the great Prince Kumbhakār(ṇ) had fallen * and the whole army of 100,000 ogres had astonishingly been overthrown, causing the mountains and the whole world to shake. * Greatly grieved and violently angry, Rāb(ṇ) summoned his soldiers to consider the situation with him. * He sent for Indrajit, his eldest son, because he had managed to seize the Lord Indr and make him captive. * "You were able to bring Indr and present him to me, to make obeisance to me and wait upon me. * Your renown will certainly last through this age and be much heard of everywhere in the three worlds, causing astonished admiration. * Now you shall take a force of gigantic *kumbhaṇḍa* ogres, bold and invincible, and go forth to

(30) devastate their territory * and destroy those ascetics, Rām and
Laksm(ṇ), destroy the numerous apes. Put an end to them with your
sharp, effective arrows!"

* Indrajit bowed and took his leave. He marched his army away,
31. with its soldiers (31) serving on the left and right, * all swaying because
of the weapons they held. Bows, arrows and cudgels were in their outstretched hands. * Some had shields, swords or buffalo-horn spears.
Some had cross-bows, spears, rocks, javelins, banners. * Indrajit, great
commander of the army, was borne upon a chariot drawn by strong
horses. * He wore garments of silk and was surrounded by ministers as
if he were the Lord Indr! * There were jewels set in gleaming arrangements. Gems, gold and pearls shone with their colourful, varied
brilliance. * There were banners, parasols and fans with long gold
handles. Bright, pinnacled umbrellas fluttered like a myriad sunbeams.
* The chariot-borne force had yoked their vehicles ready to hand, with
weapons and saddles placed just so on the golden chariots * while the
infantry marched everywhere about the whole area making the dust
rise in clouds. * And there were lions, roaring and enormous, and
32. gleaming weapons (32) for the use of the demon lord. * He prepared
his forces to the north, south and west, a vast army, impossible to
count. * To the east, to assure success for the prince as he charged, was
the entire company of mighty *kumbhaṇḍa* ogres. * As the ogres
aggressively bellowed out their war-cries, the noise of their whoops and
yells wafted as far as the land of the Brahm. * The ogre army's cry for
victory resounded confusedly in the heavens; their shrieks reverberated
deafeningly. * Indrajit, their commander, in his marvellous chariot,
with his horde of ogres, caused a great clouding over * for through the
power of Indrajit, as he stretched out his arms, holding his troops in
readiness, it became dark. The sun was hidden.

* When Rām observed the handsome Indrajit, he went straight to
the astrologer Bibhek and said, * "Who is that, riding in that splendid
33. chariot, the vehicle yoked with those fine horses of such size (33) and
of inestimable speed — * the one dressed in shining garments with
bejewelled patterns, and wearing gems, anklets, earrings and raiment
which dazzles like fire? * He wears an ornament of emeralds on his
clothing and the finest bracelets. His bearing is magnificent as, with a
triumphant gesture, he raises his bow aloft. * His force is as vast as the
ocean. Its clamour resounds deafeningly over the earth, together with
the voice of this princely, lion-like enemy. * The whole force of
kumbhaṇḍa ogres, with weapons — iron cudgels — in both hands, is
powerful enough to cleave the ground and crack it open. * As for those
accompanying the carriage, they dart hither and thither in their

(33) eagerness to be helpful. The whole enormous force, so determined, is
formidable indeed."

* Bibhek, highest prince and loyal servant of Prince Rām, placed his
hands together and respectfully explained. * "I pay my respects at your
feet, lord and master. This prince and great lord is treacherous with his
34. supernatural (34) craft. * Once King Rāb(ṇ) led a force to subjugate the
whole of heaven. It came about that the great Indr, revered god of
supreme might, * and all the gods of heaven shouted at him and came
close together, crowding upon each other. This prince shot an arrow of
manifold magic powers. * He captured the lord god Indr, whose
prowess was put in the shade. By taking Indr, he acquired exceedingly
great authority. * And that is why he has been given the name Indrajit[24]
the victorious, for, by the power of his arm, he has been triumphant in
battle. Gods of heaven or humans — * all fear him and cannot contend
against him with heroic deeds; all are agape at his greatness and come
to offer him their homage."

* When Nārāy(ṇ) had listened to this description, the expression on
35. the face of that handsome protector of men became eager. (35) "O
simian Sugrīb," he said, "go out and summon the military officers and
the men of our army." * Then Rām gave orders to his young brother
to go out and prepare the monkey army and princes, * to have simian
lords and simian hosts * assembled in readiness, brave and invincible
monkeys, of impressive might and power.

* The young prince took his leave, making obeisance, and led out
the royal army, * a throng of monkey soldiers, in whose outstretched
hands rocks were poised. * With high-pitched shrieks they were there
on the spot, fully armed with shields and swords for efficient fighting
against the ogres. * Seated on Hanumān — he being of immense
strength — there amid the teeming host, Laksm(ṇ) wore a crown and
bracelets, with brilliant armlets, glowing redly, overshadowing the
36. sun's brightness. * There he was, (36) bearing magic arrows, sharp and
destructive, with his great power for heroic deeds, out on that decisive
battlefield.

* Then the huge Indrajit, bearing bow and arrows, waved his sword
round and round, high and mighty. * Rousing his forces of the left and
right and his chiefs, he approached and surrounded the monkey army
and the lord prince. * "Hey you hermit!" he called out, "Practising
your asceticism! You do not know fear. * You are demented! How can
you stand up against my great might?" * Laksm(ṇ) replied, "Ho there!
You demon, you boast of your power for deeds of heroism just because
you captured gods of heaven. * You are stubborn in your evil ways —a
vile scoundrel. You have the idea that I am like the Lord Indr. * You

(36) are of mean origins and not very clever. How can you pit yourself against the brother of the lord? * I shall destroy your bejewelled chariot and horses and inflict upon you yourself utter destruction —
37. (37) death. * You do not know the strength of the supporter of the earth, who wields a supernatural arrow and has the power for heroic deeds."

* Just then mighty Indrajit seized a bejewelled club, stamped his feet and compressed his lips. * He ran up and hurled it at the great prince. The young prince struck out and flung the club away. * Furious and on his dignity, Indrajit took a powerful bludgeon and flung it to hit Hanumān, * who fell to his knees and then, making a great physical effort, went to ask to enter the fight himself. * Bravely he went forward at a run. "How dare you jest and joke with a sage of great power?" he said. * Hanumān seized their horses and lions, making a heap of them. He captured their elephants. He fended off and attacked the enemy, rolling them, dying, on the ground.

* Indrajit, with arms outspread, galloped off in pursuit of the monkeys, scattering them far and wide. * Then he came across
38. Laksm(ṇ), the (38) lion-like young prince. They closed with each other to contend for victory. * The gigantic Indrajit, quite fearless, was in a furious rage. He shot his arrow with a roar. * Prince Laksm(ṇ) shot his swift arrow. It intercepted the demon's shaft * and there shone forth a blaze of sunlight. The crafty Indrajit shot an arrow in reply. * Instantly, the heavens burst into flames. The young prince replied with arrows which were oceans of water * — and the magic fires of the ogre throng were doused by that most honourable and august young prince. * The huge Indrajit, wielding his bold bow, sent forth arrows which turned into thunderbolts and floods of rain. * Laksm(ṇ) of supreme powers shot an arrow which became a gale and blew away all the water. * Indrajit angrily compressed his lips and put aside his bow and arrows straight away. He drew out a flame-weapon and took aim
39. * to strike (39) the young brother of Harī — but the latter took his sword and struck out. * The other's arrows were broken and scattered in pieces! The young brother of Lord Nārāy(ṇ) brandished his triumphant sword.

* Aṅgad made the drum resound, waved his baton — the baton of war — and stamped the ground. * He went through the air, darting here and there in front of the banners on their chariots. He broke the spokes of the wheels of the vehicles and tore them away to hand down, broken. * He seized horses and charioteers, making a heap of them; he captured elephants, fended off the demons and attacked them, overthrew his adversaries completely.

9.39–51. Indrajit's arrow turns into a mesh of *nāgas* entangling Laksm(ṇ) and the army. Rāb(ṇ) sends for Sītā and, thinking that Rām is also thus captured, accuses her of vain boasting. Bibhek suggests to Rām that he should ask for help from Isūr. Rām declares that if Laksm(ṇ) dies he will destroy all heaven, except Isūr's dwelling, with his bow. The gods rush to tell Isūr, who says that Brahm is to blame because he cast the magic spell over Indrajit's arrow. Brahm asks the king of the *garuḍas* to disperse the *nāgas* and Laksm(ṇ) and the army are released.

(39) * Indrajit roused his ogre soldiers and went up into the air to
assemble the men. Reciting a magic incantation * he sent deceptive,
magic arrows, which sprang up in the form of innumerable *nāgas*
surrounding the whole monkey army. * These twined round the feet of
the two august supporters of the earth,[35] who were aghast at the craft
of the ogres, and resembled the Moon and Sun when Rāhū captured
40. (40) them. * Then Indrajit left and went back into the city, where he
paid homage to his father. * "I took the army out in pursuit of the
monkey lords and Rām and Laksm(ṇ). * I have in fact been able to
capture them. Lord King, it would be a good idea if a powerful arrow
from your own hand should destroy them." * King Rāb(ṇ) was
absolutely delighted with Indrajit. His pride knew no bounds. * "All
the godly throng gave up the struggle against you. What, after all, are
Laksm(ṇ) and Rām that they should avoid the same experience?"

* King Rāb(ṇ) sent a bellicose band of ogres to the park, to bring
back Sītā. He was beside himself with annoyance. "You deceitful
woman! You are an out and out liar! * You boasted of Rām, that he
was greater than any in all the three worlds — he was a marvel, we
heard, to be gaped at in wonder! * But now Indrajit, the triumphant,
41. has cast a spell over the arrow he has sent and (41) has captured the
whole monkey force! * He has bound Rām and Laksm(ṇ) and left
them to die. He has tied them up by the power of his arrow in a mesh
of innumerable *nāgas*. * We see now that you are unparalleled in your
wickedness. How could you be so boastful, telling me about the powers
of that ascetic?" * When Princess Sītā heard this, her agony was like
death. She trembled and was downcast. * Then she recovered her senses
and gave her mind to serious thought about the princes. * "Alas! The
two princes, then, are enduring such pain, helpless in their suffering.
* If what the ogre says is true, there is only the *garuḍa* who can help."

* Then Rām had his young brother, the prince, in his thoughts.
* Just then Bibhek returned and approached to make obeisance and
42. inform the (42) prince, "Lord, the young prince is in difficulties. He has
been defeated on the glorious field of battle. * Prince Indrajit, who is

(42) mightier than all, has wielded his bow and the arrows have all, by his
design, turned into a poisonous mesh of *nāgas*. * Only a third of an
hour and he will be dead! And the whole military force will be
annihilated too!" * The prince listened, as Bibhek described the
dreadful calamity which had befallen his young brother. * He was full
of distress and concern for the life of his brother, and afraid that he
would die. * The prince wept and beat his breast. His heart sank and
he felt a tremor of despair go through him.

* Mounted upon the monkey prince, Sugrīb, he went straight to his
young brother * and saw that that highest of princes was surrounded
by a mesh of *nāgas* which was drawn tightly round him. * He was in a
43. wretched (43) plight, quite clearly on the point of death owing to the
snake poison. * The prince was horrified and faint with anguish.
Words would not come. He trembled and shook. * He lamented most
sadly and was quite unable to keep back the sobs. * "O Laksm(ṇ)," he
said, "you who excel in goodness and wisdom, who are immeasurably
esteemed, * you have been my eyes. You have been like the eyelids
protecting my eyeballs, not letting them come to any harm, * not
letting any dirt, dust or sand enter to irritate them. * And more. You
were like my own consciousness which is attached to my body, * never
44. going very far away. And so, if you are gone, I shall not live (44)."
Rām lamented inconsolably. It seemed as though his life was at an end.

* Then the demon prince Bibhek comforted the prince, and, making
obeisance, spoke to him, "Lord, please collect your thoughts! Consider
the prince. * If you go on grieving like this, your young brother will be
dead! * Please ask for a boon from the august and noble Isūr." * The
prince then put aside his sorrowing and set his thoughts to rights. * He
stood up: "O gods," he declared, "why are you on the side of this
45. heretic ogre? * Since I have been building up virtue all the time (45)
from that first age long ago, * I ask to defeat the wicked demons
including the evil Dasamukh. Let them give in and acknowledge the
power of my right arm. * As things are, you are helping the demons
and seeming to lack righteousness! * If my young brother reaches his
time for dying, then, all you gods in the domain of heaven, * I shall
shoot my sharp arrow of great power to annihilate your domain
completely, * turning it into clouds of dust and ashes. Only the realm
of the well-established King Isūr shall I allow to endure. * The
numerous *nāgas*, strong and mighty, I shall conquer decisively as well
as all the gods. * This bow was given to me by Rāmaparamasūr, of
excessive size and power. * It is of superlative strength. I shall use it to
46. destroy the demons in Laṅkā. * With my own hands (46) I will break it
in two and throw one piece up into the skies * so that the abode of the

(46) pure and the highest point of existence, that of the Brahm, will catch
fire and come to ruin, falling down to the earth. * The other piece I
shall whirl round and fling to the glorious city of Aiyudhyā * so that
news of me will reach my mother, to say I am dead. * Thus she shall
not wonder whether I have reached that shore which belongs to the
time of death."

* Due to the prince's virtue, acquired by meditation, this declaration
reverberated miraculously. It was astounding. * The prince took hold
of his mighty bow and it seemed that on high two bright rainbows
* were scintillating, radiating a moving light, glowing like a fire which
would take hold of the whole abode of the gods. * Just then, the gods
47. of all heaven (47) in horror broke into an uproar in every celestial
place. * They could not help themselves. In their fear, they thrashed
about, anxious and afraid for their lives. * They saw Rām, suddenly so
angry, a prince of very strong determination. * Indr and the Brahm
and all the gods flew in a body to the mountain of Kailās.

* They went and informed Isūr, the great chief of sages, who was
indeed supreme in honour and prestige, * "Lord," they said, "we are in
such a fright and have nowhere to turn! We come to you for help.
* Just now Rām has been angry with all of us * and all because of the
demon Rāb(ṇ)'s mighty eldest son, a lying scoundrel of evil, crafty
ways, * whose name is Indrajit. He has dared to bring up in person a
48. force, glittering with armour, (48) to fight with the young brother of
the lord Rām, highest of princes. * Indrajit does not wage war in
accordance with the conventions which have been fixed, that is, by
using the strength and power of his right arm. * It is all incantations
and putting people to sleep and now he has despatched invincible
arrows which have turned into a mesh of snakes, known to be
poisonous. * They have slithered up through the earth and appeared to
encircle them with terrifying tightness, poisoning them with their
venom. * They are surrounding both the young prince and the monkey
force, who are scattered about there, as though dead, in great numbers.
* They are dejected, on the point of death. Now with this defeat on the
battlefield, the monkeys' reputation is ruined. * Now Rām in his anger
will raise his bow with its sharp arrows * in order to destroy us gods!
Please take pity upon us!"

49. * Isūr gave his reply: "The whole blame for this rests with (49)
Brahm himself. * That was how the mighty Indrajit obtained his fine
sharp arrow — from Brahm, who cast a spell on it for him. * Brahm
must venture into the air and go and request the king of the *garuḍas* at
the top of his Bombax tree * to come and help the young lord. Then
the *nāgas* will be shaken loose from the young prince. * If Brahm does

(49) not go and find the *garuḍa* then those *nāgas* will not be shaken loose. * As it is, Rām, the lord of men of the line of Bodhisatvas, great and mighty beyond all, is angry. He will break in two his bow of the magic arrows, * and will throw one half to the palaces of the gods to crush them to dust and scattering sand. * And more, the six far-away heavenly levels of desire will be devastated. This destruction will be entirely because of Brahm. * So, with regard to my personally guaranteeing to all the gods that they will not be brought to ruin, or
50. made homeless, * if Rām, chief of the gods, (50) throws his bow and arrows, using his great power, * in such a way that the dwellings of the gods might catch fire, I will place just one digit — my thumb — * which will be equivalent to a diamond screen so that the palaces of all the gods will not catch fire. * As to the regions of Brahm, whatever I do I cannot guarantee to protect them."

* Then Brahm heard how the lord Isūr had laid the blame on * him because he had given supernatural power to Indrajit. Brahm was full of fear and trembled all over. * He went through the air to the *garuḍa* and asked him to go and give help to the noble Prince Rām, the divine, * and told him all the facts: that he himself would be destroyed, all because Rām was displeased! * Then the king of the *garuḍas* went out
51. from his bejewelled palace and flew (51) through the wide-open skies. * His shrill cries resounded and, astonishingly, the hundred thousand vicious *nāgas* which were wrapped round the whole host of simians * and the snakes which were encircling the young brother, master of men, having wormed their way up through the earth, relaxed their hold of the army.

9.51–10.3. **Both sides prepare for battle. Rāb(ṇ) brews a snake poison to destroy Rām's army but Hanumān defeats the plan by spilling it all.**

* The two princes took their magic bows in their well-shaped hands. * Bibhek and Sugrīb drew up their forces of superlative size ready and waiting and chose out some reliable soldiers. * Some spread out in the sky straight away. Some went along the paths to prevent the approach of the demon army. * Some uprooted trees and brandished them. Some strong ones raised up mountains, forests and all, and carried them on their shoulders. * They protected their rear and every direction of the heavens: east, north and south, not letting the demons come close to their troops.

* When the demon king, Rāb(ṇ), had told Princess Sītā what was happening and she had listened and was pondering in her heart of

hearts, * just then the ogres saw the *garuḍa* chase away all those *nāgas*
52. (52) and free the whole simian force, which, * with the two princes, arrows in hand, all motionless, holding their weapons, seemed as vast as the ocean. * The ogres came to inform Rāb(ṇ) as soon as they had seen this. Rāb(ṇ) was exceedingly angry and as relentless as fire. * His ten mouths bellowed one after the other with such a roar as to demolish the mountains, trees and all!

* Rāb(ṇ) had the conch for victory blown. He took up his weapons of war, wearing garments which dazzled with brilliance. * He bawled his orders to the demon ministers to prepare the women, * the elephants, carriages and horses, the excited and varied attendant throng
10.1. and the military forces. (10.1) * When this was done, he proceeded to mount his marvellous vehicle, taking with him his chief wife. * With the uproarious army, numerous as the stars, they traversed the air and went to a huge mountain. * The purpose of this flight through the skies was to carry out a stratagem full of guile. * Reaching the top of the mountain with his august wife, Rāb(ṇ) * brewed a highly poisonous concoction for sprinkling over the 100,000 monkeys and obliterating them.

* The astrologer Bibhek, the eminently successful interpreter of the Books, who had divine sight with which to see, explained * to the master of men how things were. "Lord, I can see a wily plot being
2. defeated. * Rāb(ṇ) has taken his queen to the mountains (2) to obtain a source of power. * He will behave like a sage and practise asceticism, in respect of the five organs of sense, turning his mind towards purity. * Thus he will brew snake venom with the help of the treatises until he obtains by his craft a poison which may be described as "*nāga*-venom". * This poison has various names. It may be called "Destruction". It is of dreadful potency. * If King Rāb(ṇ) observes the tenfold laws, the regulations and all the principles and if he also practises the religious way of life, * this poison will certainly be formed and will fall down to destroy us as is his intention — and that will not bring us peace and prosperity!"

* Then the prince gave the order to Hanumān who went off through the air up to that mountain height. * Disguising himself as a Brahmin,
3. Hanumān approached Maṇḍogirī and placed himself beside her. (3) * The demon officers saw him, with fluttering eyelashes, putting his arms round her and caressing her! * Hanumān then further disconcerted Maṇḍogirī by snatching away her clothing and letting it drop. * All the ungodly creatures on that mountain — innumerable, vulgar demons — surrounded the simian * but he fended them off and broke the cauldron. The venom was spilt and lost. His plan had succeeded.

(3) * Hanumān attacked the ogre horde and then went through the air to greet Rām * and give his account of the details of the conflict on that dusty mountain top.

10.3–47. **Rāb(ṇ) sends five sons and five generals one after the other, with an army, to fight against Rām. They are defeated in turn by heroes of Rām's side.**

10.3–12. **Indrajit is killed by Laksm(ṇ). Rāb(ṇ) in his anger almost kills Sītā.**

* King Rāb(ṇ) returned to Laṅkā and thrashed about in a furious
temper. He rounded up all their arms * and gave the command to his
son, Indrajit — for he was superlative in battle and had the physical
4. stamina of an ogre in double quantity — * to marshal (4) a mighty
army, greater than before with soldiers to the rear and to the left and
right, in vast numbers, and with a force of *kumbhaṇḍa* ogres. * Indrajit
took leave of the ten-necked king, took his bow, arrows and sword,
and mounted his chariot for the departure. * The handsome Indrajit
was as radiant as the bright moon, with its wonderful dazzling light
* for he was of immense size and very good-looking. The team of
horses yoked to his chariot were of a hue like that of emeralds. * Aloft
on the royal chariot, Indrajit was truly glorious, comparable with the
bright moon. * He galloped off, whipping his horses grandly and came
quite near to that great lord, the unvanquished elder prince.

* Nārāy(ṇ)'s eyes beheld the great Indrajit standing there in his
chariot. * He saw all the attendant demons drawn up in readiness,
thick upon the ground in every direction, their weapons sticking up
closely all around them. * The clamour of this fighting force
5. reverberated afar. Their accoutrements, (5) of every colour, all
variegated, were like those of Indr. * After reflection, the prince gave
an order to his young brother. "Now, Laksm(ṇ), my beloved brother.
* I have you constantly in my mind for it is owing to the merit that we
have accumulated that we have been born together in one place. * And
you are equal to my life's breath to me. I would have you assemble the
simian force and go forth to victory. * Fight to take Indrajit himself.
You have the skill. On many occasions you have had supreme
success." * Having listened to his brother, Laksm(ṇ) put on shining
raiment of many colours and * made obeisance, taking leave of the
master of men, the lord prince, * who was exalted in his own person,

(5) exalted by his birth, exalted by the simians and by the heroic feats he performed in their midst.

* Laksm(ṇ) was like the moon on its journey. All the troops of monkeys might be compared with the stars surrounding the moon,
6. * resplendent with glorious light. (6) The monkey force carried tree trunks as weapons — a marvel! * Some bore on their shoulders immense mountains! The noise made by that boldly energetic fighting force resounded far and wide. * They reached the vulgar horde of ogres, and, in their eagerness, scrapped amongst them with thumps and slaps. * Indrajit dispatched an arrow, sharp and effective, a mighty arrow with a ferocious power incorporated in it. * Laksm(ṇ) shot an arrow which turned into fierce weapons. The ogre's arrow changed into *nāgas* all over the ground. * Laksm(ṇ) sent an arrow which became *garuḍas.* An arrow of the demon turned into crackling flames. * Laksm(ṇ) shot an arrow which became daggers and an arrow which joined them together as water, welling up like the sea. * Indrajit urged his fine chariot onwards in front of the monkey force and made repeated attacks of grim ferocity. * Laksm(ṇ), most capable leader of
7. men, was angry. Amid all the commotion he dispatched in reply (7) an arrow * which struck those of the overweening demon and tied them all together. * Indrajit urged the ogres to charge. They attacked and overwhelmed the monkeys, putting them to rout, * but, when the mighty Laksm(ṇ) held them back, the monkeys stood firm for an attack and gave their attention to it. * The simians, who looked for help to him of the race of Bisnu, seized the bold ogre's chariot and smashed it, breaking its wheels. * They destroyed the vehicle and disposed of the tiered parasols and banners of victory and the proud horses, sending them scattering off. * Indrajit galloped off, venturing right up into the sky, and dispatched an arrow of supreme power: * in dead silence and deep darkness, all the ten directions were blotted out from view! A cloud covered the sun. * Rām, Laksm(ṇ) and the monkeys gazed at the heavens and could not see the demon, though
8. the demon could see Nārāy(ṇ), his young brother (8) and the monkey host. * The young prince sent arrow after arrow whirling round while the lord of men raged furiously. * The huge Indrajit, victorious in battle, had his weapons just ready and raised them to continue the fight.

* Then, because the marvellous virtue of the two princes was supreme, exceeding that of all others, * the gods, and Indr and Brahm, helped the two noble princes, whose great glory astonished the world, to be victorious * for they bathed the faces of princes and monkeys clean and fresh * so that they saw Indrajit high up against the sky, resplendent. Laksm(ṇ) with marvellous strength * faced the godless

(8) creature, fought him and took him, for his powerful arrow was the
supreme Brahmavijit. * When the prince dispatched this fine arrow of
overwhelming power, it blew away the clouds, clearing the sky,
9. * struck Indrajit and clove him in two. (9) It was as though the skies
were rent. The earth was stirred by a tremor. * The ogre force ran back
with all their might to the city of the lord Rāb(ṇ). * Such a turmoil
arose that Laṅkā was almost in a state of collapse. People shivered and
shook in every limb.

* When Rāb(ṇ), most powerful of kings, heard of Indrajit's death
out there on the battlefield, * how he had fallen to the strong arm of
Laksm(ṇ), he was furious and stricken with grief for the beloved son of
his own flesh. * He ordered the beating of the drums to resound
throughout the city of Laṅkā. * He had Sītā brought from the park of
the Asoka trees to his assembly hall. * Rāb(ṇ) was quite distraught
about his son. He could not control his acute distress. * The ogre held
10. Sītā's head and with his right hand (10) he gripped his sword, raising
and lowering it over and over. * He debated whether to strike and cut
off her head, while holding her firmly in his grasp and imperiously
brandishing his sword.

* Then there was a royal confidant of great shrewdness, who did not
just stand by and do nothing where his master was concerned. * This
demon, whose name was Rakkhăs, made obeisance and spoke against
Rāb(ṇ), using some examples of the way things happen. * "Lord, I beg
to speak, if you would be so kind. I pray you, lord king, hear me.
* Most high lord, if you would kill Sītā, you already have her no
distance away, within your grasp but * if you do harm her and let her
perish, what, after all, will you have done to that Rām the god over
there? * Rām is like a tree, its trunk grown tall, its branches giving
deep, quiet shade. * Sītā is like a creeper growing under the tree and
11. twining round (11) and round it. * If you wish to be rid of this tree and
if you cut out only the creeper, the tree will never die. * Another
instance I offer you is this: there is a man, a physical presence, whom
another man is going to attack. * If he walks towards him and sees his
shadow and picks up his weapon to slice the man's shadow, * even if it
were broken off and crushed, he would not have scored a direct hit on
the person of the man at all! * Another instance is the following: a
huge, overpowering serpent is ready with its venom. * It bites and
slithers away. Only its tracks where it shed its skin are visible. * If you
would attack the serpent, which has slithered away, leaving only its
slough visible, and you hit at the slough and dash it to pieces, * when
12. you have hacked at this skin and scattered it in bits, you have not (12)
made a direct hit on the body of the serpent at all! * The serpent is

(12) Rām. The slough is Sītā, the precious princess, whose conduct is so proper. * If you illtreat Sītā and kill her, still Sītā, beloved of the prince, she who adds to his glory, is not the root and cause." * Hearing Rakkhăs' words, the king suddenly aspired to keep the laws. * "Well spoken, Rakkhăs," he said. "Quite right! My desires are quelled!" The king put down his sword of glorious victories * and had the Princess Sītā taken away and put in the park.

10.12–17. **Mahodar is killed by Aṅgad.**

* When he had spent his grief and was at peace again, Rāb(ṇ) summoned his soldiers, their officers and the chief ministers and had * the ogre army assembled in the royal city. Laṅkā bustled with activity. * Rāb(ṇ) beat his breast and exclaimed, "Alas! It was not right that Indrajit should fall to the might of Laksm(ṇ)'s arrow." * He
13. addressed (13) Mahodar. "I would have you give all your energy to the command of our victorious army. * You have the skill, you know, like Indrajit. There is no doubt about the glory of your deeds of prowess." * Mahodar then made obeisance and took his leave to command the ogre soldiers and great demon officers. * He ranged them in readiness, that spreading horde, thronging thick as thieves, *rākṣasas* with their weapons close together. * They beat the booming gong and drew their fierce swords. With their thick, long-handled spears they hampered and cluttered each other up. * The mighty demon prince, Mahodar, bearing a metal club, went out to fight, * his chariot yoked with an ass. He went forth proudly, venturing through the sky with his troops for all to see.
14. (14) * Rām heard the clamour of the marching demon army and its terrible reverberations in the heavens. * "O Bibhek," he said, "what troop of demons is this, that dares to come out?" * "It is Mahodar, King Rāb(ṇ)'s son," Bibhek replied with great respect. * "The mighty Kumbhakār(ṇ), his beloved son, Mahāpās, and his eldest son, Indrajit, * have all died. He is sending Mahodar to be in charge of the whole demon force to give assistance. * He is a mighty fellow too and has won many battles. He is determined and full of confidence."

* Rām sent Aṅgad, quick and dependable on the field of battle, to meet the giant Mahodar. * Aṅgad mustered his simians in readiness, took leave of the supporter of the earth and put on his sharp sword.
15. * He drew up (15) his forces of the left and right and his chiefs, arranging them in precise formation, a mighty force indeed. * Some had shields or efficient swords. Some held mountains or raised up crags

(15) upon their shoulders. * Some, with iron weapons, rushed forward brandishing them. Boulders were used as sharp weapons. * Some held clubs or uprooted trees to display their powers for victory and made their cries echo * round the great ogre horde which fended off the vast, unconquered monkey army.

* The various combatants were doggedly determined, each one. Aṅgad, of supreme might, fought at close quarters with the brazen ogres. * Ogres fought back against the mighty Aṅgad. The monkey force rushed at their adversaries alarmingly, * jeering as they joined the fray. They charged and strove for victory, blocking the enemy's way and angrily kicking and pushing and biting. * They fell in great
16. numbers to lie, steeped in (16) their own saturating, welling blood, rolling on top of each other. * The fallen covered the ground completely, both ogres and simian soldiers entangled in death.

* Mahodar and Aṅgad, there for all to see, approached and seized each other. Locked together inextricably, they fought for a long time * from end to end of the battlefield, clashing together, Aṅgad and the demon's son. * Mahodar leaped at Aṅgad with a bound. Aṅgad smashed his chariot. Crushed to bits, it hung there, destroyed. * He broke the spokes and the wheels, piling the pieces up in a heap or throwing them away. He hurled and broke and stamped and pushed and waved the pieces round, as he lashed out with them. * He hacked at the lions. They were killed. The royal chariot was scattered in pieces all around. The iron bar was detached. * He sprang forward and encountered Mahodar. He raised his sword and cut off his head. Thus
17. he achieved the annihilation of the demon! (17) * When the news of this reached Dasamukh, he was furiously angry and quivered and quaked.

10.17–20. **Atikāy is killed by Laksm(ṇ).**

* "O Atikāy, my fine son," said Rāb(ṇ), "you shall drive forth in a royal chariot to engage in battle with the monkeys and destroy them." * Atikāy took his leave respectfully and, with bow and arrows in his hands, set off in a royal chariot yoked with tigers. * He drew up the demon army, deploying all the companies of those ungodly creatures amid great commotion. * Atikāy was unvanquished, bold and brave, unflinching on the field of combat.

* Then the lord prince of noble line gave orders to the lord, his young brother. * "O noble Laksm(ṇ), I would have you take a simian army out to meet the enemy on the field of battle * and engage again in fighting to take those overweening ogres, who wield their weapons with

(17) such a high and mighty air, and with not a thought of death. * Go and
18. destroy Atikāy. (18) Let him perish by the power of your arrow!"
Laksm(ṇ) had listened to the supporter of the earth. Kneeling, he raised
his hands, respectfully taking his leave. * Then he went out. And the
sound of his progress reverberated on the ground and resounded in all
directions. * Bearing his mighty bow and arrows, he marshalled a
monkey army amid much loud shouting and clamour. * There arose a
tumult of noise as the troops beat their victory gongs and drew their
ranks together with shields and swords in close proximity. * The prince
moved forward, marching the army, fast as a hurricane in his haste to
carry out his command to fight. * He urged on the simian forces. With
much hubbub they uprooted trees — astonishing feat! — and took slabs
of rock * and went bounding through the air carrying heavy mountains
by that power of theirs which they made available to the prince.
19. (19) * Then the mighty Laksm(ṇ) approached to fight the great
ogres, hitting out with superhuman strength. * Ogre and monkey
soldiers were brought to destruction or, in triumph and with much
jeering, killed others. * With determination, they attacked, surged
forward, struck at the enemy, beat and pounded him, pushing a way
ahead energetically, imperious and forceful. * They lashed out and
leaped about adroitly. They moved forward to hammer at the enemy.
The sound of crashing boulders reverberated violently. * Monkeys and
ogres, all empowered by the books of the magic arts, were close to the
horror of annihilation! * Laksm(ṇ) came up against Atikāy. Atikāy
stretched out an arm to brandish his most powerful arrow, menacingly.
* With bows and arrows in hand, they aimed arrows in exchange
against each other, fighting with urgent haste to take the victory.
* Locked in close combat, both with supernatural powers, both with
sharp destructive arrows, they made a clamour which filled the
20. heavens. * Laksm(ṇ) (20), young brother of Nārāy(ṇ), grasped Atikāy
and, in concert with the monkeys, pressed down on him to crush him.
* Atikāy thrust out his arms, leaped away and seized the young
Laksm(ṇ) — who went off through the air in a flash! * Hand clashed
with hand, arrow with arrow. The arrows scattered far and wide so
that it seemed as if the great heavens were rent and flakes of sky were
fluttering about. * Laksm(ṇ) sent an arrow which cut off the head of
the demon prince and annihilated him.

10.20–25. **Trisir is killed by Hanumān and Usabh.**

* The evil Dasamukh was furious. Quivering, he summoned his dear

(20) son, Trīsīr. * "O mighty Trīsīr," he said, "my beloved son, so very dear
to my heart, * you are by nature a man of success and of great physical
force, mighty with the prowess of your right arm. And there is no
doubt of it: your ascetic power is extensive. * You see that Mahodar
21. and Atikāy have been lost and that their (21) respective forces are dead
too. * Please go forth and rout that army of apes and the fiend Rām,
the prince who always manages to stand his ground." * Then Trīsīr, of
massive strength, bowed very low and placed his palms together,
taking his leave. * Bearing his bow and arrows of supernatural power,
he went forth, leaping upon the well-wrought, bejewelled chariot,
* yoked with royal oxen. He had the royal army corps in readiness for
the battlefield, marshalling them and * dividing them between the left
and right with their chiefs. The clamour made by the soldiers rose up
unbelievably loud.

* Then, when Rām saw the menacing demons, huge, angry, cruel
ogres, * he wanted to go out to the field of battle. He grasped his bow
but Bibhek warned him against this. * "Lord, it is not right for a great
22. sovereign to go out to fight (22) with *him*. He is a son of King Rāb(ṇ).
* It would, I fear, cast a shadow on the glory of your heroic deeds to
fight with the son of a godless creature. * He is just like a blazing fire
which catches alight quickly and is extinguished in no time at all.
* How can you possibly be bothered with him, lord prince? I beg you,
send another one of the simian race." * Rām then addressed Hanumān
and Usabh. "You two well-born officers, * go out, join battle with the
high and mighty Trīsīr and take him! There he comes with his horde of
brazen demons!"

* Then Hanumān and Usabh, having made obeisance most
respectfully, took their swords and left. * They assembled the fighting
force with all their equipment laid out in order. They roused the
soldiers with great urgency. * The monkeys, in their excitement,
23. shouted noisily with their high-pitched voices (23) as the army was
deployed for battle in its divisions. * The soldiers at the left and right
charged, unflinching. Out they went with such a hubbub! The uproar
resounded on the ground. * As the monkeys came to grips with the
ferocious ogres, the noise rose up, a booming, reverberating din. * Its
echo vibrated in the skies, rumbling confusedly throughout the great
heavens * for they were all hurling mountains, blocking the enemy's
way by breaking off boulders. As the rocks splintered off, sparks of fire
flashed redly. * Glowing, crackling, glaring flames spread all through
the sky. Claps of thunder were heard * in the ten directions. The gods
were deafened; they cried out and flew to the regions on the outer
edges of the *cakravāla*. * The monkey force and those forces of Evil, of

(23) extraordinary might, made their attacks on each other, contending for
victory.
* Hanumān and Usabh were both full of confidence, even though
24. the gigantic Trīsīr, (24) valiant indeed, was making menacing gestures.
* Intrepid, the ogres and monkeys fought for a glorious victory to the
death, until both forces were laid low. * The fallen were littered about
in their thousands, soaked in the blood which poured all over, gushing
and spurting. * Trīsīr compressed his lips in raging fury and boldly
rushed forward. * Hanumān and Usabh, each so massive and of such
mighty strength, stayed motionless. * They had the upper hand; they
killed Trīsīr and eliminated the whole force of brazen ogres.
* When the news reached Dasamukh he wept for his lost son and
trembled in utter despair. * He was both very angry and very sad. The
evil creature could not face up to his very serious tactical situation.
25. * As he grieved for his beloved son, he felt more and more angry (25)
and simmered with rage as if ready to boil over.

10.25–27. **Narātåk is killed by Bibitr.**

* Rāb(ṇ) gave command to his son, Narātåk, who, with sea-dragons
yoked to his chariot and with bow and arrows in hand, * marshalled
his officers and forces in urgent haste. Every hand held a weapon. The
great *kumbhaṇḍa* ogres were massed together.
* Then Rām sent out Bibitr, an immense monkey lord of solid
strength. * Bibitr made obeisance, taking leave of the supporter of the
earth, and drew up his simian force, their sharp clubs ranged close
together for the encounter. * Each one was daring, brave and proud.
They were of massive size, their triumphant power astonishing. * All
were bold and skilled in fighting. None hung back overawed, none
feared the enemy's ranks on the battlefield. * Bibitr, the highborn,
26. successful simian, went forth, sharp sword in hand. (26) * With the
roar of a lion, he strode off, unflinching, and gave his mind to
controlling the monkeys for their attack on the fierce ogres.
* The unvanquished Bibitr, approaching the field of battle, was
looking forward to taking on the fight with Narātåk. * The monkey
lord faced the ogre and approached with jeering shouts. He pushed on,
pursuing the ogre and caught him up. * The daring Narātåk did not
move. Then he fell upon the officers, he fell upon the men, whisking
about like a whirlwind, * making sudden dashes, smouldering with
anger. Confused crashes and bangs echoed in the heavens. * The blood
of the ogre soldiers and of the monkeys themselves flowed constantly,

(26) spreading and bubbling up all over the ground. * They hurled
mountains, breaking off rocks. They kicked away clubs. They broke
the iron cudgels which were hammering at them. * There were loud
reverberations, crashing crags and noises of fierce beating, boxing and
battering. * There were terrifying shouts and screams, crashes and
27. cracks. (27) There was a dreadful clanging of boulders, swords and
shields one on another. * Ogres and simians were strewn thickly upon
the ground, supine, close-packed, plain to be seen. * The bold Bibitr of
many successes, greater than all in strength, brandished his diamond
sword and * approached to fight his ogre adversary, a mighty ogre
indeed. They engaged in combat, fighting for a speedy victory.
* Bodies and arms collided or took a firm grip. They rushed at each
other with violent threats and yells. * A shot struck Bibitr.
Unflinching, like a huge elephant he kicked away the weapon with his
foot. * He leaped forward and broke the other's bow and countered by
knifing and prodding Narātåk. * Bibitr hit him, threw him and sent
him flying. Then he cut his throat and thus killed off the ungodly
creature. * Having destroyed the ogre, Bibitr returned to pay his
respects to the prince, whose descent was from the Buddha.

10.28–31. **Mahākpāl is killed by Usabh.**

28. (28) * When the news reached King Dasamukh, he was both
extremely angry and sad. * He sent out Mahākpāl, who took command
of the troops amid a deafening uproar. * Mahākpāl was mounted on a
strong elephant, a wild, evil creature, standing stock still, gathering
strength. * He roared like a lion or trumpeting elephant, huge and
dazzlingly resplendent. Immense, he was, and fearless. * When he
engaged in an attack he never left the fight. He would surge forth to
overthrow the enemy in battle, an amazing sight, weaving in and out of
the fighters. * He would rush with a roar to cut off heads and gallop
29. off with them, returning in a flash. * This (29) demon commander,
Mahākpāl, was horrifyingly impressive, arrogant ogre that he was.
* Bow and arrows in hand, he marshalled the demon battle-force, who
made ready all their weapons.

* Then Rām sent out the great simian lord Usabh to meet the ogre
and fight him. * Usabh took leave respectfully and led out the monkey
force to the echo of tramping feet. * The mighty Usabh, diamond
sword in hand, shouted his orders to deploy the monkey force. * As he
roused his chiefs and his troops of the left and right, urging them to set
off, the monkeys were chattering noisily. * Holding their shields and

(29) swords athwart each other, they took up their stance with ready eagerness to give aid to the lord of the three worlds.

30. * Then Mahākpāl the brave spurred (30) on his invincible elephant towards victory on the field. * The simian force and that of the demon race, the arrogant ogres with their weapons of war, were ranged against each other. * It was as though the earth would crack and subside and the surface of this world below would sink! Such was the effect of the unrelenting battle. * Using all artifices, including the magic arts acquired by asceticism, they opposed each other with resounding bangs and shouts, hurling each other and hitting each other with mountains, * while the swish of arrows, the din of the soldiers, the crashing of crumbling crags and the clang of cudgels * resounded everywhere, together with loud shouts heard far away in all directions through the skies. * The forces of *kumbhaṇḍa* ogres and of monkeys fell and lay dead, close together all over the ground, steeped in blood.

* Then the monkey Usabh drew his sword and brandished it, shooting glances this way and that like flames, * like lightning flashes
31. (31) sparking off one after the other, criss-crossing the sky with spurts of fire. * Mahākpāl, calling out with loud jeers, grasped bow and arrows and shot directly on to * the leg of Usabh. He fell to his knees but, with a supreme effort, sword in hand, he was up and after him! * He waved his sword and swung it to strike Mahākpāl, cutting off that evil head and sending it flying, in the midst of the dreadful battle.

10.31–36. **Dūramukh is killed by Kesar.**

* When the news reached Dasamukh, his fury increased and his grief became excessive at this blow. * He addressed Dūramukh. "Look! We are at the end of our tether. The battle has resulted in a wretched
32. defeat. * The news (32) is all about our losses of life; we hear of nothing else but their supremacy. No-one has yet equalled them in combat. * We have selected all the good men we had, all of them valiant and capable — not one has managed to come back alive! * We were just now waiting for some news but we hear only of defeat. They have routed our men and destroyed them. * Now you have exceptional powers, I think, and real skill. You have been victorious in battle many times. * I would have you go and give your help. Lead out the ogre force, the proud demon army."

* Then Dūramukh bowed very low and, on his knees, with palms placed together, took his leave. * He went forth, bearing his great club, a thunderbolt of a weapon, and gave his mind to drawing up his troops

(32) in formation. * His force of *gandharvas* and *kumbhaṇḍa* ogres bore in
their hands bows, cross-bows, spears, javelins, shields and swords.
33. * The mighty Dūramukh urged on his men (33) whose ranks thickly
covered the ground, raising the dust. * He mounted his bejewelled
chariot, yoked with royal oxen of willing alacrity, bold and ready to be
off far into the air. * The evil Dūramukh marched his army off in
order to be of help to the demon king. * His men, holding their
gleaming weapons and arrows close together, resembled, as they
moved, the great, glistening ocean with its watery surface, * for, as they
glanced about, their shields and swords glittered. They called out their
fearful war cries, feeling the hatred to kill.

* Just then the prince, leader of men, Nārāy(ṇ) Rām, lord of the
three worlds, * was sending the great simian lord Kesar as commander
of a monkey force to meet the evil Dūramukh. * Kesar listened to the
34. royal order of the elder prince, lord of the world. * Then (34) that
strong and mighty monkey prince, lord of men, respectfully left and
took command of the monkey troops, * who were there in their
crowds, with hundreds of weapons, eager to give of their best. They
closed their ranks for the fight for victory and went forth.

* The evil Dūramukh drove his chariot at a gallop and came upon the simian force of the royal lord Kesar. * The ogre troops, officers and men, and the invincible monkey army hurled each other about. * The *kumbhaṇḍa* demons and the monkeys shouted and screamed in the fray, harassing each other, dispersing the enemy and battering each other down. * The armies of monkeys and ogres cut each other to pieces, hitting constantly at each other, grasping each other, angrily biting. * They lashed out; they quickly turned; they rushed forward with a great bound and fell upon each other, making onslaughts to and fro. * The clangs and bangs reverberated, making the great heaven hum. The din was loud as thunder. * A whole host of ogres attacked the monkey army — and died in that battle.

* Dūramukh was in a bad mood, his face dark and patchy as if with
35. congealing (35) blood. He roared out threats to Kesar * and beat him
with his club. The strong and mighty Kesar, great monkey lord, did
not flinch. * He held him off and, with a shout, whirled round. He
strove to turn and, with a bound, to seize * that club of Dūramukh. He
pulled it hard, first this way, then that. He surged forward, raised his
sword and struck the great Dūramukh, who was off and away,
* swooping and swerving in a powerful dive. Kesar turned and
knocked the club far away, then attacked. * He raised his diamond
sword and managed to cleave the breast of Dūramukh and kill him.

* The news that Dūramukh was dead spread widely and reached

(35) Rāb(ṇ). The whole force of *kumbhaṇḍa* demons had been annihilated.
* Rāb(ṇ) grew angry and upset. He was choking with grief and much
concerned because their evil actions * were clearly causing the ogres to
36. suffer here and now (36) with retribution upon retribution.

10.36–38. **Mukharakkhås is killed by Chief Nal.**

* Then the evil Dasamukh gave orders to Mukharakkhås, a great and fearless officer, * to gather together a multitude of ogres and vehicles in plenty, and to work out the horoscope for victory, finding the actual moment for success. * The calculations having produced a favourable time, he watched Mukkharakkhås marching off.

* Having taken leave respectfully, Mukharakkhås led off the ogre horde of great *gandharvas* and *kumbhaṇḍa* demons. * Bearing a great weapon, a magic club, the imperious Mukharakkhås roused his officers and men. * They had fire-arrows, star-bodies, arrows of diamond sharpness, great thunderbolts of weapons, of great value for achieving victory. * Weapons were of every kind, one in every hand. Each boorish individual compressed his lips in bitter hatred. * In coats of mail, or seated on caparisoned elephants, they gave their minds to the
encounter with the enemy.
37. (37) * Then Rām gave orders to the fearless Chief Nal, successful in
contests, a master of military strategy. * Chief Nal made obeisance and took leave of the noble prince. Invincible sword in hand, he went out to meet the ogres. * He held his valued weapon, a club, and stirred up the monkey throng, urging the bustling soldiers to action. * The simians, thus roused, were in a ferment of activity. They formed a sea of individuals, busily striving to attend to what was to be done. * Daring and brave, every one, they were very quick to advance, to devastate, to batter the enemy, to engage in fights.

* Mukharakkhås, the imperious chief, engaged with Chief Nal, King
Mahājambū's trusted *aide.* * Both charged forward, tough and
powerful, bold and valiant, without fault. * Thc ogre force fell upon
38. the monkeys, their clamour resounding (38) with far-away screeches
echoing back, * as though the seven perimeters were smashed and the Sea of Sīdantar were splashed in all directions amid shuddering vibrations! * It was heard in the vast heavens, crashing and reverberating to all points of the compass — a horrifying din.

* Then the imperious Mukharakkhås and Chief Nal of many triumphs fought each other, on the watch for opportunities for deeds of prowess. * Both were fully equipped with clubs for attacking each

(38) other. The sound of those blows was terrible indeed, * as though sea and sky had crashed together in a whirlwind! * Both suffered heavy blows from the clubs, as, over and over, weapon clashed with weapon, hard as diamonds. * Mukharakkhȃs attacked with a mighty effort but was defeated by the power of Chief Nal, who crushed his head in with a blow. * The head was shattered and strewn about in pieces by the strength of the mighty Chief Nal.

10.39–43. **Kumbhagadādhar is killed by Chief Nīl.**

39. (39) * When King Rāb(ṇ) heard from the demons the news that the evil Mukharakkhȃs had met his end, * he burst into a fiery rage and beat his breast. His spirits sank to his boots and he smouldered with anger. * Choking with grief, he became more and more sorrowful, moaning and groaning. * As he pondered, Rāb(ṇ) became increasingly tense, his anger knowing no bounds. He almost died of a broken heart. * "O Prince Kumbhagadādhar," he said, "you are capable of making a stand against Rām's army. * I would have you lead the ogre army. Make a proud effort and flatten that band of apes with your great might."

* Then the demon Prince Kumbhagadādhar placed his palms together and took his leave. Off he went, * his cudgel, much-valued weapon, in his hand. He picked his most capable men, who would give
40. their minds to (40) victory in the battle, * for they were intrepid, unflinching in the face of the enemy and did not call for a retreat, shaking with fright. * From among the host of tremendous ogres, very bold, two struck the gong of victory and beat the drum as a signal.

* Rām sent the mighty lord Chief Nīl as commander of the monkey army to engage the demon lord. * The high-born simian paid his respects and took his leave. * Bearing his huge diamond-hard club, he went out to marshal his army and march off to a great battle with a resounding victory. * As he made ready his force of monkeys, the deafening noise of their chattering and squealing reverberated in the heavens.

* Then the cruel Kumbhagadādhar attacked Chief Nīl, putting him in fear of his life * but the simians fell upon the demon army and
41. fiercely strove in the contest, giving blow for blow. (41) * It was as when the vast ocean was whipped by the wind, causing thunderous crashes as it destroyed an era. * The unvanquished Prince Kumbhagadādhar and Chief Nīl of many triumphs contended for the victory. * The ogre force and the bold army of monkeys struggled

(41) angrily against each other, bringing into play their different powers.
* Prince Kumbhagadādhar of great strength, and Chief Nīl, the
fearless, engaged in combat there for all to see. * Using magic devices,
they contended for victory. Jeers and dreadful howls went back and
forth. * They struck out or turned in a trice. In a frenzy they parried
and thrust. They stretched out their arms or turned forcefully to take
cover after a quick glance. * They swooped and swerved with energy.
They sprang up angrily with great bounds or flexed their muscles to
obtain maximum strength. * Each one was full of confidence, each
doing his best. Each one had great power in his right arm, the strength
to fend or attack. * Kumbhagadādhar raised his club and struck the
42. head of Chief (42) Nīl, who slipped clear away * to some distance. But
back he came, lashing out. Kumbhagadādhar in his turn was defeated
at the hands of Chief Nīl * who leaped forward, raised his cudgel and
struck the other's head — it was broken in pieces and flung far and
wide. * The evil Kumbhagadādhar was destroyed. His blood poured
out redly, seeping everywhere.

* The news reached the evil Dasamukh, whose fury flared up. A
tremor of grief went through him. * His breast was constricted with
emotion as he sorrowed deeply for his beloved sons, all ten of whom
had been annihilated.[36] * "Alas! I am without refuge. I have no one to
whom to turn! I am utterly forlorn." * The more he pondered, the
more mournful, depressed and anxious about the crisis did he become.
43. * Distraught with his great grief, he tossed and turned (43) excessively.

10.43–47. **Mālmād is killed by Satabalī.**

* Rāb(ṇ) summoned an ogre called Mālmād, a minister with the
position of military commander-in-chief. * "O mighty Mālmād," he
said, "you must go out, tough and strong, to engage those ascetics.
* Those two, the monkeys' masters, will demolish our ancient city of
Laṅkā. * You have beheld the death of all my sons and of the mighty
Kumbhakār(ṇ), together with a vast military force. * Mālmād, it is my
personal opinion that you are completely and absolutely the man I
need. * You will go out while I obtain a force from beyond the
enclosing *cakravāla*. * You will throw fire and make fire — though do
not act too hastily or urgently. You are to keep control, just aiming at
them, provoking them, plaguing them. * When I have acquired an
adequate force, we will join together and quickly capture them once
and for all. It will be quite easy."

44. * Then the huge Mālmād (44) bowed low, eager to accept the burden

(44) of giving his help. * Like a roaring lion, he went forth to draw up a
demon force ready to make their attack. * He busily split up the
soldiers into sections of the left and right, with their captains to lead
them and a dense array of weapons of every kind. * They stood in
close formation, their massed weapons sticking up higgledy-piggledy,
athwart each other, obstructively, with their tops criss-crossing.
* Javelins, metal cudgels, various diamond-sharp weapons clashed and
clanged amid the army's shouts. * Mālmād, roaring like a lion,
brandished his iron bar and shouted out to rouse the soldiers. * It was
then that the divine Rām saw the host of godless creatures, those great
kumbhaṇḍa demons — what a force they were!

* The prince spoke. "O Bibhek, my great astrologer, look! Whose
45. army is this?" Bibhek placed his palms together as he replied. (45)
"This is the demon force of the great commander Mālmād. * The great
lord Rāb(ṇ) has lost all his most powerful chiefs, evil creatures. Not
one is left. * All his eleven sons have gone.[37] Dasamukh has no one to
turn to among the soldiers of his family."

* Then the master of men gave his command to the intrepid Satabalī,
a great officer. * "O most mighty Satabalī! You are to go forth and win
a grand victory over the demon army." * Satabalī knelt and took his
leave, saluting Prince Rām. Valued diamond sword in hand, * he
organised the monkey forces. Satabalī was a capable and steady fighter,
swift in action. * Bold and practised, he had been victorious in battle.
He was a trusted soldier, successful on every occasion. * Many times
had he attacked the *rākṣasas* with fire and never given up or retreated
46. in dismay. (46) * As Satabalī marched his army to the fight, their
uproarious din was heard far and wide.

* Mālmād came down like a roaring lion and fell upon the monkey
army. They flung mountains at each other, so that, * as they fought,
monkeys and ogres, reverberations echoed clearly in all directions and
frequent tremors went through the earth. * Mālmād retreated
defensively. The monkeys, screeching and chattering, pushed him back
and rushed in pursuit, shouting at him. * They engaged at close
quarters with the ogres, all out for victory. Mālmād was scared. It
would not be easy to escape, * as the evil Dasamukh required of him.
Satabalī had chased him, dashing masterfully to the attack. * "My chief
will wash his hands of me," he exclaimed, "seeing me not only not
winning, but even losing the fight! * For the king did tell me to see this
magnificent operation safely through, aiming at them and provoking
them with vigour. * But the monkeys have turned bold. They are
constantly teeming all round and advancing upon us. They are over-
47. whelming us (47) most unexpectedly. * If I go by the instruction of His

(47) Majesty, my good reputation will have gone, because I shall have fought without victory. * The best plan for me is to endure the fight to the death and not to withdraw, following the command of Dasamukh."

* Then Mālmād jeered loudly and was charged, pushed back, engaged in a fight, pulled and hit by * Satabalī of the simian race. Mālmād stood still — and died by the power of that simian, * who took his life together with those of that whole demon force.

10.47–8. **Rāb(ṇ) assembles the remnants of his army and sends messengers beyond the *cakravāla* to ask Mūlaphalăm to bring reinforcements.**

* The evil Dasamukh, in utter fury, choked and spluttered helplessly. * He was in a daze, dizzy, unaware, with nothing to ease his spirit. * He had lost all his ten sons, dead and gone. He had lost the mighty
48. Kumbhakār(ṇ) (48). All his chief ministers had been eliminated. * The officers of the army, the glorious soldiers from the corps of ogre chariots * were completely gone. He himself was thus left desolate and Laṅkā would be utterly destroyed — the fruit of evil acts. * The evil Dasamukh struggled with his grief and could hardly breathe, so great was his trouble. He assembled the demon army, * the military chiefs and captains, who were still left after those of the simian race had killed them and reduced their numbers, * and ordered a force of evil creatures to proceed beyond the *cakravāla* to the adamantine Mūlaphalăm. * Those demons knelt and bade farewell to King Rāb(ṇ), great lord of the godless creatures, * and went off through the air. When they arrived there, they invited King Mūlaphalăm to come to them with his force of evil creatures.

Later events of the Rāma Story

(The later composition. Parts 75–80 of the Institut Bouddhique text.)

75.1–10. **While Rām is out riding in the forest, the ogress Ātul in human form mingles with Sītā's court ladies and asks her to draw a portrait of Rāb(ṇ). She does so and the ogress disappears into the picture itself.**

1. * Now the mighty Nārāy(ṇ), the magnificent, slept on his couch next
to the lady Sītā. * Torchlight flickered in every apartment of the golden
palace. All the dearly-loved ladies of the court were sitting, as always,
awake and watching. * When the resplendent sun came up on to his
path of transparent purity, there were people whose duty it was to play
music for them, the music of the trumpet and the oboe. * Nārāy(ṇ)
awoke and, abandoning sleep, he refreshed his face and went to see his
beloved young brother. Then he went to have his bath. * After bathing,
2. he put on his attire, bright with multi-coloured pattern, dressing (2)
himself in fine clothing of quality. * He wore breeches of which the
border was embroidered with pictures of sea-dragons. His tunic was
vivid with lovely flowers, the embroidered edges glittering with
diamante. * Then he put on and tucked up his splendid sarong, fresh
and bright, donned his crown — a mass of jewels — his sash and
bracelets. * On all ten fingers he wore superb rings. When he was
dressed the supporter of the earth climbed into his royal carriage.

* Oh, the magnificent royal carriage! The spokes of the wheels were
handsomely decorated. It was embellished with patterns of beautiful
gems whose brightness dazzled with flashing glints. * It was yoked with
splendid horses of very great strength indeed and was most suitable to
be the vehicle of Nārāy(ṇ) Rām. * Laksm(ṇ) was there in attendance in
3. front of the supporter of the earth. As the coachman set off (3) an
accompaniment of sonorous melodies was played on strings and
trumpet. * All the officers and men of the military escort went in
procession, rank upon rank, behind the respected king as he proceeded
on his way into the forest. * The elder and younger brothers looked
about them along the way in the deep shade of lofty trees with widespread branches. * They watched the birds darting across the sky; some
descended to perch next to their mates on branches where there was a
space in the dense forest; * green wood-pigeon, the Burmese ring-dove
and pelican; Sultan hen, heron and humming-bird; water-fowl, teal and
wild-fowl; the roller of the countryside, quail, crane and sparrow-
hawk; * parrots and lady thrushes on the *Dalbergia bariensis*, that lion
among trees; the golden goose and the ibis and peacock, bending and
bowing, swaying in a dance, springing in happy sport. * The two royal
4. brothers gazed at the whole (4) forest at their leisure, peacefully
contented, and followed their path away into the distance.

* At that time, when the king and sovereign had gone to amuse

(4) himself in the forest, his lady consort, the much-esteemed Sītā,
* remained in the fine palace grounds in company with the dearly-
loved ladies of the court, who, like young goddesses, sat in attendance
on that noblest of ladies. * It happened that she was not very content.
She became quite fretful and wanted to go off to bathe and refresh
herself. * Having had this idea, that highest of ladies suggested it to the
young ladies of the court and they quickly set out. The elderly ladies
followed along behind in a troop. * When she reached the place, the
5. esteemed queen took off her robes and went down (5) to bathe in the
water, splashing and calling out as she amused herself. * Some of the
ladies dived down and, as they surfaced, bumped into each other.
Some shrieked and squealed in their play. Still others grasped each
other in fun or, in rivalry against each other, swam down head first.
* Some splattered the water around or turned elusively, then stretched
out to grasp a hand. Some swam quite far and splashed the water all
about them with their hands. * Some danced, some made music, some
sang, the sound of their happy voices wafting away as they swam along
with the august queen, enjoying themselves in the water.

* At that time the ogress Ātul, a loathsome she-devil, a relative of
the ten-faced king, * lived down under the earth. This malignant
6. unbeliever, of evil omen, knew all about Sītā, how she (6) had come to
bathe in the water. * The ogress was angry and brooding. "I must go
and exercise a little persuasion," she said, "so as to separate Sītā from
Rām." * With this thought, the ogress made herself ready with all
speed and, with a great bound, darted rapidly upwards and arose at the
edge of the water. * She crept along the edge in among the trees, her
eyes constantly watching. She recited a magic spell to change her form.
In a trice, no time at all, it was achieved! She was just like a human
girl. She emerged quickly and went straight up to the royal consort.
7. * Reaching her, she behaved with humble docility, bowing (7) low and
making obeisance with palms placed together. "Madam," she said, "I
am arriving so late! * I seem to have done wrong. I have gone too far. I
have made a *faux pas*. I am depending on you, honoured queen, to
forgive me and graciously spare me." * The queen, most high, took her
for one of the young court ladies and so replied, * "My dear, I do not
regard that as a crime at all!" With these words, the queen went back
to her apartments.

* And then the blood-sucking ogre, evil enemy, served Sītā in close
familiarity, concealing her guile. * "Madam," she said, "I understand
8. that you (8) went to stay in the kingdom of the ogre Dasamukh, that
base and loathsome scoundrel. * Tell me, what was he like, that Rāb(ṇ),
if it please you, Your Highness? I have grown up to my present age and

(8) have never had the chance to see him, not even once!" * Then the esteemed queen, most beloved, with no idea of the cunning of that bold and overbearing ogress, who was trying to tempt her and so bring about her downfall, * spoke in explanation about that godless creature with all his ten faces and ten[38] arms and his really overwhelming power. * She said that if he wanted to make himself resemble someone else, he could be exactly like that person and no other. All the gods were agape at his deeds of prowess.

9. * And then the wicked Ātul (9) taking note of what the queen said, spoke again with her wiles, * "Madam, please favour me with this kindness: do a little sketch on this blackboard. What were they like, these ten faces and ten arms? I would like to know what he was like." * Then the noble Sītā, esteemed first consort, trusted her, feeling no doubt, and drew a picture of Rāb(ṇ). * She drew all his ten faces and ten hands, his whole form, and handed it to the wicked vampire, saying that that was just what Rāb(ṇ) was like. * And all the court ladies, young and old, came on their knees, all in a crowd, trying to be the first to look at the portrait of the king of the ogres. * "It's hateful!"
10. some said. "It's horrifying!" "He appears (10) so huge — he's sinister." "He dared to set himself up against Rām who has such power — and his whole family perished!"

* Next we shall tell of the lord of men, of the most elevated line of descent, who went on happily enjoying himself until, in the late afternoon, the sun went lower. * Then the king called together the officers and men of his large escort and, seated in his carriage, drove speedily back within the boundary of the royal grounds. * The ogress Ātul knew all about the master of men having returned. The vampire was as pleased with herself * as if she had had the chance of going to the heaven of the sixteen or to a dwelling of the *tuṣitas*. She changed her form so as to be inside the portrait of Rāb(ṇ).

75.11–20. **When Rām is arriving back, Sītā hides the portrait under his bed. It makes him sleepless and very angry with the court women. Laksm(ṇ) discovers the portrait and Sītā, seeing that her women will be blamed if she keeps silence, admits that she drew it.**

11. (11) * Then, when all the charming court ladies who were there in attendance upon their mistress, the king's consort, noticed that the ogress Ātul had disappeared, * they realised that she was a demon, most treacherous, and each one of them was full of fear. They cried out and fled, trembling in every limb, and fell down all in a heap leaning

(11) upon each other. * Then the lovely chief wife, Sītā, learned that the
serene king had reached the entrance to the royal grounds! * She took
the blackboard to efface the portrait of Rāb(ṇ) completely. She wiped
it and washed it with water but it did not come clean. The picture
became clearer and clearer! * The queen was afraid of the great power
of her husband. Trembling all over, in her fear, that esteemed lady
took the blackboard and hid it under the fine royal couch in their room.
12. * (12) And then, when it was time to go to bed, Nārāy(ṇ), renowned
all over the world, arrived at the decoratively bejewelled mounting
block. * The bright moon and the stars had risen to beam brilliantly.
The king descended from his jewelled carriage and entered the
apartment. * He climbed on to his fine royal couch but he tossed and
turned, disturbed in his sleep as though he was being bitten all over by
little mosquitoes and by poisonous flies settling on him. * He was very
restless and as hot as if set on fire. He sat up and lay down again on his
splendid royal couch. * He opened the fine window casement to let the
air blow pleasantly on to him. It would make the burning heat abate
13. and soothe him. * The breeze blew on to him (13) but the king felt even
more excessively hot! He caught sight of the attendant ladies and
became very angry. His face flushed red. * "You concubines—" he
said, "why on earth have you come flocking round like this? Do you
mean to mock me with this behaviour?" * Saying no more he promptly
grasped his weapon and, drawing it, pursued them, intending to end
the lives of the beloved court ladies! * Then the dear ladies went pale
and faint with the fearful shock, overwhelmed by the king's power and
authority. They trembled all over. * Some cried out, quivering in every
limb, anxious and afraid for their lives. They ran out of reach of His
Majesty, the noise of their commotion resounding afar. * When he saw
14. all the ladies, so terrified, running out of his sight like that and (14)
hiding away, the king burst into a fit of rage, like the fire which ends
an era with its blaze. * With boiling anger in his heart, the king waved
his sword rapidly round and chased the ladies, to strike them. What a
commotion!

* Then Queen Sītā, noble consort of great esteem, saw her husband,
head of the three worlds, whirling about in pursuit of the court ladies
in this fashion. * She was aghast! Full of fear, she told one of the
women to go and ask the young Prince Laksm(ṇ) to come at once.
* The woman bowed and bustled off with all haste, as was Her
15. Majesty's wish. (15) * She crept up to the noble prince, bowing low,
and told him what had been happening, all the facts without any
omission. * The younger brother, highest of princes, was horrified and
afraid when he heard this. He made himself ready in a moment and

(15) hurried off. * Arriving in the presence of his elder, he crouched on his
knees, making obeisance at the queen's feet, amid the throng of dear
court ladies. * Seeing Laksm(ṇ) there, the queen said to her young
brother-in-law, dear to her heart, in explanation, * "Just now the king,
most high, was sleepless. He became angry and chased the women
16. away (16), causing much consternation and noisy turmoil! * I asked
you to come and discuss it because you are as close to me as my own
heart. Please will you go and see him at once; then his anger will abate."

* On hearing this, the young Laksm(ṇ) bowed and took his leave
and went out immediately. * Coming to the noble king, he raised his
hands in greeting and bowed, clasping the other's feet. "Victorious lord
and elder," he said, "why are you so angry?" * And then, seeing the
young prince, the high-born Lord Harī came to himself. * He
17. explained, "My own dear brother, (17) I went to my couch to sleep as
always but * my mind became red hot as if a fire was raging furiously
all round me. What could be the reason for this? Please go straight
away and find out." * Then the young Laksm(ṇ), dearly loved, made
obeisance and took leave of his elder and went, in accordance with his
wishes, * to look in every room of the palace. And he went and opened
out all the curtains and looked under all the covers. * He saw nothing.
Then the great prince stooped down and went under the noble king's
bed. He saw the blackboard stuffed under the couch of the great king,
* with its portrait of the loathsome Rāb(ṇ)! The young brother was full
of fear. "Whoever could have thought of doing a thing like this?" he
18. said. * "If (18) I were to put it away out of sight, I am afraid some
calamity might befall the king." With these thoughts he hurried off
without delay to present it to his elder.

* And then the lord of men, the highest-born king, looked at the
portrait of the arrogant ogre and his anger flared like fire. * He spoke
to the court ladies. "Ho there! You! You treacherous trollops! Which
of you drew this portrait and tucked it away out of sight like this?"
* All the court ladies, overawed by the king's authority, came to attend
upon him in great alarm, unable to collect their wits. * For if they told
him the straight truth, they were afraid that the blame would be laid
upon the chief consort. They looked at each other and did not know
whether to reply or not. * The king questioned them many times and
19. had no (19) word of reply. Very cross, he stamped his feet. They bowed
respectfully, each one silent.

* And then the noble lady Sītā saw how angry her lord the king was
and considered the situation carefully. * "If I remain silent it looks as
though the court ladies will be punished and then there will of course
be retribution to come in the future. * And further, people will speak ill

(19) of me, saying that I did wrong and, though I was at fault, stayed silent,
letting others suffer the dreadful consequences." * So thinking, she
approached her dear king, creeping on her knees and bowing low. She
said, "May it please you, I realise that, in drawing that portrait of
Rāb(ṇ), I committed an offence against your authority * but there was
a girl asking about the appearance and name of that godless creature
and she pleaded with me to draw him, there among the dear ladies of
the court. * I drew him on the blackboard and handed the finished
20. picture to her (20). When she had looked at it she completely disappeared! All the women were shocked and alarmed. * I tried to erase
the portrait with water but it did not go away. It was clearer than ever!
When you arrived at the mounting block, I slipped it under the bed."

75.20–27. **The angry Rām orders Laksm(ṇ) to take Sītā away and kill her. Laksm(ṇ) takes her into the jungle but, believing in her loyalty to the king, does not wish to carry out the order, especially as the queen is pregnant.**

* And then, hearing this, the king of the three worlds which spread
over the universe raged furiously and pointed his finger at her in his
anger. * "So!," he said, "this woman is no good! She is of base origin
and evil omen. Just because I took pity on her, she dares to act like
this and has no fear. * Secretly she draws a picture of her lover, to
amuse herself gazing at it in rapturous delight. For pity's sake! I
thought you were true to me. That was why I went after you and
brought you back to care for. * I waged that war with no regrets for
loss of life — and, two-faced, you turned away from me! If you were
going to yearn for that godless creature, why on earth did I bring you
21. here?" (21) * The king then told his young brother, "Madam Sītā is
unworthy of our love. I cannot possibly keep her with me. Take her
away and kill her. * Do not let word of it reach our parents, the elders.
You are to cut out her liver and bring it to me, so that I may see how it
is that she can have had such temerity."[39] * Then Laksm(ṇ), that young
brother so dear to their hearts, saw how angry his elder was, telling
him to kill Sītā. * He trembled inwardly with fear as if a sword was
cutting off his head. He wanted to plead for her life but he could see
how furious was the king's temper. * He simply set himself to do what
he was commanded by the king, leader of the world, who wielded
power: he took the queen right away out of sight of their sovereign
lord.
22. * In secret, then, the young brother made obeisance (22) at the feet

(22) of the chief consort. "Alas! What past action has pursued you and has now caught up with you to cut you off like this? * If I were to beg his forgiveness for your crime, he would be still more violently angry." He spoke and then lamented sadly, his whole body drooping limply. * Then the lovely queen, the chief consort of high esteem, spoke to the serene young prince, "His Highness will not be so indulgent as to spare me. * I was wrong to draw Rāb(ṇ), that is true. But I was quite without the feelings of a lover. I told him exactly what had taken place but the king did not believe a word! * He told you to kill me. In his furious temper he did not listen to what I said. It just seemed to him completely false! I shall endure death in accordance with my fate. * It
23. is normal for mankind in this world (23), once they are born, to die, every one. Where will you take me to execute me?" Then Laksm(ṇ) felt sorry for her. Amid tears, he told the dear queen that he would take her beyond the metropolis * because from where they were, in the city, he was afraid that the news would spread to all countries in all directions and people would speak slander and calumny. * As he spoke, tears fell from his eyes. He led the chief consort out through the city gate and into the jungle. * The prince reached an area which was safe from danger, where there were trees of deep quietness. He took the dear queen to the foot of a mountain and halted.

24. (24) * And then the much-esteemed chief consort, the lady Sītā, having given full vent to her grief, instructed the young prince as follows, * "My own precious brother, I take leave of you now. We have grown used to sharing our sorrows together but today, it seems, we shall be in separate places. * My guilt in drawing the portrait of that godless creature was not such as to merit death. However bad my behaviour has been, you, my beloved young brother, have completely understood what was in my heart. * If I am to die, then, with that goodness on which I depend, kill me quickly in accordance with my dread fate."

* Then the young brother, whose glory was resplendent, wept and wailed, as be heard the queen's words. He said, * "Your Majesty is true
25. and good. I believe (25) everything and have no suspicions. Dasamukh took you to Laṅkā but you were able to protect yourself. * All the gods and anchorites in all places believed in your supreme virtue. They said that, if there had been any doubt of it, when you stepped in the fire[40] you would have died. * And now it is only because of some bad fate from long ago that you are brought here to undergo a grim punishment. Please go free and follow your destiny." * Even while speaking the prince was plunged in grievous lamentation, most pitiably, prostrated at the feet of the royal lady and faint almost to the point of losing consciousness.

(25) * Then, when the lady Sītā saw her dearly-loved young brother-in-law grieving with bowed head and brought so low, * she soothed him, saying, "Good brother, it is fitting that you should feel merciful. But
26. the king has told you to kill me — so how (26) can you let me go? * If you go back to the city now, what about having my liver? It will be seen that you have deceived the highest of princes and you will suffer blame for it. * Your kindness to me makes me feel deeply — indescribably — grateful. Do not let me suffer. Please kill me as fast as possible." * And then the young Laksm(ṇ), master of men, made obeisance and replied, "How can I bring myself to execute you? * And a further consideration: Your Majesty is carrying a child and nearing your full time. Take pity upon that precious, lovely infant within your womb. * Surely your life cannot come to an end? I feel pity, great pity, I would have you go off and follow your destiny. I shall return to the city. * I shall inform the king that I have killed you. Whether this offence which I shall commit is a right or wrong thing to do — what of it? I beg to repay my debts of gratitude to you, Your Majesty. I am not concerned about my own life."

75.27–39. **Sītā tries to make Laksm(ṇ) do his duty by speaking roughly to him. Finally Laksm(ṇ) strikes but the sword turns into a garland. Encouraged by this miracle, they part company, she to wander onward, he to return to the city.**

27. * And then that lady of high esteem, Queen Sītā, realising the import of her brother-in-law's reply, gave thought to the matter * as follows, "Alas! Laksm(ṇ) here is far too concerned about coming to my aid. He cannot cast away my life because his heart is so full of pity. * I must deceive him, then. I will speak roughly and inconsiderately to him, using some craft, and thus I will make him angry. * Then he will stop being sorry for me and will put an end to my life." With these thoughts, she spoke. "Laksm(ṇ), why this delay? * You are the executioner, with orders from our sovereign lord. You had better do as our master bids. Why ever do you keep on putting it off? * I am the prisoner, after all. The king told you to raise your arm against me but, to judge by what you have been saying just now, you are behaving far
28. too much as if (28) you were on my side! * And, more than this, I know what is in your mind. Do not let yourself feel like this. You saw how quiet it is in the forest and have been speaking in innuendoes to me like a philanderer!"

* Listening to the queen, his elder, the prince felt acute stabs of pain

(28) in his heart, as if a sharp arrow were shot straight at his very vitals. * He fell flat on the ground, his face quite blank. He turned the matter over in his mind and could see that it really did seem to be as the queen had said. He thought, * "It has long been an axiom of this world — and it is a golden rule when judging behaviour — 'If only two people come into the jungle, there is no one to know whether they behave well or ill'. * And usually men and women are doing something not so impeccable! If, then, I am a true friend towards my revered elder, who
29. will believe that I behaved honourably? (29) * I had better kill her, then, and so avoid all recrimination." With this intention, he raised the sword over her threateningly, to cut off her head. * Then he thought of the darling child in the womb of the queen. He became burning hot as if a fire had flared up in his breast. * He wept tears which ran all over his body and was unable to control his limbs. The sword dropped out of his hand, as his whole frame drooped limply. * The prince came to himself with a start and sat up. He made a great effort to concentrate and expiate his sin with regard to the queen, so that there should be no retribution. * For it was Rām's order to him and there could be no question of failing to do it. He grasped his sharp sword, intending to execute the queen. * He raised the sword over her but then suddenly
30. looked at (30) the chief consort. It was not right to end her life. He stayed still, feeling miserable. * But there was another thing: he was afraid of his treasured elder brother. He made a great effort to be resolute. He rose up, seized the sword, closed his eyes and swung it down with a rush — * and the sword dropped from the prince's hand! He thought he had killed her and fainted, losing all consciousness.

* And then, when the young prince, so serene, had taken his sword to end the life of the lovely chief consort of high esteem, * by the great power of her good faith and the goodness of the precious infant she bore, the sword turned instantly into a garland of flowers on her neck!
31. * She saw her young brother-in-law, highest of princes, (31) unconscious in a faint and concluded that he was dead. She bent down and put her arms round him * and said, amid her tears, "Alas! my dearest young brother! You are constantly in trouble because of me. When we were on that journey far away and our elder went after the deer, * I was cross with you, my dearest. You never made me suffer for it! You went to fight at Laṅkā and were hit by the arrows of those vulgar, godless creatures * on five occasions without being killed. You gained glorious victories, were eminently successful and on your return enjoyed a time of leisure and contentment. And now, how can it be that so soon afterwards you are dead? * All this is because I mis-treated you! The king told you to execute me and now, my beloved young

(31) brother, my treasure, it is you who die in my place, taking no thought
for yourself! * This good deed of yours to me is unequalled. If you
32. have died and are leaving this place, I beg (32) to die with you, my dear
one." * The queen lamented over and over again, tense with emotion,
in great anguish. She beat her breast. Then her head fell forward as she
fainted.

* Dew fell and in no time at all the chief consort felt completely
refreshed! She regained consciousness and put out her arms to embrace
her dear young brother-in-law. * She touched him, found his body
warm and knew that he was not dead. She raised her hands and
declared before all the gods in their dwelling-places in the ten
directions, * "O gods, as I have been true to the powerful Rām of the
line of Harī, I ask that this dearly-loved young brother may escape with
his life and live." * After making this prayer, she felt the body of that
33. highest chief, her (33) cherished young brother-in-law. It seemed as
though refreshing water was running all over him.

* And then the serene young Laksm(ṇ) regained consciousness and
saw that his elder had not died. * He was quite overcome with joy. He
asked the dear queen, "How can it be that you did not die? * May it
please you, that weapon of mine, that sword, is exceedingly sharp. If it
were to cut solid iron, all would be cut into little pieces. * Your
Highness, that garland of flowers which you are wearing round your
neck seems to me to have a supernatural air about it." * Then, the
34. highly-esteemed lady Sītā (34) replied, as she heard this, "When you
were trying to kill me just then, * I thought I really *was* dead. But by
the power of my good faith, your sword did not come near me! * It
turned into this garland of flowers and went round my neck." As she
said this, the queen took it off and handed it to her young
brother-in-law.

* The beloved Laksm(ṇ) took the garland of flowers from his
respected elder * and it changed back at once into a sword, in a flash!
Regarding this as a most miraculous occurrence, Laksm(ṇ) placed his
palms together acknowledging her virtue. * "Your Majesty, you have
spoken the truth; this is clear proof of it. You are a jewel without stain,
worthy of praise beyond all others in the world. * This miracle will be
heard of throughout all the three worlds, reaching every point of the
35. compass! When you set out (35) on your way, I can see there is nothing
for you to fear. * Go now, madam, and may you have happiness! May
you have no misfortunes! I would take my leave, bowing before you,
and return quickly so as not to be overtaken by the dawn." * Then,
listening to her young brother-in-law, so dear to her, the noble queen,
the elder, shed tears and sobbed with grief. * "My precious young

(35) brother, so dear to my heart," she said, "I will set out, yielding to fate. I will endure my sorrows and journey to distant places. * I am only concerned for you, returning to the city of Aiyudhyā; for what will you do about the liver to give to our elder? * The king will say you cheated him and he will be extremely angry. You will probably be killed there and then! So tell me, have you any ideas about what to do?"

36. * Then Laksm(ṇ) reflected. "Dear lady, do not worry at all," he said. * "I am thinking only of you, so precious, for you will now be deserted and alone, exposed to the rain, the wind and the sun, journeying along the way in adversity. * Turning your head, you will see no companion. Your feet will swell with bruises and blisters." * With this, he bowed and placed his palms together, making obeisance at the feet of the queen. The tears falling fast, the prince forced himself to set out. * But as he walked away he looked back and saw the dear queen, sorrowful and trembling in fear. He ran to her and clasped her

37. feet. (37) * Lamenting, he raised his hands and pleaded with all the gods who lived in the forests, among the crevasses and the jutting crags of the mountains, * including Indr, greatest and noblest lord of men, Virūpakkh of heroic grandeur, Viruḷhak and Dasarath; * and also Isūr himself, who was supreme during the three eras over the sixteen divine lords, together with the gods of the ten directions. * "I beg to leave the noble queen in your care, placing her with all of you gods. Please rally to her side and protect her so that she may be free from fear and disaster." * With this prayer the prince walked away into the distance, far from that queen of great beauty, hastening on his way with

38. determination. (38) * As he journeyed along, the supporter of the earth wept. Seeing the moon, bright in the sky, he quaked inwardly, thinking deeply about his elder. * Now she would be journeying alone, forlorn and isolated in the forest, having no one to go along with her as her companion. * And so it was likely that animals and birds might attack her or harass her. She would sleep directly on the ground, in great discomfort and distress. * "Alas! How she is to be pitied! How will she endure this fate? Who will help her to overcome her terror? Who will take her away and look after her? * And then, she is near her time. To walk along at all may well be impossible!" Grieving, the prince journeyed on, his hands brushing away the tears.

75.39–42. **Indr helps Laksm(ṇ) by producing a dead deer whose liver Laksm(ṇ) cuts out to take to the king, pretending it is Sītā's.**

39. * And then the Lord (39) Indr Kosī was sitting in his bejewelled

(39) palace, Bejayant, the gods thronging round him in attendance. * It
came about that he felt uncomfortably hot, not at all at ease, and that
he therefore opened his divine eyes and looked about at every dwelling-
place. * He saw that the young prince was returning to the city of the
serene king and that he did not have the liver of the lovely queen to
present to him. The latter would be very angry. * And further, there
was the lady Sītā in the very depths of despair with nowhere to go.
Moreover, she was very near her time. * "The lady will have pain all
over her body and shortly she will die in the forest. I must go and help
them both and not let them be in such terror." * With these thoughts,
he came down from his seat, with its three decorated sides richly
covered in gold, and, flying through the air, arrived on earth in a
40. moment. (40) * There and then, he created a deer which died just on
the path by which the prince would be returning to the city. * And then
the most elevated prince of great might had spent his grief and become
calm. He was proceeding on his journey * when he saw the deer lying
in his path. Approaching, he could see that it was definitely dead. The
prince was very pleased indeed. * "I must take its liver to present to
that highest of princes and tell him it is the liver of the dear consort,
which I have brought to him as he commanded." * With this thought
the serene prince, so handsome, grasped the deer firmly with one hand
41. and drew his sword to cut out its (41) liver. * Having managed this, the
protector of men proceeded on foot to the city, carrying in one hand
the deer's liver. * Arriving, he bowed and made obeisance at the
sovereign's feet and, amid the throng of ladies of the court, he
presented the deer's liver. * Then the king, Nārāy(ṇ) of noble descent,
received it. He just took an overall look at it, assuming it was the liver
of his consort * and with no thought that it was the liver of a deer. He
spoke straight away. "Greetings, my own most lovable brother! Come
near and look closely at this. * This liver is most unusual; it is like the
liver of a wicked beast. So that was why she was fickle and loved the
42. (42) godless creature, was it? * Both you and I were deceived; we did
not realise how wily she was." With these words he went into his fine
royal bedroom.

75.42–51. **The queen bewails her plight. Indr transforms himself into a buffalo which leads her to a hermitage. There the sage, Vajjaprit, hears her story and uses magic to produce a hut in which she can live.**

* And now we shall tell about the noble queen. When she had watched constantly until Laksm(ṇ) was out of sight, * that lady heard

(42) the droning sound of the large cicadas, noisily buzzing along her path
and reflected, her face downcast in gloom, on her pitiful loneliness.
* When she looked about there were owls, rollers, gibbons and ghost-
kites sending out loud calls and responses to each other in those
desolate, jungle-covered mountains. * The *Centropus sinensis*, water-
fowl, jungle-fowl, quail, cranes, humming-birds and herons came down
to perch on branches near together, preening their feathers in play.
43. * Elephants, rhinoceros and big tigers ran (43) thundering along, swift
in pursuit of each other. The queen felt faint with fear and turned this
way and that, weeping miserably. * The noble lady made a supreme
effort to marshal her thoughts. "It will clearly be impossible to stay
here. * I am alone too and a woman — I shall surely be eaten by the
animals! I must leave at once and find another place to stay." * Such
were her thoughts. Then she raised her hands above her head and
prayed to all the gods before proceeding on her way.

* As she walked along the royal consort grieved. The tears flowed
44. freely. Desolate and forlorn, she choked with sobs. * "Oh (44) wretched
me!" she cried, "what evil deed is it for which atonement has not been
made? It is not right that I should be in such terror and grim
destitution. * I have already been cast out from my home once to come
and live in the jungle. Now this makes a second time. However shall I
manage to keep alive? * Alas! My young brother-in-law!" she
lamented. "Now you are going back to the city without the liver to
present to our sovereign. The king will surely punish you." * The
queen was most distressed by these thoughts, almost at the point of
death but she felt pity for the child in her womb. Why should it die
with her? * "Oh, by the power of the goodness of this innocent child,
most dear to me, I beg the gods all to come to my aid and ward off this
danger." * As she lamented, with tears flowing freely, trickling down
her face, the noble lady struggled to journey on through the forests and
by the mountain gulleys, jutting crags and ravines.

45. (45) * And then, after Laksm(ṇ) had gone, the Lord Indr Kosī transformed himself. * In an instant — no delay! — he changed himself into
a buffalo, with head aloft, held erect, walking towards the queen. * The
buffalo came right up to the chief consort and asked, "Why are you
crying so sadly as you journey along on your own * with no servants?
In what direction, in what place do you live? How is it that you are not
afraid of animals attacking you? How dare you travel alone in the
forest?" * Then, hearing the great buffalo's words, the noble lady,
46. much-esteemed Sītā, spoke (46) in reply to him. * "I am the chief
consort of Nārāy(ṇ)," she said. "That respected lord and master of
men made his dearly-loved brother bring me here to punish me.

(46) * Laksm(ṇ) tried to kill me but I did not die and he let me go on with
my journey in the direst destitution, alone, wandering in the forest. * I
beg you, Brother Buffalo, kindly spare a thought to helping me. Show
me the way to the dwelling of some great hermit, that I may entrust my
life to him." * And then the great buffalo, Indr Kosī, heard the royal
consort of great esteem and felt pity for her. He thought, * "If this is
how things are, I will take her straight to the hermitage of a pious
anchorite." With this thought, he led the way for the queen as quickly
47. as possible. (47) * Light was breaking as the buffalo Kosī conducted the
queen to the hermitage of a most august sage of great learning, said
goodbye to her and returned to his dwelling.

* Then, as the unblemished queen looked at the hermitage of that
sage of understanding, her joy was beyond comparison. * All the
suffering and sorrows of the chief consort were eased and without any
delay she went to make obeisance and salute the sage of piety[41] and
power. * Vajjaprit, observer of the code of ascetic behaviour, looked at
the esteemed lady and had a feeling of doubt and suspicion. * He
questioned her. "Greetings, O lady of perfection, comparable in
48. grandeur with the full moon. (48) How is it that you dare to journey in
the forest and come here all alone? * And your name — what is it? In
what city do you live? What is your desire in coming all the way here?"
* And then that beautiful and much-honoured queen explained what
had happened. * "Lord, my name is Sītā. My station in life is noble. I
am the consort of Nārāy(ṇ) of great power and virtue, who rules royal
Aiyudhyā. * On a certain occasion I happened to be feeling
uncomfortably hot and irritable. I went out to bathe in the water.
* There was a loathsome she-devil who disguised herself as one of my
daily attendant women. She had me drawing a portrait of Rāb(ṇ). And
I trusted her, thinking her to be genuine! * When I had finished the
49. drawing, I handed it (49) to her straight away. She looked at it and
disappeared! I do not know where she went. * When I tried to wash off
the picture of the godless creature, it would not come clean! It became
clearer and clearer. I put it under the bed of my dear king. * He saw it
and was displeased. He let it assume the dimensions of a heinous
crime, saying that I had turned to another, that I loved a godless
creature. * He told his young brother to execute me and end my life
but the sword turned into flowers, a garland round my neck.
* Laksm(ṇ) saw this and gave up the attempt to kill me; he let me
journey on alone in the jungle. I came here and saw your noble self. I
beg you, may I put my life in your care?"

* And then, hearing the whole story, the righteous hermit felt sorry
50 for that (50) noblest of queens. * "Alas!" he said. "Rām the divine did

(50) not, in his excessive anger, reflect about the time when Rāb(ṇ) took you far away and he waged war, followed you and destroyed the demons.[42] * Why did he not think of this? Because of some bad fate from long ago. It shall be my duty to look after your precious child, ensuring that there shall be no imperfection in the task." * When this conversation was over, the great sage recited in prose from the Veda for increase. Instantly there appeared a hut * for the queen to make her home in, there beneath the trees. It was decoratively created by skilled craftsmen, with fine cushions and pillows, mattresses and pretty
51. foreign coverlets. * And then the lady (51) Sītā took up residence with the pious hermit, making it her habit always to be dutiful towards him, * letting nothing trouble him, as if he were her own father. She brushed, swept and tidied his cell; she drew water in readiness at all times. * When the queen's time had come, the full ten months having passed, and she was about to give birth to her offspring, her whole body was racked with pain. * Then the great hermit of piety knew that the noble queen would have her treasured child. * He came out of his hermitage with many troubled thoughts. He took water and, with trembling lips, his mouth pursed,[43] he made haste to sprinkle it on the queen.

75.51–57. **Indr sends his four wives and the goddesses down to earth to help Sītā when her son is born. Sītā laments, when they return to heaven, on the loneliness and poverty of herself and the child.**

* And then, as the Lord Indr Kosī was resting on his bejewelled seat
52. in his (52) decorative palace, Bejayant, * with the divine *apsarās* all round him in orderly array to attend upon him, it came about that the seat became hot, with a raging heat as though it were on fire. * The lord therefore opened his divine eyes and looked at Sītā there, about to have her dear child. He urged his four wives * and all the heavenly goddesses to come down from heaven with him. All the divine beings together therefore used their powers to fly down through the air. * They reached the hermitage without delay and saw the queen, in pain all over her body, trembling violently, on the point of death. * Lord Indr told the four wives and the goddesses to give aid and support to
53. the lady to relieve her agony. * (53) Sujātā and the other three wives with the divine *apsarās* approached to cosset the chief consort. Some raised her, some supported her with arms about her and that dearly-loved lady was able to give birth to her son very quickly. * Then Lord Indr Kosī saw that Queen Sītā had had her child and * he blew on the

(53) conch, making sonorous notes which wafted through the trees. It was
Sujātā who took the precious baby, so dear. * She took water to bathe
him, then laid the darling loved one down carefully on a bejewelled
crib * with a piece of fine, soft bark-cloth beneath him. * When the
little prince was all fresh, she put him where his mother could see him
inside the noble hermitage.
54. (54) * And then the lady Sītā gazed upon her beloved son of glowing
beauty. * She bent to clasp him in her arms, embracing him closely,
tenderly kissing that child, so dear to her. Gladness filled her heart as
she tended him so that nothing untoward should come his way. * The
majestic Indr, manifest lord of men, and all the gods came to be with
the queen. * Happy and excited, they all offered their congratulations
and gave their blessing to the infant, that he should have splendid
power like his father, exceeding all others in the three worlds. * When
they had given their good wishes, Indr and all the gods said farewell to
the queen and swiftly returned through the air to their palaces.
55. (55) * And then, when Indr had returned to his heavenly home, the
lovely Queen Sītā could not see anyone at all. All alone and weak,
seeing only the little prince, she sobbed convulsively, in very low
spirits. * She held her precious son in her arms, free from harm. She
put him on her knee and kissed the dear child tenderly, crying in her
great misery. * "My child, why did you have to be brought into
existence like this, separated from your father and with your mother
constantly suffering unhappiness and danger? * It was when your
mother was living in peaceful serenity in the royal palace far away, my
56. heart's darling, that you should have been born! * Wet-nurses and (56)
nannies would have combined to take care of you, my treasure, and the
three grandmothers would have cherished you, letting nothing upset
you. * But, as it is, here I am, your mother, destitute! I suffer excessive
hardships. It is by your own merit, my love, that the gods have been
here to help you, * causing clothing to appear and rugs and coverlets
for you, my dearest — while mother is in the most dreadful state of
poverty, without a single possession! * I have only the ring on my
hand. My gift to you will be in accordance with our destitute state, my
treasure! * I ask that you may have great prowess, that your fame may
reach all points of the compass." Then the queen put her fondly-
cherished son down to sleep and went out.

* She went to the hermit's dwelling, greeted him with palms placed
together and said, "Lord, I take my leave of you. I shall go to the
57. water's edge. (57) * May I put the little one in the cell and leave him
in your care? It is so isolated here. Some danger might threaten him."
* And then, straightaway, the sage Vajjaprit spoke. "O, Your Highness,

(57) * do go, of course. Just put the boy there. It shall be my task to look after him. Do not be at all worried."

75.57–76.5. **Sītā leaves her son in the care of the sage, while she goes to bathe but later fetches him, unseen by the hermit. When the latter realises that the child has gone, he creates a similar child.**

* And then that pre-eminent lady of high esteem took leave of the hermit and started out. * Walking to the foot of the mountain near the edge of the water, the queen watched a family of monkeys bounding about at play on the branches of the trees. * Their young ones hung on to them, either in front or on their backs, and they jumped about
58. plucking fruits (58) of various kinds. "You monkeys there!" said the queen. "Why do you carry your children like that? * Those babies have only just opened their eyes. Why do you not give more attention to them and keep an eye on them? You jump about so playfully on the branches of those trees. I am really horrified! * No animals, great or small, do this jumping about, thoughtlessly amusing themselves with their young holding on to them front and back."

* And then the monkey mother had heard and she replied, "Our children are brought along with us — and quite right too! * In the old days, folk used to say if there was any trouble, *we* would not have to be afraid, because our children came with us. * Now you are just a foolish human, you who turn to us and say we are ignorant! You humans are irresponsible. You do not know how to give proper care. You have
59. abandoned your child and left him in the cell. (59) * The ascetic will close his eyes to meditate. If an animal hovers near it may attack and carry off your child to eat — for the sake of its stomach you will lose your child!" When she heard what the monkey said, Queen Sītā was panic-stricken. * "Oh! Oh! I have left my child with the noble hermit, just as the monkey says — and he is always busy meditating with his eyes closed!" * With this thought, that lady went up from the water and returned to the hermitage and the cell. * When she arrived she bent with outstretched arms to embrace her son and fondle him lovingly in her arms. Putting him on her hip, she quickly returned to the bathing pool.

* And then the good hermit was sitting or pacing to and fro in
60. meditation, his eyes closed and his thoughts concentrated. (60) * When after some time he came to himself, he opened his eyes and looked about and saw that the precious child had disappeared! The sage was horrified! * "Alas! The child which the queen left in my care! What

(60) creature could have come and taken him away? How one must pity the
boy! However could I lose him like this? * And now no doubt his
mother will be back and will scold me roundly. She will grieve
excessively. She will be at the point of death." * Even as he thought
these thoughts, he took his walking-stick and walked with trembling
limbs round the hermitage and the hut but he saw no precious little
prince. * The hermit walked about looking for him earnestly, hot and
flustered, in an agony of remorse. He considered the situation carefully. "What I must do * is to carry out a sacrificial rite and by magic
create a replacement for the prince. I will just put him there for the
queen. Then she will not have to suffer this dreadful sorrow." With this
61. idea the *ācārya* (61) drew a picture of the dear infant on a blackboard
and made a fire round the magic image.

* Now Queen Sītā had walked to the edge of the water, singing a
lullaby to her dear baby. * Then she went to bathe in the water and
washed the little prince all over. This done, she returned to the hut.
* Arriving there, the queen, most high, made obeisance and placed her
palms together in greeting to the great hermit in the *sālā* outside the
hermitage. * Just then Vajjaprit, who observed the rules of behaviour,
62. was beginning the magic rite in the *sālā* (62) and, looking up, he saw
the esteemed lady, her cherished son upon her hip, coming straight
towards him! The hermit questioned her. * "You gave me your
instructions. You put your child here for me to look after. When did
76.1. you come and take him away without telling me, * (76.1) giving me
such a fright? There was I, bustling about looking for him — I nearly
died! I was just beginning this rite to produce a replacement for your
son as quickly as possible by magic. * But now your son is alive and
well and my anxiety has gone from me. Now, madam, please take good
care of your little treasure and I shall have a chance to meditate."
* With these words he took the drawing up to rub out the picture of
the prince then and there before the eyes of the queen.

* Queen Sītā bowed low before the sage in salute and eagerly pleaded
with him. * "Lord, why rub it out? Do by your magic make another
child for my boy's sake! He would be just right as a companion to be
2. with my son." * The good anchorite listened to her and (2) readily
replied, * "Very well, then! That is quite satisfactory. Think no more
about it, Your Highness. I will begin the rite, concentrating, reciting
and using the sacred sayings." * He put the picture in the fire and it
burned up, glowing redly. By the divine power of the learned magic
spell, he caused a miracle to take place. * The sky was darkly overcast
and dimmed, just as if it were night-time. Soon there was a little light
and there appeared the form of a boy. * When the sage performed the

(2) incantations for totally extinguishing the fire, rain fell, pouring down in quantity. He approached and took the child, bending over him as he held him tenderly in his arms. * He handed him to the queen with these words. "Regard him as the young brother of your son, just as though he were from the same mother."

3. * And then the much-esteemed (3) Queen Sītā received the prince and bent to embrace him lovingly. * She put them down to sleep, those two precious sons, whose delightful beauty was like that of gold, just polished with sand — for both of them were of remarkable comeliness. * Their bodies were fine and rounded — Bisnukār himself might have fashioned them. They resembled each other in every respect. The queen cherished them, keeping them from all harm. * "Dear lord," she said, "today is indeed a good day! I would like to bestow names straight away on the two boys." * Then the good hermit considered what would be an auspicious time to choose for giving names to those treasured sons * so that they should have happiness and prosperity and, in accordance with their descent from great kings, should be able to govern their kingdoms in complete content. * The elder was given
4. the name Rām-Laksm(ṇ), a fine son, (4) clearly intended by nature for success. The younger, who was produced magically by means of fire, was called Japp-Laksm(ṇ). * Thus both princes would be able to continue the family line, endowed with power and prowess unequalled in the three worlds. * The lovely queen, greatly esteemed, saluted the serene hermit, feeling a joy which could not be equalled, * and, carrying the two princes, most high, one on each hip, she left the anchorite's dwelling and went to her own, to live as was her wont. * When she reached home the queen fed her babies at the breast and kissed her splendid, delightful sons. She loved them with all her heart and cherished them, letting no harm come to them. * Whether it was morning or evening, she never grew in the least tired of her darling sons. She cared for them and protected them at all times with unruffled calm.

5. (5) * And the two princes grew into fine, handsome boys. * They would go off together, elder and younger, to play, morning and afternoon, at the usual amusements near the paved area round the hermitage. They enjoyed themselves, untroubled in their happiness. * The lovely queen, much-honoured, lived with the ascetic, possessed of wisdom, as with a noble father. * She dutifully attended upon him at all times in the morning and evening, seeing to it that nothing annoyed him. Every day she swept and brushed and tidied the whole place where he meditated, pacing to and fro. * Having done this, that lady without blemish would go to gather fruits of the forest bringing them each time to offer to the anchorite.

76.6–18. **The sage instructs the boys, teaching them to use the bow and arrow. Finding them apt pupils, he makes them magic bows. They shoot a huge *Barringtonia acutangula* and shatter it with far-reaching noises.**

6. * The queen's sons were now ten years old (6) and of a physical beauty and grace superior to that of all others in the world; * the queen loved them as dearly as her own life. She took them to the great sage and respectfully said to him, "Dear, honoured lord, these princes have now reached the age of ten. * They do not yet know the Treatise on the Supernatural Arts which would be useful to them if some overweening enemy should come to attack and overpower them. * I beg you most kindly to instruct the boys, grandfather, and give them some training that they may learn the arts and ward off dangerous enemies." * Then
7. that best of sages (7) spoke to her. "O madam, do not fuss! * It shall be my task to instruct and train the princes in the whole of the three Vedas, exhaustively, so that they shall have pre-eminent powers." * As she listened to the sage, possessed of wisdom, the lovely queen of great esteem felt an unparalleled joy. * She admonished the princes, both of them so innocent and dear, * "Now, children, do your best and settle down to your studies as quickly as I could wish you to do." With these words the esteemed consort, dearly loved, bowed and took leave respectfully, returning to her own home. * And then the sage, so good, had the two noble princes reading and learning the Books of the three
8. Vedas (8). * They also acquired the mighty, supernatural power which comes from divine incantations, the Pali sayings. They learned too the art of the bow and of the sharp arrow. They learned everything without any omission. * Thus the two dearly-loved princes learned all the Treatise on the Supernatural Arts with the good sage and, owing to the cleverness which they had in all their senses, their brilliant intelligence and their wit of lightning quickness, they had no difficulty, no frustration. They learned right through to the end of the three Vedas.

* And then, realising that the scintillating intelligence of those beloved princes was superior to any in the whole world, the good hermit * made bows out of bamboo to give to the dearly-loved boys, the elder and the younger, with three arrows each, * sending them off
9. (9) to learn to shoot, rivalling each other as they practised; for the hermit had introduced to them the magic craft which brings victory, all of it without any omission. * So the two princes, highly delighted, received the bows from the good hermit. * They bowed very low, making obeisance, as they dutifully took leave of the sage, diligent in the ascetic practices. They set off, there and then, * and proceeded

9) until they reached a place beneath great trees with deep, silent shade, a
place for meditative pacing to and fro. They plucked flowers and
placed them a hundred yards away, suspended in a row. * They raised
their bows and, closing one eye, set their sharp, powerful arrows,
aiming at the flowers, and drew their bow-strings smartly. * The
10. arrows (10) flew straight there and detached the flowers, which fell to
the ground. The boys playfully aimed their arrows, trying out their
skill, laughing and clapping their hands in delight. * When the sun was
lowering its rays in the afternoon, Rām-Laksm(ṇ), descendant of a
powerful line, urged his dear young brother to return to the hermitage.
* And then the sage Vajjaprit saw that the two lovable boys were
capable and tough, with the strength for heroic deeds * and thought,
"Just so. These two boys have the courage needed to carry on their
line. They are by nature lords of the earth. * The proper thing for me
to do, then, is to make bows and arrows of real power for them by my
11. magic." * With this in mind the ascetic, possessed of (11) noble
benevolence, built a fire and concentrated his thoughts for the
recitation of the magic words. * By the power of the teaching of the
best and highest of lords and through the efficacy of the ascetic
practices, the fire flared with blinding brightness * and there appeared,
while this was taking place, rising in the midst, a god who bore in his
hands six arrows and carried on each shoulder one bow. * The hermit
was overjoyed when he saw this. He stretched out his hands to take the
bows from the middle of the fire. The god was gone! * Then he handed
the bows and sharp arrows to the two boys of royal lineage and
addressed them. "Now, dear grandchildren, with regard to these
arrows: * suppose some malicious military force were to make a
12. vicious attack on you, (12) some dangerous enemy, intent on putting to
the test his physical strength — they would give up and surrender to you!"
* Then both boys made respectful obeisance in homage to the good
hermit. They readily took the bows and the sharp powerful arrows
from his hands. * Then they bowed and placed their palms together
and, prostrating themselves at the hermit's feet, said, "May it please
you, reverend sage, your goodness to us is outstanding, without
comparison. * One might take the sky, the sea, the earth to compare
with it but they would not be equivalent. Only our very lives would be
equivalent and these we would entrust to you, grandfather." * With
these words, the two well-born boys took their leave without delay and
13. went out of the leaf-thatched *sālā* to return to their mother. * The (13)
queen, realising that her two beloved sons already knew the three
Vedas through to the end, * that they were brilliantly clever in the
supernatural arts with those victorious arrows and that everything was

(13) as she had desired, was delighted beyond all comparison and made a great fuss of her two treasured sons, so dear to her heart. * Then Rām-Laksm(ṇ), so tough and strong, and Japp-Laksm(ṇ), his invincible young brother, bent to clasp the knees of their mother. * Both princes eagerly spoke to her. "Honoured lady, we beg leave to go and amuse ourselves in the forest, * looking at the four-footed and two-footed creatures and the trees. That will give us great contentment. We shall come back in the afternoon." * And then their royal mother
14. (14) had heard what her two offspring said and gave her reply, * "If you would go and amuse yourselves looking at the trees and their fruits, then go, my cherished darlings, but do not go too far away while you play. * For one thing, I am afraid you might come across a godless enemy or a malicious host of buffalo. As you go along, keep an eye on each other. Do not be careless, my treasures!"

* And then Rām-Laksm(ṇ), tough and strong, and Japp-Laksm(ṇ), his beloved young brother, respectfully took leave of their mother, * grasped their bows and powerful, magic arrows and set out with eager footsteps, pre-eminent in strength and virtue, moving like royal swans. * The two princes, like roaring lions, looked at all the variety of trees, whose branches spread round with pleasant shade, giving a deep
15 (15) quiet. * Some of the fruit was almost ripe, some fully ripe, some just new and small. Petals and pollen, fallen from some trees, were wafted by the breeze, diffusing that essence of the flowers, their fragrant scent. * The princes went along by way of the mountain gulleys, passes and crags, so remote. There was a stream whose water flowed clean and pure. The princes drank and rested. * Birds flitted hither and thither, first one, then another, pecking at objects of all kinds and sending out their calls in answer to each other. * Animals of every kind were shepherding their mates with loud cries, one following another: hares, wild oxen, great tigers, rhinoceros, roebuck, woodland deer. * There were elephants in rut, struggling, trumpeting, running with deafening din. There were the fabulous scaly dragon-headed quadrupeds, and goat-antelopes all moving along with their own herds.
16. * The two royal (16) princes explored the forest enthusiastically and went further and further. Finally they reached the Hemabānt, where * they saw a *Barringtonia acutangula* of gigantic size. Its foliage hid from sight the lofty sun; its girth was about a hundred thousand armfuls! It was the king of all trees. * Rām-Laksm(ṇ) said to Japp-Laksm(ṇ), "O dear young brother of noble qualities, I would like to make the attempt with my sharp arrows to shoot at this tree and destroy it, to see whether * it would split or not. I want to know the supernatural power of this arrow of victory so that I may see clearly

(16) with my own eyes what might is in my hand." * Such were his words. Then the prince took his bow — looking very like his father — and swiftly swung it up and, putting a sharp arrow close to it, gave a smart twang to the bow-string.

17. * The arrow struck the trunk of the *Barringtonia* — it collapsed (17) on the ground in little pieces! The noise reverberated, as a tremor passed through the earth. In all ten directions there was a violent quivering. * The tremor was felt away in the *tuṣita* heaven and by all the gods who dwell in the celestial regions, by the *gandharvas*, by the fair-winged *garuḍas*, by the *nāgas* and by all the great kings in the cities. * All heard the mighty, thundering boom, such almost as to overturn the earth, as though a massive rain-storm in the sky was beating the earthly regions with excessive ferocity. * The marvel caused consternation. In every single inhabited place men were horrified. They shivered and shook in fear for their lives. * The gods left their dwellings and came down. Goddesses floated down on the clouds — having this power through meditation. Young *garuḍas* fell out of the Bombax trees. And all devilish creatures were scattered far and wide. * As to the human beings, men and women, they went in terror this way and that, parted from each other. The whole host of *nāgas* rushed to hide down in Pātāl. * The
18. herds of (18) animals which lived upon the earth — regal lions with manes and strong elephants — all roared as they ran here, there and everywhere to tuck themselves away safely in confined spaces in gulleys and crevasses. * Birds, male and female, called loudly and flew away from their homes, almost senseless in their fear of the quaking and trembling and the clamour. * The arrow was shot and such was the result! Then the two dear princes saw the tree reduced to little bits like dust by the power of that superlative magic arrow * and they both clapped their hands with joy, laughing loudly. They decided to return home, picking fruit from the trees: * ripe durians, mangosteens, *Willughbeia cochinchinensis* and mangoes. They wrapped them up in the hems of their robes and gathered frangipani and *Michelia*. Then they went back to the hut.

76.18–25. **The boys tell the sage and their mother about the tree. They learn from their mother more about their family history.**

19. * Arriving there, the two princes bowed low (19) in obeisance on their knees, showing their devotion to their revered teacher as they presented the fruit and flowers to him. * The sage, who had power through his acquired virtue, had been watching the two boys as they arrived at the

(19) *sālā* in the hermitage. * The serene, good anchorite questioned them,
"When you went to amuse yourselves in the forest, I heard a most
astounding noise * like ten thousand thunderbolts! A tremor went
through the earth; it quaked violently. There were reverberations on the
ground and in the sky. All the trees were shaking. * I realised that it was
a remarkable event. Now, were you boys trying out the powers of the
supernatural arrows? Was that why the sky became overcast? During all
time there has never been such a phenomenon!" * And then the two
20. princes, palms placed together, replied, "We (20) went as far as the
Hemabānt, serenely free from mishaps. We saw a gigantic *Barringtonia*.
I shot at it for fun, to try out the power of my right arm and because I
wanted to know the might of the sharp arrow. * And, entirely due to
your virtue, holy one, to your powers, grandfather, that tree could not
hold fast. It collapsed, reduced to little bits like dust." * As he listened to
the two princes, the learned ascetic was delighted beyond comparison.
* He stroked and patted the boys and said, "Children, that tree was as
old as earth itself! * It was created, a mighty king among trees, together
with that lord of mountains, Sumeru. No one — even with superlative
physical strength — could destroy it. * But now you have acquired the
power through your asceticism! You have been able to obliterate this
tree, my grandson. It is impossible that anyone is your equal." * Then
21. (21) the hermit gave his blessing, wishing them great glory and success,
that they might quell their enemies everywhere into submission and
fearful acknowledgement of their power.

* And then, having received this blessing the two noble princes took
their leave respectfully and went back to their home. * There, they
bowed and placed their hands together, making obeisance at their
mother's feet, and told her their story, how they had tested the power of
the victorious arrow. * And, listening to her cherished sons, so dear to
her heart, their lady mother was as pleased as if she had received a gift
from heaven. * She kissed her two precious children and stroked them
all over, those beloved sons, cooing over them. "My darlings," she said,
22. (22) "most dear to my heart, * it is owing to your origins that you have
this present strength and this surpassing ascetic power. * When you shot
your arrow and destroyed the *Barringtonia*, the whole world felt a
tremor, as when your respected father went and raised the bow in
Mithilā. * You have indeed great power — but do not go off playing, my
sweethearts, for every day I am deserted and so far away from the city."

* And then the virtuous Rām-Laksm(ṇ), strong and mighty, learned
all about their circumstances for he bowed low and asked his mother,
* "Madam, concerning His Majesty, sustainer of the earth, in what
kingdom does he live? And what is his name? Will you tell me, mother,

(22) please? * What was the reason why you came here alone like this and
23. stayed in the middle of the forest, destitute (23) and in extreme hardship?" * And then, when she heard her child ask these questions about
what had happened in the past, the queen, * with tears welling up and
falling freely, sobbed in great distress. She bent to embrace and kiss her
dear sons and then explained to them as follows.

* "My dear children, your father is Nārāy(ṇ) himself, who wields
supreme power. He came from the ocean[44] and was born into a family of
supreme kings. * He was called Nārāy(ṇ) Rām, the strong and mighty,
whose deeds of heroism abound. He ruled Aiyudhyā, a delightful
country, being the grandson of Ajapāl * who had three sons, fine men of
superlative power. Rām was the son of King Dasarath. I lived in Mithilā
but * your father managed to raise the bow and bring me to this
24. kingdom to join your grandparents. After a little time, he (24) came to
live in the jungle. * Dasamukh stole me and took me away to far-off
Laṅkā. Your noble father and Laksm(ṇ), his young brother, * marched
their army of monkeys, with its four fighting corps, in pursuit of that
king of the godless creatures, to fight against him, cut off his whole race
for ever and bring me back to the city. * As time went on, battles were
fought. Your two uncles set out to march the mighty army and fight,
seizing the chance to do great deeds of prowess. * They were able to
capture Laṅkā and Malawa for the king, their handsome elder brother.
As for Aiyudhyā, it resembles the far-distant heavens! * My children,
when I was carrying you, so dear to my heart, in my womb, your
victorious father went to amuse himself in the forest. * A she-devil came
and, changing her form to look as if she were one of the dearly-loved
25. ladies of the court, she came and chatted to me, persuading me to (25)
draw a picture of the loathsome Rāb(ṇ). * His Majesty was furiously
angry and gave orders for me to be put to death! And so it was that I left
the city and came to live here." * When he heard this, the high-born
Rām-Laksm(ṇ) was stricken by grief, distressed by choking sobs. * As
he thought with pity of his mother the tears welled up and flowed freely,
streaming over his face, while his limbs trembled violently.

76.25–37. **Rām consults his astrologers about the remarkable noise which all have heard. It is decided to try to find the potential enemy by attaching a message to a horse and letting it go at will. First Hanumān fetches Bhirut and Sutrut from Kaikes.**

* Then Nārāy(ṇ) of illustrious might, seated upon his bejewelled throne with his ministers ranged in attendance upon him, * had heard

(25) the deafening noises reverberating through the heavens and felt the
tremor which went through the ground so that the earth almost turned
26. (26) over. * And all the Brahmin elders and astrologers and ministers
of royal descent and all the beloved ladies of the court and the young
girls were pale and faint with fright and much perturbed. * The entire
population was fleeing in turmoil. Trumpeting elephants ran pell-mell
in the chaos which resulted. Appreciating what a phenomenal event
this was, * the king ordered a messenger to rush off with all speed to
summon the astrologers with their Brahmin scriptures. They were to
come at once. * The messenger knelt in obeisance, taking his leave, and
ran off with all haste and urgency. * Arriving, the official gave his
27. message. "O astrologers, (27) His noble Majesty bids you go quickly
this instant." Then, hearing of the king's summons, the chief
astrologers * grasped their blackboards and almanacs, busily made
themselves ready, each one, and went with all speed up into the palace
with its bejewelled tiers. * When they reached the court of the pleasant
hall, they crept up to pay their respects and sat down according to their
ranks and sections, attending upon their sovereign. * And then the
28. king, Nārāy(ṇ), observing the arrival of his astrologers, (28) eagerly
addressed them. * "O astrologers, a marvel occurred today. A violent
tremor went through the earth. Pray work out the explanation at once
from your volumes of the Jyotisār."

* Thereupon the astrologers made their calculations, checking all the dispositions produced by the books of learning. When they had their conclusions ready they respectfully informed their honoured sovereign, * "May it please you, as to this marvel, according to what is written in our almanacs and in the Brahmanic scriptures and judging by our observations, it is just as when Your Majesty and your young brothers, * all four of you, were testing out arrows for your father. A tremor went through the earth and it shook violently like this. * Lord, to our way of thinking, it would seem that there is someone of great physical power amusing himself with a victorious arrow and that was how this
29. marvel took place. (29) We would suggest, Your Majesty, that you
should arrange for a written message to be attached to the neck of a horse, which would then help us. We would make a wish and let the horse go.[45] Have Anujit go with the horse. * We should say, 'If you are kindly disposed towards our lord, then you should at once pay honour to the horse reverently in accordance with our traditions. * If any person, lacking in respect and deference towards our lord's virtue, manages to seize the royal horse and amuse himself by mounting it, feeling no fear of our lord's prowess, * such a person is a trouble-monger, intending to attack the king. Let such be captured and brought

(29) forthwith to be presented to His Majesty'." Then the king, Nāray(ṇ),
master of men, readily replied, "O astrologers, your idea is excellent."
30. * Next the king gave orders (30) to the son of the Wind to go to his
victorious young brothers, Bhirut and Sutrut, far away in the kingdom
of Kaikes. * "Tell the two princes to come without delay because I
would have them set out to quell an enemy." And then the mighty
Anujit received the king's order with all its content. * He bowed and
took leave respectfully and, controlling his limbs, he made his tough
body go through the air with surpassing speed straight to the kingdom
of Krasiṇ. * Arriving there,[46] they bowed in greeting and, making
obeisance with palms placed together, spoke. "Our elder brother, the
31. king, has sent (31) Anujit here. He would have us, his two servants, go
to the royal capital, Aiyudhyā, because he intends to assemble an army
and march forth to quell an enemy." * And then the king of the land
of Kaikes, learning all the facts, spoke as follows, * "According to our
understanding of the situation, it seems probable that this will be a
major war. Go now — and may you perform heroic deeds and
vanquish all your dangerous enemies!" Then the respected Bhirut and
Sutrut took leave politely and returned to their golden apartments.
32. * Next they sent off an official (32), devoted to the throne, to
organise a military force immediately. * The latter made obeisance at
the feet of the noble princes and hurried off as he was bidden with all
speed. * When he reached the ministers, he told them, "His Majesty
bids you prepare all your forces * because the princes are to march to
Aiyudhyā. He bids you prepare at once with no delay." * The ministers
heard and busied themselves, giving orders to all their auxiliary forces.
33. The elephant corps were to prepare their bold elephants, (33) attaching
their fine trappings. * The officers of the royal chariots had the vehicles
ready all spick and span, yoked with splendid horses, decked in their
dazzling trappings, brightly sparkling. * The whole infantry force, with
weapons of every kind visible in their hands, were there in their proper
sections with their appropriate chiefs. These were the divisions of the
auxiliary forces. * And there was music too: the army drums, the
beating drums, the Malay drums, the tambourines, the stringed,
crocodile-shaped zithers and the *ramanā* drum. Their melodious notes
wafted on the air. * Umbrellas and many-tiered parasols, opened to
shade Their Royal Highnesses, dazzled with their brightness. When
everything was completely ready they came to the front of the king's
court.

* Then the two elevated princes prepared themselves, putting on
their crowns set with sunstones, their sashes over one shoulder and the
34. bracelets on their arms. * They put on breeches and (34) their sarongs,

(34) tucked up, and they donned tunics of striking magnificence. Having
dressed, the two princes stepped forth and mounted their royal carriage
for the departure. * Oh the royal carriage! It was so fine, superior,
splendid, resembling the Bejayant of Indr come down to earth. * Gongs
were struck and drums beaten for the four army corps of officers and men.
What a din reverberated on the ground! * The charioteer, seated at the
front of the royal carriage, drove off speedily. The great prince, Sutrut,
bearing his sharp sword, sat in the front of the carriage of the other
honoured prince. * After some time they reached Aiyudhyā, halted their
35. various troops and went into the city to greet their elder. (35) * They
entered the palace, bowed with hands placed together and sat in
attendance upon the king amid the assembly in the magnificent hall.

* Then Nārāy(ṇ) Rām, looking for them, perceived that those great
princes, his young brothers, had arrived as was his desire. * That scion
of the line of Nārāy(ṇ) spoke. "Greetings, my young brothers! I
consider what has recently happened to be a phenomenal event.
* There were reverberations in the skies and a most violent tremor
went through the earth just as when we tried out our strength for our
father's sake. * I judge that there is some base man of erring, wicked
ways, coming to assault our boundaries. There can be no doubt of it.
36. * So I have had (36) my chief ministers, my wise men, poets and
Brahmins, all pondering. They are going to attach a message to a horse
and let it go off. * Then I am sending you, my dearly-loved brothers,
and the mighty Anujit to follow the horse, watch and intercept it, so
that we shall at last know what is happening. * If anyone dares to
capture the horse and amuse himself by riding on it, then that person is
my enemy. You will seize him and bring him here in all haste." * Then
young Bhirut and Sutrut heard and made obeisance, saying to their
noble elder, * "Lord, when this phenomenon took place and there was
an earthquake and excessive reverberations, we heard it and were
afraid. We thought of coming to you! * And now, most high, we have
your orders to command your ministers and soldiers, to follow the
37. royal (37) horse and waylay it. * We would ask to undertake what
Your Majesty, our master, commands, even to the point of losing our
lives. We would not have Your Majesty feel any anxiety."

76.37–42. **The message is placed on the horse's neck, prayers are said for the discovery of the potential enemy and the horse is let loose. Hanumān follows. Behind him come Bhirut and Sutrut with the army.**

* Hearing his young brothers, Nārāy(ṇ) Rām was thoroughly pleased.

(37) * He gave a coat of mail, set with brilliant diamonds, which had been presented to him in the forest by Akat, to Bhirut and a coat of mail from Indr * to Sutrut. He provided for their protection every kind of weapon and wished them power and success. * Then he gave the word to a captain, Sumantăn, to prepare the swift horse, attach the written
38. message and let it loose, as had been arranged. * The two (38) younger brothers knelt, raising their cupped hands, and received the bejewelled coats of mail. * And Sumantăn, the captain, bowed too, taking his leave, and marched out of the gilded court building to the victory pavilion * where he made ready the royal horse, putting on the fine, decorated saddle, the stirrups and the handsome fringed bit. It was as splendid as a horse from heaven. * A clerk quickly prepared the message, inserted it into a golden cylinder and attached it to the neck of the splendid horse as His Majesty had commanded.

39. * And then the (39) astrologers with their Brahmanic scriptures passed the leaf-shaped candle-holder round the swift horse fully seven times. That was the completed ceremony. * As they put the message on the horse they made a wish by the power of Nārāy(ṇ), their superior, before all the gods, asking them to help: * "If there is any person of overweening confidence in his prowess and power, in whatever direction he may be, please, O gods, indicate that direction. * Let the horse move towards him, straight to the very place, quickly and accurately, in accordance with our wish. Let there be no going astray." * When they had finished their prayer, the astrologers watched and saw an extraordinary phenomenon. The sky did not have its usual aspect, with the sun's light glowing redly. * The astrologers looked at
40. the sky (40) in every direction. It was absolutely dark! But soon there appeared in the East the forms of the two boys. * The astrologers had the drums and the gongs beaten with a resounding din and the military officers let the eager horse loose. * The splendid steed, of tremendous power, arched its neck to look in all directions. Then it was off, quick as lightning — * like a regal lion, long-maned, leaving its lair — after circling three times to the right and turning to face the East. * The gods who produce inspiration entered the mind of the horse. It went straight along by the mountains and entered the forest ways.

41. * When they had let the swift horse go, Hanumān (41) of the simian race left Aiyudhyā immediately and followed behind it, * crossing gulleys and open forest, keeping a close watch. Going neither too near to it nor too far from it, he stealthily kept an eye on the horse. * Then, after Hanumān left to follow in the track of the swift royal horse, those supporters of the earth, Bhirut and Sutrut, * elder and younger, assembled all their officers and men and, bearing their bows and

(41) victorious arrows, mounted their bright chariot. * Oh that brilliant
chariot! The spokes of the wheels were delightfully wrought in design,
sculpted as sprigs of flowers like a transformation of the pattern of a
42. sarong, all covered with gold. * It was yoked with splendid horses. (42)
Lion-like, the younger brother was in attendance in front of the other
prince. The charioteer drove off, speeding into the distance. * White-
tiered umbrellas set with jewels were fixed wide open, their fringes
shading the noble princes. The trumpet, conch, gong and oboe played
decorous music harmoniously together. * The whole densely-packed
force raised a clamour which resounded in the heavens. Earth
trembled. Every hand held a weapon. * The two noble princes followed
the path into the distance and arrived at a plain beyond the mountains,
impressively vast.

76.42–52. **The boys go off again into the forest where they observe the trees and animals. They find the horse, catch it and, in spite of the warning in the messsage, ride it.**

* Then, in the fine *sālā* the two boys of superlative power were
asleep with their mother. * When it was almost daybreak and the
course of the sun was glimmering with light, they awoke, rose, washed
43. their faces (43) and took their victorious bows. * They made obeisance
before their mother. "Madam," they said, "we take our leave and go to
the forest. We shall look for every kind of fruit to pick. We will return
when the sun is just inclining a little." But then, when she heard her
sons bidding her goodbye, their royal mother was extremely upset.
* She felt a dreadful quaking in the pit of her stomach and experienced
stabs of pain, jabbing like sword-thrusts at her heart. * She shivered in
distress, all her skin gooseflesh. Her eyelids flickered. She realised that
this was a most unusual occurrence and said, * "My children, when
you tried out the arrow a tremor went through the earth and there
were loud reverberations. I was so upset! My heart was breaking. I
have not been able to put it out of my mind, not for a single day. * I
44. am afraid news of it may have reached those kings who have the (44)
power for deeds of heroism and they may march their armies to the
attack, capture you and take you away for punishment! * I, your
mother, would die! Do not go there to play, my dearest loves. Please
do as I say." * Then the two boys, so dear to her, were quite downcast.
"Madam, dear honoured mother," they pleaded, * "we are not so bold
as to go far away. We play only round about here. And even if some
dreadful enemy should come to attack us, * there's no need to brood

(44) anxiously about it. We are not at all afraid. We will return to the hut
when the sun is just inclining a little."
45. * Then, seeing her cherished sons full of gloom (45) and wheedling
and pleading to go, the queen * embraced them, dear innocent sons,
and wiped away their tears, saying, "O children, apples of mother's
eye, * is it not true that fighting on the field of battle and the deployment of troops is very difficult? You are still very young. You have not
come up against it even for the first time. * But I will not prevent your
going. Off you go — and take care of yourselves. Go together all the
time, younger with elder, and constantly keep an eye on each other.
* Please, my treasured darlings, come back early. Do not stay until
evening. I always have fears for you!" * Then her two sons, most high,
bowed and placed their palms together. Carrying their bows and
46. arrows they went to the *sālā* of the hermitage. (46) * There they bowed
dutifully and said, "Honoured grandfather, we would respectfully take
our leave and go to play in the forest." * Then the best of sages spoke
to them. "Well, grandchildren, go and play — and may all go well! * If
some army of devils of ill intent approaches you in enmity, may you,
by your heroic deeds have them defeated, giving up the struggle,
broken into submission and surrendering to the might of your right
arm!"

* Then the dear princes received this blessing and set off. * They
went into the forest to a remote part, most awesome. They followed a
47. regal avenue among lofty (47) trees of equal height with deep shade.[47]
* Fig-trees sprang up there, small bamboos and sagoutiers, * eaglewood, litchis, mangosteens and sapotilles. * Herds of animals were
audible everywhere as they ranged about; some were mounting their
mates, staying in the shade to lose heat. * Elephants guided their mates
away from the various groups in the herd. They travelled a great
distance to feed on the far edge of the forest. The chief of the herd,
head aloft, would mount a mate or take some grass. Some trumpeted,
some ran far away. * There were rhinoceros and roebuck, great tigers,
jackals, wild dogs, monkeys, deer, large and small, iguanas, wild oxen
and hares, regal lions, young elephant-lions. * Strong young buffaloes
48. with black necks,[48] in rut (48) confidently butted each other. The
princes enjoyed themselves watching as they went through the forest in
that remote place.

* And then Rām-Laksm(ṇ) of glorious power caught sight of the horse, walking straight towards them, * its body white, its head black, its mouth red. Decorative trappings, all burnished, had been put on it and its movements as it walked were swan-like. He realised that it was special, like no other animal. * And so the elder prince pointed it out

(48) to his young brother. "My dearest brother, what is this exceedingly
strange animal with such fine trappings on it? * Never yet in all this
long time that we have been coming here to play have we seen such a
beautiful wild animal as this! * If it is as I think, this is not a wild
animal. This animal, it would seem, has someone who looks after it.
49. No, this is no wild animal. That is how it comes to have (49) such fine
trappings as these. * We must chase it and make it captive. Then we
will take turns at riding it. It will be even more fun than usual if we can
go for rides in the forest." * With this idea the boys pulled up creepers,
all they could hold, and twisted them into strong ropes. Then they ran
to intercept the splendid horse. * When they had managed to catch the
king's horse the princes were highly delighted. Elder and younger, they
gazed without stopping * at its soft mane, its waving tail, its perfect
stance and form and its trappings, fit for a noble king, engraved and
set with gems. * They looked intently at its headstall on which a design
of fig-leaves and stars was clearly visible and at its saddle, decoratively
50 patterned, and they saw the tube (50) with the letter tied to the neck of
the horse, hanging down. * Then the elder prince of the ten powers
detached the tube and saw the writing on a gold-leaf scroll. He opened
it out to read at once:

* "Message from His Majesty Nārāy(ṇ), highest of princes, whose
power extends through the three worlds which reach to the shores of
the ocean. The gods of the ten directions * invited this prince, scion of
high descent, to come and be born in this world to vanquish the
treacherous demons of villainous crimes who oppressed the whole
world. * And all of them gave up the struggle and were beaten by his
prowess. This prince now rules the city of Aiyudhyā. His name is Rām,
the king.[49] His strength and might are the greatest in the world. * The
king heard the dreadful noise of the supernatural arrow when a tremor
reverberated through the earth. He felt suspicion and has therefore let
51. this swift horse set off. (51) * Let anyone who is well-disposed towards
our noblest of lords prepare to make an offering to the swift horse in
accordance with traditional procedures. * Anyone who catches the
horse and goes for a ride on it, having no fear of Rām's prowess, is a
traitor to the great king. His Majesty will have him executed."

* When Rām-Laksm(ṇ), the elder master of men, had read what was
in the letter he told his beloved young brother, "This animal is called a
horse. * In the message they say that if we catch the horse and ride it
we are traitors and they will kill us! * Well, *we* are not afraid! We have
caught it and we will have a ride in the forest. If its owners come and
ask for it we shall simply give it back. * If they are setting themselves
52. up as our enemies, then leave it to me, your elder! I will (52) finish

(52) them off." * With no further words or delay the prince sprang on to
the horse, looking as handsome as his honoured father. Truly they
were without difference. * In his left hand he held the reins, in his
right, his victorious bow and arrow. His dear young brother walked
along behind the royal horse.

76.52–77.7. **Hanumān makes two vain attempts to capture the boys. They tie him up and scratch a message on his face. He finds Bhirut and Sutrut and tells them what has happened.**

* And then Hanumān, strong and mighty in deeds of heroism,
overtook the splendid horse and saw the treasured young princes,
* one walking, one riding on the horse, distinguished by their most
attractive good looks, bows in hand, looking like Indr Kosī himself
come down from heaven. * "What king's sons are these," Hanumān
thought to himself, "coming to play in the forest on foot, without any
military escort? * And another thing: was it these very boys who
53. demonstrated their arrows of victory (53) and is that why they dare to
catch the swift horse and have a ride on it, without fear of Rām's
prowess? * If I try to take their lives they will certainly die — but I
ought to capture them and take them alive to present to His Majesty,
supporter of the earth." * With these thoughts that scion of simian
descent, the monkey prince, stopped, sidled round the trees and sprang
out to catch the two princes. * Rām-Laksm(ṇ), strong and mighty in
deeds of heroism, * finding himself thus made captive by a monkey,
shook all over with fury. * Taking his bow of the powerful arrows, he
whirled it round and hit the monkey Hanumān, flinging him down flat
in a faint on the ground by this use of his power for mighty deeds.
* "Did you see that?" said the prince to his beloved young brother.
"What kind of monkey could it be that dares to try to capture us like
54. that and thus meet its own end? (54) * Its whole body is arrayed with
fine, decorative silver jewellery. I find it very unusual, not like
ordinary, everyday monkeys." * Saying no more than this, the prince
urged his brother to enjoy a ride on the splendid horse and they
continued along the isolated path.

* Then the Wind-god blew on Hanumān and that truly powerful being recovered consciousness at once. * He thought, "It *was* these boys who came out to test their sharp arrows! Their power is superior to any in the world. They gave me a whack which nearly killed me! * Since they are very small indeed in stature, how can they have such great strength? In the circumstances I had better think up a trick. * I

55. will change myself so as to pass for a jungle monkey (55). I will go up
to them and speak to them and beguile them into forgetting themselves.
I shall be able to capture both of them." * With this idea, the monkey
prince, scion of simian descent, controlled his body, raised his hands
reverently and made a wish. By the use of incantations, he changed his
form. * All of him was transformed and he became a little jungle
monkey plucking fruit. He made his way along from tree to tree and
came out in front of the splendid, swift horse. * Then, taking some
fruit, he went up close to the boys and behaved in a most friendly
fashion, chatting very pleasantly to win the princes over to him. * "I
like you, royal masters, so I have brought all this fruit for you to eat,
56. for your pleasure." (56) * Assuming that he was a jungle monkey,
Rām-Laksm(ṇ), the victorious elder, laughed gaily and said, * "You
have brought us this fruit because you think *we* eat such things! Take it
away to store as your own food. You have given us great pleasure.
* Did you see, just a moment ago, how a white monkey, a wicked,
pernicious beast, seized me when I was on that royal horse? He was so
bold and aggressive! * I struck him with my victorious bow and he fell
down flat, dead. Now *you* have a face such as one can take to. One can
trust oneself to you, you being a jungle monkey."

* And then Hanumān, hearing all that was said to him, replied to
the noble prince, "That white monkey was a town monkey, * may it
57. please you, (57) he was no jungle monkey. That was why he was so
bold as to attack you princes. If he died it served him right!" * Even as
he spoke, he pressed closer, pretending to be very affectionate, and,
with tongue in cheek, he laughed gaily in his attempt to beguile them,
77.1. not letting them be aware of his real feelings — (77.1) * for Hanumān
was in fact extremely annoyed. Then, controlling his limbs, and
compressing his lips, he whipped round with a sudden spring, grabbed
at the two boys — and missed!

* And then Rām-Laksm(ṇ), with the strength for mighty deeds, gave
a swing with his swift bow — and Hanumān fell flat on the ground!
* His form rapidly changed back to that of the son of the Wind-god.
Japp-Laksm(ṇ) fell into a terrible rage and struck a second blow at
Hanumān. * Rām-Laksm(ṇ), who bore the bow with ease, said, "My
beloved brother, it was this very monkey who captured us — and we
2. struck him a deadly blow! * How is it that he did not (2) give up the
struggle but transformed himself into a jungle monkey to come and
make us captive again? Let's do him to death once and for all!" * Then
Japp-Laksm(ṇ) respectfully replied, "If we kill him probably we shall
never hear of him again. * Now this monkey seems to be a very special
one. He must have a master who looks after him. We ought to tie him up

(2) and then let him go off and look for his master again." * Rām-Laksm(ṇ),
of superlative toughness and strength, heard and agreed with his
brother, dear to his heart. * He dismounted from the horse's back. The
two of them with outstretched arms pulled up creepers and tied the
monkey's hands behind his back. * They busily broke off sticks and
3. scratched letters on his face saying, "If (3) among all the immortal
gods, whatever their number may be, those gods of might and power,
* from the realm of Pātāl right to the *tuṣita* heaven and to all the
sixteen heavenly dwellings, if any one of them, not being in fact his
master, * should try to untie him and pull him out, cutting him loose
by any means whatever, let the bonds not be freed from his body! If
that god is really his master who looks after him, let them be undone
as is his wish." * Having scratched this on his forehead, the princes
thumped and walloped him, saying, "You obstinate ape! Such a
nuisance! Go and tell your master to come. We will stay here and wait
for him."

* And then Hanumān of simian descent, tied up most uncomfortably
owing to the strength of the two princes, * with a blot on his
escutcheon, his reputation for physical strength dimmed, felt very
miserable and experienced great pain. After struggling for a very long
4. time without managing to extricate himself, he set off home. (4) * He
jumped about, turning from side to side, and tugged at the creepers
which were bound round his body until he was exhausted — he could
not break them. * Hanumān grew more and more frustrated and tense.
"Oh dear me!" he thought to himself, "never before have I reached
such straits! * Even when I fought against Indrajit and he shot from his
powerful arm an arrow which struck me down and I lay upon the point
of death and he had me surrounded and captured by his whole force
* and they all worked together twisting chains round me, binding me
very tightly, even then I was able to kick the whole force down dead in
a trice and shake the chains off. * But now it is a most remarkable
thing. The creepers are no thicker than a whip and yet I cannot wriggle
free from them; they seem to tighten more and more." * Hanumān was
5. much dismayed by these thoughts. It seemed as if (5) he would die.
Ashamed before all the gods of the ten directions, he walked along in
tears, all woebegone, a sorry sight. * After a little while, as he made
progress, he came across the army. Hanumān was so embarrassed that
he hung his head as he approached Bhirut, sustainer of the earth.

* The two princes were just then driving along in their royal chariot,
urging the whole host of the army to follow the royal horse and cut off
its progress. * As they journeyed along the way their keen eyes caught
sight of the royal simian Hanumān, all tied up. * Startled, the two

(5) noble princes dismounted from their glorious chariot and questioned
6. Hanumān, * "My dear fellow, you are tough and strong. All the gods (6)
fear the power of your arm. You defeated all those godless creatures of
ill omen — their blood was like a sea! * Bodies of ogres slumped down
dead in a tangled mass, littered about the city of the demons. But now
— tell us, who was it who made you captive and tied you up like this?"
* And then Hanumān of superlative might replied to the noble princes,
"May it please you, I * saw as I went along, two princes who have the
great strength which comes from merit. Intrepid, they caught our
splendid horse and went for a ride on it without fear of the king's
virtue! * When I crept along and came up close to them and jumped up
and seized one of them from the back of the swift horse, those two
boys beat me until I nearly died! * After I came to my senses again, I
gritted my teeth and forced my body to change into a small jungle
monkey and I went up to them and chatted pleasantly with them —
7. deceitfully for, (7) with a spring, I seized both of them. But they
grabbed their bows and, whirling them round, they both, elder and
younger, struck me. Once again I was at death's door! * They captured
me, tied me up and then spoke with excessive impropriety, suggesting
that I should come and inform our noble king and that *he* should go
out and match his might against theirs!"

77.7–12. **Bhirut and Sutrut cannot untie the bonds. Rām sets Hanumān free, hears his tale and sends him, with Bhirut and Sutrut, to fetch the boys.**

* Then Bhirut and Sutrut fell into a rage as they listened to the
monkey. * They seized the creepers to undo them, pull them away —
but they could not do it! They took their victorious swords and * both
sawed at the creepers but they could not be broken through. It was
miraculous. They paused and caught sight of Hanumān's forehead
with the writing scratched on it. * Reading it, they understood every-
8. thing. "To write such a message was indeed rebellious! (8) It is clear
that they have no respect for Rām's perfection. * We are not your
masters, Hanumān, so off you go quickly and inform the lord, our
sovereign, that he may know this news."

* Then the son of the Wind was downcast, ashamed in front of all the officers and men. He almost sank into the ground. * "Oh dear me!" he said, "now I really have disgraced myself in a big way! If I go through the air I shall be embarrassed in front of the gods. If I go on foot I shall be embarrassed in front of the humans! * And if I avoid

(8) going to the respected king, most high, I shall be more and more in
pain, being bound so tightly. I shall suffer the most dreadful anguish."
* With these thoughts, he bowed and took his leave of the two younger
princes and set off across the forest from that distant region towards
9. the city of Aiyudhyā. (9) * When he arrived Hanumān went to attend
upon the noble lord king, bowing and keeping his face cast down,
ashamed in front of the lesser and greater officials.

* And then the king, Nārāy(ṇ), master of men, looked eagerly at the
high-born simian and observed * that he had been tied up with bonds.
He boiled with rage and urgently enquired, "O brave Hanumān, * you
are so strong, my dear fellow! All the gods in their thousands — more
than that, millions — of dwellings have never come anywhere near you
in strength! * You quelled the wily, godless creatures. They resigned
themselves to defeat, recoiling from the power of your right arm. But
now, when you went after the swift horse, who dared to capture you
10. and tie you up? * And these creepers (10) — they are as slender as a
whiplash. Why can't you undo them? They merely bring shame upon
your glorious name, making you as common as a jungle monkey —
even more so." * As he spoke, the king saw the writing scratched upon
the monkey's face and when he learned what it said he was absolutely
furious. * He stamped his feet and his eyes blazed like red suns flaring
in his face. "Well! Who is this person, so confident in his own power
that he does not give thought to the fact that he will die for it?" * The
lord and sovereign undid the creepers and took them off the monkey,
able to do this as he wished through his great powers.

* Then the high-born simian, Hanumān, bowed very low at the feet
of the king, much embarrassed in front of all his ministers, * and
11. managed to tell him (11) what had happened — all about the two boys,
the whole story without any omission. * "My dear sovereign, I never
besmirched your honour, whether I was to live or die. I have now
brought it very low but, before long, please be indulgent to me."
* Then, hearing what had happened, Nārāy(ṇ), renowned throughout
the world, was even more furiously angry, like the fire which burned
everywhere at the end of an era. * "So! They were little lads, were
they? And how did it come about that they had such power and
courage? O brave Hanumān, back you go, at the double * and order
my two young brothers to march the army, all four categories, and go
with you to capture the two horrid boys and bring them back for me to
12. have a look at them." * Then the son of the Wind bowed (12) and took
his leave with respect, accepting the royal command. He went through
the air in a trice. * Reaching his destination, he bowed at the feet of the
two noble masters of men. "Your elder, the king, sends me with a

(12) message, Serene Highnesses. * He would have you march the army with all four branches, officers and men, and follow the boys and take them by force." * Learning this, the young Bhirut and Sutrut disposed their forces instantly there and then. * An advance party, bearers and a reserve force came thronging in vast numbers, jostling each other. Hanumān led the noble princes in pursuit of the two boys.

77.13–26. **The boys confront the army, refuse to give their names and claim that their actions were justifiable. They fight Bhirut and Sutrut, using magic, and overcome the whole army at one point. All revive, however, and Rām-Laksm(ṇ) is captured and taken back to Rām while Japp-Laksm(ṇ) runs away.**

13. * And then Rām-Laksm(ṇ), whose descent was from the Sun, was riding the splendid horse, amusing himself most contentedly, * when he saw the royal monkey bringing the ministers and soldiers. "Here's the monkey coming back," he told his handsome young brother. * "He is returning once again with a whole army in divisions. Their ranks, in close formation, are extensive. The monkey is a captain. * Well, I have no fears. I want to try out the power of my right arm." As he spoke he dismounted from the swift horse and stood facing the army, * bravely bearing his bow, as intrepid as a roaring lion. Without delay, he
14. sweetly enquired of them, (14) * "What is your intention, Your Highnesses, in bringing your army here? Do tell us that we may know."

* Then the princes, Bhirut and Sutrut, heard the two boys[50] speaking so boldly, lion-like. * Their bearing was decorous. Their build was similar to that of Nārāy(ṇ) of great power. * "Are they of our own lineage," they said, "or are they the sons of a king, * coming to seek instruction in the noble arts from some good sage? Why do they go on foot, just the two of them, with no accompanying escort? * They are so small; we really should perhaps take pity on them. How can they have this surpassing power and speak with such insubordination? They show us no respect, no doubt of that!" * With such thoughts, the princes,
15. great overlords, replied, "Greetings, you two boys! (15) What are your names? * And your father and mother — what are their families? In what thoroughfare or city do you live? Kindly inform us. * And how is it that you boys are so brazen? You just seized this horse without the slightest compunction and went for a ride on it! *And* you tied up the son of the Wind-god and beat him almost to death! * You made marks on his face, words saying that he should go and find his master. Now, by the order of our noble king we two have brought all our officers

(15) and men * out here to surround you both and make you captive and take you to present to His Serene Highness, whose role it is to be the lord of the world."

* Then, hearing this, Rām-Laksm(ṇ), who had the strength for mighty deeds, replied, "Do not ask our names, O princes. * We were
16. walking through (16) the forest enjoying ourselves and not doing the slightest harm — but if you want to fight us, we on our side will not shrink from it. * This horse had no one to look after it. It came along, right there on our path. We two brothers saw it and together we caught it and rode it. Now, what wrong did we do? * As for that white monkey, he's a wretch! He's big, bad and horrid. He took us off the back of the horse, so we beat him to the point of death. * Later on he turned into a jungle monkey and made us captive. We dealt him two blows, made marks on his face and tied him up but we spared his life. And you say we did wrong. Hmm! * Why did you not investigate this instead of nipping off home, misrepresenting the matter as though we were in the wrong and marching here to surround us and capture us? We *are* afraid of you, I'm sure!"

* And then Bhirut replied, "Now, you boys! You are being very silly
17. * not to fear (17) the perfection of the noble master of men, Nārāy(ṇ). On that swift horse's neck the king attached a royal message. * We are speaking to you as friends. Why did you speak so thoughtlessly? You are so very young. How will you be able to match your lives against his?" * Then Rām-Laksm(ṇ) replied, "Do not, O Serene Highnesses, be so confident in the power of your hand! * The message, we thought, was astonishing. It is not according to the rules of fair play to let a horse go off to find a person and then make that person a criminal. Is this really within the bounds of honourable behaviour? * It may be that the lord Rām, a sovereign of power and prowess, being Nārāy(ṇ) in changed form, has descended to give attention to his kingdom * and has been able to quell all those evil godless creatures, loathsome wretches, and kings of ill-repute who lack virtue and that they have
18. thus come (18) under the power of his hand. * But *we* are not slaves of Rām! He has despised us — regarded us as small fry — but we are strong and can destroy. * We feel sorry for your host of men. Why should they come and die like this? We two and you two princes will join combat together and see what powers we have." * The princes, Bhirut and Sutrut, raged furiously as if a fire had broken out and was consuming their whole bodies.

* Then those sustainers of the earth took their bows and sharp, magic arrows and shot at the boys to kill them. A violent noise reverberated! * The sky became overcast with darkness and was

(18) disturbed with movements all the way to the celestial regions. There
appeared a strong rampart enclosing the two boys! * And then Rām-
Laksm(ṇ), strong and mighty, his face flushed with anger, trembled in
19. every (19) limb. * He shot an arrow which instantly shattered the
strong rampart, dispersing it in little bits as fine as ash! A tremor
moved through the earth. * Then Bhirut, seeing the prince break up the
rampart with his arrows, * shook with fury. He took his bow with its
effective, magic arrows of victory and, using his power for heroic
deeds, aimed an arrow in answer. * There was heard resounding
through the skies a dreadful, echoing din. The arrow turned into *nāgas*
which pursued the two boys, spitting out their venom all over the
ground. * But when Rām-Laksm(ṇ) of magnificent power saw the host
20. of *nāgas* spitting out their venom (20) and moving in pursuit of them in
this way, * he was most amused and enjoyed watching them, quite
unafraid. He shot an arrow which turned into *garuḍas*, regal birds,
* which chased the *nāgas*, swooping down to snatch them and carry
them off to eat. All the *nāgas* met their end as they fled in every
direction. * Seeing the prince's arrow turning into *garuḍas* and
pursuing all the *nāgas*, the two magnificent young brothers of Rām
* angrily grasped their efficacious arrows and, dismounting from their
vehicle, approached to fight at close quarters for victory. * Bhirut,
tough and strong, with his mighty arrows, joined battle with the
powerful Rām-Laksm(ṇ), while Sutrut contended against young Japp-
21. Laksm(ṇ). * The four devotees of asceticism, with the power (21) for
heroic deeds, clashed body on body, might on might, provoking each
other in the contest of physical strength. * Then the all-powerful Rām-
Laksm(ṇ), whose descent was from the Sun, shot his victorious arrow
at the two princes and, owing to his power for deeds of heroism, they
fell. * For he shot an arrow which became, by its invincible power, a
mesh of many thicknesses and went round and round the soldiers, all
the various forces. * And then the officers, senior and junior, were tied
up in bonds, trembling in terror. * They fell and lay writhing on the
ground, tossing and turning, or trying to run away, pale with fright,
the white of their eyes showing, their cries echoing through the forest.
22. (22) * Then the son of the Wind saw that Bhirut and his young
brother, struck by that sharp arrow, had fallen and were lying there on
the ground * and that their men were tied up in tough, constricting
bonds. Hanumān was very cross indeed. "So!" he said, "I am a
military officer of our respected great king * and I will endure death in
order to have good reputation for ever after this." * With this thought,
he changed himself into an awe-inspiring shape. Reciting divine
formulae, he transformed himself * into a body with eight outstretched

(22) arms and four faces! He stood there in this transformation like Brahm[51]
the mighty and then he approached and seized the two boys. * The two
noble boys found themselves made prisoner when the monkey sprang
23. towards (23) them but * managed to leap up quickly and swing their
bows to strike Hanumān. He fell instantly and lay faint and shaking all
over.

* Then the princes, Bhirut and Sutrut, who had been struck by arrows, were not dead, owing to the efficacy of the coats of mail given by their elder brother. * They came to consciousness and both struggled to get themselves upright. Bhirut said to his young brother, "We * have always, on every occasion that we have fought, managed to achieve what we desired but these youngsters are quite out of the ordinary — that is clear! To what king can they be related? * Or is it perhaps Isūr there in the arrow to destroy us and that is why these arrows have such power, striking us and sinking into our bodies,
24. * causing us sharp, stabbing pains? (24) Poison has spread right
through us. I feel ashamed before all in the three worlds." After these words were spoken, the princes murmured divine incantations of speedy effectiveness * three times through. They felt their bodies — the arrows had melted into thin air! And all trace of their wounds was gone! * Looking round, they saw Hanumān, looking like a dead soldier, and all the officers and men with their hands tied. * Their two Serene Highnesses raised their hands and pronounced a prayer. "By the power of Nārāy(ṇ), who, in another form, came down to take upon himself the care of our realm, * would that we might help this monkey-born one, that he may rapidly have life again and, as for the men and officers, may they manage to be free in accordance with our prayer."
25. * Having expressed this wish, those royal sustainers of the earth (25)
took aim with their sharp, efficacious arrows and shot them into the skies. A deafening noise rang out * and there arose a breeze which blew on to Hanumān who regained consciousness and did not in fact die. As for the snare, it disappeared from sight * and the arrow flew on towards Rām-Laksm(ṇ), high-born prince, who took the force of it. As it fell from his hand he fell over and lay there on the ground.

* Then Hanumān, whose powers were superlative, trembled all over with fury. He leaped up and flew through the air in a flash. * Springing forward to catch the two of them, he succeeded in catching only Rām-Laksm(ṇ) — Japp-Laksm(ṇ) managed to run off into the forest
26. — and took him to present to the princes. (26) Bhirut and young Sutrut
were in a mighty rage. They ordered the whole force and their officers * to grab hold of him, this loathsome young enemy, drag him triumphantly away, bind him up mercilessly, make him suffer as he

(26) deserved. * This done, they set off with the army, officers and men, they themselves travelling in their royal vehicle, on their return journey to the city.

77.26–33. **Hearing what has happened, Rām orders Rām-Laksm(ṇ) to be kept in fetters in a cage for three days and to be publicly reviled. The populace secretly pities him. The gods come down and make him comfortable.**

* When they reached the outskirts of the capital, the two serene princes, sustainers of the earth, dismounted from their carriage and went into the golden reception hall to attend upon the king. * Arriving there, they raised their hands with palms placed together, making obeisance respectfully at the feet of their elder. They informed him
27. about the boys fighting against them, (27) setting themselves up as adversaries. * "They have great power in their right arms. They shot arrows to kill us and to bind up our men. Hanumān, too, nearly died! * Through the power of your virtue we did not die but we were able to capture only the elder of them; the younger ran off and disappeared from sight." * Then Nārāy(ṇ) of most elevated might, became red in the face as he listened to his blameless young brothers. * The lord king impressed upon them his command, "Now, ministers and all of you officers and men, * this is a brazen rascal. We cannot spare him. Please remove him as quickly as possible. Make him suffer, let him endure hardship. * Give him all five devices for restraint.[52] After that let officials take him round the city to be publicly reviled before all the
28. (28) people. * Then put him in a cage and keep him there for three days. Don't be in a hurry to kill him. After that let the executioners take him away and finish him off." Then the chief ministers of the four administrative departments received the command of the master of men and led Rām-Laksm(ṇ) away.

* Arriving in the city they had auxiliary soldiers putting the restraints on the precious young prince, putting him in chains with a weight attached to his neck, * putting all five kinds of bond on him. Then the officials took him without further ado on public show, doing what the king had ordered. * They carried all kinds of vicious
29. implements (29) clashing against each other and impeding each other. They struck the gong for the public revilement in the squares of the city as they proceeded round the metropolis. * Then the whole population, male and female, were secretly communicating with each other. They nudged people or drew them to one side and whispered,

(29) * "You see that handsome prince? He is like the full Moon in the
hands of the godless Rāhū, hidden so that her brightness cannot be
seen." * "His appearance suggests a superior position. He is good-
looking and attractive." "He is very like His Majesty, the lord above
our heads." * "Oh I am so sorry for him!" "Of what king's family is
he?" "Why ever did he show off his power for great deeds? He has
caused his own death!" * Some of them had food which they wanted to
give the prince but they did not dare for fear of the military officers, so
30. they told (30) each other not to do so. * The whole population, in a
tumultuous, disorderly crowd, followed to watch them. They pitied the
prince and sadly bewailed his lot.

* Then, when the executioners had taken the prince on show round
the city, they came to a place used for punishment where they speedily
made their arrangements, placing a large cage there for the beloved
prince. They did not execute him. * Then each day the executioners,
their swords drawn, gleaming white, and held close to each other, sat
31. and kept a keen and careful watch over him. * The dear prince (31)
suffered his terrible punishment in wretched despair. * He wept
miserably, his breast constricted with choking sobs. He cried out,
addressing his revered mother and the sage of great piety. * "O good
mother," he said, "your loving kindness has been abundant indeed.
You have cared for me tenderly, never letting anything trouble me.
* And now I have reached a state of destitution and am undergoing the
greatest hardship. It is because of a past action from long ago that I
have to endure this. * It has caught up with me and is destroying my
life. It has separated us, made me abandon you, dear mother, and so I
do not have you to take care of me. * Alas! Now both of you, I expect,
are constantly looking out for me, imagining that I am on my way
back and will return to you. * You do not know I am dying, about to
leave you there in that dense forest. You must be sadly distressed as
32. you (32) constantly look for the arrival of your lost son! * Alas! My
dearest, darling brother, you ran away and were separated from me.
Are you alive and well or did you die? * I pray that you managed to
escape and reach our mother's home to be a companion for her, not
leaving the hermitage but staying nearby." * The prince wept about the
whole situation, oblivious of all else in his distress. He sank down in a
dead faint, his head slumping forward.

* And then the divinities who dwell in heaven and those whose
attention is given to the protection of capitals * saw how Nārāy(ṇ),
who held great sway, did not recognise his own dear son; and how he
was having his military officers carry out his execution * and those
33. gods were quite perturbed, every one, (33) and sped down through the

(33) air, leaving heaven to come to the prince. * When they arrived the gods produced various things through the power of their virtue. They placed a shady parasol, in tiers, bejewelled, to screen the sun's rays so that they would not reach him. * They loosened all his bonds. They applied nectar all over his body. Some wafted him with fans to make him pleasantly cool. * And they brought divine food which had an exquisite flavour for the boy to eat, to keep him alive.

77.33–46. **When Japp-Laksm(ṇ) arrives home and tells the story, the sage is able to assure the queen that Rām-Laksm(ṇ) is still alive although in trouble. The queen gives Japp-Laksm(ṇ) her magic ring and he sets out to find his brother. He reaches Aiyudhyā.**

* And then the young Japp-Laksm(ṇ) had stood beside the path in terror, watching and thinking hard. * When he saw them capture his elder he almost died of distress. He might have returned, summoned
34. his strength and fought against them but he saw that their forces (34) were far too numerous. * He stayed there hesitating, in the depths of despair. When the sun was going down he returned to his mother. * As he went hurrying along he saw his elder's bow. He picked it up and carried it on his head, weeping miserably. * "Alas, elder brother!" he cried, "you must be experiencing terrible fear. Are you alive or dead? You are lost to me. * I would go off after you to help you and join you in death but I am sorry for our revered mother. She would not know what happened. * Oh why did we spoil our good name just as though we were not full-grown men — simply letting them capture us! We
35. have been disgraced before all (35) three worlds. * Alas! We must have parted little birds from their partners and that is why we are experiencing retribution, in my being separated from you, elder prince. * In this remote place you and I have come and played every single day, picking fruit to give to our mother and the revered sage, so peaceful with his precepts. * But now we have an enemy, a low, disreputable, worthless enemy who has contrived by deceit to beguile you and take you away captive for punishment. * Oh, as soon as our mother sees me arrive back home she will ask after you, my elder, and when she hears about you she will almost die of grief." * The younger brother in increasing distress lamented about all these things with a heavy heart. He was faint and trembling but, * when he had spent his
36. grief, he felt better. (36) Without delay he went to inform his mother at the hut in the hermitage.

* And then the revered ascetic and the noble queen saw her son full

(36) of trouble. * Suddenly fearful, they questioned him in haste. "Darling child, why are you weeping so sadly? Tell us, where has your elder gone? We cannot see him returning." * Then Japp-Laksm(ṇ) replied, grieving as he did so, "Madam, we went off to play in the forest. * As we walked along we came across a horse. My brother caught it and rode on it. We saw a message on the swift horse's neck saying that it
37. was the mount of Nārāy(ṇ). * Then there was a white monkey (37), a mischievous, inconsiderate wretch who, with a leap, seized hold of my brother. My brother struck him down dead with his bow but, * a little while later, he changed himself into a jungle monkey and came to us, all friendly. He captured us again — that made two occasions! My brother was extremely angry. * He dealt the monkey a blow and tied him up, a prisoner. He made marks on his forehead and let him go away to his own part of the country. But he came back with some princes and a whole large army! * They fought us and managed to get their hands on my elder. I do not know whether he is alive or dead. I fled away and was separated from him."

* And then, learning the whole story, his esteemed mother fretted in an agony of despair, almost dying. * "O my dear, innocent son! What retribution has caught up with you, my loved one? I told you not to go
38. to the forest (38) but you did not heed my words. * Alas! The whole reason for this was that when you were trying out your arrows there was an earthquake and loud reverberations. Most likely news of it reached the respected king and he thought to wage a victorious war * and so he sent off Bhirut and Sutrut and the son of the Wind in person to keep the three worlds in subjection, destroying any godless creatures of erring ways. * And you are so small! Why did you fight against that power which comes from merit? Now, my own darling child, you are defeated by their ascetic power for heroic deeds. * O my son, now deprived of your mother, when I left the city, I went on foot through the jungle, carrying a child, and came here to live with this best of sages. * When you were born and I beheld a son I was so delighted! I looked after you tenderly, day by day, like an animal crouching protectively over its young." * The lady bewailed again and
39. again, her breast tight with emotion (39). In dire distress, she completely lost consciousness.

* And then the aged anchorite, most respected, seeing the lady in such wretched misery, faint and trembling, on the point of death, * was suddenly alarmed. He seized some water and, reciting a divine incantation from the scriptures, sprinkled it all over the royal consort. * The esteemed lady Sītā then rapidly returned to consciousness and bowed low at the feet of the revered sage. * She spoke with deference.

(39) "Dear lord, if my son loses his life I cannot live either. * I beg you to
40. take pity, to give some thought (40) to helping me. Please meditate
immediately now so as to help your grandson that he may live."

* Then the sage, with his clear understanding due to meditation, saw
the queen's abject misery as she thought about the imminent death of
her son * and so he contemplated in accordance with the treatise on
the rules for sages and learned through his divine understanding and
power the whole situation, without anything lacking. * He told the
dear lady, "With regard to your beloved son, a dire misfortune has led
to his undergoing a severe punishment but he is not in fact dead * so
do not grieve so sadly, madam, as though there were no possibility of
release. Soon the dear young prince will have happiness beyond that of
41. all royal princes." (41) * The dearly-loved queen of great esteem heard
what the sage said but still felt some misgivings. * "O my darling child,
what hardships you must be enduring! The sage says you are not dead.
Are you really alive? * My child, I am in pain, in anguish. My heart is
torn to pieces just as if someone was cutting my throat with a sharp
sword, causing jabs of dreadful, poisoning pain. * My beloved, if you
are in fact dead I pray to die with you. Let me not endure this fear, my
dearest, or undergo this suffering."

* And then Japp-Laksm(ṇ), her dear son, remonstrated with his
42. esteemed mother, "Please be calm. * If you grieve like this (42) you will
not know bad from good! I shall take leave of you with respect and
quickly go back after my elder brother to look for him. * I offer my life
in payment of my debt of gratitude to you. Let me take on this task.
As soon as we meet each other I will return in all haste." * And then
the queen had heard her most lovable, precious son. She spoke. * "For
you to go after your elder, my own darling, seems to be absolutely the
right thing — but I am worried for you. You are still very young, my
precious. * And another thing: just being able to see your face, little
one, warms my heart — but now you would go away from me again,
43. leaving me bereft. * If they (43) capture you they will not keep you
safe, my love. They will surely kill you both together. My sorrows,
multiplied, will weigh heavily upon me."

* Then the prince heard his beloved mother and, bowing respectfully,
replied, * "Lady mother, in this world men can never escape death.
* May it please you, there is another thing: living is never free from
effort. But if a dangerous enemy does come to harass me with his
threats, he will not be able to do so. * You just stay here, mother. I beg
to take my leave now. If I do not see my elder I shall go on after him
until I die." * Then, as she heard her dear, lovable son, the queen did
44. not dare to stand in his (44) way. * She took off her sunstone ring of

(44) beautiful pristine gold and handed it to her dearly-loved son, instructing him as follows: * "O my child, this ring here has mighty powers and can manifest great deeds, laying low all the ten directions or hurling to pieces a hundred million wicked men. * If you were in prison with chains, locks, handcuffs and pillory restraining you, these things would open up, be visibly broken to bits, totally unable to impede you. * You take it to your elder and he will be able to escape from his perilous situation." This instruction given, the lady and the sage gave their blessing to the boy: * "May you find your elder brother. If an enemy attacks you, may he be dismayed by the power of your virtue and be defeated."

45. * And then Japp-Laksm(ṇ) (45) bowed his head and, making obeisance, took leave of his respected mother and the good anchorite. * Carrying Rām-Laksm(ṇ)'s bow, he set out from the hermitage with determination, though much affected by his grief. * As he journeyed he felt sad, upset and in low spirits. He thought of his fine elder brother who usually came with him to enjoy himself in this remote region. * As he looked about he saw herds of animals, male and female, calling as they shepherded their mates and his eyes flooded with tears which rolled all over his face. * "O dear elder," he said, "are you alive or dead? I am afraid wicked men are ill-treating you, trying to kill you." * The prince heard the cries of the animals. In that remote, deserted
46. place it seemed as if the voice of his respected elder (46) was calling him. He stood, looked about * and strained his ears to listen but what he heard was definitely the calls of the forest animals. He felt despondent. Gloomily he pressed on with his journey. * As he progressed, Japp-Laksm(ṇ) saw the forest glade where they had captured his brother and bowed his head in sorrow. * But soon, having given vent to his grief, he pulled himself together and concentrated on the journey. He proceeded with speed and arrived in Aiyudhyā.

77.46–78.3. **As Japp-Laksm(ṇ) listens to the crowd speaking of his brother's imminent execution, Indr sends Rambhā to help him. She takes to his brother a pitcher of water in which Japp-Laksm(ṇ) has placed the magic ring. Rām-Laksm(ṇ) uses the ring to break his bonds and escape. Reunited with his brother, he returns to the forest, intending to destroy the enemy before returning home.**

* The prince gazed at the great variety of people who thronged there in noisy commotion. "If I go into the city," he thought to himself,
47. "this will be spoken of among the city people (47) and then I shall most

(47) likely be put to death — with nothing achieved! * I will therefore stay close and listen to the ordinary folk talking to each other about what is being done to my brother." * With this idea, the prince stopped there and hid under the shade of a fig-tree beside the gate. Then he raised his hands respectfully, addressing all the divinities. * "I pray all of you elevated deities, who dwell in the sixteen celestial regions, and the most high Indr to descend and help me at this time, * so that I may find the prince, my brother, and I pray too that none of all these people shall see me."

* And then the people were going in and out of the gate in great
48. crowds. * Everyone had seen Rām-Laksm(ṇ) (48) and all were sadly troubled and afraid for him. They were talking to each other. "It makes you feel sorry for him to look at his face." * "That poor little prince! They say that tomorrow the king will have him executed." "It is not right that he should die." * When the dearly-loved Japp-Laksm(ṇ) heard all that the people were saying to each other, * he was terrified. He trembled all over his body and almost died with grief and anxiety for his elder.

* Then Indr, most high, was seated upon his throne in the heaven of the thirty-three. * It came about that he became boiling hot. He was
49. not at all comfortable (49) or at ease. He opened his divine eyes, directed his gaze upon all the cities of the world * and saw the young prince Japp-Laksm(ṇ) who had come in pursuit of his elder brother, master of men, afraid to enter the city and grieving sadly outside its boundaries. * "Oh dear," he said, "Nārāy(ṇ) of the ten strengths will be able to see his son! I must help the poor boy at once, then, to avoid being condemned to punishment." * With this thought, the lord spoke to Rambhā. "Now, the respected King Rām does not know that it was his son * whom he ordered to be seized and brought to him for punishment and he will certainly not forgive him. And now Japp-Laksm(ṇ) has come after his victorious elder. * He is staying in hiding in a place
50. (50) outside the city and does not dare to enter it. You must therefore show him sympathy and go down quickly at once to help him."

* And then the dearly-loved goddess, Rambhā, took leave of the respected Indr and sped down through the air from her dwelling-place. * She floated swiftly through the sky and reached the royal city of Aiyudhyā. Then that lovely lady transformed herself * into a human, a young girl of pleasing appearance. She carried on her hip a pitcher for water. With her hands outspread to adjust her balance, she gracefully swayed to and fro. * When she came near the city gate she looked
51. about her and perceived young Prince Japp-Laksm(ṇ) (51) under the fig-tree, most unhappy. * She questioned him. "What has happened to

(51) make you so distressed? Do tell me." * Then the cherished young
brother had heard her and replied, "Here outside the capital I * have
been hearing everything people said. 'There is a brave boy,' they have
been saying, 'who rode a horse, seated on the saddle of the serene king!
His Majesty is going to have him executed.' * People are going in
hordes to look at him. They go right up to where the boy is — except
for me. I stay here and weep." * And then the divine Rambhā of
decorous form replied to the prince, most high, "That prisoner * has
already had the five bonds put on him. Tomorrow morning they will
52. execute him. (52) Goodness me! His features and build are just like
yours! * Don't go near to look at him, little one. Suppose he ran off,
you might be captured and put in his place! There's no point in making
your own way to your death! * I urge you not to do so because I am
sorry for you. Do keep back in there and be safe. *I* will draw water and
take it as alms for the prince."

* Listening to the goddess, Rambhā, Japp-Laksm(ṇ) felt cheered and
pleased. * All his grievous sorrows melted into thin air. Then the
younger prince spoke to her. * "Young lady, I am most grateful to you
for this splendid idea because I have journeyed on foot in the sun and
am weary with the hard physical effort. * I would ask to make merit
53. too, (53) in conjunction with you. Let me not be entirely lacking in
good deeds. Please give me the pitcher * and I will take it and draw
water for you — and you take it into the city to give it to the
prisoner." * Then Rambhā replied to the prince, "A very good idea!
* It would be hard to find anyone brave enough to go and give alms to
this prisoner." The goddess hurriedly handed him the pitcher. * Then
54. the young Japp-Laksm(ṇ) took it straight to the water. (54) * As he
was drawing water at the edge, he took the valuable, jewelled ring with
its marvellous power for great deeds, * and dropped it into the pitcher.
Then the young prince reverently addressed all divinities, calling upon
them to be witnesses. * "If the water reaches the prince, whether he
drinks it or uses it to bathe, I pray that this bejewelled ring shall go on
to his finger, * and that he may escape from his terrible punishments
and from all his bonds." Having made his prayer, the prince returned
to the city gate, carrying the water on one shoulder. * Once there, he
handed the water to the lovely Rambhā, saying, "Do take it quickly
and give it to the young prisoner."

55. (55) * Then that lady of the celestial regions took the pitcher of
water, put it on her hip and went into the city. * Reaching the place,
the heavenly lady of excellent qualities spoke to the guards. "This
prisoner has been directly in the sun and its heat is excessive. * I can
see that with all his bonds he is suffering. I have brought water for him

(55) to drink or bathe in for I am very sorry for him. It will be a very
satisfactory work of merit. * Please open up for me to go in. I will
share the merit with you." The goddess smiled and, with sideways
glances, addressed them laughingly and pleasantly. * Then, not
knowing she was a goddess, the four executioners joked and laughed
56. with (56) loud merriment. * "Where do you come from?" they asked.
"Come over here, sweetheart." "Is this young prisoner a relative of
yours or does he belong to someone else?" * "Fancy your not thinking
it too much trouble to draw water and bring it here for him!" "We do
feel pleased that you are sharing your merit with us. Your kind heart
has no equal." * "If we can all be friends together, trusting each other,
this will be the best good deed there ever was!" * Then the young lady
pretended to be coy. She chatted in a friendly way, smiling with
sideways glances and swaying to and fro, and then, laughing easily, she
quickly went in.

* "Dear little prince," she said when she reached him, "why ever
57. have you been put in bonds to suffer this hardship (57)? * I felt sorry
for you so I fetched this water for you to drink and bathe, to keep you
alive. * All these chains and locks they have put on you will suddenly
be loosened. Your body will be freed of its fetters." * And then, the
prince had listened to her, not knowing she was a goddess. He eagerly
took the pitcher * and poured water over himself, bathed his face and
drank. Immediately he stopped feeling hot; his whole body was cool as
if it were the ambrosial water of heaven. * The prince saw the
58. burnished ring on his finger, as if someone had put it on — (58)
through Indr's power to perform miracles. All his bonds suddenly fell
apart * and the unblemished goddess became invisible to everyone!
The prince escaped from his harsh confines, looked at the bejewelled
ring * and understood: his mother had sent his young brother off after
him straight away; he had journeyed with all speed and here he was!
* The prince then addressed the goddess. "I'm overjoyed! You have
helped me to escape from this danger. My debt of gratitude to you is
enormous." * At this, the lovely goddess replied, "Do not stay here
59. long, dear boy. I will take you away, * a long way, (59) outside the
boundary." She took the prince away in all haste after that and
* explained the way to him as they walked along. Then the lady from
glorious heaven went through the air to her celestial dwelling.

* The treasured prince gazed after the goddess. She was out of sight in the twinkling of an eye! * He stopped and wondered. As he thought about it, he was not in any doubt: she was, he concluded, an unblemished lady from heaven who had come down to help save his life. * The prince, master of men, walked on, his face happy with

(59) excitement — for it seemed he had had a gift from Indr Kosī! * As he went he looked along every street and pathway seeking Japp-Laksm(ṇ).
60. (60) He followed every alley-way but could not find his beloved brother. * "O my dear brother," he said, "have you really come to the city?" He constantly looked and looked until he had gone right outside the city gate. * And then the beloved Japp-Laksm(ṇ) was in close hiding, listening to everything that was said about his brother, when * he saw that highest prince, his elder, walk out past the boundary! He ran to clasp his feet, weeping and almost dying as a result of his troubles.

* And then Rām-Laksm(ṇ) bent to embrace his young brother and coax him out of his unhappy mood. * "My dearest brother," he said,
61. (61) "no man or animal of any kind has ever escaped retribution and passed beyond the danger of it. * As to the possibility that I might lose my life, I never thought of it. I thought only of you, my beloved younger, for I was afraid you might not manage to reach our mother. * As you came to look for me now, who told you the way? How brave you were to make your way through to here from so far away!" Then the handsome young brother respectfully told his glorious elder of what had passed during that time. * "Lord, when they captured and took away Your serene Highness, I went alone running into the forest.
62. * I returned to tell mother. When she (62) learned, she was extremely upset. Then I took leave of that dear one and came on this journey to look for you. * Mother gave me the sunstone ring of beautiful design
78.1. so that if I did find you I could present it to you, my lord. (78.1) * When I reached the place where they had captured you, O lord and master of men, I saw your bow, which had fallen on to that very path. * I picked it up and brought it along. As I journeyed across the forest I said, "If I do not see him, I shall kill myself." * But by the power of your merit, highest prince, I arrived here on the outskirts of the city and saw that very special young lady walking along with the pitcher on her hip. * She told me she was going to draw water to give to the prisoner but she would not let me go there. * When I heard what she said I was delighted. I talked to the young lady and asked to take the pitcher to draw the water for her. * Then I dropped into the pitcher that beautiful sunstone ring of great value, praying to all the gods of all
2. places in the ten directions * that it would reach (2) you, highest of princes, without fail, just as I prayed." As he told the whole story to his elder, he presented him with the bow and its sharp arrows.

* And then Rām-Laksm(ṇ) took the bow and eagerly replied, * "That young lady who fetched the water was no human of this world. She was a goddess from glorious heaven who came down to

(2) help me and free me from punishment. * And further: it was owing to
the great loving-kindness of our respected mother, which exceeds all on
land and sea, and owing to your goodness, dear brother, in coming to
help me, through your love for me, that I have not been killed. * Now
that I have escaped with my life, I should be ashamed and chagrined
indeed if we were to depart. It would seem that we were cringing with
fear. * I would rather give up our journey home, stay here and retaliate
3. with a definite attack. I shall aim an arrow to destroy (3) the whole
race." * With these words Rām-Laksm(ṇ), most elevated descendent of
the Sun, led his handsome young brother off on their way there and
then. * When they reached the deep, silent jungle the two dear noble
princes stopped to rest beneath a shady tree.

78.3–12. **When Rām hears that the executioners have lost Rām-Laksm(ṇ) he has the army made ready and marches out with it to fetch the boy himself. The boys go out and stand facing the army. The men are afraid of them.**

* And then the executioners were suddenly aware, looking round,
that they could not see the prince * or the girl who had come to offer
him water! They had completely disappeared both at the same time.
Horrified, the executioners fled, each separately, in consternation.
* They ran to look in every road or way, in every building, every
construction, thoroughfare or edifice, in every Brahmin monastery or
4. convent of elderly ladies (4). They poked into every nook and cranny.
* Some looked in the stables and in the elephant-drivers' quarters.
They questioned all the people — but they said they had not seen them
at all. * They looked everywhere, inside and outside the city, but could
not find the noble prince. * "Alas for each one of us!" they said. "We
shall surely die, all of us together!" * "Now we cannot remain silent.
The only thing we can do is to go straight to the military authorities."
With these thoughts the executioners went, there and then, to call upon
them. * Arriving, they informed the four senior chiefs of staff, "May it
please you to look upon all of us with favour. The prisoner has
5. disappeared!" * When the four chiefs of staff heard this (5) they were
terrified. Hastily they made themselves ready and went to inform His
respected Majesty. * On arrival they crept towards the king to have
audience of him and informed him of all that had taken place
concerning the prince. * "Lord, begging your indulgence, the prince
has just disappeared! A girl came with water she had drawn for him.
They both disappeared completely! * The executioners, terrified, ran to

(5) look for him along every street, in every alley and by-way, inside the
city and outside, to satisfy themselves. They caught no glimpse of
him!" * Then, hearing this, Nārāy(ṇ), renowned throughout the three
worlds, fell into a furious rage. * Full of disapproval, he crashed his
6. hands together (6) and said, "Right! Off you go at the double, all you
army chiefs! * Put fetters on the executioners, tightly so that they will
not make a habit of this! You must prepare the various armed forces in
their sections ready for action * for I shall march them out to capture
this unprincipled young fool and bring him back to execute him
together with the wretched executioners."

* And then the four senior chiefs of staff respectfully took their leave
and went straight off to carry out the royal order. * They sent for
chains, locks, pillories and handcuffs in quantity as soon as possible
and put them firmly on the executioners, handing them over to officials
7. to guard. * Then they gave their attention to the preparations (7) and
gave orders to officers and men. The elephant corps were to make
ready the bold elephants with their gold seats, beautifully engraved,
* with swaying cane ropes to fasten them, with tusk covers, sheaths
and fine muzzles set with gems of genuine worth. Officers were
mounted, vigilant, on their heads, * dressed in trousers and coats of
mail, with elegant sashes crossed this way and that. They had splendid
gold hats, brightly glinting, set with jewels in striking patterns.
* Elephants in their thousands were made ready with their trappings.
The glorious officers, so capable, were mounted on elephant-back,
elephant hooks in hand, to control them from behind. * As for the
cavalry officers, their equipment was magnificent! They put on saddles
which glittered brilliantly, stirrups and fine fringed bits, * seed-filled
"bells", front cords and martingales. They tightened the chest and
belly cords — all new to accompany the master of men of glorious
8. renown, their splendid king. * The fine officers, all seated upon (8)
royal steeds, drove forth, wearing tunics of precious gold and hats set
with intersecting lines of gems. * They bore stones, spears and fans
which they brandished round and round. As they went in procession,
rank upon rank, behind their king, the impression they gave was as of
a sheet of metal. All were well trained — insuperable! * The
commanders of the royal chariots were provided with fine vehicles, of
which the curved shafts were rearing *nāgas* — *nāgas* which seemed to
be alive and conscious! — * painted all over with gold, of matchless
beauty. The officers were standing in the carriages, one foot in front of
the other, holding their goads, their arms raised, ready to threaten.
* The whole infantry force, in their various companies with their
officers, bearing their full range of arms, were close behind with their

(8) commanders. * And then there was the music (how the sound of it
resounded!): an orchestra composed of trumpet, conch, oboe and
Javanese and Mon drums. * The white parasols, sunshades and
9. umbrellas in readiness, row upon row (9) for the use of the princes,
massed closely together everywhere, might have accompanied Indr!

* Then His Majesty, Nāräy(ṇ) Rām, protector of men, of widespread
sway, and his three handsome younger brothers put on their apparel,
* decorative rings, covered with perfectly-set gems, bracelets on their
arms, earrings like those of the gods, * breeches, tucked-up sarongs and
tunics, bright and costly. All four princes were splendid beyond any
others in the whole world. * Having finished dressing, Rām went forth
with his dearly-loved young brothers, intrepid like a roaring lion, to take
10. up his position in his chariot and drive off at high speed. (10) * The
soldiers of all the four army corps were sounding gongs and beating
drums and providing all kinds of music which echoed afar. * The sky
became overcast, dark and misted over and loud, booming noises
resounded. There was a shuddering and shaking as in a violent storm as
* the four royal princes left the city boundary. Their forces, bold and
keen, produced a deafening din with their cheerful confidence. * As the
king, Nāräy(ṇ) Rām, proceeded to march the army, the noise of the
densely-congested host reverberated throughout the forest.

* And then, when the two little princes, under the shady branches,
heard this great hubbub, * they looked up and saw the whole tumultuous
11. force, in a dense, winding throng. (11) They saw the four dearly-loved
princes seated in their chariots, victorious arrows in hand. * They saw
him of the simian race marching in front of those carriages! "We have
what we desire!" said Rām-Laksm(ṇ) to his dear young brother. * "I shall
aim my efficacious arrow of victory and shoot it to destroy the princes and
the monkey. Do not worry, young brother." * With these words he took
his bow and, like a roaring lion, quite without fear, he led his dear brother
out to stand facing the army! * Then the troops who formed the
spearhead, going in front of the royal personages, saw the two boys and
were bewildered, pale and faint with fear. * They were so startled that
they halted just where they were, not daring to march forward, each one
with the whites of his eyes showing, overwhelmed by their heroic power.
12. (12) * Seeing the army dismayed and disordered, Bhirut, so strong and
bold, took a quick look. * He observed that it was definitely the two boys.
Then he informed his elder, master of men, "Lord, this is the very lad who
ran off and disappeared and whom we could not find. * He has come
forth to stand blocking our path. When he sprang up in front of our men
and their officers, all became scared stiff and are in a state of
consternation. They dare not advance!"

78.12–23. **Rām and Rām-Laksm(ṇ) shoot arrows at each other of which the magic properties cancel each other out or turn harmless. Rām finally prays that, if the boys are of his own lineage, his arrow shall become food. It does so and he asks the boys who they are.**

* Then Nārāy(ṇ) of supreme power heard his dearest of brothers and
looked at the two boys, * so fair of form, so comely, tall and straight
of build. There was no one in the world to be compared with them!
13. * They bore themselves like roaring lions, unflinching, both (13) of
them, intrepid, superior as the moon which shines there in the heavens,
beaming down on every place. * If you looked at the younger, he
seemed like the elder, not a whit different; and their movements and
stature were the same. They looked most lovable. * What king's sons
were they, then, so surpassingly clever at the magic arts? When he had
looked at everything about them the respected king felt some
misgiving. * "It seems best to me, seeing the situation and considering
it carefully, to produce a sharp arrow and send it to tie up the boys and
bring them here for questioning about their family line." * With this
thought, he who was by descent the lord of men drove his chariot
further on. Then the serene king, highest of princes, held the arrow,
took aim * and shot it — it turned into multiple snares which tied the
boys up tightly. A tremor went through all the ten directions owing to
the power of the lord king.
14. (14) * Then Rām-Laksm(ṇ) of superior power shook with fury in
every limb. Grasping his effective arrow of victory, * he shot it as a
reply, using his heroic powers. The earth trembled violently. He raised
his diamond sword and cut the snares to pieces. * When Nārāy(ṇ) Rām
saw that by the boy's power all those snares were scattered in little bits,
* he said, "Well, wicked boy! You are no bigger than a fly! How can
you commit such powerful acts of aggression? * I am like the god of
Death coming after you to take your life." With this, the king aimed
15. his sharp arrow * and shot it. It turned into a fire (15) which glowed
and burned up mightily, filling the skies with fierce crackling noises.

* Then, observing the fire, Rām-Laksm(ṇ), the victorious elder, turned towards his young brother and told him, * "Now you just take note of his various powers. I shall test my right arm against his." So saying, he seized a sharp arrow, closed one eye and sent it speeding away. * It turned into rain falling all about them from the skies and dampening down the ring of fire. It extinguished it completely — it was no longer to be seen! * Laughing, he said, "Hail, great conquering king! You have boasted of the power of your hand, said that there is none to equal your physical strength. * You think because we are

16. young (16) you can come here aggressively to attack us. With your
armed force to depend on, you are not afraid of us, not even as much
as a hair's breadth. * Here you come, driving up to us, all of you — or
are there still more to come? Even if you came with everyone, the whole
land, there would not be enough of you against our right arms! * We
may be small but we are like diamonds, clean and trenchant, ready to
make sharp cuts. On that previous occasion the two princes came to
know our mighty powers. * Now *you* have made the effort to follow us
here to fight us and make us captive. Have you yourself great power,
then, surpassing that of the princes, do you think, sire?"

* On hearing this, King Nārāy(ṇ) Rām became angry, his face flushing
17. redly. (17) "You wicked, ill-fated boys!" he said, "I am like the mighty
god of Death coming after you to execute you. * You two are like
gnats, so confident that you have no fear of fire. Or rather, you are like
horrid crows. How could you be set beside the sunstone?" * With these
words, the king firmly took up a position, placing one foot in front of
the other, controlling his limbs. He stretched out an arm with the
efficacious arrow high up, took aim and shot it in the direction of the
boys. * It turned into numerous *garuḍas* which were all about in the sky.
They swooped down low, swiftly swerving, and surrounded the boys.

* Then Rām-Laksm(ṇ), strong with the power for deeds of heroism,
saw these royal *garuḍa* birds all around them, thick upon the ground,
* seized an arrow and shot it at them. It turned into a whirlwind and
blew the birds away. The royal *garuḍas* were all destroyed, scattered in
18. all directions, lifeless. (18) * And then Nārāy(ṇ) the king shook with
anger in every limb. He shot the victorious arrow, Ārriddhacandr,
* which made a resounding, booming noise as if to turn the three
worlds over, as if to break up the mountains and forests — but it did
not go near the boys! * Rām-Laksm(ṇ), strong with the powers due to
merit, saw the king's arrow burning its way through the forests and
mountains, reducing them to dust * and took the sage's efficacious
arrow to destroy that of the king, shooting at it through his mighty
power. A tremor went through the three worlds. * The arrow went
19. flying afar, keeping close to (19) that of the king. The prince, furiously
angry, humbly asked for a boon. * "I ask that this next arrow of mine
shall by my merit have the power for a mighty deed, to destroy those
royal persons over there, all four of them, utterly." * Having said this
prayer, he shot the arrow. A tremor went echoing through the earth.
The whole heaven was clouded over and there were loud reverberations. * The arrow flew off and went round the esteemed king, lord of
men, to the right, turning into decorative flowers in quantity, heaped
up all around him as an offering!

20. * And then, seeing the boy's arrow changing into (20) garlands of
flowers, the lord of all the three worlds * realised that it was a miracle.
He felt serious doubt and misgiving. "Hmm!" he thought, "I am he who
destroyed all the godless creatures in the three worlds. * Their blood was
like a sea; one would not know how to calculate its quantity. It is strange
indeed that a mere boy no bigger than my thumb is not destroyed by my
arrow! * Now is he the treasured scion of some great lineage of the three
worlds? Under the circumstances I will offer a prayer on the strength of
my virtue, a solemn declaration: * if they are the sons of some ordinary
king, I pray that Brahmās here may kill them, that they shall not live in
body or soul, but * if they are in fact of my lineage, I pray that my most
superior, effective arrow shall change into a variety of foods as an
21. offering to the boys." * Having offered this prayer, Nārāy(ṇ) (21) took
the invincible arrow and without delay sent it swiftly up aloft, directing
it towards the two boys. * Instantly the arrow turned into things to eat,
an offering to the noble boys. And a parasol, decorated with crystal, was
there, opened to shade them from the sun.

* Seeing this marvel, Rām-Laksm(ṇ), the strong and mighty, spoke.
* "O most lovable Japp-Laksm(ṇ), have you seen this, dear brother?
That arrow which I, who am strong with the power to do heroic deeds,
shot to destroy him — * why did it change into roasted grain and
garlands of flowers? And that arrow which the great king shot directly at
22. us * turned into food and a fine, shady parasol! (22) It is because of our
merit, dear brother. Come, let us enjoy the meal." * Then the respected
Nārāy(ṇ), strong in might, saw that it was exactly as he had prayed. He
was delighted, his heart overflowing. He addressed them. * "Greetings,
young princes! We are waging war against each other, competing at
close quarters with the strength of our right arms. * Our arrows are
battling against one another, each with its individual power. But it
would be better to give up and be friends. Why fight? It just causes us
physical toil. * I would like to become acquainted with you and be
friends, in accordance with the good manners of convention. Come now,
put aside your anger. Do not harbour revengeful feelings. * Now, to
proceed. Tell me, what are your names? Your parents who have lovingly
23. cared for you and your whole (23) family and kin — where do they hold
sway? * And your teacher who has instructed you in the books of
learning, what is his name? Come, tell me, what is your reason for
coming to this forest?"

78.23–36. **When Rām-Laksm(ṇ) reveals that Sītā is their mother, Rām asks Laksm(ṇ) about her execution. He is overjoyed to learn the truth and**

asks Rām-Laksm(ṇ) to take him to Sītā; he will bring her back to rule the city. Suspicious of his intentions, the boys set off quickly for home, trying to avoid pursuit.

(23) * When the noble boys had listened to this, Rām-Laksm(ṇ) said to
his dearly-loved young brother, * "Now he is asking our names and
those of our parents and kinsmen. If we do not tell him I am afraid he
will continue to be suspicious of us, yet, * if we tell him frankly, we
shall look very foolish, as if we are afraid of his might, and that will
bring us the criticism of others. * So we will wait for a moment. Let
24. him tell first, and us (24) afterwards." * With this idea, the young
prince replied affably, "Respected lord king, whose role is that of lord
of the three worlds, * you asked just now, highest of princes, about our
descent. I would inform you, esteemed lord, so as not to go counter to
your wishes, * but you, being the important person, should tell us first.
We, the young ones, will inform you afterwards."

* Then the respected Nārāy(ṇ), strong and mighty, had listened to
the boy's reply. "Well!" he thought to himself. "How does a small
child such as this come to know so well how to put his case and use his
wits with such lightning speed to get out of a situation? * If I do not
give him an honest answer I shall never know his descent!" With this
25. thought the noble king (25) informed them, * "I am called Rām, a
name which is indeed renowned in every direction. I am a part,
separated, of Nārāy(ṇ) and I came to rule the city of Aiyudhyā. * As to
my three young brothers, one, most lovable, is called Laksm(ṇ). This
brother is called Bhirut, master of men, and that one, Sutrut. * We are
concerned with the care of this second age and have quelled the
godlesss creatures of overweening pride. Tell me, now, what are your
names? Come, tell me instantly."

* And then the virtuous Rām-Laksm(ṇ), strong and mighty, had
listened to these honey-sweet, friendly words of His Majesty the King,
* presenting the facts quite clearly, telling his name and giving the
26. information too about his country — everything (26) without omission.
* He had learned about the king, sustainer of the earth — that he was
in fact his own father! He was dismayed into silence, hanging his head,
his whole body inert and limp. * He thought of approaching to pay his
respects but was troubled by the thought that the king, master of men,
would undoubtedly make him take him to his mother. * "He will have
my mother executed without any investigation and he will take us away
and punish us mercilessly. * If, in accordance with correct and friendly
behaviour, I tell him the truth, news of it will reach my revered mother
and she will be very angry. * So I had better be evasive, not completely

(26) clear about it." With this idea, the noble boy made his reply to the great king.[53] * "My name is Rām-Laksm(ṇ), descended from the Sun. I am of high esteem and mighty in deeds of heroism. My younger
27. brother is called Japp-Laksm(ṇ). Sītā is our respected mother. (27) * With regard to our father and protector, sire, I do not know him at all. They say he is a king, ruling the city of Aiyudhyā, mighty and powerful beyond all in the world. * As for the teacher who gave us our instruction from the books of the magic arts, he lives in the forest, far, far away and is by name the righteous sage, Vajjaprit."

* Then the king, Nārāy(ṇ) Rām, had listened. "How can he possibly say such things?" he thought to himself. * But then, after serious consideration, he felt a great joy. Turning to Laksm(ṇ), master of men, he questioned him. * "My young brother, I commanded you to take the lady Sītā to some remote spot in the jungle and execute her. * You told me you had killed her in accordance with my order and also that it
28. was Sītā's liver which you brought home (28) as proof. * But now this boy tells me he is the son of that very Sītā! I am strangely confused. Is this true? Or what are the facts?"

* Then Laksm(ṇ) had rapidly understood. As he had listened to his victorious elder, he had rejoiced, though he also felt afraid of his authority. * He looked at his nephew, carefully observing his whole form, and was inwardly delighted. Tears flowed from his eyes as he made obeisance at the feet of his sovereign. * "Lord, when I took your wife away to execute her out there along the forest way * and raised my sword to sever her neck, it turned into a garland of flowers round her throat and the princess did not in the event die. * I realised on reflection that this was truly a miracle and so, begging your forgiveness
29. (29) and mercy, I let her journey onward. * When I was on my way back I saw a large deer dead under the branches of a sacred fig-tree. I went and * scooped out the animal's liver to take the place of the liver of your dearly-loved wife and brought it to you, dear, respected king. I deceived you with a lie. * I beg your indulgence concerning this serious wrong that I did you, deserving even of death. Let it not be long before you look kindly upon me and mercifully forgive me." * Then, hearing his young brother, Nārāy(ṇ), master of men, was delighted beyond comparison but, * as he thought of how he had punished his own son,
30. his limbs trembled and tears poured down his cheeks (30). He addressed his much-loved young brother. * "It was because she had spoken the truth that the treasured lady did not die when you tried to kill her and your sword turned into a garland of flowers! * And another thing: the merit of your nephew supported her so that our family line might be continued. And then you came by the animal's liver — it was a god

(30) who made it appear! * Then another thing: the queen had taken shelter with an ascetic of exceeding goodness and kindness and so was delivered of her son, most dear to her heart, in the *sālā* at the hermitage. * I was indeed wrong! I was extremely angry, quite beyond the limits of proper behaviour. I did not ask the queen any questions and thus it came about that we were separated." * As he spoke he cast aside his bow and sharp arrows and came down from his chariot. His three beloved brothers walked along behind him, their glorious elder.

31. (31) * When they were near, the high-born king spoke. "Greetings, my son! Do not feel any doubts. It is I who am your father. * Your mother was my consort, whom I tenderly loved and protected. Acting upon the pronouncement of your grandfather, we came to Mount Trīkūṭ, * three of us with Laksm(ṇ), your uncle. All dressed as anchorites, we dwelt beside the river, concentrating daily on the building up of our asceticism, but * Dasamukh came and stole away your mother, taking her off to far-away Laṅkā. I waged a victorious war, destroying all his kin, * and brought your mother here to rule the kingdom of Aiyudhyā. Some bad fate of the beautiful queen made her draw a portrait of Rāb(ṇ) and * when I saw it I was furious. I told Laksm(ṇ) to take her life. And
32. in all this, it was your merit, my dearest, (32) that helped your mother so that she did not die. * Then, destitute in the jungle, she had hardships and troubles to endure. Truly I was wrong. I beg you, my dearest, to find it possible to forgive me. * Please take me to see where your mother lives. I shall prepare to take her back and bring her to rule in the city."

* Then, having listened to the lord, his father, the treasured young prince respectfully rejoined, * "Lord, my mother has been brought low, really degraded and debased. The three of us have suffered, left on our own, having only the *ācārya* to whom to turn. * We have journeyed on foot, looking for fruit to eat as our food. Our respected mother has brought us up and looked after us in a state of daily deprivation. * When we went off to play and saw the horse and caught it together and rode it,
33. they said we (33) were committing an offence against the noble king and they had your orders to bring the army to surround and capture us. * They took me away and punished me severely, with no enquiry in accordance with the law. It was by the power of my merit that I did not die but managed to escape from that terrible punishment. * And now you come and tell me a lie, saying that, being my father, you will take us to the city! That, great king, would not be at all suitable. * You are superior in greatness and prestige, grand and noble while we are destitute. How can we dare to set ourselves up beside you? * Please turn round and go back home. Do not try to persuade us. We humbly beg your leave to go."

(33) * Nārāy(ṇ) the king, strong with the power of his magic arrows, had
listened to his son. Eager to win the boys over, the sustainer of the earth
34. then said, * "O my sons, my dear children, (34) both of whom I truly love,
come, hear the whole story. I shall tell you it this instant. * On a certain
occasion I heard the confusing sound of a powerful arrow, booming in all the directions. I thought an evil godless creature had come to
attack the royal city. * I gave orders that a horse should be released and
thus I met you lovely young children. But, owing to the effect of retribution from time past, I was unable to recognise you. * When this present
critical situation developed I marched all my available troops to wage war
on the field of battle. * O, my children, my powers are equalled by no one
else's. I was born to be the highest of well-born lords and to reduce every
land to a state of subjection. * All the *gandharvas* of all ranks and the gods
in the celestial regions will hear your names and will bow low in
35. submission, shivering, their skins all gooseflesh. * Now, my (35) darling
children, your powers are equal to mine. You have become leaders of the
world, continuing the line of the most supreme lords."

* And then his beloved son had listened and replied with respect,
* "Lord, you have spoken most fittingly. It was as though I had not
understood and so you explained everything to me, beginning with times
past; * but all this is only your side of the matter, Your Majesty." Even as
he spoke, he took his young brother by the hand and went off into the
forest. * And then Nārāy(ṇ), most strong and mighty, and his three
younger brothers and Hanumān of the simian race, together with the
36. minister Sumantăn and all the military officers (36) saw the distrustful
princes hastily setting off together on foot and * could not keep back their
tears. All felt very sad, their limbs going quite limp. The king set off after
the boys. * Rām-Laksm(ṇ), whose strength and might were due to his accumulated merit, saw that the king was following them and would soon be catching them up. * The prince made a dash for it, bounding away across the open country and through narrow ways in the forest, taking along his young brother, dear to his heart, making straight for the hermitage. * When they reached it they halted and stayed still. Stealthily, they looked for their father. Seeing that he was indeed coming quite close, they stood guard at the entrance.

78.36–53. **Rām follows the boys home and halts his army near the hermitage. The sage acts as go-between. He fails to persuade Sītā to return to Rām but does prevail upon her to see Rām in person.**

(37) boys, dear to his heart, travelling through remote passes and ravines.
* Arriving in a forest of high trees with a thick entanglement of
branches up above, he had looked round and seen the sage's hermitage
with its lotus pool, a peaceful, pleasant place. * Not daring to enter for
fear of the righteous sage, he halted his military force just there in front
of the hermitage.

* The princes, distinguished, magnificent, most high, approached the
queen, their respected mother, to greet her. * They made obeisance,
bending low upon their knees, with hands raised in the lotus position,
their eyes brimming with tears, sobbing and choking with the emotion
38. in their breasts. (38) * And their respected mother clasped her dear,
lovable sons in her arms, * caressing them all over and kissing her
precious children. She spoke sweetly, saying, * "My son, on that day
when I heard the news about you, that you had quite definitely been
captured, I was stricken by grief, to the point of death. * When he had
told me, your young brother said goodbye and went off after you with
my valuable jewelled ring which I gave him to take to you. * But tell
me, when they had taken you away to punish you, how did it come
about, my darling, so full of grace, that you managed to meet with
your dear brother?"

39. * Then Rām- (39) Laksm(ṇ), princely descendant of the Sun, had
listened to his respected mother in the midst of his distress. He replied,
* "When I caught the royal horse, the great prince whose name is Rām
and who rules the city of Aiyudhyā, * sent two younger brothers to
bring up the army with its four corps. They fought us and made me
captive, took me away and gave me terrible punishment; * they had
five kinds of restraint put on me and let me be reviled in all the
market-places; they put me in a cage and kept me alive for three days.
The next morning they were going to execute me. * But owing to the
power of my merit, a disturbance caused heat to reach heaven and a
divine lady, wife of a god, came down to help save my life! * She gave
me water to drink and bathe in and my body was freed from the
fetters. As for your bejewelled ring, it was on my finger as though
someone had put it there! * So I realised that you, mother, most high,
40. had sent my young brother after me (40). Then the divine girl led me
quickly away * and without delay she returned through the air while I
walked through the city looking for my dearest young brother; and we
found each other at the boundary gate. * I took him away from the
city and we halted under the shade of a tree. We very much wanted to
retaliate, using the power of our right arms. * In a little while, the four
princes came after us, bringing their vast army with its four corps to
fight us and wage a war of victory, and * there was a quaking and

(40) reverberation; the heavens were obscured; the noise was deafening! We sent arrows in reply to each other many times, contending and provoking each other, each the other's equal. * Very soon, Rām cast aside his arrows and asked about our family line. He told us that he is
41. the father who begot us. * And now (41) the four princes and all the chiefs of staff of the four army corps have followed us and have halted in front of the hermitage under the fig-tree."

* And then the esteemed Queen Sītā, learning that her husband had followed them, was very angry * and felt a terrible anguish as if a sword had cut into her heart. "O children," she said, "my dearest darlings, why do such dreadful things befall us? * We had departed from home and come to live in the jungle with only the good sage. Why did he follow us to oppress us? It seemed as though our merit would keep us from danger. * When I consider the whole situation, I have had enough of it. Even in 10,000 years or more, I shall not forget it, my children. It would surely have been better to have endured death! * What he did to me has not, as you see, brought me to ruin but he is pursuing *you* to harm you and I am thinking only of you, my dear
42. sons, because you are without (42) anyone on whom to depend. * Alas! We know no happiness, then! We have only sorrow and trouble." Even as she bewailed, she clasped her dearly-loved sons to her, her face downcast in gloom.

* Then King Nārāy(ṇ) Rām heard his wife's woeful sobbing. * His heart almost broke owing to the sorrow he felt for his dear consort. He sobbed in great distress of mind, the tears pouring down his face. * Then His Majesty spoke. "My dearest, all this situation is due to retribution. That is how all this has arisen. * The power of your truthfulness, my dear wife — for you were without lust or stain — and the goodness of our beloved, darling child have made possible the continuation of our noble family line. * I myself, as I now see, was in
43. the wrong. (43) Do not blame me, my darling. Think of the time when we were destitute together, far away from the city. * I beg you, my own precious partner, come out, open the door. I will come and tell you about my sins." * Hearing her husband's honeyed words of friendship, the noble queen * thought of taking pity on him but in her inmost feelings she was not appeased. She considered the matter seriously. * "This king has been extremely good to me but, if I go, if I comply with his request, I shall be ashamed[54] in front of that lord." * With this thought the august lady made respectful obeisance to the sage. "I beg your indulgence, grandfather. Please be so kind as to do the talking for
44. me. * Please go and (44) ask the king what are his intentions in bringing the four army corps all the way here."

(44) * Then the renowned sage had listened to the beautiful queen. He
took his walking-stick, opened the door of his cell and looked out.
* He regarded the four resplendent princes, immaculate as the
burnished sun, beneath the shade of the fig-tree, * their faces downcast
in gloom, as they gravely pondered. * He knew that these noble princes
were excessively troubled. * Thinking with sympathy of the respected
king of the line of Nārāy(ṇ), he came down from the hermitage, went
to the place under the branches of the fig-tree * and sat down with
45. them. He asked (45) them, "What is the business concerning which all
you princes have come here?" * Then all four masters of men bowed
their heads low, making obeisance to the *ācārya*. * Nārāy(ṇ) spoke
respectfully, "Lord, you, who have the power due to acquired merit, I
have learned that when the queen came to live in your care * and when
she gave birth to the lovable boy too, you cherished her tenderly. You
have been extremely kind. I have come to pay homage to you. * A
further matter: I would ask you to come to my aid, to help me contrive
to have the queen back in the city, in charge of the beloved court
ladies. * And more, I would beg to ask a question, though you may
46. think this is not very (46) proper: are both the boys this lady's children,
revered *ācārya*?" * Then, hearing the questions of His Majesty,
protector of the world, the sage, whose powers came from acquired
merit, informed him straight away, * "Prince Rām-Laksm(ṇ) is the
queen's son. His young brother I created to be a companion to her
child. * He is by name beloved Japp-Laksm(ṇ). The queen has tended
them with equal care." He felt pity as he spoke, for Rām had come
upon such troubles. * "Wait a moment. I will go and give some advice
to the lovely Sītā. It will be of some help to you." The sage of great
wisdom returned to the hermitage.
47. * There, he told the queen (47) what had taken place with Rām. "He
pleaded with me, as with a grandfather, weeping and grieving about the
whole situation. * Do listen to what I say, madam. Do not be angry.
You would best join your husband and return to rule the kingdom."
* Then, having listened to the *ācārya* of great wisdom, the lovely Sītā
respectfully replied, * "Grandfather, you do not comprehend my
wretchedness. He said my wrong was excessive. He ordered me,
without the least compunction, to be struck down, regarding me as
wicked, accursed. * But now he says I am good; he will take me back
to rule the city. I beg you to have pity on me, grandfather. To satisfy
48. me, go and question him again!" * And then the sage (48) who
observed the code of conduct, listened to the dear lady. "I have had
quite enough of this!" he said. * "Bossing me about like this! I am like
a boat for hire. I give a lift to one lot of people, then the other hires

(48) me. First one, then the other. You have no pity for me!" So saying, he
left the cell.

* "Now," he reported, "Queen Sītā says that you, sovereign lord,
said she transgressed the limits of good conduct. * In your fury you
had no mercy. You ordered her execution. And now, why do you
change and become so affable towards her?" * Then King Nārāy(ṇ),
master of men, gave the matter serious consideration. * He had been
excessively thoughtless when he had punished his consort. He felt very
upset but made an effort to control his feelings and replied, * "It is
49. indeed true that I was wrong. I do not deny it (49) at all, venerable one.
All depends on your indulgence towards me. Forgive me, save me,
have pity! * Help me to persuade the blameless lady to let me see her
and speak with her in person. Then her anger may abate." * Then the
good sage replied to Nārāy(ṇ) Rām, laughing pleasantly, teasing him,
* "All these orders! You allow me no rest. I cannot get away from you
even to sleep." Then with that the sage returned to the hermitage.

* There, he said, "You asked me to go and report to Lord Rām. He
accepts that he has been wrong. * O madam, you should be kind and
pity our respected great king. He asked me to plead with you. He
50. wants to come and speak with (50) you. * So do not be so cross. Listen
to what I shall say to you. You are a heavenly lady whose magnificence
excels all in the three worlds. * You came down to earth to look after
the kingdom in its entirety, preventing the occurrence of calamities.
Come now, be more compliant. Do not be angry towards the king."
* Then the esteemed Queen Sītā had listened to the ascetic as he told
her what occurred with her husband, * how he had admitted his guilt
and wrong-doing and was enduring great unhappiness. She thought of
the king's goodness to her, her heart bursting with emotion. * It would
be right to let the august king come to the hermitage, then. She would
like to hear what the esteemed sovereign had to say — how he would
explain his actions! * With these thoughts, she bowed, paying homage
at the feet of the righteous sage. She sobbed, unable to produce the
51. words which she had in her mind. * Thoughts came to (51) her all over
again about the king's guilt and her heart was full of emotions: she did
not want to see the king and yet she could not bring herself just to do
nothing at all about it. * She spoke, "Grandfather to whom I owe so
much, I feel great shame but I cannot forbid him. It would seem
impolite under the circumstances. * I beg you to be so kind as to return
and speak to His Majesty respectfully inviting the master of men to
come if he so wishes." * And then the anchorite said, "Well then, I will
just look for some areca and take out one chew, all ready." * The sage
took a mortar, crushed the areca and put it to the back of his mouth.

(51) Chewing with relish, he grasped his stick and went off in haste.
52. * Arriving, the sage informed the king concerning his consort. (52) "The lady Sītā sends me, Your Majesty, to take you in at once."

* And then the respected Nārāy(ṇ), strong and mighty, heard and was overwhelmed with joy. All his sorrows slipped away. * He gave instructions to his three young brothers to organise the soldiers of the four army corps to concern themselves with the construction of a pavilion to be placed at the foot of the mountain.

* This instruction given, he went, like a strong lion, proceeding swiftly behind the ascetic of right conduct. * When they had almost reached the treasured lady, the sage, whose power lay in the precepts, cleared his throat[55] and said, * "Now, husband and wife will speak
53. directly to each (53) other. Do not come sidling up to me. You must depend on your own individual ideas. * I would have had you be friends at the beginning but you were not! Why were you so cross with each other? You ordered me about mercilessly. I have failed utterly to concentrate on my meditations!" * With this, the sage immediately took his walking-stick and went into the forest with the two young princes walking along behind him.

78.53–79.12. **When Rām asks her to return with him Sītā angrily refuses, blaming him for believing her unfaithful in spite of the evidence of Hanumān's visit to Laṅkā and her ordeal by fire and pointing out that she is destitute now and unfit for court life. Rām asks to take the boys with him, thinking that she will soon follow them. When she refuses this, he says he would rather die than return without any of them. Sītā gives in to this and tells the boys. They are unhappy about parting from her.**

* And then the respected King Nārāy(ṇ) entered and stood before his consort. * He looked attentively at the queen, observing her whole appearance, and saw that she was thin and that, owing to the physical toil and hardship, her radiance was impaired. * Feeling pity for his sweetheart, the king sobbed with a full heart and wiped the tears from
54. his eyes. (54) * Then that lady of high esteem looked at King Rām as he wept so miserably. * She raised her hands in greeting, with tears pouring down her cheeks, feeling shamed in the eyes of her royal husband of many victories. * She made an effort to suppress her feelings, the anger and pain in her heart. She turned her face away and did not even glance sideways at him. So embarrassed was she that the words would not come. * Then the high-born lord of men spoke. "Greetings, my most beloved sweetheart. * Do not be angry and frown

(54) at me, my dearest treasure! In doing you that wrong, I did indeed
55. commit a crime * but all this was due to a bad fate of long (55) ago.
This led me into such an excess of temper that I ordered your
execution, my love. * Owing to the power of your truthfulness, when
Laksm(ṇ) struck you did not die. And the merit of the child in your
womb came to your help in a most miraculous way. * But from that
day, my dear, I have mourned without any respite. And my dear
mother has been exceedingly angry with me. * She said my anger was
unseemly and, whether you were in the right or wrong, whether you
were bad or good, where would I find anyone like my beloved? She
lamented repeatedly every day. * When I let the horse go, offering a
prayer, and met our son, most dear to my heart, and learned that you,
my precious, had not died, my joy was unparalleled. * O my love, I
was indeed wrong. All depends on your forgiveness. I beg you, my
treasure, to return to rule the capital."
56. (56) * Then, hearing this, the queen of high esteem was extremely
angry. She placed her palms together and said, * "Lord, your words
sound well because you know how to excuse yourself from guilt but if
you had any mercy in you, I would never have been in this state of
79.1. hardship! (79.1) * And another thing: when I was in Laṅkā, the
kingdom of the arrogant Rāb(ṇ), you had Hanumān venture through
the air to apprise himself of my whole situation, * as to whether I was
bad or good. And, though you knew the answer in your heart, still,
when the victorious war was over, you made me step in the fire.[40]
* And I did indeed do so, for your sake, taking all the gods to witness
and Earth as well. And you brought me to our kingdom. * Now, after
all that, why was your mind not clear of any suspicion and doubt? As
it is, I am bereft; I have only the *ācārya*. I have traversed the forest on
foot looking for fruit to pick for our food and have had no one to look
after me for ten full years now. * I might have met with a hunter of the
forest or a *gandharva* or a dreadful godless creature. *You* would have
suspected me of impurity and have been even more annoyed than
2. before, I suppose! * And a further point: you (2) have great influence.
What lack of royal ladies is there? — whereas I am debased and of
erring ways and live a life of destitution in the jungle."

* Then the high-born Nārāy(ṇ) said, "O beloved treasure, do not mock me. * If, my darling, you do not accept that we can be close together again, then take this sword and sever my neck so that there will be an end once and for all to your anger and no trace of suspicion in your mind. * As for me, where could I find a woman of your character? Please find it possible to forgive me! Think of the time when we were destitute together. * O my darling, you and I were of one and

(2) the same thought; of one and the same body. You ought to have
compassion for me, my treasure, because I have treated you with
kindness too."
* The chief consort, dearly-loved, heard her husband's words and
3. bowed, to speak in (3) reply. * "Lord, what you say sounds very well —
all affectionate words of honey, the sweetest of foods, but when you
have eaten it you are sure to have a stomach-ache! * When one thinks
about it one really must laugh. It is impossible to refrain from mirth!
You see me as a lowly creature. You just say what you feel like saying.
* Are there women in this world who strike men? I find this suggestion
unusual. If I could do that I should not be in my present state of
hardship! * I was born into this life with a bad fate which I shall
endure until I die. Your merit and mine, esteemed king, are probably
at an end now. * Do return to your home and your kingdom and
govern your people. Do not be troubled about this. * I shall stay here
in this state of poverty and care for my beloved children, turning for
4. help to the sage of great goodness to the very end of my life. (4) * And
one more thing: would you please, my sovereign, just be so kind as to
give my greetings to the two mothers."[56]
* Then the respected Nārāy(ṇ), strong and mighty, had listened to
his consort's reply, her decision not to stay with him. * However much
he might cajole her, the lady was not agreeable. Satisfied that this was
so, the noble king was grim and withdrawn, uttering not a word. * He
pondered deeply. "My beloved wife holds most firmly to her words as
if they were inscribed on stone. * And so I have in mind to ask to take
to the city only our two august children, so dear to us, letting her stay
alone in the forest. * If children and mothers are separated by a great
distance they usually fret and feel bereft and are quite unable to stay
5. (5) where they are and so * all this anger of hers will simply abate and
disappear. Then I shall send my forces to fetch her to the city." * With
this idea the king said, "Well, my dearest, lovable wife, if you will not
return I shall ask only for our dear sons. * I will take them away and
care for them instead of you, my well-born treasure, so that they will
be able to continue the family line in their role as lords of the world."
* And then the lovely consort had listened to His serene Majesty.
Hastily she bowed and replied, * "Lord, I am a poor person. I am not
sure that the children are your own dear sons. I would ask you, master
of men, to look at them with care this instant. * These children are not
6. like you. Perhaps they are King (6) Rāb(ṇ)'s? Why ever, great king,
would you take them? And their mother is an evil good-for-nothing!
* They are descended from wrong-doers; it would not be right for you
to show them such kindness. When you took Rām-Laksm(ṇ) away to

(6) execute him the whole kingdom knew about it. * If I give them to you,
sire, I am afraid you may become angry and my children will be
eliminated without the slightest investigation!"

* Then Nārāy(ṇ), strong and mighty in the power which comes from
acquired merit, had listened to what the queen had said and his feelings
were almost at boiling point. * And so he replied, "What *is* the good,
my beloved wife, of your deciding to stay here and saying things to
cause me pain? * I am only asking to take the children. How can you
7. forbid it? If you do, I ask to die. What good is there in living, (7)
shamed before the populace throughout the country? * Alas! I, who
am of the race of supreme kings, enjoying the greatest prestige and
superior possessions, resemble now the man in the street, enduring the
most excessive grief! * If I return to the kingdom I shall be ashamed
before all the gods of the realm. Thus, if I do not have what I want I
would prefer to die here. That would be far better. * You will remain
here happily after me. Please take good care of the dear children."
With those words, he wept and writhed in agony.

* And then the esteemed lady Sītā looked at the king, her husband,
as he wept in this state of extreme wretchedness * and considered
seriously. "This great king, becoming a separate being, came to
suppress a terrible threat and to make our kingdom his concern. * The
8. gods in their (8) aerial palaces, and the sages, were all pleased. Now
these lovely princes are the sons of our sovereign * and will be able to
continue the family line. They are the dearly-beloved of the three
worlds, the city's crown, excelling all; they will rule glorious Aiyudhyā.
* And if I do not give them up, it looks as though the king will kill
himself!" With these thoughts, the lady bowed at the feet of her
husband * and said, "Our dear offspring are as much to me as my own
life but I shall offer them to you, respected king. I give them up as is
your desire." * With these words the queen called to her dear sons,
highest princes. "Boys! Come in quickly to greet your father."

* Then the two gifted princes had heard their mother calling them
9. unmistakably and came in haste together. (9) * They raised their hands,
palms together, making respectful obeisance to their parents, and sat
there in attendance. * Their victorious father bent to embrace his dear
sons and caressed them all over. * He looked at Rām-Laksm(ṇ), his
beloved son, and at Japp-Laksm(ṇ), the high-born younger brother,
both so noble and good-looking, and covered them with kisses. * He
made a fuss of them, putting them on his knee, taking a sideways
glance at his wife. His eyes brimmed over with streaming tears as he
sobbed in great distress. * Then the queen, their mother, spoke to
them. * "My children, His Majesty is now asking me for you. He will

10. take you to stay (10) in the city of Aiyudhyā. * If I were to try to
prevent him I am afraid he would be very upset. Now do go with the
victorious king — and behave yourselves! * You must endure this and
allow me to stay where I am. I shall suffer here in accordance with my
own destiny, my children, for always until the end of my life, relying
upon the sage whose righteousness is renowned."

* And then the two princes had listened to their respected mother's
words. * The noble boys wiped away their tears, flowing freely because
of their affection for her, and said, "O mother, * honoured lady, you
have only us two as your companions. If you let us go, how will you
live alone? * And another thing, we have never repaid our debt of
11. gratitude to you; and this, mother, is extensive. And (11) our indebted-
ness to the righteous sage is incomparably great."

* At that point, as she listened to her darling sons' replies, their
mother felt utterly miserable. She struggled to give a reply. * "My
dearest sons, so gifted, I cannot help your going. That would be to
oppose what the serene king has said. I fear His Majesty would be
upset. * O my treasures on whom I have depended, have no thought
for me. You must endure this and let me live in the forest, suffering my
fate, until I die. * The king will take you away to his home in the city.
You will take over from our sovereign and govern the realm of
Aiyudhyā." * Neither of the dear princes dared resist the royal order.
12. They went, as the queen (12) had said. * They clasped her feet and
wept, crying out over and over loudly, trembling violently. With faces
full of gloom, they became faint.

79.12–24. **Rām tells his sons that he will take them to meet their grandmothers and then, if they miss Sītā, they may return. Sītā gives them advice and they part company. The uncles and Hanumān are delighted with them. The party returns to the city.**

(12) * And then the esteemed king and queen saw their offspring sobbing
miserably in their unhappiness. * The king embraced his dear sons and
spoke persuasively to them, his tears brimming over. "O children, do
not be sad! * Come, listen to your father. I will tell you about your
mother here. We were in love, caring for each other as much as our
own lives, * at that time when we left the city and came and endured
the hardships of the jungle. But now there is some dreadful fate which
has caught us up and is separating us again. * I admit that I have been
13. truly in the wrong but the queen is not (13) being the least bit indulgent
to me. Although I have pleaded with her many times over, she will not

(13) agree to return. * So I am asking only to take you dear children and
present you to the three grandmothers. If you miss your mother, then
you shall be brought back again."

* Then the two princes, greatly beloved, had listened to their
respected father's honeyed words of friendship. * They had spent their
grief and felt calm. Both the beloved princes paid their respects to the
king indicating their loyalty and agreed to conform to his command.
* The dear queen saw her much-loved sons consenting to the lord's
command and bent to embrace her high-born offspring. * She spoke to
14. them, instructing the (14) dear children, "My sons, off you go and serve
the esteemed king with dutiful care! * Never fail to go and attend upon
him. Do not be forgetful concerning state business. And another thing:
your dear grandmothers are most important people in the capital.
* You must be diligent in paying your respects to them, both of you,
and in serving them. You are not to give them any worry or cause them
annoyance. * And further: please, my darlings, entrust yourselves to
your uncles and to the ministers of the army and the soldiers and
officials inside and outside the city. * Do not speak rudely or behave in
a rough, bullying or arrogant manner. Whatever a person's fault,
serious or slight, deep-seated or superficial, be patient and keep calm.
* My children, if there is a war, do not be scared or dismayed. Go out
to the fight on behalf of the dear king; your good name will still be
known in the future. * And then, my sons, so dear to me, so lovable,
15. show mercy to the people. Just be (15) aware of their troubles. Then
serene contentment will be yours. * You are to be the bejewelled
parasol which protects the whole of the three worlds. You will ward off
all base enemies, that they may not be able to oppress you." * The two
treasured princes paid their respects to their serene mother, making
obeisance as they received her words of counsel. They were sobbing in
distress.

* And then the righteous sage, in the forest beyond the terrace of his
cell, was counting his rosary beads with eyes closed. * When the sun
inclined and it became cool, as its rays were dimmed, he took his stick
and returned to the four royal personages. * And King Nārāy(ṇ) Rām
16. bowed in homage before the ascetic (16) of superior magic powers. * "I
have been talking just now with the lovely queen," he said. "I am very
much indebted to you, dear grandfather, incomparably so. * I used my
persuasive powers with the august lady but she has made up her mind.
All she will do is to allow the beloved children to go back with me."

* Then Rām-Laksm(ṇ), descendant of the Sun, and Prince Japp-Laksm(ṇ) saluted the sage, weeping miserably. * "Lord grandfather,"
they said, "we beg to take leave of you and go to the city of Aiyudhyā

(16) with the respected king of high esteem. * We would leave our mother
in your care, revered sage, asking you in kindness to keep her safe and
17. treat her with compassion." (17) * Then the *ācārya* saw the beloved
princes weeping in excessive grief. He comforted them. * "Boys, boys!
It shall be my task to take every care of your mother, just as you would
do. Don't worry about that at all." * The sage gave them his blessing,
wishing them great prosperity, renown and physical prowess for their
future as lords of the kingdom and * the two beloved princes bowed
upon their knees as they received it. * Making obeisance to their
mother and to the sage of great perception, they said, "Lord, begging
your favour, we humbly ask to take our leave."

18. * Then the king, (18) Nārāy(ṇ) Rām, having made obeisance before
the sage Vajjaprit, * said, "Well, my dear, delightful wife, stay with the
ācārya of great perception — and may you prosper and be happy! * I
will say goodbye and return to my home in my kingdom. Do not
brood about the boys, my lovely treasure." * When he had spoken, the
tears poured down, making his face quite wet. In his pity for his
consort, his whole body drooped limply. * Making a great effort to
control his limbs, the handsome royal lord took his two magnificent
sons back to the pavilion.

* And then Bhirut, the elder, and the young brothers, Laksm(ṇ) and
19. Sutrut, (19) highly delighted, * came forward on their knees in
confused haste and clasped their dear nephews, soothing them, each
one, making a fuss of them, kissing them all over their faces. * "O
beloved, gifted children!" they said. "We uncles did not know you! We
went and engaged with you in the fight. It seems it was by some merit
of ours that death was avoided. * All was achieved through the gods
miraculously affecting the thoughts of each of us. Thus it is that we are
united together and our family line will be continued."

* The two princes saluted their three uncles and, making obeisance,
begged for forgiveness. * "Lords, we did wrong. We exceeded the
limits and were in error. We attacked you, respected princes. Our
20. wrong has indeed been excessive. * But all this, serene princes, (20) do
quickly forgive us! Do not let it be a cause for hatred and enmity
against us in the future!" * Bhirut and Sutrut were highly delighted.
They replied to this with honeyed words. * "Treasured children, most
high, do not be in the least troubled. We uncles do not place any blame
upon you at all, precious ones."

* Next Hanumān of the simian race, Sumantăn and all the soldiers,
in a state of pleasurable excitement, * approached on their knees to
pay their respects to the dear boys, most high. They crowded into the
pavilion in order to praise their powers, acquired by meditation.

(20) * Hanumān raised his hands in salute and bent to clasp the boys' feet
21. (21), humbly expressing his excuses for the wrongs which he had
committed against them. * "Lords, I did not know that you were of the
line of the serene princes! I started to fight against you and was
aggressive, attacking Your Highnesses. * With regard to all this, I must
depend on your forgiveness for my wrongs that I may continue as your
humble servant throughout the remainder of my life."

* Then Rām-Laksm(ṇ), descendant of the Sun, made his reply to
this. "Greetings, royal simian, Hanumān! * It is quite usual, when
waging war, not to treat the enemy with respect! Everyone goes
straight for victory — they always have done, since times long past.
* You, sir, and we ourselves all performed deeds of prowess. Why
should any blame be attached when it was merely because we have
22. never met each other? * So now, then, do not feel (22) doubtful or
troubled about it. You shall be the dear, respected king's servants,
every one of you, to the end of your lives."

* When the strong and mighty Nārāy(ṇ), most elevated, saw how his
serene young brothers and he of the simian race * were delighted with
his offspring, he was overjoyed. The king then spoke to his minister
Sumantăn, * "Now I shall return to the city. Please prepare our four
branches of the army for immediate assembly here." Sumantăn bowed
down low, accepting the command, and went out to busy himself with
23. the preparation of the soldiers. (23) * They were divided into sections
of the left and right in accordance with tradition. They made the
chariots ready, yoked with their horses, and brought them to present to
the sovereign. * And then King Nārāy(ṇ), master of men, his three
younger brothers and his sons * put on all the equipment intended for
their personal use. This done, the four elders mounted their splendid
chariots, * while the two boys rode on huge, lordly elephants, driving
off with the esteemed king as he returned to his kingdom. * The
ministers, the officers and the cavalry thronged round and the whole
host of soldiery went in procession on both sides of the way. * As he
24. journeyed along by way of forests and mountains on a remote (24) and
difficult path, the king thought of his consort and was constricted with
emotion. * He saw birds flitting this way, then that, swiftly swerving
downwards to grasp the branches of the forest trees. He pointed them
out to his darling sons to encourage them. * "Children, look at the red
parrot, that lion among birds, and the blackbird, the green wood
pigeon and the Burmese ring-dove. Look at the white ibis, the goose
and the peacock, * the roller, the quail, crane and heron; the pelican,
Sultan hen, great ibis and cuckoo; the wood pigeon close in among the
leaves. They are calling along the deep forest way." * All the four

(24) branches of the army, bold men one and all, were full of eager enjoyment.
Some picked fruit and brought it to offer to the boys. * The king led away
his lovely sons, so dear, and they enjoyed themselves contentedly. Traversing the more remote parts of the journey, they came close to the city.

79.25–32. **The grandmothers hear Rām's news and welcome the boys, who tell them about their life in the forest.**

25. (25) * Then the people, both men and women, knew about their
sovereign bringing his sons into the kingdom * and were delighted and
full of welcome, every one. In the various thoroughfares there was a
commotion as, with their children on their hips, the wives ran in a body
to see their powerful king. * They sat at the roadside, close together in a
dense crowd. Their belongings had fallen down, misplaced, unheeded.
Each tried to be the one to have the best view. * The procession going on
foot in front of the king reached the palace gate in two magnificent
columns, with parasols in bejewelled tiers and long-handled fans spread
out. * All was splendid: the chariots, the soldiers of the ten divisions of
the army, Rām with his arrows, his sons like the moon on her course; the
royal Bhirut. * Splendid too were Laksm(ṇ) on his chariot and the
26. much-esteemed Sutrut for (26) they were scions of a lordly race, more to
be admired than any in the world. * The people clamorously offered
their good wishes for great prosperity, praying that the respected elder
prince might become the bejewelled diadem of the land.

* And then the virtuous Nārāy(ṇ), strong and mighty, arrived in the
royal city together with the four army corps. * The six royal persons
dismounted from their chariots[57] and the young princes were taken into
the turreted palace with its bejewelled tiers to wait upon the mothers.
* There, they raised their hands in greeting, bowing in obeisance before
the three mothers, highest of princesses, and sat together in attendance
upon them.
27. * Then Kosakalyā, serene matron, (27) and the lovely Kaikesī,
together with Sramud * saw their four dearest sons bringing in the two
beloved boys, endowed with the most charming good looks, splendid
beyond all in the world. * The ladies looked at their whole appearance
— so similar to that of the beloved son, Nārāy(ṇ), and the two of them
indistinguishable from each other — and were astonished. * They asked
questions of their sons. "Greetings, dearest darling children! When you
marched the army off to capture those vulgar enemies, * did you
manage to do so, then, beloved sons, and have thus returned? But where
did you find these two boys?"

(27) * Then the king, Nārāy(ṇ) Rām, had listened to the three mothers'
28. questions (28) and gave reply. * "Ladies, I marched my men after the
dear boys and we met in battle. We tried everything but neither won nor lost! * Then I asked about their place of origin and their family descent and I learned about my beloved Sītā. When Laksm(ṇ) tried to kill her she did not die! * She went to take shelter with a revered anchorite of great righteousness and kindliness who lived along a far-off forest path. And there she bore this son. * Through the goodness of the righteous sage, she had no dangerous illness and brought up these boys to the age of ten years. * This one, her beloved son, is called Rām-Laksm(ṇ). The younger one, the dearly-loved Japp-Laksm(ṇ), was created by the sage as a companion for him. * I went to where the *ācārya* was and I met my consort. I pleaded with her over and over but
29. she would not (29) consent to come back here. * Then I just asked my
dear consort for these darling sons." Even as he spoke, he was distressed, his eyes brimming with tears.

* When they learned that the boys were the sons of the queen, the great joy of the three respected mothers was unparalleled. * They bent to put their arms round them, making a great fuss of them. Half-embracing them, they put them on their knees and spoke to them, stroking them. * "Being so small as this, however did you have the strength to equal that of your father? It was due to the fact that you are to be the highest lords in the three worlds. * O children! When your father ordered that terrible punishment, to kill your mother, we grandmothers had no inkling of it. * Only when the day's first light
30. was clearly breaking through did we know (30) from the court ladies
that she was just then to be executed and that she was gone from the royal palace! * We bewailed. We were so sad. No one could have said we were content or happy. We thought only of the lovely queen. We never stopped thinking about her. * By that power which comes of merit, good fortune came the way of the queen and she did not die; separated from us, she went on to live in the jungle, enduring the direst of hardships."

* And then Rām-Laksm(ṇ), young descendant of the Sun, bowed respectfully and spoke to the grandmothers about the destitute state of his respected mother. * "Ladies, the queen is suffering distress of the grimmest possible kind, in abject poverty. She is emaciated and her body is disfigured. She has no clothes to wear. * When our august
31. father took it upon himself to bring us here, our mother (31) was
inconsolably grief-stricken, remaining there all alone. * O she will surely feel very heavy of heart, so forlorn is she, seeing only the righteous sage as her daily companion. * In the early days, when we

(31) were far away from father, we suffered hardship in the forest but now that we are reunited with him, we are bereft through being separated from our mother." * Even as he spoke, the tears welled up and he wept in utter misery. His whole body trembled violently as he fretted, faint and shivering.

* And then the three grandmothers, of elevated status, embraced their lovely grandchildren and, with tears of grief, lamented, * "Alas, darling daughter, in such poor circumstances! How can you be reduced to such wretchedness? You were accustomed to a constant state of well-being; you were used to being surrounded by possessions. * You
32. had great prestige. Your attendants, the court ladies, (32) those charming unmarried girls, were there, morning and evening, never shrinking from doing whatever you, dear daughter, asked of them. * Alas! When you went anywhere you would have mounted soldiers going in front and behind and at each side of your carriage, so that you might enjoy yourself contentedly. * But now, precious daughter, so wretched, you are suffering dire hardship in the jungle! This situation is due to some retribution from long ago. That is what has caused you to endure these misfortunes."

* Seeing the great sorrow of the mothers and his children, King Nārāy(ṇ) Rām * comforted the five princes and princesses so that they spent their grief and it was gone. Then that victorious great king bowed respectfully, taking his leave * of the mothers and led his sons, so dearly loved, back to their splendid palace.

79.33–44. **Rām organises companions for his sons and holds a feast in their honour.**

33. (33) * There, seated on the elevated throne with its three faces, all gold, the serene king spoke to his minister Sumantăn. * "I would have you choose a hundred and forty-eight well-born princesses of noble family to be companions for my dear sons * and find a thousand young boys of fine, handsome appearance, of families of the very highest rank, * selecting them for their good looks and decorous appearance. They must be neither too short not too tall and aged just ten years. They shall serve my lovely sons." * Receiving this order, Sumantăn bowed before the serene king with palms placed together, and left the palace to make arrangements in accordance with the king's
34. wishes. (34) * He chose princesses from noble families (all of which had their chronicles) and he chose boys from the best military families. All the chosen ones were just ten years old. * Having found the complete

(34) number of boys and girls, the senior minister Sumanatǎn took them on foot in a great throng to present them to the sovereign.

* And then Nārāy(ṇ) of magnificent power saw that the light was turning to darkness, as the sun was setting * and the clear moon and stars were rising brightly. He took his two offspring to the fine couches in his usual sleeping quarters. * The king tossed and turned in his sleep, his heart heavy with his troubles. He put his arms round his
35. dearly-loved sons, (35) one on each side of him. * The tears welled up and flowed freely as his thoughts turned to his chief consort. Sadly he addressed his beloved wife, far away in the hermitage. * "Ah! By this time you are asleep. Or are you troubled by your grief? Or are you angry with me? Or has your anger subsided? * Alas! As I reflect further I am puzzled. Because of some past misdeeds on both our parts I am parted from you, my treasure. You are far away and have abandoned me! * I must have separated some creatures from their mates and so I have been separated from you, my little one, do you not agree? But I have not yet had enough of being with you and loving you." * The king lamented from deep dusk until far into the night, when, curling up protectively near his two sons, he slept deeply, heedless of all those thoughts. * When the sun broke through, with radiant light and one heard only the music
36. of the strings, trumpet, conch (36) and cymbal in melodies played for enjoyment, * Nārāy(ṇ) awoke and sat up. He washed his face and bathed. He put on his splendidly-patterned clothing so as to be impeccably dressed and set out, taking with him his dearly-loved sons, to sit in the golden hall amid the groups of attendant ministers.

* His three younger brothers and the royal minstrel bowed before him, indicating their loyalty, and sat in attendance on Nārāy(ṇ). * People whose duty it was to do so played a musical accompaniment, of which the thrumming sound was heard afar. The singing was like the music of the distant heavens and thus enhanced the king's grandeur. * Then Nārāy(ṇ), the powerful, the high-born, spoke what was in his mind, uttering honey-sweet words. "Now, * you page, off you go as
37. quickly as possible (37) to summon the astrologer with his Brahmin scriptures. He is to come at once with all haste." * The royal orderly, bowing and making obeisance, took his leave, as he received the king's order and sped away most readily. * Arriving, he explained his errand. "O astrologer, the lord king has sent me to summon you at once." * The chief astrologer, hearing the order of His Majesty, the respected lord, busily made ready his learned books and went back with the royal page.
38. * There, he dutifully crept up to (38) the serene king who wielded mighty powers and, amid the groups of military officers, respectfully listened to what he had to say.

(38) * Then, seeing the astrologer, King Nārāy(ṇ) Rām spoke to him
earnestly. * "O astrologer, I would have you calculate the times which
are auspicious in accordance with the light or dark fortnight. What day
would bring good fortune? I intend to hold the ceremony of the tying
of hands[58] for my dear sons." * The astrologer, thus bidden, set out his
formulae for recitation with regard to the days, in accordance with the
horoscopic rules. He set out the Great Era. He deleted or added hours,
he did multiplications, he calculated urgently. * When he had found
the time which, with the moon favourable, would quite clearly be
excellent in all respects, he humbly informed his sovereign, "May it
please you, this morning[59] is an extremely good time. * It is the
39. fifteenth day (39) of the dark fortnight. The time in every way coincides
with good fortune. If you hold the ceremony it will be blessed with
happiness and prosperity." * Then the virtuous Nārāy(ṇ), strong and
mighty sovereign, had heard the astrologer. He spoke to Sumantăn,
commanding him * to go as quickly as possible and make all the
necessary preparations for the games and festivities to be ready in good
time for that morning.

* Then the minister Sumantăn bowed, respectfully took his leave and
went quickly away. * When, soon afterwards, he reached the courtyard
he gave orders to the ministers. Each of them was to organise the
arrangements in accordance with his particular responsibilities, so that
all would be as His Majesty commanded. * They built a turreted
40. pavilion with bejewelled tiers, (40) sculpted and painted over with gold,
with awnings from which were hung garland upon garland of
decorative flowers. * There was every kind of cover, mattress, silk
cushion and rug; and pillows edged with wool. There was a most
superior and elegant offering made from the banana plant and, to
complete all, the candle-holder for passing round the candle. * In front
of the pavilion they constructed shelters facing this way and that, for
entertainments and games, with a scaffold of flowers all placed together
in sections according to their various colours. * Then they opened up
the royal enclosure, flattening the earth and decorating the area with
splendid banners and parasols. There were pavilions for the food
provided free and stalls for drinks all over the city!

* When dawn broke and the sun's radiance shone in the heavens, the
mighty King Nārāy(ṇ), supporter of the earth, awoke and left his bed.
* Joining the three mothers and his high-born younger brothers, he
41. gave an order for (41) water to be brought, drawn from the five rivers,[60]
* and sprinkled it on the two young princes. Powder was smoothed on
them, oil was sprinkled on them and they were perfumed with flowers.
They wore the finest jewellery, including earrings shaped like

(41) Phyllanthus flowers. * They wore decorative rings and ornaments
covered with patterns of jewels. Their sarongs were embroidered, with
flowers arising vividly from the weaving; tusk-shaped sequins caught
the eye on the border of the cloth. * They wore tunics on which
flashing gold was prominent, sparkling most beautifully. The
magnificent splendour of the two august boys, so dignified, was heard
of far and wide. * They were like the divine Sun, sitting in his royal
carriage driving forth. Or rather, it was as though the Moon on her
course had come down to earth! * When the seven royal persons were
arrayed, the dear young princes were led off to mount the royal
42. carriage. * The mothers and the king, so elevated, (42) together with
his serene young brothers, mounted their vehicles and set off. * The
ministers, the royal family and the Brahmin priests of ancient descent
went in procession on either side of the way in closely-packed, separate
columns. * The music of the strings and of the trumpet resounded.
Umbrellas and many-tiered parasols were opened out. People held
long-handled fans of mulberry-leaf shape and sunshades of gold cloth.
There was a great clamour and the earth reverberated loudly. * When
they reached the pavilion itself the king had his beloved sons ascend
the bejewelled throne and sit beneath the white umbrellas. * When the
auspicious time arrived, the Brahmins uncovered the offering. They
placed a gold candle in the candle-holder and all of them passed it
43. round * fully seven times. Then (43) the royal grandmothers and their
father approached to tie the dear children's hands * and to pray that
they might possess superior ascetic powers, excelling all in the three
worlds; that they might come to be the people's overlords; * and that
they might have long lives of peace and great prosperity, a billion and
a million years of life without encountering troubles, sorrows, sickness
or danger.

* When the ceremony was over the king let the festivities begin with
all the amusements and shows of various kinds: the puppets, the duel
dance,[61] the *yike*,[62] turning somersaults and sitting cross-legged with
mortars. * The *mańgram*[63] music echoed through the place. People
walked the tight-rope, performed the Annamese opera, and, with
shrieks and screams, contended against each other in spinning tops,
with the tops all a-tremble. There was Chinese and Chatri[64] dancing.
44. * There were Javanese, in pairs or singly (44) most cleverly holding up
their shields and whirling them rapidly round. There were people
boxing adroitly against each other and there were fighting elephants.
There was every kind of contest. * When the whole programme had
been gone through completely the three grandmothers and their
relatives returned to their homes, * while the highest of kings, the lord

(44) of men, took his lovely, treasured sons back to their palace to be all
together as usual.

79.44–80.1. **After some time, Rām overhears the boys express their grief about their mother's loneliness and sends them with Sītā's women to see Sītā and ask her to return. If she will not do so, they are to leave the women there as companions for her. They arrive at the hermitage and speak first with the *ācārya*, then with Sītā.**

* The king cherished his two beloved sons tenderly without mishap
over a long period and gave his attention to the government of the
kingdom. * One night, the noble sovereign took his dear children to
45. their sleeping quarters. * On his comfortable couch, with pillows (45)
and mosquito-nets with gold thread and wool edging, he curled up
protectively near his august sons, who were sound asleep. * In the
small hours, the elder boy was miserable. He woke and was most
unhappy, missing his mother. * "Alas, mother!" he lamented, "we are
separated from you by such a great distance! We have abandoned you
to your life with the sage. You must surely be full of grief. * Sorely
troubled and forlorn, you will be thinking of us, your much-loved sons,
with yearning. * O mother, highest of princesses, we used to attend
upon you constantly at all times. Now you have only the *ācārya* to
look after you day by day. * We have come here to lead a pleasant life
46. of ease in company with our father — but we have left you (46)
deserted in your forest glade." * The prince lamented about the whole
situation. Choking with grief, he embraced his younger brother and
moaned beside their couch.

* And then Nārāy(ṇ) of magnificent power, on the royal couch
which was for sleep, started awake. * His ears unmistakably caught the
sound of his son's plaintive address to their mother in the far-distant
hermitage * and he felt pity for the dear boy, the apple of his eye.
Tears of distress flowed as he thought tenderly of them, trembling with
the anguish of his emotions. * The king comforted his two sons,
47. stroking them all over. "O dearest darlings," he said, "I (47) feel very
depressed each day. It is my own bad fate, children, which is causing
me to suffer deep sorrow. * Now, my little ones, do not weep and
grieve. I shall have you taken to see your honoured mother." * He
consoled his dear sons, whom he loved so much, talking to them kindly
until, when dawn broke through, he went out to sit in his delightful
hall.

* The people whose duty it was to do so, the orchestra with drums,

(47) gong, strings, trumpets and decorous conch, played an accompaniment
for the dear king. * His young brothers, the chief ministers and the
military officers, in endless lines, were seated in attendance on him.
48. * Then the high-born Nārāy(ṇ) (48) spoke. "Greetings, Sumantăn! I
would have you go and prepare a force * because my sons are to go
away to visit their mother. Elephants, carriages, horses and everything
the princes will need . . ." * Sumantăn bowed respectfully before the
serene king, most high, and left then and there. * He prepared his
soldiers, a vast cavalry force. Processional objects were carried in every
hand as they came in dense formation, thronging close together.
* There were round umbrellas and many-tiered parasols, spread stiffly
out with hanging fringes, opened for use against the sun; there were
long-handled fans and fans of mulberry-leaf shape in readiness, as
though it were a procession for Indr. * And they prepared splendid
49. horses, (49) noble, felicitous beasts, putting on their magnificent,
patterned harness which sparkled with burnished brilliance. * The
masters of the royal carriages decked the vehicles with decorations of
pure gems; the shafts were rearing *nāgas* which seemed like real, live
ones! * Then they made arrangements for all the music, the playing of
the trumpet, the conch, the drum and the gong. When all was finished,
Sumantăn took them to pay homage to the king.

* Then Rām of the three worlds, whose renown was heard of all over
the earth, turned to the elderly ladies, * suggesting that they should be
away with all speed to make ready the young ladies of the court; and
he sent his treasured sons, most high, to pay their respects to the
50. mothers. * Next, the lord king (50) gave instructions to his children.
"When you are there, please put in a plea for me with your mother.
* Tell her of my great grief and pain, of how I think of the dearly-loved
queen and my heart never forgets her. * Say that if that dearest lady
does not consent to come back, your father will most likely die; he
cannot live. * Everything depends on you, my treasures. Do your best,
my dearest little ones, to think of a way to make your mother come
back to the city. * There is another point, however. If the lovely queen
decides to be unfriendly towards me, then, my darlings, let her keep
with her the dear court ladies." * The king had given his instructions in
full detail. His heart was full and he was much upset. The three royal
persons grieved, unaware of anything else.

51. (51) * Having spent their grief and feeling easier, the two dear
princes bowed low in obeisance with palms placed together, taking
leave of their father, sustainer of the earth. * Bearing their magnificent
accoutrements of great beauty and their bows with arrows of supernatural power, those leaders of men, mounted on swift royal horses,

(51) led all the court ladies away. * The two princes rode on their fleet
horses, leading the whole vast force, which came along in columns, one
succeeding the other. * The grandeur of the princes, their magnificent
personal appearance and their noble lineage were talked about far and
wide, for were they not the sons of Nārāy(ṇ), strong and mighty
beyond all in the world? * The court ladies, riding in carriages, drove
off on the journey, all dotted about the wooded hillsides; there was no
52. chance to stop and rest. * The two happy boys (52) eagerly pressed on,
traversing the jungle, following their route. * When they were nearly at
the hermitage beneath the branches of the large fig-tree, they halted the
military force and dismounted from their splendid horses. * The two
princes, most high, took the court ladies to pay their respects to the
serene, good anchorite in the fine *sālā*. * There, they raised their hands
in greeting, bowing low in obeisance and offering candles, joss-sticks
and garlands. Respectfully they asked him all about himself. * Then
53. they took leave of the revered (53) *ācārya* and took the ladies to where
their respected mother sat in the hermitage. * Approaching upon their
knees, they clasped her feet, making obeisance to their honoured
mother, humbly indicating their devotion.

* And then that royal mother looked at her two dear sons and at all
the charming court ladies * who had come and was delighted. She bent
to embrace them, showing her close attachment to them. She kissed her
beloved sons, so dear, and spoke honey-sweet words to them.
"Greetings, * my children. After you had gone I suffered sheer anguish
in my yearning for you. Every day I have thought about you and
missed you, looking out for you in case you came. * But now I can see
54. (54) you, my darlings. Here you are! My joy is without parallel.
Nothing could be compared with it." * Then the court ladies in tears
crept up on their knees to greet her and asked their beloved queen her
news and told her about themselves. * "O every one of us thought on
that night that you had died," they said. * "We have been unhappy all
the time, mourning you in deepest sorrow, missing you sadly, beloved
queen, never failing to think of you one single day, * until we saw your
sons arriving in the city and learned about you, that you were alive!
Then each one of us was relieved of her sorrows and felt overjoyed.
55. * O mistress, you are accustomed to living in a fine palatial (55)
dwelling, surrounded by us, in magnificent grandeur. * How can you
now be brought so low, suffering sorrow and hardship like this? Your
appearance is quite changed. The brightness of your face is marred.
* Now you eat only the common fruits of the jungle, lacking in
flavour." Even as they spoke, they clasped the queen's feet and shed
tears of grief. * When she saw all her women weeping and wailing as

(55) they said this to her, the noble queen * sobbed in great distress, the
tears brimming over and pouring down. She made an effort to speak.
"Greetings, ladies. It is some bad fate of mine * which has caused me
56. to be far away, to have left happiness behind me (56) and to have come
to live here and undergo these troubles alone. Day by day, I ponder
about impermanence. Once one is born, nothing is certain.
* Happiness and sadness are no different from each other. Do not
grieve for me or think sadly about me. I entrust my sons, so dear to my
80.1 heart, to all of you. (80.1) * Please, ladies, do this for me: just give the
boys a little instruction about affairs of state, important or trivial. If
you love them and care for them, your kindness would be without
parallel."

80.1–13. **When the boys ask Sītā to go back to Aiyudhyā, she says she will not go back unless the king dies, in which case she will go back for his funeral. She refuses to accept the court ladies as her companions. They all return to give the answer to the distressed Rām.**

* And then the two princes respectfully informed their honoured
mother of how matters had been progressing. * "Madam, when we
arrived in the city of Aiyudhyā together with our three uncles and the
king, our father, * he took us to pay our respects to the three noble
princesses, most high, the grandmothers. They asked us questions,
heard all about us and * wept copious tears of sorrow, quite
inconsolably. They grieved without respite about your absence. * All
the seven royal persons, kindly forgiving us, fussed over us and made
2. sure we were not troubled (2) in any way. * May it please you, our
father was most unhappy. Every day he was afflicted by his grief. He
was never without trouble. * The three grandmothers and the rest of
the family missed you and so our noble father told us to set * out and
come here to ask you to go back to your home in the far-away
kingdom. If you do not grant our request it is likely that our father will
die! * And we ourselves are not happy either. Every day our wretchedness weighs on our minds. With regard to all those wrongs done to
you, what you have said about them is quite true. * But we do ask you,
mother, to consider at length His Majesty's wish to be reunited with
you. He sent us to ask you to go there. * Surely, under the
circumstances, you could bring yourself to forgive him and take pity
on the two of us?"
3. (3) * Then, hearing her dearly-loved sons relate how her respected
husband had sent them to take her back, * Sītā was beside herself with

(3) fury. "My children," she replied, "I am so pleased with you, coming to
your mother, * but, as to the lord, your father, he said I had
transgressed the law and was accursed. He blazed with wrath and told
Laksm(ṇ) to do away with me. * What good quality does His Majesty
see in me now to make him bewail my loss and feel my absence? * If
the king had forgiven me and been merciful, if he had taken pity on
me, his servant, I would not be in these grim circumstances. * And
when he ordered my execution, everybody knew about it. I was
disgraced in the eyes of the ministers and soldiers and of the populace
4. everywhere, (4) even the lowest of them. * So have no doubt about it,
young princes, I have no wish to return to the city. I shall stay here in
accordance with that fate of mine from long ago. I would rather die
than go to see him, though, * if His Majesty did in fact die, children, I
would return then to do honour to the noble king's remains."

* Then the princes had heard their mother's point of view and seen
how angry she was and how she absolutely refused to return. * They
bowed low at her feet and sobbed in great distress. Again they pleaded
most earnestly with her and tried to persuade her. * "Lady, may it
please you, if you do not grant our request, we, being your servants,
5. dare not force you against your will * but our honoured father (5) gave
us instructions, requiring us to let you have the young ladies of the
court to live here and be your servants." * Then, when the esteemed
lady heard that her husband had told them to offer her all the dear
ladies of the court, * she embraced her dear, lovable sons and spoke in
reply, "Children, I am most grateful for the kindness of the noble king
* but I have lived here for ten years, taking refuge with the sage of
superior knowledge; I have gone alone on foot foraging in the jungle
and have brought you up to the age you are now. * Tell me, children,
whom should I have to come and stay with me? Why cause them
6. hardship just because of me? * Now please go back and inform the (6)
dear lord, our serene king, that I simply do not accept them and I
would not have him worry about me."

* The princes had listened to what their mother had said and did not
dare to compel her. They bowed their heads, downcast in gloom. * In
their hearts they were in anguish. They were stricken as though by a
sharp arrow, full of sorrow, the two of them, their limbs trembling
violently. * "Alas!" they said. "There is no happy solution, then. There
is nothing but unending trouble. To live is to be a burden to the great
earth. It is much better to die. * O we are so miserable! How can we
endure this retribution? Every day we feel full of trouble. And we do
not know where to go. * While we were there, father was unhappy.
7. Now we come here and (7) mother is not content." * As they spoke,

(7) the princes were writhing on the ground with anguish, almost losing
consciousness.
* Then the esteemed chief consort, the lady Sītā, saw her most
lovable sons stricken with grief and cast down in gloom and
* comforted the two dear children, stroking them all over and putting
them on her lap. She spoke sweetly, * "O children, do not be so
inconsolably miserable. Come now, go back and speak to the king,
that he may learn my answer. * If you miss me, my two darlings, just
take leave of His Majesty and come back to visit me."
* The beloved princes heard their respected mother's soothing words
8. (8) * but were disturbed by a confusion of emotions, their hearts full to
breaking point. They wept copious tears in depressed silence, unable to
speak. * Then, after raising their hands and bowing to take leave of the
anchorite and their mother, they left the cell and the hermitage. * The
princes were leading the court ladies away when they caught sight of
the honoured lady, her whole body drooping dejectedly. They ran
9. unhappily to clasp her feet and (9) * pour forth all their sorrow. Then
they struggled to control their limbs, mounted their splendid horses
and drove off with all speed.
* When they reached the city they dismounted from their swift steeds
and led the court ladies in to attend upon their father. * There, they
raised their hands in greeting, making respectful obeisance, amid the
groups of young women, before their dear father. * The virtuous
Nārāy(ṇ), strong and mighty, saw his two beloved sons arriving back at
10. the palace. (10) * "Well, my children," he enquired of those lovely
sons, "you have made the journey on my behalf to make my plea to
your mother. * Was she content or was she angry? What was her
instruction to you? I have been watching out for you constantly. I
simply longed to know what had happened."
* Then the two dearly-loved sons, making obeisance, informed their
father of what had transpired. * "Lord, you were so understanding and
compassionate as to send us to visit our mother in that far-off
hermitage. * We respectfully pleaded with her. We said the supporter
of the earth was almost dying as he daily grieved for her and that he
had sent us to ask her to go to him. * Our mother said that, while you,
11. highest of princes, are still alive, she absolutely refuses to return (11).
* If you were really to die, she would then come straight back to do
honour to your remains. * We pleaded with her over and over. We
offered her all the court ladies but she was quite resolved; she refused
absolutely to have them." * As the princes spoke, they were suffocated
by sobs, in great distress. The tears flowed all over their sad faces
because they loved their mother.

(11) * Then the high-born lord of men of great prestige had heard his treasured sons, so gifted, telling him all the news. * His heart trembled violently and until the sun lowered its rays and dusk turned to
12. darkness, he struggled to control his grief. * Then he went (12) into his sleeping quarters and thought about his wife, so dear to his heart. * He tossed and turned again and again in his inconsolable sorrow, almost dying, as he thought with wistful longing of his beloved sweetheart. * "Alas, my dearest love," he lamented, "many times have we been destitute, you and I. We used to suffer our troubles together, living out there in the jungle. * The three of us[65] were of one heart and mind, having the same daily life. Why, my love, dear to my heart, have you now cut yourself off from me like this? * Ah me! I used to see you and talk to you, my treasure without blemish. I used to be united with you in love. We were so gay and happy. Everything was perfect." * The
13. king (13) thought mournfully of those early days, unable to sleep at all. His face expressed his sad foreboding. His limbs trembled violently.

80.13–25. **Rām has a funeral pavilion and urn prepared to trick Sītā into returning. Hanumān fetches her to attend her husband's "funeral".**

* When the sun was already radiating its light, he awoke, bathed his face and went to sit in grandeur in the delightful hall. * Taking his place on the bejewelled throne beneath the white umbrella, the serene king, Nārāy(ṇ), gave his orders to his young brothers, * the minister Sumantăn and the monkey prince, Hanumān. "The royal lady is now in a furious temper! * I sent my sons to ask her pardon but she has no forgiveness in her. She says that she will come only if I die — to pay her respects to my corpse! * So will you please give your minds to the
14. speedy preparation (14) of a funeral urn and a cremation pavilion, without letting the whole population hear about it. * I intend to trick her into thinking that I am actually dead. Then it will be possible to persuade her to come to the city." * The three younger brothers, Hanumān and the minister Sumantăn approved of the king's plan. * They raised their hands and bowed, taking their leave, and went out at once.

* Arriving in the courtyard, Hanumān of surpassing powers paid homage to the gods of all ten directions in the three worlds and recited
15. the divine incantations for creation by magic. (15) * There instantly appeared a splendid, gold pavilion of superlative brilliance, its pinnacle as high as the sky, and a funeral urn, decoratively set with gems. * The base of the pavilion was directly supported by *garuḍa*-motifs, with tier

(15) upon tier of lotus petals in a splendid design and a chain of jewels
intertwining, forming an embossed edge. * Then above there was a
white umbrella with its separate tiers, one upon another. It seemed that
a celestial palace had come down on earth! * Sumantăn readily
organised men and supervised activities, placing officers on guard
there. * Some of the officials, not knowing about the king's trick,
loudly bewailed his loss with much commotion. * Others knew and
16. worked in silence (16) at whatever task they had to do. As for the
populace, they were afraid. Mournfully they asked questions of each
other.

* Then the three brothers, Sumantăn and he of the simian race had
finished their preparations and returned quickly, * reporting, on
arrival, "Lord, noble king, the cremation pavilion has now been made
ready as was your command." * Learning the facts, Nārāy(ṇ), strong
and mighty with the power which comes from meditation, was highly
delighted. * In excited anticipation, he seemed to see the beloved form
of his wife. He gave orders to certain women in whose loyalty he had
17. complete confidence * to go and tell the elderly ladies (17) and the
charming court ladies to prepare, every one, to mourn, to weep and
wail and keep watch in accordance with the royal manuals. * "And
when the queen arrives, please, all you ladies, mourn. And do take the
princes a long way away to play." * The women took leave respectfully, hurriedly made themselves ready and went to the resplendent
cremation pavilion to do as their sovereign had commanded.

* Then the virtuous Nārāy(ṇ), strong and mighty, spoke graciously.
"Now, Hanumān, * I would have you go to the hermitage of the
greatest of *ācāryas*. Persuade the queen. You have wits — use them."
18. * When he had given his instructions, the esteemed king went (18) out
of the golden palace all alone to the cremation pavilion.

* And then, when the king had gone, the simian son of the Wind,
strong and mighty, bold as brass, manifested his power. * Controlling
his body, he took up a stance, solid and mountain-like, and then took
flight to that far-distant place, the hermitage of the best of sages. * On
arrival, Hanumān behaved, as he entered and saw the honoured lady,
as though he were bereaved and in deep mourning. * Then the lady Sītā
19. saw the royal simian thus weeping in sorrow. * Round-eyed (19) with
terror, she trembled in every limb. She questioned him urgently in her
uncertainty. * "O bold Hanumān, what is the purpose of your visit,
that you come like this, weeping and wailing? Please tell me as quickly
as you can." * As he listened to her, the son of the Wind lamented
more and more. Then he said to the most estimable queen, * "Madam,
from the time when our sovereign, your husband, mightiest of all in the

(19) power gained by virtue, came to visit you * and returned home, he
has never been at peace. He has been grieving most wretchedly. He
became very thin and suffered from an illness. His face turned
blotchy and dark. * He forgot all about the administrative work of a
20. king. He avoided all nourishment. He lamented night and (20) day.
Then he sent the princes off * to come and plead with you, asking
you to cast away your anger, inviting you to go to the city and be
with him just as you were before. * When the princes returned and
informed him that you had decided to stay, your husband bewailed
more than ever. Eventually his life came to an end. * Now his three
younger brothers have taken upon themselves the burden of the
kingdom in joint council with each other and were intending to hold
the cremation ceremony for the sovereign. * The three mothers said
they must not, they must wait for the queen. They sent me, therefore,
to invite you to come quickly to pay homage to your deceased
husband."

* And then the Queen Sītā of high esteem, knowing nothing of their
21. artful trick, writhed in an agony of grief, utterly downcast. (21) * "O
dear master," she mourned, "your power exceeded all in the three
worlds. Gods, *garuḍas*, *gandharvas* — all had contentment owing to
your virtue. * How can it be that you have now died, my precious love,
that you have left the city, abandoning the young ladies of the court,
that your life is thus reduced to nothing? * Alas! My innocent, darling
children! You must be sorrowing in bereavement, then, having lost
your father and having no one to whom to turn! * Oh fate caused me
to change my feelings and abandon you, my precious love, living in the
jungle with no possibility of seeing your face." * The lady lamented,
thinking with yearning of her husband. Her heart was almost breaking
22. as, shaking violently, she became faint. (22) * When the queen came to
herself again and rose up, she made every effort to control her
thoughts and then took Hanumān, the simian, to the *ācārya*. * There,
the queen saluted him, bowing in homage, and respectfully related to
him the whole story as Hanumān had told it to her. * "Lord, I am here
now to beg to take leave and go to the city to attend the cremation of
the serene king and seek expiation of my wrong deeds."

* Then, when the righteous sage had heard, knowing nothing of the
trick, * he beat his breast and shoulders and trembled with fear in
every limb. "Alas for Rām, the noble king!" he said. "It is not right for
23. him to come to (23) this. * I said you ought to be friends and you were
not. You argued with me, did you not? And now this has happened to
your husband. Where can you find him now? * Alas! Men, sages, gods
everywhere must feel chilled. Vile enemies will come to pester and

(23) oppress the three worlds. * Ah! I am sorry for the princes, fatherless now. They must feel their bereavement deeply. Do hasten, madam, and return to them." * The tears of the esteemed royal consort brimmed over then and fell streaming upon the ground. * She took leave of the lord sage on her knees and then left the cell and the hermitage, with Hanumān following close behind her.

24. (24) * When they were beyond the terrace the monkey Hanumān said to her, "Madam, respected queen, if you go on foot like this along the ground * the path is laborious and long. You will surely be in physical distress as you walk along. Please sit on my hand. It will be very quick. I shall fly there in an instant." * With these words the great lord of the simian race demonstrated a transformation of his body. He recited divine incantations of the most superior kind. * By the power of Nārāy(ṇ)'s divine magic Hanumān changed himself so that he was as big as a mountain of the Hemabānt, the palms of his hands like the earth's surface. * This done, he invited the queen to take her place. He was like King Rāb(ṇ), Dasamukh, going through the air, holding in his
25. hand the lessed Queen Umā, to offer her to Isūr. (25) * Hanumān went through the air and arrived quite soon in the city of Aiyudhyā * where he proposed to the chief consort that she should go to the cremation pavilion.

80.25–35. **When Sītā laments beside the funeral pavilion Rām comes out to comfort her from where he was observing her. She runs away from him. When she sees that she will be unable to avoid capture she prays that the earth will open for her and descends to the land of the *nāgas*.**

* And then the noble queen, so dear, stepped into the decorated, gold pavilion, mourning most sadly as she did so. * And all the family relations and the ladies of the king's court and every one of the elderly wives of the ministers * caught sight of the blameless queen of great beauty and watched her come to the splendid cremation pavilion, her face downcast in great despondency. * Seeing how thin and disfigured she was, not at all as she had been wont to be, they wailed with much
26. ado, in their (26) pity for their dear queen. * When that lady, most high, heard the court ladies grieving, she thought that they were mourning His Majesty Nārāy(ṇ). * She trembled in every limb. She paid no attention to the others as, round-eyed and with her thoughts in disorder, her body limp, she forced herself to go forward. * Reaching the bejewelled funeral urn, she writhed in anguish, her head drooping. She beat her breast until it was red and she rolled on the ground.

(26) * "Alas, my precious love," she bewailed, "why are we now
separated? I pray that I may die too, O king, to be joined with you, our
lives as one. * Your goodness to me was greater than the ocean and
27. more extensive than the broad earth. These things are not (27) equal to
the immensity of your kindness. * Alas! When we three[65] set forth,
leaving the city boundary, we travelled on foot across the jungle,
enduring harsh sufferings of every kind, * eating only the fruits of the
trees, putting on the garb of ascetics, until the ungodly Dasamukh stole
me away to the city of Laṅkā. * Then you quickly had the idea of
building the causeway in order to bring the force of monkeys across,
follow me and fight. And you destroyed their whole race and King
Dasamukh was eliminated. * I was able to be united with you, my love,
my heart's darling; and you brought me here to rule over the kingdom
of Aiyudhyā. * Trouble arose because that horrid vampire, so wicked
and deceitful, persuaded me to draw the portrait of Rāb(ṇ). Thus it
was that I was separated from you, my king and husband. * You
followed after me and pleaded with me over and over again; and it was
28. because I refused to come here (28) that you suffered death. * Why
have I never known happiness? Why have I known only suffering?
What is the good of living in dread? It would be far better to die."

* More and more did the queen bewail as she thought things over
and more and more distressed was she in her pity for the king. She beat
her breast in anguish; then she felt faint and lost consciousness. * Then
the virtuous Nārāy(ṇ), strong and mighty, who had been sitting beside
the bejewelled funeral urn close to the curtain, * heard his chief
consort, so precious, lamenting about that time when they were
destitute, and could not control his will. He came out, there and then.
29. * Seeing his wife in a faint, he (29) trembled in anxiety. He went up to
his dear wife, took her in his arms and put her on his lap. * As he
wiped away her tears he thought that the queen had died. His heart
quaked with dread. * He moaned and cried aloud, feeling her loss
acutely, indifferent to all else in confused oblivion.

* Then the blameless queen came to herself and saw the king.
Furiously angry, she sprang up and ran quickly away from him. * "So,
my lord, great king and master of men," she said, "that was a mean
trick, wasn't it? Do you find it acceptable? Esteemed king, * why did
30. you not consider your shame in front of the army and (30) the vassal
princes? And the gods of the ten directions of the three worlds? They
will speak slightingly of you." * At this Nārāy(ṇ) Rām hastened after
the queen * and spoke honey-sweet words. "My dearest, most delightful
wife! The tradition in this world (that husband and wife stay together)
goes back far into the past. * Now you are my partner. How could

(30) anyone say anything against *my* behaviour? It was you, my treasure,
who decided to stay away from me." * As he spoke, the lord king had
approached near to her. He hurried round the cremation pavilion in
31. pursuit of his beloved wife. (31) * The esteemed lady Sītā ran away
from him and replied, "Lord king of great victories, * that was because
an end had come to our living, you and I, in one home as formerly. Do
not force me, esteemed king." * As she spoke she ran away, her beauty
like that of Mekhallā when she tantalises Rāmesūr in the heavens.[66]

* Then Nārāy(ṇ) of magnificent powers had listened. He reflected.
* "When I try to cajole her like this she does not feel any love for me. I
32. will think of some other way of speaking to her so as (32) to beguile
her and catch her." * He summoned the lords, his young brothers, and
the simian Hanumān to help him catch the lovely queen and prevent
her from escaping. * Soon after he spoke, the four noble princes were
all running after the chief consort, intercepting her and blocking her
way. * The king called out to her, "My dearest little love, why are you
running away? Come here, my treasure. * How is it that you have no
compassion, that you do not feel the slightest pity for your husband?
Where would you find two people who were as one, like you and me?"

* The treasured lady respectfully replied, "Dear lord, I shall not
make such a mistake (as to fall into that trap). Noble king, * you are
33. making a public exhibition of yourself in front of the people (33). Do
not trouble yourself to try urging me against my will." * "O my heart's
darling," the king replied, "do stop just where you are now! Do not
run away!" * and he rushed off to chase after his beloved wife. It
looked as though he was just about to catch up once and for all. He
took hold of her — but she was away, out of reach of his arms.

* Then, when his young brothers and the simian saw the noble
consort running far away from their sovereign, * they had approached
to help him, running to intercept her and bar the way in front of her,
34. to keep the queen back and not let her escape from her husband. * (34)
Glancing about her as she ran, the noble queen could clearly see that
the young brothers, endowed with great qualities, and the monkey
Hanumān * had come in pursuit and cut off her route in front and
behind, stationing themselves to block her way. She could not proceed.
Feeling furiously angry, * she raised her hands reverently and said, "By
that power which I firmly hold through my good faith, I pray that the
earth * may open up a way for me to go to the *nāgas* to escape from
the serene king." And instantly, as she finished saying this prayer, the
earth opened up a way.

* Then the sovereign had pursued his chief consort and intercepted
her in the fine cremation pavilion. * When he had come close to her,

35. the serene king had managed to seize (35) her hands but she had flung his hands away and made a way down into the ground. * Unable to catch his consort as was his intention, the king was in mental agony. He trembled violently in every limb.

80.35–48. **The king of the *nāgas* offers Sītā a home in his palace. Hanumān is sent by Rām to find her and is able to tell Rām that she will be looked after well. Rām, in despair at his separation from her, writes a message and sends it, attached to his arrow, to Laṅkā and from there down into the underworld.**

* And then, when the noble lady arrived in the land of the *nāgas* she proceeded into the city. * Biruṇ, king of the *nāgas*, supporter of the earth, was standing by his palace window, attended by a host of court
36. ladies. * Looking out, he saw (36) a human lady, faultlessly fair. In wonder, he came out from the palace straight away, * went up to her and questioned her. "Greetings, delightful lady, whose beauty excels that of all women, exceeds that of the young goddesses! * Your name, madam — what is your name? And from what kingdom do you come? For what reason have you journeyed alone to come to us here?"

* Then the noble queen of great beauty replied and told him, "Sītā is my name. * I am the consort of Nārāy(ṇ) whose mighty power stretches over the world and who gave part of himself to come here, with the name Rām, head of the three worlds, to suppress the ungodly
37. creatures." * And (37) the much-admired lady told her whole story. "I am in a most difficult situation and have come down here to ask for refuge in Pātāl." * Then the *nāga* king, Biruṇ, heard the name of Nārāy(ṇ), protector of the earth, whose role it was to be lord of the three worlds. * Having heard the whole story, he had no hesitation about believing her. He bowed before the respected queen and said, "Clearly this is the absolute truth. * Madam, one might think you were the mother of the gods! Now, feel no anxiety. I invite you to live here peacefully." * With these words, the king of the *nāgas* took the honoured consort to the turreted palace, all his ladies following behind
38. the queen. (38) * There, he told his chief consort, Ratanā, to go in at once and assign to Sītā a thousand court ladies, * who would arrange suitable apartments for her in the palace, provide everything needful and be with the queen, so fair, every day to do her bidding.

* Then, having heard what her husband said, the chief consort, Ratanā, went in to make arrangements in all haste. * When she had had all the things that might be required put ready, she invited the

39 noble Sītā to go in and take up residence there in peaceful serenity. (39)
* And the noble queen, so lovely, lived in that palatial home in the
kingdom of the *nāgas*. * No illness assailed her. Her thoughts were
only of her beloved sons; she never let them be out of her mind.

* Then, when his wife, so dear to his heart, had fled to the kingdom
of Pātāl, Nārāy(ṇ) of great strength and might * ordered the strong and
mighty Hanumān, so immense and superb, to follow the queen and
40. find out where she was. (40) * Receiving the royal command, Hanumān
took leave of His Majesty and went off. He darted through the air and
then made a way down through the earth. * When he reached Pātāl
and saw all the *nāgas*, he magically caused his person to be screened
from view, invisible. * This done, he of the simian race journeyed on
directly towards the city of the king of the *nāgas* and went with all
speed in search of the dear queen. * As he quickly turned in one
direction or another through the royal city, he could not see her. He
41. entered the palace grounds of the *nāga* (41) * and went into the palace
where he saw the dear consort seated upon a decorative, bejewelled
throne with *nāga* handmaidens all round her. * Hanumān made
himself visible once again in the form of the son of the Wind god * and
approached close to the dear queen, saluting her with palms placed
together.

* Then that royal lady of great esteem caught sight of Hanumān out
of the corner of her eye. * She fell into a furious rage. She was so upset
that she was at breaking point. "So! You beast!" she said, "you vilest
of vile scoundrels! * First you pretend to mourn and tell me my
husband is dead, practising deception upon me and humiliating me
before one and all, * thinking that, being a woman, I would be swayed
42. by (42) beguiling speeches — it was only through the power of my
merit that I managed to escape and reach here! * And now you have
followed me like a shadow and intend to tell me lies. I shall not believe
a word. Go away, ape! Do not stay here. * If you continue to persecute
me, I shall take you by the throat with my own hands this very instant
and drag you out of the way, wretched ape, and no mistake!"

* The bold Hanumān, strong and mighty, heard what the queen
said. He made an effort to explain. * "Madam, most high, I am at your
service. When my mistress has cause for sorrow I am distressed to the
point of death. * All the royal family are most unhappy. If our king is
reunited with you, dear lady, we shall be delighted, every one of us.
43. * That was why I played a trick on you. I wanted you to be in (43)
complete harmony with the king, your husband, as you were in the
beginning. * I will serve you out of gratitude to the end of my life. And
also, I ask you, please, to forgive me. * At this very moment your

(43) husband, our dear king, is most deeply troubled. He just sent me down
here after you to find you, Your Highness. * He wants to know about
his wife and the place where she has come to stay. And His dear
Majesty would have me return and inform him."
* Having said his say, the simian bowed, taking his leave, and swiftly
went to the king of the *nāgas* who was outside those apartments.
* Hanumān approached and joined the king on the seat where he sat.
44. With honey-sweet words (44) he chatted with the sovereign. * "Our
honoured queen, the consort of Nārāy(ṇ), highest-born prince, whose
role it is to be lord of the three worlds, has now * come down to take
refuge with you. Will you please, my dear fellow, just do our dear king
the favour of keeping an eye on his lady?"
* Hearing Hanumān's request, the king of the *nāgas*, imperious and
mighty, gave reply. * "O bold Hanumān," he said, "soldier of the
esteemed king, when you return, inform His Majesty * that I send my
respectful greetings to that noble sovereign, most high, and that I
45. would not have him troubled by any anxiety (45) concerning his queen.
* I shall take good care of her, regarding her as a mother and not
letting that estimable lady suffer any annoyance or upset." * Hanumān
had listened carefully to the message and was highly delighted. He said
goodbye most warmly and * went off through the air, leaving the well-
constructed palace with its fine decoration. All in a moment, he made a
way upwards through the earth. * Arriving back, he raised his hands in
greeting and bowed, indicating his devotion. "My sovereign lord," he
said, "Her Highness your consort * went down to the kingdom of Pātāl
and is in the *nāga's* residence. His court ladies are all round her sitting
in attendance, to look after her and be at her beck and call. * The *nāga*
Biruṇ sends his greetings to you, noble king, most high, and says you
46. must (46) not be troubled by any anxiety."
* When he heard Hanumān's message, that serene and respected
king was most despondent, his face full of trouble. He sobbed in great
distress. * When the sun's light was extinguished and the darkness of
sunset had come, the king went to his fine couch in his sleeping
quarters as always. * He tossed his head to and fro on the pillow and
was convulsed with sobs as he thought of his wife, the tears flowing
without respite. * He bewailed loudly, "O my darling, why did you
decide to be so cold to me, to abandon me to a life on my own? * Alas!
When King Rāb(ṇ) stole you away, I was not in such anguish as this.
47. Now my heart is bursting with emotion. I am distressed (47) to the
point of dying. * What can I do, my treasured love, to make you come
and share my couch? From this day onwards I shall never be able to
see you, who are so dear to my heart. * O now your feelings and your

(47) thoughts, your own self and the place you live in will be so far away, so
remote from me. * From now on there will be nothing — only the
sound of your name. And you and I, my precious, cannot be united as
we always used to be." * The king grieved from the first watch until
the small hours. Then, losing all consciousness of himself, he fainted,
his head drooping.

* When the light of morning shone clearly the king regained
consciousness and awoke. He pondered inwardly. * "For me, things
48. have turned out very strangely, (48) most unusually. There is only
Bibhek who can calculate my horoscope and know my future." * With
this thought the supporter of the earth took in his hands the arrow of
power and at once went out to the courtyard. * He wrote a message
and fixed it to the point of the swift arrow, so bold, and shot it to the
land of Laṅkā. The arrow of power flew far and fast, * resounding like
a hundred thousand thunderbolts, and a tremor went through the earth
such as to make it overturn! The arrow went in the direction of the city
of Laṅkā and then fell into the kingdom of the *nāgas*.

1. The list consists of *Citrus, Xylopia, Aglaia, Baccaurea sapida, Payena elliptica, Willughbeia cochinchinensis* and *Feroniella lucida.*
2. i.e. "furrow" (Skt. sītā).
3. This is not mentioned in the narrative nor in the account given by the envoy.
4. The connection between the name Rām and the possession of great power is not, so far as we know, due to any meaning in the Sanskrit word rāma. We assume, therefore, that an association with powerful figures of Sanskrit literature, whose names include the name Rāma, is felt.
5. The text on pp.20 and 24 suggests that the company halted at the gate of Mithilā. We now have to assume that a temporary encampment was made there.
6. In Buddhist teaching these are: slight interest, momentary joy, an oscillating interest, ecstasy and a suffusing joy.
7. i.e. the infantry, cavalry, chariots and elephants.
8. This simile is echoed on p.48,1.6, where it again refers to Rām and Laksm(ṇ) leaving Aiyudhyā.
9. Traditionally in Cambodia magic men have blown spittle over sick people to heal them.
10. A messenger from a king would bring a pair of golden sandals and ceremonially offer them to the recipient of the message, thus proving that he really came from the king. The sandals would then be returned.
11. i.e. rebirth in hell or as an evil spirit, as a devil or as a four-footed animal.
12. In fact it is the elder whom she approaches first (p.5 of text).
13. This is a reference to a hand movement in the ballet in which the arms are held down straight and the hands, at right-angles to the arms, are spread out. (Pou, personal communication).
14. All our I.B. editions refer to 12 directions instead of the usual 10.
15. This is a small, leaf-shaped metal candle-holder which is passed round at ceremonies.
16. The distinction is drawn in this conversation between the polite and virtuous behaviour and the intelligence of the nobility (to which the egret belongs since he has a city) and the rough manner, lack of morality and unintelligence of the commonalty (with whom Rām seems to the egret to have some affinity since he was so foolish as to let Sītā be stolen.)
17. i.e. Rāhu, a demon by birth, who, when he disguised himself as a god and stole ambrosia, was split in two by Viṣṇu. In astrological tradition he is the enemy of the sun and moon.
18. The following names of trees are omitted from the translation, replaced in this stanza by "all manner of trees" and in the next stanza but one by "various plants":- *Livistona cochinchinensis, Dipterocarpus*

intricatus, Fragraea fragrans, Mimusops elengi, Ochrocarpus siamensis, Clitoria ternatea, Citrus, Xylopia, Aglaia pirifera, Baccaurea sapida, Payena elliptica, Willughbeia cochinchinensis, Feroniella lucida, Oroxylum indicum, Popowia diospyrifolia.

19. These are the names of the six levels of the heaven Kāmāvacar referred to in the next stanza.
20. A particularly insulting affront in Cambodia.
21. The five alloyed metals are copper, brass, tin, lead and iron.
22. Hanumān's change of mind may be explained as follows. The snore came from the female sleeper. Human ladies do not snore; it must therefore be an ogress. Sītā is safe, then.
23. This action is under any circumstances a gross insult in Cambodia but, when done by a woman to a man, it is also likely to reduce his magic powers. (K.H.)
24. Indrajit means "conqueror of Indr".
25. The meaning of the name Atikāy is in fact only "of extraordinary body or size".
26. It seems possible that "flower-stones" may be a reference to the Skt. word for "topaz", puṣparāga, literally "flower-coloured".
27. These are pearl, topaz, garnet, diamond, emerald, cat's eyes gem, coral, sapphire and crystal.
28. i.e. with five parts of the body: two knees, two feet and the head.
29. The military exercise described in this not very clear account (pp. 36–8 of the text) does not follow Jambūbān's suggestion very closely.
30. We take the meaning of this verse to be that the waves rose so high that the bed of the sea was momentarily left empty of water.
31. There are omissions of detail in this stanza and in the next stanza but one. In order to understand how Rāb(ṇ) intends that Aṅgad should be received by him and give his message and yet should be killed, as he has just suggested, *before* reaching the palace, we must assume that the room he intends to have preepared for Aṅgad's reception (see next stanza but one) is between the palace and where Aṅgad is. Pou clarifies the narrative by inserting "Mais d'abord" at the beginning of this present stanza and we follow her idea.
32. cf. passages on the modern inscriptions of Angkor in which all the Buddhas, past and future, are referred to as "grains of sand", implying, as here, "as numerous as the grains of sand". e.g. Inscriptions Modernes d'Angkor No. 4, B 11. (Lewitz 1971:108).
33. The various translations used for references to Kumbhakār(ṇ)'s unusual weapon are: "club" (moṅ 8.68;9.14;9.26); "pike" (sūlī 9.16, laṃbaeṅ 9.24), "combined missile and pike" (mūl sar sūlī 9.15) and "club-missile" (moṅ sar 9.23).

34. According to the text, Bibhek did not in fact come over to Rām's side until Rām had already crossed the ocean and was in Laṅkā.
35. It seems best to make the narrative consistent by taking these two victims to be Laksm(ṇ) and Aṅgad so that at p. 40,1.3, Indrajit is mistaken about the identity of Aṅgad as he tells Rāb(ṇ) what he has done, and Rāb(ṇ), at p. 41, l.1 of text, repeats the mistake. Then p. 41, l.11 of text makes sense.
36. The ten sons are not all accounted for in our text. Sahasakumār's death was related at 6.39. At 10.14, Bibhek tells Rām that Rāb(ṇ) has lost his son Mahāpās as well as Indrajit. Between 10.14 and 27 the deaths of four further sons are accounted for. The four demons whose deaths are related between 10.28 and 43 were not sons of Rāb(ṇ).
37. The text is inaccurate here. Ten sons and one brother were lost, as is stated on p. 47, last line - p. 48, line 1.
38. In fact, as is mentioned at 4.5, Rāb(ṇ) had 20 arms.
39. This is a reference to the belief, (evidenced at 75.41) that a person's liver will give an indication of the character of that person.
40. This is a reference to the ordeal by fire to which Rām subjected Sītā to test whether she had been faithful to him while she was in Laṅkā. This part of the story is lacking in our text.
41. Both sīl "piety" and silp "supernatural art" occur frequently from here onwards with reference to the sage. Owing to their identical pronunciation their spelling has been confused in the MSS, the I.B. text having silp more often that the Paris MS. Translations have been chosen according to context.
42. The train of thought here is: since Rām went to all that trouble to fetch you back from Rāb(ṇ) he should at least have reflected before deciding to have you executed.
43. i.e. in readiness to blow water over the sick person to cause healing by magic.
44. A reference to Viṣṇu who still sleeps in the sea.
45. cf. the practice, known in Cambodian legends, of discovering the proper person to be king, when no rightful heir was available, by letting a horse, carriage or elephant set off without a rider or driver. The person who should rule would be nearby when it stopped.
46. Our text omits any account of Hanumān giving the message. We now find Bhirut and Sutrut informing their father of its content.
47. In this and the next stanza the following plants are mentioned:- *Croton jouffra, Dalbergia cochinchinensis, Xylia dolabriformis,* a variety of fig, *Pentacme siamensis, Sindora cochinchinensis, Melanorrhea laccifera, Aporosa sphaerosperma,* a variety of small bamboo, *Melaleuca*

leucadendron, Seriops roxburghiana, a fig-tree, *Sagus rumphis, Crudia chrysantha, Azzadirachta indica, Syzygium, Garcinia ferrea, Erioglossum edule*, a variety of eaglewood, litchi, *Nephelicum cochinchinensis, Aglaia*, a variety of *Bovea burmanica*, a variety of *Aegle marmelos, Aegle marmelos*, Sapotille, *Pouteria*.

48. Black colour in the neck and arching of the neck occur in the mating season.
49. The boys do not apparently react to this name, although their mother told them (at 76.25) that their father was Nārāy(ṇ) Rām.
50. Precision about the person or persons speaking is not a characteristic of Khmer narratives! It does not therefore seem careless to the Cambodian reader that, although it is Rām-Laksm(ṇ) who is said on p. 13 of the text to address the army, the princes are said on p. 14 to hear "the boys".
51. In Cambodian literature Brahma is usually understood to have four faces. K.H.
52. These are itemised by the queen (p. 44 of the text). They are prison, chains, locks, handcuffs and pillory.
53. Rām-Laksm(ṇ)'s reply is not in fact very "evasive" since he reveals his mother's name and the fact that his father rules Aiyudhyā (which Rām has just said he himself rules!) We must assume that by "evasive" he meant not too direct or blunt.
54. The reasons for both Rām-Laksm(ṇ) and Sītā speaking of shame if they comply with Rām's requests are to be gleaned from the text at various points here and at 78.54. They are that they were too poor to associate with court people; that, having been wronged, they would be debased by behaving as friends again; and that (in Sītā's case) she looks less beautiful now.
55. The character of the sage was gently ridiculed in the performances of the Reamker.
56. Omitting Kaikesī? Other references are to the "three mothers", e.g. p.13,1.3.
57. There is a discrepancy here since the boys were said on p. 23 of the text to be mounted on elephants.
58. At various ceremonies thread is tied round the wrists to bring good fortune.
59. It seems best to take this as "this morning (which you may see on the calendar)", i.e. a future morning, since on p. 40 of the text we find Rām rising at dawn for the ceremony after the completion of the preparations for the feast.
60. The country of the five rivers, according to literary tradition, was the Punjab. The Khmer readers or audience would be likely to imagine a place in Cambodia, however.

61. vīsai. Dr. Manas Chitakasem informs us of a Thai entertainment, wīsǎy, seen only at the royal tonsure, which consists of a mimed duel, danced by two men, one of whom has a short and the other a long weapon. Thai sources state that the form wīsǎy is a corruption of Malay pisay (perisai) "shield". The dance is believed to have come from Malaya.
62. The name of a popular form of theatre. See Pou 1982:257, n.4.
63. Name of a kind of music performed on drum, gongs, oboe and bamboo clappers. See Pou 1982:257, n.5.
64. A kind of dance-theatre of Thai origin connected with the Manorā story. See Pou 1982:257, n.8.
65. i.e. Laksm(ṇ) as well as Rām and Sītā.
66. According to Cambodian legend, this demon contended against the sea-goddess, Mekhallā, for possession of a jewel which could grant all desires. The goddess won but the demon is still pursuing her through the sky. When it rains his axe gleams or resounds as it is thrown.

List of Preferred Readings and Emendations

Only important cases of faults in the printed text (i.e. those which affect the translation) are given below. Thus, for example, constant misspellings of tanū 'body' as dhanū 'bow' and *vice versa*, which the context clarifies, are not noted here.

The source of the chosen reading is indicated either by a date (i.e. of the I.B. edition) or, if Pou's text is followed, by her name or, if we have emended the text, by the word 'Emendation'.

Part	Page	Line	Chosen reading	Source	Rejected reading
1	2	9	phgaṅ'	Pou	phtuṅ
	7	6	and *passim* gị ṭă	Pou	git ṭă
	8	1	neṛrati	Pou	nehṅati
	10	7	ṭaṃloeṅ	1937	juṃloeṅ
	12	7	snām	Pou	sthān
	15	8	chnāk'	1937	chlāk'
	18	9	guor	Pou	gū
	19	4	thbaṅ	Pou	khbaṅ'
	21	10	ṭiṅ jaṅ	Pou	jiṅ phaṅ or joeṅ phaṅ
	23	7	kranuon	Emendation	tranuon
	24	7	ṭiṅ	Pou	jīṅ
		10	ṭiṅ	Pou	jīṅ
	25	4	ṭiṅ jaṅ	Pou	jīṅ phaṅ
		7	paṅsu	1937	paṅg
	28	3	prāl	1937	prās
	30	4	gāppī	Pou	gā pī
	32	1–2	bhūvanārth	Pou	bhāvanā
		3	mahindr nā dī	Pou	mahīnadī
	37	11	ṛsyā	Pou	drṛsyā
	43	8	dhluṅ	1968	thluṅ or chluṅ
	44	1	gaṅ	1937	gaen
		2	bak	1968	brak
	46	4	par(i)cār	1961,1968	paricāg
	48	1	rāmā bīrottam	Pou	rāmā bhirottam
	50	11	got go	1937	got to
		12	ma	1937	kă
			khmoc	1937,1968	khloc
	51	2	căkk cān'	1937	căkk cān
		3	jalakā	Emendation	jalikā
	52	7–8	mohanamidh	Emendation	mohinamiddh
	55	2	kāt'	1937,1961	ktāt'
	58	9	jraek	1937,1968	jraeṅ

Part	Page	Line	Chosen reading	Source	Rejected reading
2	3	1	pupphā	Emendation	Pūphā
	7	5	ārambh	1937	āramm
		9	jhī̤	1961	jhị̄ṅ
	10	3	kuṇḍī	1961	gandī
	11	11	guo nā	1937	gaṇanā
	15	10	paṃruṅ	1961	amruṅ
	16	10	upades	Pou	abhides
	18	7	mān	1937	prāṇ
	20	2	rām	1961	rīem
	29	2	rapoy	1937	poy
	37	8	banlī̤	1937	banlịk
	44	3	khloc	1937	khmoc
	47	9	it spoey	Pou	jā troey
	50	1	cacoek paṃpaek sruk des	Pou	paṃpaek nūv kulabhines
	55	9	uccās	Pou	opās
	59	11	ka	Emendation	kă
	61	1	sānt	Emendation	sān
	64	8	pruoñ	Pou	broñ
	66	3	kram	1937	krum
	67	1	uccās	Pou	opās
		3	narabin	1937	narabind
	75	6	buṅ	Pou	baṅs
	76	9	gar	Emendation	gal’
	79	5	vanāsray	Emendation	vaṇṇāsray
		10	rām	Emendation	rīem
	85	3	saṃpūṅ	1961	paṃpūṅ
	86	3	sūl	Pou	mūl
3	1	2	ya(k) ma(k)	1967	ya ma
	4	2	jot	1964,1967	jog
		5	isīsar	1937	as’ sar
	5	9	yaksādhirāj	1961,1967	yasādhirāj
	9	1	prājñā	Pou	prāthnā
		11	kar	1937,1967	ka
	10	4	randaeḥ	1937	randaḥ
	12	5	got	Pou	khot
	15	3	svaeṅ	1961,1964, 1967	lvaeṅ
		11	prasiddhi	Emendation	prīsiddhi
	17	4	sīkhar	1937	sirakhar

Part	Page	Line	Chosen reading	Source	Rejected reading
(3)	19	10	asurās	1937,1967	asurasar
		11	ṭāp	1964,1967	ṭāc
	20	1	baṅ' boḥ	1937,1967	ban' bor
	21	3	maraṇā	Pou	kaniṭṭhā
			mūḷhā	Pou	molā
		5	niradukh	Pou	rūbhīniradukkh
	22	5	brae	Pou	brai
		5	saṃsae	Pou	sāvsai
		5	trae	Pou	trai
	23	9	phlāñ	1937	phlāy
	25	6	ṭa	1937,1964	ṭī
	26	12	praṇamy	Pou	bar brahm
	28	1	jāñ	Pou	jā
		3	siddhikar(ṇ)	Emendation	siddhi braḥ kar
		8	suparṇ	Emendation	supār
	31	4	kar	1967	ka
		4	kāṃmā	Pou	kām
	32	6	krīdā	Pou	kradā
	33	8	cpaṅ	Pou	sram(ṇ)
	34	8	bed	Pou	koet
		11	jāp	1967	phlā
	35	5	bhloeṅ	1964,1967	tloeṅ
	36	4	ktau	1964,1967	khlau
	37	2	saṅhā	Pou	sāhār,sāhās
		3	mig mās	1967	mit cās
	39	4	doep	1964,1967	dep
	40	2	amar riddhī	Emendation	amariddhī
	43	3	ñāti ṭă	Pou	yādasu
	44	10	phñoe	1937,1961, 1967	dhvoe
4	6	9	paṃruṅ	1964,1967	aṃruṅ
	7	2	drust	1967	drūst
	10	6	paṅ	Pou	paṅ'
	12	11	bidagdh	Pou	bidåks
	14	2	maithilī	Pou	maidhulī, maidhūlī
	15	3	muḥ nir bhăy	Pou	mān bhoc bhăy
	16	7	buj	Pou	bhoj(jh)
		8	traleṅ	1937,1964	krai laeṅ
	17	8	yās'	1937	yal'
	20	9	sot	1937	lot

Part	Page	Line	Chosen reading	Source	Rejected reading
(4)	25	7	tāṃṅ	Pou	tāṅ
		8	aṃbal'	Pou	kambal
	26	4	phkāp'	1964	phgāp', phkā
	36	4	bo bai	1937	bodhi bai
		8,9	ṭor	1967	tor
		11–12	trāṃ traeṅ	1937	traṃ traeṅ
	37	5	mahiṅsārāj	Pou	mahiṅsāsārāj
	39	3	rabind	Pou	rūbin,rūbind
	43	12	utpāt	Emendation	utpādr(v)
	44	12	khlāṃṅ	Emendation	khāṃṅ
	45	6	dvā	1937	dvār
		6	me sakti sūl bī	Pou	merasak sal' bī
	51	5	seyyā	Pou	sayā
		10	adhammisvar	f.n. in I.B. text	adhammismar
	52	6	bhimukh bān	Pou	dhīmukhabānar, dhimukhabān
		11	ṭī	Emendation	tī
	57	12	ṭoer	1961	coer
	59	1	jātī	Emendation	jāt
		2	thṅai	1937	thlai
	60	4	jātī	Emendation	jāt
	67	6	sānt	1937	sān
		6	bāl	Pou	vā
5	10	8	sur	Pou	sūry
	17	10	thbaṅ	Pou	khbaṅ'
	33	12	skal'	Emendation	skār
	36	8	mit	Emendation	mitr
	38	5	bibhnāl'	Emendation	bibhāl'
		11	sikhar	Emendation	siṅkhar
	45	2	svādhyāy	1937	sādhyāy
	47	3	bhār	Emendation	bhāb,bhārā
	49	12	ḍik	1937	ḍim
		12	gandhī	Emendation	gandī
	50	9	saeb	1937	sab
	51	9	ādhipatā	Pou	ādhidhātr(i)
6	2	10	narapā	Pou	narapā(ti)
	3	7	samrās'	Emendation	samaras
	6	9	saṃṛddhi	Emendation	sūm ṛddhi
	13	3–4	saṃṛddhi	Emendation	sūm ṛddhi

Part	Page	Line	Chosen reading	Source	Rejected reading
(6)	14	5	bal	Pou	das
	15	7	siṅhasūr	Emendation	siṅhasuor
	17	11	yal'	Emendation	yal
	19	3	luḥ	Emendation	lị
		9	līlā	1959,1961	selā
	20	2	bejarā	Pou	bejr tā,bejr ṭā,bejr trā
	28	11	rīem	Pou	rām
	29	1	nāy	Pou	chāy
	33	7	mān	Pou	maṭṭh, m̈aṭṭh
	34	4	banitā	1961	panatā, banatā
	35	2	ruos rān'	Pou	rukhachand
	37	1	randeḥ	Emendation	randaḥ
		6	phnaek	Emendation	bhnaek
	39	3	baḥ	1937	braḥ
	42	10	senī	Emendation	asanī
	43	10	rị	Emendation	rī
	44	4	rị	Emendation	rī
	50	3	pratehār	Emendation	prātehāry
	51	2	khaṃ	Emendation	kha
	52	11	bīr ṭaṇṭap'	Pou	sāmsip bīr
	55	12	catu	Pou	das
	56	9	raṅāp' raṅoe	Alternative reading in printed text.	aṅgoep aṅgīer
	57	1	cho	Pou	sara
		5	ṭāl'	Pou	ṭāl
	60	10	pad	Pou	putr
	61	6	krajūr	Emendation	traṭūr
7	1	5	bidagdh	Pou	bidakkh
		8	pramān	Emendation	bramān
	6	1	sakti	Emendation	såkkh
		2	tpoeṅ	1937	mpoeṅ, mīoeṅ
		9	masār	Emendation	maṅsā
	7	6	bablau	Emendation	balhau
		10	bruy	1937	bruoy
	18	10	narap	1962	narup
	20	19	putr	Pou	braḥ
	28	6	asubh	Pou	osubh
	29	3	bịṅ	1962	bīṅ
		3	nibaddh	Emendation	nibatr

Part	Page	Line	Chosen reading	Source	Rejected reading
(7)		6	isūr	Emendation	asūr
	33	3	bidagdh	Pou	bidakkh
		6	dūl	1962	duol
	36	4	phlūv	Emendation	bhlūv
	38	12	banlā	Pou	pandāt’
	39	5	narapind	Pou	narabandhu
	40	8	prasap’	1937	prasap
	41	5	byūha ma(k)	Emendation	byūhamar
	42	2	anant	Emendation	ānand
	44	2	nūv bā-nar	1937	nūv-nar
	45	7	joeṅ	Emendation	yoeṅ
	47	7	parākram	Emendation	paramakram
	50	5	mangị	Pou	prāṇ trī
	53	4	sabd	Emendation	sabv
		9	gadā	Emendation	gradā, kradā
	54	2	cāt’ dăb	Pou	catudăb
		8	raeṅ	Emendation	reṅ
8	1	5	bidagdh	Pou	bidăks
	2	11	jotisāstr	Pou	jogasāstr
	3	2	siṅ bakradhā	Pou	sịk bāk’ kryādhā
		4	bablau	Emendation	balhau
	4	1–2	lagnā	Pou	lakkh(ṇ) gnā
		2	koet bibarṇ	Emendation	ketu bibarṇ
		9	sūryakānt	Emendation	sūryachān
	9	8	mak leḥ mak luoṅ	Emendation	maleḥ maluoṅ
	10	5	sau khum lagnā	Pou	saur khum lakkh(ṇ) gnā
	16	11	taskar	Emendation (PRK)	tastar
	19	8	sānt	1959,1962	sān
	26	3	krok	Emendation	krodh
	32	1	nab	Pou	nup
	33	11	paribar	Pou	par bal
	40	9	bī	1959,1962	bīr
	41	6	balakkar	Emendation	balaskār
	47	3	noḥ	1962	doḥ
	55	5	paṃruṅ	Pou	aṃruṅ
	56	9	krās’	1962	krā
		11	paṃbār	Emendation	paṃbā
	57	5	vak’	1959,1962	vuk

Part	Page	Line	Chosen reading	Source	Rejected reading
(8)	58	6	prāṅg	Emendation	prāṅg(ṇ)
	60	5	masār	Pou	maṅsā,maṃsā
	61	6	uccās	Pou	opās,obhās
	66	5	rī	1962	rị
	68	11	moṅ	Emendation	moṅg
9	2	2	cancaeṅ	Emendation	cañcoeṅ
	14	5	kolāhal	1962	kohal
	25	1	(Omitted)	(Text uncertain)	asanī
	28	5	suriyodhujdhar	Pou	suriyodhādhar
	31	5	kāsā	Pou	kāsā(v)
	33	6	gị	Pou	patī,tī
	34	2	ṭă	Pou	upa
	39	5	gị yodh	Pou	tī yoc
		6	cāp'	1937	cāk'
		7	bairī	1937	bherī
10	2	1	samār	Pou	sammā
		2	sāstr	Emendation	sās
		3	ṭal'	Emendation	tal
	4	3	thkān rath yātrā	1937	thkān yātrā
	6	12	samār	Pou	sammā
	16	11	loek	Pou	loe
	26	6	nāy	1937	bāy
	27	7	gī rū	Emendation	gī ro
	30	9	ranāp	Pou	ranāp'
	33	2	ruos	1959	rūs
	34	1	sahass	Pou	sahăss
	35	7	loek khăn	1962	loe khăn
	40	3	gaṅ	1937,1959	ṭaṅ
		4	nīl	1937,1959	nal
	43	3	krīdā	Pou	gradā
	45	12	bhlịk	1937,1959	klịm
	46	11	ghvāl	Pou	jvāl
	47	6	jhān	Emendation	jhāñ
	48	3	vinās	1937	ranās
75	2	3	knuṅ knak'	1959/ Emendation	knaṅ knak
	6	1	khịṅ	1937	nịṅ
	27	12	loek	Emendation	loe
	46	1	vịṅ	Emendation	rịṅ

Part	Page	Line	Chosen reading	Source	Rejected reading
76	4	6	isīsīlā	Emendation	isīlā
	20	1	sānt	1959	sān
	28	3	jotisār	Emendation	jogasāstr
		12	leṅ	1959	laṅ
	31	3–4	ae braḥ kaikes bhūmī	Pou	braḥ bhirut braḥ sutrut kaikes bhūmī
	38	6	ṭaek jhnān'	Emendation	paek ghnān'
	41	11	knak'	Emendation	knak
	43 44	2 10	dandan'	Pou	dan'2
	56	12	buṃ gị	Pou	gị
77	8	2	oey	Emendation	hoey
	20	5	rūt	Emendation	ruot
	40	4	thlā	Emendation	klā
78	7	10	ṭaek jhnān'	Emendation	paek ghnān'
	8	12	ṅār haṅsā	Pou	ṅāhiṅsā
	27	4	isīsīlā	Emendation	isīlā
	50	11	kruoñ	Emendation	kruoy
			isīsīlā	Emendation	isīlā
	55	3	nā(th)	Emendation	nā
79	15	9	dandan'	Pou	dan'2
	24	4	norī	1962	nārī
		7	slok	Pou	lok
	26	8	prāṅg	1962	prāṅg(ṇ)
	28	8	janmā	Emendation	jansā
	39	12	prāṅg	Emendation	prāṅg(ṇ)
	43	9	yīke	Pou	pīkae
	48	9	āsā	Emendation	assā
		10	kluṃ	Emendation	klaṃ or klam'
	51	4	naranāth	Emendation	nanād
	52	6	sīl	Pou	silp
80	38	9	yak	1937	yal'
	39	9	nāṅ nāṭ	1959	nāṅ nā
	42	4	raeṅ	Emendation	reṅ
	48	1	bibheksā	1937	bibhaksā

Glossary

Words contained in the Glossary are almost exclusively (i) not given in the Khmer dictionaries (or not given with the meanings required for the text), (ii) not deformations of Skt.or Pali words and (iii) not derivatives of Khmer bases (which may be obsolete but which may be found by reference to other derivatives). The words given are chiefly obsolete Khmer words or usages and words of Thai origin (in connection with which I have been most grateful to the late Mr. Peter Bee and to Dr. Manas Chitakasem). Some other entries take the place of notes to the translation, in which the general reader would not be interested; they are in fact explanations of certain translations.

kaṅkāñ' Var. of aṅkāñ' "ripples".

kaṇṭhas Taken to be a deformation of kaṇṭhakas ,N. of a horse of the Buddha. Translated "splendid".

kandrok and kandrot Alternative readings in I.B. text at 1.44 in list of musical instruments. drot occurs similarly at 2.27. kan drot occurs in the poem, *Bhogakulakumār* (I.B. edition, p.77.1.14) in a list of musical instruments. The instrument at 1.44 is made of bak (var. of bamboo).

kass Interpreted as being < Skt. kaṣ "to scratch, kill".

kāsā(v) We follow Pou (1977a:52,n.3) in understanding this as a deformation of Skt. kāśi "silk".

kuñcae "lock" (Thai).

kuṇḍakār We have followed Pou's interpretation of this word as being < Skt. kuṇḍa "hole in the ground" and karman "rite". cf. also Skt. homakuṇḍa "hole in the ground used for the sacred fire for oblations" (M-W).

kuoñ jalī It is clear that the word añjali is present in this sequence but whether kuo stands for guor "decorous" is not clear.

ker We follow Pou's interpretation of this as < Pali kira (a word which indicates the beginning of a narrative).

kola Taken as equivalent to kolāhal "commotion".

kautār "window" (Thai).

kuṃṭiṅ cf. kaṃṭiṅ "indebted "in Mod. Khm., "bond, contract" in Mid. Khm. Here translated "guarantee".

kradūs Interpreted as "hurl oneself about" from use with kradā (itself understood by reference to Mod. Khm. kradī-kradā "move this way and that".)

kriṣ Pou attributes this tentatively to Skt. kṛṣ "drawn along". MEF reading kroes could perhaps be justified as being < roes "to pick up"?

krai Mod. Khm. kamrai "profit" suggests an earlier meaning "over and above" for this word, which needs the translation "superior;master" in Reamker.

klāṅ "middle" (Thai).

kliṅ "sunshade" (Thai).

kluom klāt' Known only from the occurrences at 8.20 and 21. "Cut off" suits the contexts.

kh

khā "crush". A guess from the context *re* the preparation of areca.

khāv "news" (Thai).

khum	Interpreted, by reference to Pou's translation and note (1977a:215,n.3), as forming a compound (from Thai) with preceding sau ("impure + oppress") and thus giving the sense "unfortunate conjunction".

g

gandhan	*pro* gandharb. Reflects Thai pronunciation of this written form.
git ṭă	Occurs in I.B. text *pro* gī̤ ṭă "that is to say; in fact". The two particles were much used this way in Old Khm. They are not found in Reamker after the first few Parts.
guḥ	cf. Old Khm. gus "utterly (emphatic particle which refers to the preceding clause)". Here, emphasis is given to "highest merit, blessedness".

ṅ

ṅaṅ	"martingale" (Thai).
ṅā haṅsā	haṅsā "Mon" (See Pou 1982:225,n.1). ṅā also occurs in a list of drums in the poem, *Bhogakulakumār* (I.B. edition, p.77,1.15).

c

căkk cān'	"cicada" (Thai).
caṅ	4.51. Taken as = caṅ gaṃnuṃ "start a feud".
cer	(1.) "to proceed" (2.) "to transgress" (3.) "long (of time)". For meanings (1) and (2), which occur in the first six Parts, cf. Old Khm, cer,cyar. For meaning (3), which occurs in Parts 75–80, cf. Mod. Khm.
caṃnat	Taken to be "place where one moors (a boat)". cf. Mod. Khm. Pou interprets it as < Old. Khm. camnat "established area, village".
chmāt'	Tentatively translated "provided" as if from cāt' "to organise, dispatch, arrange".

j

jur juk	"in quantity, springing up all around". See Angkorian inscription K. 144 (9) where juk jūr describes creepers and thorns springing up in the jungle. (Coedès 1964:34).
jū,juo	Occur in the negative. "not in fact".

jotrī	Tentatively translated "shining" as though the form represents either Skt. jyotis or Pali joti "light".
jaṃbāy	Taken as being related to sbāy "to sling over one shoulder and under the opposite arm".
juṃbā	"llama" (Thai).

ñ

ñiṅ	. "near" (Old. Khm. ñyaṅ id.)
ñāṃṅ	See Pou (1977a:54,n.2) where this is identified with the Mid.Khm interrogative particle of the same form.

ṭ

ṭă	Used much more widely than in Mod. Khm. and much less precisely than in Old Khm. Often seems to function merely as a filler of a syllable required by the metre, e.g. deb ṭă munī "divine king", braḥ ṭă bhirut "Lord Bhirut".
ṭaṅhoem sar	Translated "wish of one's life" by guesswork. lit. "mindful of one's life's breath".
ṭaṃpār	5.44. "sheet,surface", here = phdai "surface,womb".
ṭān	9.37. The meaning "rise and go" is required by the context. ṭān may be a var. of ṭāl, q.v., with final n *pro* l under Thai influence.
ṭāl	In Parts 1–10, the meaning "make a ready move towards, move off with eagerness, be eager to" seems to fit most contexts. cf. Mod. Khm. āl "be in a hurry to, rush off to" rather than ṭāl "to spread (like fire)". See also under ṭoḥ.
ṭoem	Occurs frequently with the meaning "matter,matter concerning".
ṭīev	"only one" (Thai).
ṭaeṅ	"red" (Thai).
ṭoḥ	"to move" rather than, as in Mod. Khm. "to shake off". e.g. ṭoḥ dăb "march the army away", toḥ ḷoeṅ "to get up" and ṭoḥ ṭāl "to set off".
ṭāṃ	"black" (Thai).

ṇ

ṇal'	The I.B. text spells this word so that it looks like a Khmer word. The meaning "very much" would fit all occurrences. See Pou (1977a:28,n.5), however, where she relates it to Skt. anala "fire"; hence "burning with (anger, etc.)".
ṇā	"front" (Thai).
ṇūn	"reinforcements" (Thai).

ṇāy	At 79.10. represents repeated final consonant n of preceding word plus āy.

t

taṅ	6.36. Construed as repeated final consonant t of preceding word and the word hoṅ with h absent. Pou's text has hoṅ.
tān'	7.6. Represents the pronunciation, needed for the rhyme, of the second, usually unpronounced, syllable of rat(n).
tralaeṅ	"public place of punishment". See Pou 1982:210,n.2.
trā	2.70;6.23. Translated as being equivalent to Mod. Khm. luḥ trā tae "to the point that".
truoc	"to supervise". (Old. Khm. form)
traitā	"second age of the world". Occurs *pro* traitāyug or with yug preceding, in Parts 1–10.

th

thaṅ	"belly" (Thai).
thbaṅ	"organise troops". Meaning taken from contexts. See Pou 1977a:12,n.4.
thlā	Occurs *passim*, as does phlā, as an attribute of sar "arrow" or khăn "sword". The translation of either form as "sharp" is based on Mod. Khm. mut thlā "id.", on the phrase khăn jăy bejr thlā "victorious diamond sword", on the occurrence of phlā with phlāñ "destructive" and on the Mod. Khm. derivative panlā "thorn".
thvāt'	Occurs alone frequently in early Parts where "directly, immediately" suits the context, e.g. 1.32. īlūv thvāt' hoṅ "this very instant".

d

daṅgeṅ	79.36 and 46. Translation "play (music)" taken from very clear contexts.
drot	See kandrok and kandrot.

dh

dhārā	Occurrences in Parts 1–10 may represent either Skt./Pali dhārā "stream" or Skt./Pali dhara "supporting; earth" or Khm. dhār, dhā for which the meaning "big" is taken from occurrences with dhaṃ.
dhuj	"banner" (< Pali dhaja).

n

nǎṅ	"royal carriage" (Thai).
narasīh	lit. "lion of a man" is translated "lion among birds" and "lion among trees", *faute de mieux,* in the contexts where it occurs.
nā	Occurs with its Old Khmer meaning "rank,grade" at 1.32;78.34. oy nā at 7.44,11.2 and 4, might be construed "(to whom we) have given responsibility".
nī	8.5;9.9;9.12. cf. Old Khm. nī, probably "each,distributively" as now in nimuoy "each". Ref. is to the preceding word in Old Khm. as in the Reamker occurences.
nūv	Occurs with modern meanings "and" and "with" but is also sometimes, as in Old Khm., equivalent to nau "on" (2.16) or nịṅ "will,intend to" (1.39).
nai	In addition to usages similar to those in Mod. literary Khm., nai occurs in Reamker as a particle joining verb to object (1.28;1.52;2.10) and as a phrase-final particle with backward reference to a noun, "of that one, of him/her".
nau	As in Old Khm., nau may be the spelling representing nūv, q.v., with its meanings as for Mod. Khm. nịṅ (1.45).

p

paṅgat'	We follow Pou for the meaning "belt" which she refers (1977a:25,n.5) to Old Khm.
paṅ-āt	Occurs in every case (1.22,23 and 25;76.29) with pramāth (sometimes spelt pramād). Taken, therefore, as equivalent to Mod. Khm. nāṃ ārth "cause trouble".
pas'	"to grind" (Old Khm.)
pād	2.25 and 84 = pāduka "sandal".
pindā	All occurrences are with piet or piet pien "to oppress". pindā is assumed to add to this meaning. Possibly the form is < Skt. pīḍā "harm" directly, as pīet is generally assumed to be.
pī	Occurs sometimes with its Old Khm. sense of "so as to" (e.g. 1.29, 1.8) but usually links an epithet to a preceding noun.
pussavī	Translated, *faute de mieux*, as if it represented puṣpī. (Suggestion of I.B. editors).
paek	77.12 "to bear" (Thai bɛɛk? Suggestion of Dr. Manas Chitakasem).
praces pracās	Unknown. The bases creḥ "to hew" and crās "to push against" have inspired our translation "kick and push".

praveṇī	Has the Mid.Khm. meaning "family line" (see Lewitz 1970:112) rather than the modern meaning "tradition, protocol".
prahās	Perhaps phonaesthetic of sound of fire. cf. hās (laughing sound).
plāk' plīoeṅ	Translated "excessive". Possibly from Thai plaʔ "to let go free" and plyaŋ "to squander". (Suggestion of Dr. Manas Chitakasem).

ph

phgaṅ	Occurs as in Mod. Khm. meaning "to begin" and "to raise (and direct towards); to raise the hands in offering or salute" but in at least 3 contexts phgaṅ seems equivalent to the particle phaṅ "also". (4.12;4.31;7.28).
phlā	See thlā.
phsoḥ	"to be missing, to fail to be there". Translated to fit the context but cf. soḥ "(not) at all".

b

banālī	Taken as a deformation of Skt. vanālaya "forest habitation".
bahul baho	Taken to be a reduplicative form based on Skt. bahu-la "dense, thick" and used to mean "deeply,fully" *re* thought.
bā	"to fend off". cf. Mod. Khm. bār in kārbār "to defend".
bibarṇ	For some occurrences (3.5;3.39; 10.25) taken as being *pro* bibardh (< Skt. vivardhana "prosperity") since "of varied colour" does not suit the contexts so well and the two words would have the same pronunciation in their Khmer naturalised form.
bibhin	Derived from Mod. Khm. bhin "distinguishing mark", this Skt.-like form serves as a reduplicative for bibhed "differentiated" and bibhăl, "distinguished to avoid confusion".
besabarṇā	Taken to be a deformation of the name, Vaiśravaṇa, god of belongings. Pou's text has phies barṇā. See Pou 1977a:40,n.3.
buṃ jū, buṃ juo	"not really, not in fact".
baḥ	"advance upon, attack". Contexts require intentional rather than accidental encounters as in Mod. Khm. usage.
brahā	"great". Translation based on compounds given in VK and on Pali brahā id.
blay	"mouth organ". See Pech Sal: 25–6.

bh

bhaṇācāry "teacher of the Brahmin race". We have taken bhaṇ as representing bandhu (the aspiration being due to Thai influence). VK cites brāhmaṇabandhu "of the race of Brahmins". For a different interpretation, see Pou 1977: 62,n.4.

bhā dāy Unknown.

bhiniskram "leaving this world" (< Skt. abhiniṣkram).

bhimalai Pou relates this word to Pali bhīmala "frightening".

bhisamăy "remarkable" < Skt. vismaya "surprise".

bhul Contexts require a variety of translations: "move with a sudden rush", "appear suddenly", "burst forth", "produce", "dazzle", etc.

m

makuṭ "high", "prince" as well as Mod. Khm. dictionary meaning "crown".

man gị "now it is a fact that". cf. Old Khm. man gi.

markal' "perhaps;might have". Probably to be regarded as prefixed m before kal' "one way, one possibility". See Pou 1977a:157,n.2.

mā,mār,māl māl occurs followed by mās, translated "all gold". All three words occur in contexts where "great" or "many" is required.

muḥ Represents Mod. Khm. moḥ in moḥ mut "bold" and moḥ "that is".

mūt "in the least". See Pou 1977a:247,n.1 and 248,n.1.

mīoeṅ "city" (Thai).

mohanamidh "drowsiness". Strictly, if analysed as mohana "erring" and midh "torpor", this is "drowsiness due to errant ways".

mrāṅ "however;by some method". See Pou 1977a:44,n.1.

yant trī For yantrī (Skt. yantra) "mechanism". Here taken with spaek to mean "leather puppets".

yamanā, yamunā Though not known except as the N. of a river at 1.5;3.19, this is taken, at 2.32 and 6.37 as the N. of a kind of cloth. cf. khīen yamanā "yamanā cloth" in the poem, *Buddhisen* (I.B. edition, p.2,1.2).

yubhā Taken as = yubā "young" (Skt./Pali yuva) with aspiration due to Thai influence.

yogantarakappanās "which ends an age within an era". Taken to be Pali yug "age", antara "within", kappa "era", nāsa "destruction".

r

rapāl	Meaning "succession,procession" taken by reference to rāl "to spread". The word occurs on IMA 31 A 1.27 with the meaning "constantly,in succession".
ramanā	N. of a small drum. See Morton 1976:77–8; 108–11.
rān'	Several occurrences in Parts 9 and 10 require a verb "to rouse" or a sense of "urgency" rather than Mod. Khm. meaning "quickly, in good time".
ruom	The occurrence of ruom ās(n) "take a seat" at 77.51 led us to treat yak āsanā ṭă ruom raṅ at 4.4. as having the same meaning.
roḥ	(1.) "murmur,buzz" required in some contexts. (2.) At 10.11 roḥ may be compared with Old Khm. roḥ "in accordance,like that".
ṝ	At 76.19. the occurrence at the beginning of a sentence is like the Mod. Khm. use of toe "tell me; now...?"

l

lalaep	Taken as "to deceive" cf. laep-khāy Mod. Khm. "to mock".
luḥ	The Old Khm. meaning "as far as (a place)" occurs as well as the Mod. Khm. meanings of luḥ "as far as (a time)", "to submit to", "on the point of" and the meaning of loḥ "noisily (of quarrelsome speech)".
leṅ	With laṅ or alone, leṅ may have the sense "try out one's powers against".
laeṅ	3.6;7.36. "let (him,them,you,etc.)", followed by verb. cf. Old. Khm. use of leṅ.
leḥ	(1.) "so;thus;(in a question) how?" cf. Mod. Khm. mleḥ "thus". (2.) 8.9. "a little,slightly" (?) cf. Mod. Khm. les id.

v

vipaṅ'	Reduplicates vipatti/vibat/"misfortune", echoing the Skt. prefix vi and recalling, together with/vibat/the Khm. compound /bat-bɔŋ/"to lose, cast away".
vīsai	"duel dance" (Thai). See n. 61.
vutt	"time,occasion". cf. Old Khm. hvat.
vuddhāsuddhāy	"submerged in liquid". Very tentatively, suddhāy is taken as locative of Skt. sudhā "liquid" and vuddhā is taken as a deformation of vuḍita or vruḍita "submerged".

S

sakal	"satisfied". cf. Mod. Khm. skal' < Skt./Pali sakala "whole".
saṅgaraṇī	Skt. saṅkaraṇa "mixing" would help more than saṃgaraṇa "agreement". Clearly "mixture,connection" is needed.
saṅhān	"destroy". The final n which saṅhār has here, due to Thai influence is needed for the rhyme.
sammā	"suitable,capable". We follow Pou 1977:237,n.1. in relating this form (samār in her text) to Skt. samartha id.
sādar	"happy,eager". cf. Skt. sādara "respectful;intent upon". Reamker meanings are closer to the idea of "intentness", "eagerness" and thus "joy" while Mod. Khm. usage reflects Skt. idea of "respect".
sān	2.16. occurs *pro* sār "message,prayer", Thai influence accounting for the final n.
sāpāl	The meaning of the preceding word, sansaṃ "to accumulate bit by bit" would be completed if sapāl meant "merit". Might it be a deformation of Skt. supāra "bring to a prosperous conclusion"? Confusion between final r and l is common in Mid. Khm.
sāmāl	"vassal". See Pou 1982:273,n.2.
sāvaḷik	Translated "boys" at 79.33 rather than usual "girls" to fit in with prus on p. 34,1.3.
siṅ	This pre-verbal particle constantly occurs when a plural subject is separated from the verb by other words. It has often been translated by "all". Occurrences have been observed, particularly in Part 4, where, with a singular subject and a verbalised noun as predicate, siṅ seems to imply "wholly". e.g. 4.10. siṅ jhām "(her face) all blood".
subhak subhāj	The translation "now separating, now mingling" has been extracted by reference to Skt. su "well", bhakta "divided" and bhāj "forming part of".
sūmai	"speech, message". Pou (1977:3,n.5) relates the form to Mid. Khm. samay "speech,message" < Skt.samaya id.
soḥ sā	Regularly modifies a preceding attributive verb giving the meaning "utterly, extremely" but occasionally has the role of attribute as at 8.60: aṅgad soḥ sā "the prodigious Aṅgad".
smer	"secretary'. cf. Old Khm. sir "to write", with agent infix m.
smoḥ smān sar	"warmly welcoming". Seems to be a combination of smoḥ sar "joy" and smoḥ smān "free,clear,utterly".

syāt	Taken to be Skt. "perhaps (a word occurring in formulae)" (M-W.). Translated "formulae".
slai	"rock" (Thai form < Skt. śaila). See Pou 1977:197,n.1.

h

hak'	"turn somersaults" (Thai).
haṅ	"you (derogatory)". Now only addressed to women.
hāt' poy	"Annamese opera" (Vietnamese). See Pou 1982:257,n.7).
hūrȧk	"armlet" (Guesdon). Short form of bāhuraks id.
huoṇā	"chief" (Thai).
hoñ	Not known. Possibly alliterating with hoṅ and the last syllable of the previous word, hā.
hmak	"cloud" (Thai).
hmū	"group" (Thai).
hmuot	"unit,company" (Thai).

a

akkho	For akkhobhinī "a number followed by 42 ciphers". (Pali)
aṅkae	"belt". Pou (1977:71,n.2) refers the form to Skt. aṅka "flank".
appades	Taken as being < Skt. apadeśa "indicating" and translated "of special intent" and "instruction".

ā

āc	At 2.10 buṃ āc has the Angkorian sense "to be possible not to, not to have to".
āraṅ	"apparatus for distilling alcohol" cf. raṅ "to filter".
ārām	The translation "ornament,accoutrement" suits all contexts (1.47;4.5;9.33;79.41) < Skt. ārammaṇa "dependent"?
āsā	(1) *pro* ass "horse". (2) "auxiliary", "available" cf. Mod. Khm. yak āsā "bring help".

i

isuorgā	"heaven". Looks like a play on isūr "Śiva,lord" and suorgā "heaven" or a contraction of the two.

u

uk	"chest" (Thai).

Names of Journals are abbreviated as follows:

AAK	*Arts et Archéologie Khmers*, Paris.
ASEMI	*Asie du Sud-Est et Monde Insulindien*, Paris.
BEFEO	*Bulletin de l'Ecole Française d'Extrême-Orient*, Paris.
BSOAS	*Bulletin of the School of Oriental and African Studies*, London.
JA	*Journal Asiatique*, Paris.

Works to which reference has been made

Coedès, G. 1964. *Inscriptions du Cambodge* Vol. 7, Paris: Ecole Française d'Extrême-Orient.

Guesdon, J. 1930. *Dictionnaire cambodgien-français.* 2 vols. Paris.

Lewitz, S. 1969. 'Note sur la translittération du cambodgien'. *BEFEO* 55:163–69.

Lewitz, S. 1970. 'Inscriptions modernes d'Angkor 2 et 3'. *BEFEO* 57:99–126.

Lewitz, S. 1971. 'Inscriptions modernes d'Angkor 4,5,6 et 7' *BEFEO* 58:105–23.

Lewitz, S. 1973. 'Inscriptions modernes d'Angkor 26,27,28,29,30,31,32,33' *BEFEO* 60:205–42.

Martini, F. 1938. 'En marge du Rāmāyaṇa cambodgien'. *BEFEO* 38.2:285–95.

Martini, F. 1950. 'En marge du Rāmāyaṇa cambodgien (suite)'. *JA* 238:81–90.

Martini, F. 1978. *La gloire de Rāma (Rāmakerti).* [Translation into French] Paris.

Monier-Williams, M. 1976 *A Sanskrit-English Dictionary.* Oxford University Press.

Morton, D. 1976. *The traditional music of Thailand.* University of California Press: Berkeley.

Nong 1961. *Bhogakulakumār.* Phnom Penh:Institut Bouddhique.

Pech-Sal 1970. *Aṃbī laṃnāṃ saṅkhep nai bhleṇ khmaer.* [A short description of Cambodian music. Khmer text] Phnom Penh:Institut Bouddhique.

Pou, S. 1977a. *Rāmakerti (XVIe–XVIIe siècles), traduit et commenté.* Paris: Publications de l'Ecole Française d'Extrême-Orient, Vol. 110.

Pou, S. 1977b. *Etudes sur le Rāmakerti (XVIe–XVIIe siècles).* Paris: Publications de l'Ecole Française d'Extrême-Orient, Vol. 111.

Pou, S. 1979. *Rāmakerti (XVIe–XVIIe siècles) Texte kẖmer publié.* Paris: Publications de l'Ecole Française d'Extrême-Orient, Vol. 117.

Pou, S. 1982. *Rāmakerti II (Deuxième version du Rāmāyaṇa khmer). Texte khmer, traduction et annotations.* Paris: Publications de l'Ecole Française d'Extrême-Orient, Vol.132.
Rīoeṅ Buddhisaen 1964. Phnom Penh:Institut Bouddhique.
Rīoeṅ Rāmakert(i). (Reamker) 1937–1969. Parts 1–10, 75–80. Phnom Penh: Institut Bouddhique.
Vacanānukram khmaer. [Khmer dictionary] 5th edition, 1967. Phnom Penh: Institut Bouddhique.

For a full general bibliography attention is drawn to the recently published inventory of works on the Khmer Rāmāyaṇa by Pou, Sunnary and Haksrea given in the list below. Otherwise the works cited below have either been regularly consulted as tools in the preparation of this translation or have a direct bearing on points made in the Introduction.

Brunet, J. 1969. *Nang Sbek* [French text] Berlin. [Illustrated description of the Cambodian shadow-play.]

Brunet, J. 1969. *Nang Sbek* [German text] Berlin [Content as for last entry].

Commission des Moeurs et Coutumes du Cambodge. 1964. *Rapāṃ prajāpriy khmaer. Danses Populaires.* [Khmer text] Phnom Penh:Institut Bouddhique.

Groslier, B.P. 1965. 'Danse et musique sous les rois d'Angkor'. *Felicitation volumes of Southeast Asian Studies presented to H.H. Prince Dhaninivat.... on the occasion of his eightieth birthday.* Vol. 2:283–92. Bangkok: Siam Society.

Groslier, G. 1921. *Recherches sur les cambodgiens.* Paris. [Contains illustrated descriptions of Angkorian dress, weapons, musical instruments, etc.]

Headley, Robert K. *et al.* 1977. *Cambodian-English Dictionary.* 2 Vols. Washington: Catholic University of America Press.

Huffman, F.E. 1977. *Aksarsāstr khmer. Cambodian-English Glossary.* New Haven and London: Yale University Press.

Krasem 1966. *Padānukram Rāmakert(i).* [Glossary to the Reamker]. Phnom Penh:Institut Bouddhique.

Lewitz, S. et B. Rollet. 1973. 'Lexique des noms d'arbres et d'arbustes du Cambodge'. *BEFEO* 60:117–62.

Martin, M. 1971. *Introduction à l'ethnobotanique du Cambodge.* Paris.

Martini, F. 1952. 'Note sur l'empreinte du Bouddhisme dans la version cambodgienne du Rāmāyaṇa'. *JA* 240:67–70.

Pou, S. 1975a. 'Les traits bouddhiques du Rāmakerti'. *BEFEO* 62:355–68.

Pou, S. 1975b. 'Notes de morphologie khmère'. *ASEMI* 6.4:63–9.

Pou, S. 1976. 'Recherches sur le vocabulaire cambodgien IX'. *JA* 264:333–55.

Pou, S., Lan Sunnary and Kuoch Haksrea. 1981. 'Inventaire des oeuvres sur le Rāmāyaṇa khmer.' *Seksa khmer* 3–4:111–26.

Przyluski, J. 1923. 'La légende de Rama dans les bas-reliefs d'Angkor-Vat'. *AAK* 1.4:319–30.

Rāmker (Rāmāyaṇa khmer). 1969. Phnom Penh: Commission du Ramker, Université Royale des Beaux Arts. [Contains accounts of popular performances].

Simmonds, E.H.S. 1961. 'New evidence on Thai shadow-play invocations'. *BSOAS* 24.3:542–9.

Tandart, S. 1935. *Dictionnaire cambodgien-français.* 2 vols. Phnom Penh.

Thiounn, Samdech Chauféa Veang. 1930. *Les danses cambodgiennes.* Hanoi.

Vidal, J.E.,F. Martel and S. Lewitz. 1969. 'Notes ethnobotaniques sur quelques plantes en usage au Cambodge.' *BEFEO* 55:171–232.